IN THE HEAT OF AFRICA'S UNDERDEVELOPMENT

Africa at the Crossroads – Time to Deliver

John W. Forje

Langaa Research & Publishing CIG
Mankon, Bamenda

Publisher:
Langaa RPCIG
Langaa Research & Publishing Common Initiative Group
P.O. Box 902 Mankon
Bamenda
North West Region
Cameroon
Langaagrp@gmail.com
www.langaa-rpcig.net

Distributed in and outside N. America by African Books Collective
orders@africanbookscollective.com
www.africanbookscollective.com

ISBN-10: 9956-550-95-7

ISBN-13: 978-9956-550-95-1

© John W. Forje 2019

All rights reserved.
No part of this book may be reproduced or transmitted in any form or by any
means, mechanical or electronic, including photocopying and recording, or be
stored in any information storage or retrieval system, without written permission
from the publisher

Acknowledgements

Although small, it is precious and held in high esteem.

In The Heat of Africa's Underdevelopment could not have been written without accumulating tons of debts to many people known and unknown to me. Without doubts, my greatest debt is to the many journals, organizations, scholars, and writers who have ventured into this area with vast literature which in various stimulated as well as crystallized my thoughts including with whom I sharply hold different views on the continents current state of underdevelopment and exploitation; and how to find a way out of the prevailing dilemma.

My special thanks go to Professor Njimanted who found time in the wake of his increasing work load to write the foreword; to my wife, who in spite of academic commitments pushed many ideas into my head; and the children and grandchildren, Gert, Ellinor, Lina, Noah and William for being wonderful, helpful and providing supportive assistances in many ways ever since I scribbled the first lines of this publication; and to friends and family members who pushed me along.

Many thanks to my publisher and especially colleagues and students for the motivation. To readers, for sacrificing their time in browsing through the pages of the book so that we can jointly make a significant difference and contribution in building the Africa We Want. Have great fun as you read through my rambling thoughts and let us all collaborate in building a great continent.

JWF

Table of Contents

Preface

The ever growing disparity in living standards between the developed and developing polities constitutes a striking feature of life on Planet Earth. This publication is an attempt to highlight some of the factors dividing the worlds apart. A new North-South synergy is needed in creating a balanced world at peace with itself. As long as more than half-the population of the world go to bed hungry there can be no peace. A sting rich world and a sting poor world cannot cohabit peacefully. How to build a more equitable and balanced world is the challenge facing us. It is not that such a world cannot be constructed. It is a question of overcoming our current egoistic attitude. What is happening is that there is in us and in inside the weird world a monster of greed haunting us. Can we have a new mindset that small amount of love, of give and take, of caring for one another? We need to embrace and practice our long-aged concepts of ['ubuntu', 'harambee' and 'batho pele'] among others in creating, and consolidating the new world order. Africa missed out on its most articulated development plan (Lagos Plan of Action –LPA); we equally missed out in the Millennium Development Goals (MDGs) and run the risk of missing out in both the SDGs 2030 and AU Agenda 2063 if the right policy measures and implementation strategies are not put in place now.

Everything that happens to Africa especially the stinking poor afterwards bears the stamp of not only the moment but inhibits long-term consequences even for the stinking rich. But in life, there are always patterns, however shallow, and they have a way of finding the stinking poor and neglected silent majority that one day things will get better. It is hoped a new vision, mindset and new ways of doing things emerges as we ponder through the different pages of the book. Just only a tiny fraction of the tips of the iceberg of the continent's problems are taken up in this publication. Each chapter is well documented and can be read independently as discussions on numerous historical examples and contemporary situations pertinent to the subject without missing the very essence of the focal direction of the book which is educating the African public to articulate and own its development trajectories. Africa is underdeveloped. But it does not mean the people cannot rise again to claim its place among other nations of the world. It requires serious structural modification in our current mindset, thinking and actions which calls for total involvement of every citizen.

This book could not have been written without accumulating heavy debts and the support of the various authors and sources, some known and unknown to me. I am grateful to all who directly or indirectly contributed to seeing the fruition of the publication. Needless to state that, the author alone remains responsible for the shortcomings of the publications. The book is intended for both experts and the general leader. The ideas advanced here are strategies and pathways for dealing with the problems we encounter, such as poverty, corruption, the distribution of power, deterrence, good governance, health, human capacity building and other tactic efforts necessary for a systemic structural-functional governance construct for the continent.

Foreword

In the Heat of Africa's Underdevelopment: Africa at the Cross-roads, Time to deliver is an interesting book written with wisdom, rigour, skills and intellectual insights into the subject matter with a lot of reflection to the age of the author as well as his experiences. Other text books on the issue of underdevelopment are somehow difficult due to the fact that they look abstract even when all the illustrations have living examples drawn from the African continent. It is within this background that this book is conceived to provide readers with the time situation of the countries in the African continent.

It identifies the potentials of the African man-made and natural disaster which could be examined under the paradox of curse against blessing. It provides a breakthrough in its comparative approach in overcoming the issues of underdevelopment which has to do with general poverty, resources underutilisation, dualistic economies, and exports bias and import concentration not leaving out culturalism.

The book highlight issues of underdevelopment with focus to the mineral resource and manufacturing backwardness, wrong educational practice which enhances exploitation hence high degree of planted inequality as a fertile environment for underdevelopment. It also reminded Africans of the position of the endogenous growth hypothesis to African development as it is the case with the previous and their current dependence on the exogenous paradigms.

John W. Forje (PhD) has acknowledged the fact that students and some users of developmental texts are bored by the volume of some of these texts and the difficulties associated with the extraction of the relevant substance since one has to read through so many pages to get the real message. These made the readers and learners sometimes confused rather than strengthen their understanding of the subject matter.

This book, *In the Heat of Africa's Underdevelopment* is easy to understand as dates, maps, tables, etc. are carefully explained to capture the interest of the users. An important feature of the book is its visibility, comprehensiveness and chronological presentation of the chapters and the visual instructional materials that follow. The book attracts the interest of all social scholars, some of which include the government, geographers, political scientists, economists, sociologists, historian's, entrepreneurs, managers, undergraduate and post graduate students in all fields of applied and management sciences. Furthermore, the book is very relevant to that studying conflict management. At the end of every chapter, all the referencing cited in the body of the work and the maps are well coloured depending on the information in question.

The book provides facts and figures about Africa between 2000 and 2015 as such could be used for literature review and factual provision about Africa. Though no attempt is made to exhaust knowledge in each of the areas, the degree of extraction is remarkable as efforts have been made to cover substantial basic ideas through extensive library survey and experience. By implication, the book therefore is well conceived, carefully thought out and well written.

I hereby fully appreciate the level of intellectual commitment of Dr. John W. Forje and his success in coming out with this vision. I strongly belief the author has made significant network in ventilating the copies of this book throughout Africa and beyond. Preparation of a text book of this capacity, magnitude and focus with all the contemporary applications requires unconditional acknowledgements.

Professor Njimanted, Godfrey Forgha
Head of Division, Tertiary Science and Technology
Department of Economics Science
Higher Technical Teacher Training College Bambili
University of Bamenda,-Cameroon
20th June 2017

Introduction

Dangerous Crossing or What?

Africa remains the richest natural resources continent on Planet Earth; yet the least developed. We are faced with dangerous crossing if Africa has to join the now exclusive club of the developed world. Africa is an interlinking continent. It is the junction of physical and human geography, a reservation of resources (as noted above and only to be used by the developed world), a cultural geometric meeting or clashing point Because of the varsity of its natural potentials; it remains the most conflict prone continent. Here the views of Muzawazi (2017:43) are worthy of reflections: *"One of the most fascinating things about Africa is the remarkable contrasts that formulate the image of the continent in the world, but the poorest in the world are found there. This is also the oldest human society, yet the least developed. This is why I went on a journey across the African continent, to try to understand these simple yet intricate 'wonders of Africa".*

African Union Agenda 2063 – Some Key Projects – Conflict Agent Type

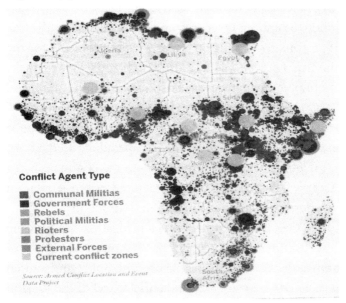

Conflict Agent Type

- Communal Militias
- Government Forces
- Rebels
- Political Militias
- Rioters
- Protesters
- External Forces
- Current conflict zones

Source: Armed Conflict Location and Event Data Project

"Today, around the world, Africa is the last frontier of development; a land of hope, opportunities and possibilities where humanity can find new solutions without repeating the mistakes of the past. The knowledge base exists, what is missing are the linkages that can only come through dialogue. If Africans fail to share their experiences and neglect to carry out research on the issues confronting them peace, security and ultimately, human development will continue to evade the continent. We can and must strive to turn our natural wealth into palpable benefits for the people of Africa. A strong wind is currently blowing throughout the continent: – Where leaders are now accountable to the people – is the surest guarantee for peace and security" (Sirleaf and Obasanjo, 2017:34). Apparently, the mere availability of resources tends to provide a fertile ground of triggering conflicts rather than promoting sustainable development. One of the most important and contentious issues Africa faces in the natural resources sector is how to reverse the misfortunes of exploitation and 'bringing governance back' in ensuring that the benefits accruing from the continent's providential endowments create new opportunities and positive multiplier effects for both citizens and the state (Ndiaye, 2017:35).

Silencing of the *'guns'* and putting an end to the various conflicts as early as possible will accelerate the movement of the continent to a capable developmental state. Security and conflicts are two issues that require serious attention. Insecurity and conflicts hinders the free movement of persons and goods but creates more problems for the continent – the fleeing of people to more safe boards which equally generates xenophobic tendencies against migrants and refugees. Africa is the most conflict-prone region in the world with 9 out of 16 UN peacekeeping missions around the world totalling 103,000 troops and personnel and with a combined operating budget of USA$5.87bn. In 2009, illicit small arms trade on the continent had a value of USA$30m. These arms are manufactured not in Africa but Europe; not for development, but for human destruction.

In short, the West is part of the forces instigating the growing conflicts on the continent through the manufacture and supply of weapons of human destruction. The arms used are not manufactured in Africa. But these conflicts keep the industrial wheel of the West in constant rotation. They inflict sufferings to the people in developing countries. Just as it was done when the colonizers drew lines on the map of Africa and allotted territories to themselves without any regard to the peoples who lived there. And so the saga continues of the so-called *'the legacy of the Dark Continent'* now structurally transformed into the paradigm of the *'Hopeless and Forgotten Continent'*.

The African saga is best captured in the words of Lt. Gen. Remeo Dallaire in this two lengthy quotes from his book *"Shake Hands With the Devil and They Fight like Soldier, They Die Like Children"* in (Meffe 2017:31-33). "Still at its heart the Rwandan story is the story of the failure of humanity to heed a call for help from an endangered people. The international community, of which the UN is only a symbol, failed to move beyond self-interest for the sake of Rwanda. While most nations agreed that something should be done they all had an excuses why they should not be the ones to do it. As a result, the UN was denied the political will and material means to prevent the tragedy."

And *"The global village is deteriorating at a rapid pace, and in the children of the world the result is rage. It is the rage I saw in the eyes of the teenage Interahammwe militiamen in Rwanda, it is the rage I sensed in the hearts of the children of Sierra Leone, it is the rage I felt in crowds of ordinary civilians in Rwanda, and it is the rage that resulted in September 11. Human beings who have no rights, no security, no future, no hope and no means to survive are a desperate group who will do desperate things to take what they believe they need and deserve."*

Ending Africa's wars is a must for the continent to regain its dignity and sovereignty. The dark sides in the advances in science and technology have only added to the horrors of mechanized warfare and cruelty on scale hitherto unknown to the world. "Decolonisation, the Cold War and the dissolution of old world political structures laid the groundwork for a general global malaise that materialized into several avoidable human catastrophes, during which the UN acted as little more than accountants of slaughter. No part of the world experienced this more cruelly than Africa. Early failures of international arbitrators and peacekeeping in Katanga and Biafra left a stain on the UN emblem, while later conflicts in Angola, Sierra Leone and Somalia exposed their impotence. The 1994 Rwandan

Genocide provided a startling reminder of the gross inefficiencies of international diplomatic bureaucracy, and the manner in which broad policy can dehumanize the individual and lay waste to even the best intentions. It reminded the world that the true enemy of humanity is not evil, but rather the indifference of good leaders, and a lack of empathy translated into direct action" (Meffe, 2017: 34-36).

There are too many pirates plundering the flames of ethnic and linguistic rivalries. The plundering forces in East and West are driving the continent into abyss. Africa has long been considered the *'chasse privée'* (private hunting grounds of the West.). The new invasion is not coming only from the West, but the East as well with China leading the resources plundering spree in the name of being the friends of Africa. At the same time Africans are fleeing to the West encouraged by the 'Green Card Syndrome" and 'poor services delivery at home'. Before, the West arrived and forced us into slavery. Today, we beg the West to be their slaves. What then is wrong with Africa? Is there a future for the continent? Yes, there is a future but we need to get our priorities right; develop our human intellect and make the best of our human and natural resources. It means unravelling the natural resources curse and having total control over these resources. "We need to look at the issues holistically and also what needs to be done differently and how. We need to ensure that the proceeds from natural resources are well managed" posit former President of Nigeria, Olusegun Obasanjo. In the same vein, former United Nations Secretary General, Kofi Annan, asserts that; *'Africa's rich coastal waters have long been plundered by foreign fleets, fishing illegally. Now global initiatives are gathering forces that aim to end such plunder and protect the livelihood of coastal communities."*

In spite of this dangerous crossing saga, a few are more even determined to see Africa embrace the basic tenets of democracy and functional administrative structures that places the life and interest of the people first. To be a slave or not to be, the heat is on for a radical, constructive and progressive developmental change in the ultimate sustainable quality welfare for all citizens. It is the developed polities which produces, creates, invents and imposes what can be seen as the 'African Problem' on our historical conscience. Hidden behind the 'African Problem' of underdevelopment, exploitation and destruction is the reality, the 'Western Problem' which comes from a conflict of interests between West and the African people. In the same manner, it can be said, that Africans have failed to exploit the *'late comer advantage'* and their natural resources to bargain for a better deal in transforming the continent. A number of countries are making progressive strides towards the democratic and good governance nexus, for example, Ghana, Botswana and Mauritius.

However, three outstanding deficits are poor leadership, the state of endemic poverty and legalized corruption that continues bleeding the continent to death. Addressing these critical issues will go a long way in accelerating the continents strive to being a high quality services delivery continent. These together with other shortcomings need urgent attention without which the cancer of underdevelopment will destroy the region. Increasing Africa's trade calls for free movement of people and goods. Currently, it is difficult to travel within and between African countries. Free movement is hindered by two major factors, poor road, rail and air transportation, and the issue of visa restrictions. Presently, only the following 15 countries on the continent that Africans can travel to visa-free or get visas on arrival: Seychelles, Mali Uganda, Cape Verde, Togo, Guinea Bissau, Mauritania, Mozambique, Rwanda, Burundi, Comoros, Madagascar, Somalia, Benin and Ghana, representing only 28% of African nations. On the other hand, Africans need visa to travel to 55% of other Africa countries in total; Benin and Ghana are the two countries to have opened their borders. While Seychelles is the only country that has complete open access and requires no visas for African citizens. This is the time for all African countries to come on board and accelerate the free movement of African people and goods across the continent.

Table 1: Trade – The AU want Intra-African Trade to Increase.

TRADE

The AU want intra-African trade to increase from 14% to 50% by 2050

Cross-border trade indicators by selected sub-regions

REGION	TIME TO EXPORT (DAYS)	COST TO EXPORT (USD PER CONTAINER)	TIME TO IMPORT (DAYS)	COST TO IMPORT (USD PER CONTAINER)
SADC	31.2	1,856.3	38.0	2,273.3
COMESA	32.4	1,915.3	38.3	2,457.5
ECOWAS	27.6	1,528.1	31.6	1,890.0
CEMAC	35.2	2,808.8	44.0	3,721.4
Middle East and North Africa	20.4	1,048.9	24.2	1,229.3
East Asia and Pacific	22.7	889.8	24.1	934.7
South Asia	32.3	1,511.6	32.5	1,744.5
Latin America	19.0	1,310.6	22.0	1,441.1
Eastern Europe & Central Asia	26.7	1,651.7	28.1	2,457.5
EU	11.5	1,025.3	12.1	1,086.5
OECD	10.9	1,058.7	11.4	1,106.3

- AfDB believes that the economy would be boosted by 25% if trade on the continent was made easier
- "In Africa, the average customs transaction involves 20-30 different parties, 40 documents, 200 data elements (30 of which are repeated at least 30 times), and the rekeying of around 60-70% at least once." – WEF
- "If you want to send a shipment to the Democratic Republic of Congo, you will spend 804 hours (33½ days) on paperwork, inspections and waits for approvals. Your cost will be $3,900 – not including tariffs and transportation. That same process takes a day or less in Austria, where your cost to comply with documentation and inspections will be about $1." – WEF

Continental Free Trade Area (CFTA)

- After meetings at the end of last year, the AU are hoping to launch this sometime this year.
- There are currently 14 different trade areas on the continent. Though the Tripartite Free Trade Area (COMESA-SADC-ECA) covers 26 countries.
- UN estimates that the CFTA could stimulate intra-African trade by up to $35bn (52%) annually by 2022.
- Could lead to a $10bn decrease in imports from overseas, boosting agriculture and industrial exports by $4bn (7%) and $21bn (5%) respectively.

Source: Credit - New African No.569 February 2017 Agenda 2063 Key Projects., pp31

A number of fundamental key projects must be embarked upon apart from that of building the human capital and ensuring the existence of a healthy citizenry. Without a healthy population, transformation cannot take place in a sustainable form. Some of these key projects include infrastructure – roads, railways, seaports, harbours and airports among others. Security and conflict – the need for guns to be silent across the continent before 2025; the free movement of goods and people; and increase in inter-African trade see Table 1: Trade – The AU Want Intra-African Trade to Increase from 14% to 50% by 2050. For example, how long does it take to ship goods to the Democratic Republic of Congo, Cameroon, Chad, Central African Republic, and how long does it take you to collect these goods? Administrative red-tapes and corruption hinders progressive development

It is easy, of course, to blame our forefathers for being ignorant of trends of events: in reality, there is no excuse for what could be seen as our folly to continue treading in the footpath of our forefathers. We have acquired western knowledge; live in the developed countries, and our leaders travel there; some of these leaders have the west, as their first homes and rule their countries from abroad; they see the good and bad sides of western life-style but behave worse than our fore-parents who never travelled abroad. This is the hour for us to realize that progress lies in working together, developing a critical mindset and focused on coming out of the current dilemma we find ourselves in. We can only progress if we pull ourselves together, cooperate, reconcile our differences and to convert our current resources as a *'curse into a blessing'* for the welfare of the people. In short, turn the resource curse into a boom is what Africa at this stage should be gunning for. Inputs for development include human capital (skilled manpower) resources and focused vision.

African states, with shorter histories of independent governance, are clearly subject to all forms of pressures, including energy pressures. It is relevant to note that Africa is arguably caught in a modern version 'Great Game' This time between China and the United States. Evidenced by Us military interest in Africa (such as United States Africa Command), through the Obama administration – continuing policies from the Bush administration is primarily interest in reducing politically-motivated violence, there is, of course, a keen desire to maintain a stable flow of energy resources out of the region.. As part of its strategy for the region, the Obama administration is keenly interested in promoting African states' intrinsic ability to resolve domestic issues. The Chinese not this US interest, increasingly devoting China's own considerable resources to the region (Derdzinski & Porreca, 2017:61; Holslag 2009; and see chapter One in this publication).

What is common among all African states, is that they have attracted international attention for both market potential and extractable wealth, Jonathan Holslag contends, 'Despite changing interests, perceptions, and means, China is and will remain dependent on the good will and collaboration of other players to help safeguard its economic interests in Africa. In fact, it will be the main stakeholder in terms of maintaining peace, social stability, good governance, and equitable development in its partner countries (Derdzinski & Porreca (2017:62). There is an urgent need for a common vision to harmonise diverse efforts into one coherent movement toward shared goals. As a common sense of purpose emerges and takes root among more and more individuals, and understanding of how different efforts can reinforce one another becomes sharper, increasing numbers are able to find the unique contribution they can make.

Building Tomorrow's Africa Now

Building tomorrow's Africa begins today. Implying we have to unity, integrate, connect, engage and innovate now. The continent has to step-up its efforts in educational or human capital development, health and infrastructure revolution. Our commitment has to be total and focused. We have to be productive. Build a healthy citizenry and ensure that our resources are properly utilized and no African left behind as we march towards the promised world of quality services delivery. More than half-a-century has since gone when most African countries gain their independence. The life and status of the rural people have changed little since the departure of the colonial masters. So the simple question – what have the rural population gained from shaking off the shackles of colonial governance?

As antidote, the experience of Muzawazi Tapiwa Kwame (2017:39-43) tells it all: *"Day 43: Monday 10 May 2010 – 50 years after independence, the black man is still second class on his own soil. One would think that for a black man traveling on African soil, life would be easier than for aliens from beyond the oceans. Not until you visit the Nigerian Embassy in Bamako, Mali. Upon inquiry, the never-smiling visa officer informed me that visa for Zimbabweans could be collected only the next day. But my German friends had been informed that their visa were collectable in three hours. This kind of second-class treatment for blacks has repeated itself in different ways throughout the journey."*

Infrastructure

Development requires infrastructure and Africa suffers serious deficiency in this respect. Without adequate infrastructure – factories, roads, railways, air transport etc. with strong structural-functional institutions sustainable developmental transformation can hardly come the way of the continent. In the words of football star, Pele of Brazil; "success is no accident. It is hard work, perseverance, learning, studying, sacrifice and most of all love of what you are doing or learning to do." Nigerian Novelist Ben Okri asserts that; "the most authentic thing about us is our capacity to create, to overcome, and to endure, to transform, to love and to be greater than our suffering."

Institutions

Strong and independent institutions (universities, legislatures, legal and justice system, administrative bodies etc.,) are imperative in piloting the policy directions of the transformation of the continent. The renowned psychologist and Pan-Africanist, Hilliard Asa notes that; *"the education of African people is an urgent necessity. It is a matter of life and death. We cannot abide another generation of children who have no identity and who are ignorant about Africa."* Most African institutions remain weak and corrupt and politically influenced unable to take an independent objective course of action in defence of the people and nation. Capacity building provides the way forward. We people of Africa must be poised in building institutions of higher learning that are uniquely Africa, without down grading the scientific quality of knowledge, informed by the needs of the continent's economies, and within reach of many youths as possible.

Our universities must focus on the schilling of labour and, in tandem offering relevant market skills needed to survive in the labour market. Our institutions of learning must train and graduate students who are job creators and not job seekers in the public sector. This is the only way our institutions of learning can emerge as vital but critical drivers of national development and usher Africa into a new era of prosperity and better livelihood. Many small businesses, however, may not have the luxury to train an individual for a prolonged amount of time. Additionally, within the global market, a lack of necessary technical skills means these small businesses are not readily able to compete regionally, or even internationally. Fortunately, there is an increasing in the penetration of high-speed internet connectivity, as well as partnerships between companies and communities where they offer training and monitoring opportunities, African governments must ensure greater investments in human capital development than the weapons of human destruction which occupies a high priority position on the annual budgets of many-an African country. It is extremely crucial for African small business owners to be cognizant of the possible learning curve that may come with taking on new additions. The issue of skilled labour is paramount in the sustainable transformation of the continent

The Diaspora- The Sixth Region

There is a thriving Diaspora willing to help or encouraged to be partners in the development of the region. For now, the Diaspora as the sixth region of the African continent remitted a value of USA$64bn in 2013 and this amount could rise by USA$10bn annual through securitization and rise up to USA$20bn, including diasporas bonds. So far, the continent has failed in the area of domestic resources mobilization for its transformation but tends to rely on foreign handouts for its development which can be non-forthcoming a times. In line with this is the urgent need to diversify our activities rather than reliance on the export of raw materials to the developed countries.

Diaspora remittance is of vital importance to African countries with a note of caution. Caution in that it depends on the status of the Diaspora to their respective host country. Things can change dramatically in the host country inhibiting the employment status quo of the people, which in turn reduces their possibilities of remitting money home. While properly utilising the opportunities offered by the Diaspora adequate measures must be put in place to take care of the rainy days as well as for the mobilisation of domestic resources. The Diaspora is equally vulnerable to any form drastic changes taking place in their countries of abode. Being on the front line, they are the first victims of any bullets. It is therefore vital for African countries not to put their hopes and dependency on the Diaspora as the source for the continent's transformation.

The Diaspora, African Renaissance, Pan-Africanism and a United continent has much to do with the views of President Julius Nyerere when he asserted on the meaning of an Africa: "that an African was not defined by the colour of his/her skin. An Africa is anyone who has made Africa his /her home and is struggling for the rights of his/her country. We are all on God's land, under God's sky and breathing the air created by God. When we fight for right we are fighting for the rights of all human beings because all of us have been created to fight for our rights. Therefore Africans unite; liberate ourselves from the shame of foreign rule (Shivji, 2008:30). Develop your continent. No other country will do that for us.

United Nations SDGS 2030:

The United Nations Millennium Development [MDGs] is now history. Was the MDGs a misunderstanding or did African countries see it as means of receiving more foreign assistance? Did African leaders negotiate the MDGs out of the barometer of fear or focused with how much would get into their pockets. Business as usual Nonetheless, the creation of Agendas 2030 forged a new way of engaging on global issues for humanity's future. Here is where we see the link between UN Agenda 2030 and African Union Agenda 2063. The MDGs had to be replaced with something concrete and achievable. There was a 'strong pushback' against the idea of expanding of the eight MDGs from their focus on poverty and health issues to the more encompassing idea of promoting sustainable development, a concept that includes a much broader notion that couples a push for overall economic growth with a strong environmental protections The SDGs were seen as a direct threat to countries that had invested in the MDGs – which meant most member states. Developing countries feared that funding would be cut off if the agenda was going to be universally applicable (Dodds et al (2017).

Few African countries realized the vision embodied in the MDGs Agenda. Other factors contributed to the goals having serious negative impact on the livelihood of the people. Between 2000 and 2015, poverty was not halved on the continent. Rather it increased. The continent stings with corruption and poverty leading to poor living conditions. Will UN Agenda 2030 turn-around the plight of the continent?

Agenda 2063 harps on issues whereby natural, financial and human resources are managed with integrity, transparency and accountability for efficient and effective services delivery, sustainable economic growth and development. While AU Agenda 2063 is road map for Africa becoming a capable developmental state echoing the ideals advanced in SDGs 2030 – effective, accountable and development oriented institutions, efficient and strong bureaucracy among others. Will the SDGs and AU 2063 go the same way like the MDGs? What lessons did Africa learned from the MDGs? What must be done to ensure that the goals of SDGs are realized? How can SDGs be structurally linked to Agenda 2063 and national development agendas (NDAs)?

AU Agenda 2063

No doubt, Africa stands at the cross-roads between decay and development. Now is the period to lay out a people's agenda. The challenge is how to marry the three forces together; i.e. National Development Agendas (NDA for example Kenya's 2030; Cameroon 2035 etc.); UN Sustainable Development Goals (SDGs) 2030 and African Union Agenda 2063. Turning to the AU Agenda 2063, the continent is completely disintegrated as traveling from part of the continent to the other is a night mare. Even traveling with a country is no easy task. For example, it takes three hours by road from Bamenda (North West Region) to Bafoussam (West Region) of Cameroon a distance of less than 100kms. The Central African Region is the most disenclaved part of Africa. The Trans-African Highway and Railway road should be accelerated linking Banjul to the Horn and Cape to Cairo. Africa's Integrated High Speed Railway Network (AIHSRN) and the Trans-African Highway are needed to facilitate the integration of the continent and the movement of goods and people. Some of the envisaged infrastructural activities would include:

* Plan – 4 - longitudinal north-south and 6-latitudinal east-west continental railway network – to be implemented over a period of three planning horizons, until 2065;

* Feasibility study – currently being carried out – investigating issues of traffic demand, costs and revenue, routes, rail technologies and financing;

* Five year action plan signed in October between the AU and China, head contractors of the project;

* First part of the project completed was the Addis Abba-Djibouti railway, a 656km line. The first African cross-border electric train;

* Hurdles – lack of standardised operating equipment and differing gauges for the tracks *(New African, No.569, February 2017, An IC Publication, London, p30)*

Road, railway, air, sea, and river transports are not the only vital infrastructure items enshrined within Agenda 2063. Attention should be focused on other items mentioned in the agenda that would propelled the continent into prosperity

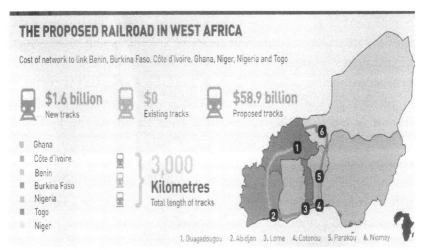

THE PROPOSED RAILROAD IN WEST AFRICA

Cost of network to link Benin, Burkina Faso, Côte d'Ivoire, Ghana, Niger, Nigeria and Togo

$1.6 billion New tracks | **$0** Existing tracks | **$58.9 billion** Proposed tracks

Ghana
Côte d'Ivoire
Benin
Burkina Faso
Nigeria
Togo
Niger

3,000 Kilometres Total length of tracks

1. Ouagadougou   2. Abidjan   3. Lome   4. Cotonou   5. Parakou   6. Niamey

Source: Kuwonu Franck (2014), West Africa: New Railway Network Aims to Boost Inter-regional Trade, African Renewal, December 2014, pp8-9

National Development Agenda (NDAs)

The five Year Development Plans that characterized the structural-functional basis of most countries on the eve of independence was abandoned by many countries. The advantage of these five Years National Development Plans (NDPs) acted as a check on government's performances. It ushered some degree of balanced development in society. In Cameroon it was abandon due to articulate self-interests – the politics of favouring some regions over the others. Bring back the 'Five Year Development Plan' to rekindle hope for participatory development and equitable distribution throughout each country.

There is a denial of equal opportunity and development on-going in many parts of the continent. The different national development plans [2020, 2030, 2040 or whatever the case envisaged by African countries] should hook-up with UN Agenda 2030 and AU Agenda 2063. The realisation of national Development Plans is prelude to attaining the objectives of SDGs 2030 and AU Agenda 2063. Today African countries find themselves in dynamic contexts demanding constant adaptation. The effects of the global financial crisis are still smouldering and important lessons should be learned more specifically how to prudently manage national resources to bring joy and greater dividends to the people.

The dwindling and unpredictability of development assistance compels African countries to look inwards for domestic resources for the care of her citizens. The unstable and inefficient management of resources compels African countries to critical revisit and restructure their management strategies of resources. It is therefore imperative for the sustainable and efficient management of national resources and the achievement of at least 12 out of the 17 United Nations Sustainable Development Goals (SDGs) for African countries to strongly focus on a number of inter related input factors among which is that restoring and maintaining the health of the natural resource base is not only needed to adequately feed current and projected populations, but to provide a better quality of life in the years to come..

Energy

There can be sustainable development without sustainable energy supply to power Africa's industrial take-off. Africa's energy deficit cannot propel it to an emerging economy. Yet the continent is rich in energy resources potential ranging from gas, coal, hydro, wind mills, to, solar energy. These sources of energy need to be adequately exploited to power the industrialisation of the continent and to improve on the living style of the people. The sustainable and successful exploitation of these sources of energy require knowledge in advanced technology and skilled human capital currently lacking in Africa. These energy sources calls for huge investment.

For example, the construction of Inga Dam hydroelectric plan in the Democratic Republic of Congo (DRC) is estimated to cost about USA\$100bn, and the number of people that may have to be relocated (about 60,000) during construction of the two planned phases of a total of 7. The expected generation capacity is 40GW, equivalent to 20 large nuclear power plants. World Bank estimate of DRC hydroelectric potential is 170GW. The estimated percentage of Congolese population without electricity is put at 85%. The power generation potential for selected Sub-Saharan African countries by technology is depicted below. World Bank estimate of Congo's hydroelectric potential is 170GW

Power generation potential for select Sub-Saharan African countries

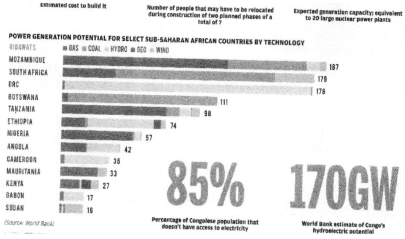

POWER GENERATION POTENTIAL FOR SELECT SUB-SAHARAN AFRICAN COUNTRIES BY TECHNOLOGY

Country	Estimated cost to build it	Number of people that may have to be relocated during construction of two planned phases of a total of 7	Expected generation capacity; equivalent to 20 large nuclear power plants
MOZAMBIQUE			187
SOUTH AFRICA			179
DRC			178
BOTSWANA		111	
TANZANIA		98	
ETHIOPIA	74		
NIGERIA	57		
ANGOLA	42		
CAMEROON	35		
MAURITANIA	33		
KENYA	27		
GABON	17		
SUDAN	16		

(Source: World Bank)

85% Percentage of Congolese population that doesn't have access to electricity

170GW World Bank estimate of Congo's hydroelectric potential

Source: New African, No.568 January 2017, London, pp10

Technological Capability

Advanced technologies carry with them the promise of technology 'lap-frogging' that should enable African countries to jump over certain steps in the process of industrialization, thereby avoiding the burden of going through every stage in development experienced by the current industrialized countries. According to Bhalla (1996) and many others, (Freeman, 1989, 1994, Forje, 1989; Bessant and Cole, 1985) three interpretation of the concept of 'leap-frogging' are advanced; namely:

- implies narrowing of gaps between countries at different stages of development;
- involves the adopting of advanced technology in the 'leap-frogging' countries ahead of the more industrialized countries; and
- developing countries jumping some steps and avoiding the passage through the difficulties experienced by the current industrialized countries.

The availability of new and emerging technologies provides the new comers (Africa) with a major advantage over the established industrialised countries. For African countries, advanced technologies, such information and communication technologies – e.g. mobile phone network, provide a new set of opportunities for improving their economic competitiveness, and enhancing their capability for innovation and technological progress and sustainable development. African countries that do not join the new technology bandwagon are doom to failure. The reality is that African countries are empowered with their 'late-comer advantage' and failure to make a proper use will be their bust.

Healthcare

The continent has the world's poorest healthcare system. The Ebola outbreak in West Africa, the growing increased in other diseases intensifies the need for building a strong health system. The continents maternal mortality rate is the worse with a country like Malawi registering about 16 die daily from childbirth and pregnancy-related complications, while there is a massive out-flux of Malawian nurses to the West. Not only nurses are fleeing. The same goes for doctors and other health personnel. The active recruitment of health personnel trained by poor countries by wealthy nations creates serious disparities whereby developing countries are in essence subsidising health delivery services to citizens of rich nations. The development of a country is accelerated when its population is strong, educated and healthy. This is not the case with Africa. Here is where Africa should make us the 'late-comer advantage' by exploiting the advantage of new financial and technological solutions in solving its health related problems.

Access to Capital

Africans must device a means of having access to capital in financing their basic needs developmental activities. If we are to promote small business and be part of an innovative entrepreneurial society, we cannot go on depending on external financing sources. Mobilising domestic resources is crucial in the building the Africa we want without leaving any one behind. The continent's local financial institutions, the tontine, njangi house, credit unions are sources to be improved and encouraged through good government policies. Whether it is for marketing purposes, buying in large quantities to cut down costs, building houses, sponsoring children to schools, research, or even hiring extra help, the difficulty in accessing capital stifles many young businesses and other development related activities.

This can be attributed to many reasons, investors being weary of various risks, or even the way the entrepreneur packages their product due to limited training. In Africa in particular, the region suffers the negative branding that has been attributed to it for ages now that has kept investors at bay. Government regulations in facilitating the promotion of small business and other economic activities are primordial. Facilitating small business operations is a win-win for most countries, especially African countries. African government should by now realise this reality. African Governments should position themselves as resource, and not another obstruction for the growth of small enterprises.

With the spread of technology coupled with the ever increasing rise of globalization, interest in the continent has peaked albeit many still tread with trepidation. It is now up to African governments and various regional bodies to make themselves attractive investment disseminations so as to increase the inflow of potential investors. How can the continent make the best out of the continent's sixth region – the Diaspora in facilitating access to finances?

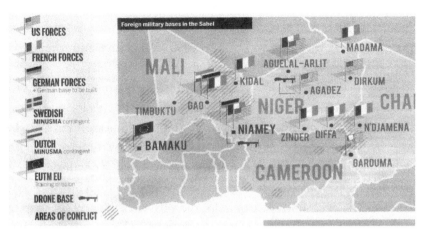

Source: Keenan (2017) "War Games in The Sahel", New African No.568, January 2017, pp39

Apart from silencing the guns, security also requires a number of interrelated input factors; job security, health security; water security, housing security, food security and name the rest as well as other forms of warfare, terrorist attacks. The displacement of millions of people fleeing violence puts security in the centre of all activities. That is why it is important to build the necessary capacities to evade insecurity in society and work harmoniously toward shared concerns and peaceful coexistence. Do we need foreign military squads to keep peace, security and harmony in our backyard and at what cost?

Development cannot take place in a conflict-prone country and under the siege of foreign military bases or occupation. When justice fails to exist, the rise to inequality increases creating room for various forms of decedent groups which eventually destabilising the country. It comes as no surprise of the increasing number of rebel groups across the continent. It gives rise to various forms foreign interventions – see map on foreign military bases in the Sahel. The Democratic Republic of Congo, Somali, and Sudan provide a good example. The spread of small arms is a common place in many of these countries rendering life very unsafe for citizens. These arms are not locally manufactured but imported draining the meagre resources of the country and subjecting the citizens into deepened poverty and poor quality livelihood. While appreciating the efforts of the developed countries in providing some safety nets for African countries, one should not be silent of the fact they are also part of the rising problems of conflict .and insecurity on the continent. Increasing inequality, rising perceptions of corruptions, accelerated poverty among other ills contribute have all contributed to the deterioration in the overall decline in security and quality welfare.

The Leadership Challenge

Africa is faced with a serious leadership challenge. The founding fathers with their good intensions had their own shortcomings. The shortcoming of leadership left a big vacuum. How to close that gap is the question. The emerging young leaders face a world of greater complexities, confusion. Africa's future equally depends on its leadership vision, have a message and be conscious of the mission. Who should be able 'effectively express their passion for the people, love and fear of the Lord and with positive responses from citizenry? Therefore, the continent is great need of:-

---

Africa is in need of=======➜*
- leader as seeker;
- leader as strategist;
- leader as seer;
- leader as servant (not as master)
- leader as strong one (not a dictator)
- leader as shepherd
- leader as sustainer;
- leader as spokesperson

(See Levine 1981; Bass, 1985, Banniss, 1986; Campolo, 1983; Ford, 1991 ;)

Being in the throes of change, the first question is where are the leaders? What is leadership? Why a new type of leadership nexus now? These and many other soul search questions need soul searching answers. To begin with, leaders take the lead, i.e. they initiate ideas and advanced strategic plans; second, leaders move people to follow them by showing them consideration and good character. Thus different leaders behave in different ways, and as such, there is no single style of leading. Thus leadership is contingent on circumstances and that what works in one situation may not work in another. In a letter from Abigail Adams to Thomas Jefferson in 1790: Adams stated; Great necessities call forth great leaders." Perhaps the creeping crises facing Africa will yet produce a new wave of visionary, servant leadership with a responsive citizenry.

Effective leaders pass on these values not only through their performance, but mostly out of what they are as human-beings (Ford, 1991:67). At this critical juncture of the continent's transformation, the challenge for developing future leaders is an even greater one. We therefore, need transformational leadership as that kind of motivation which raises the consciousness of people about what they want (Bass, 1985). By and large; 'transaction leaders work within the situation; transformational leaders change the situation. Furthermore transaction leaders accept what can be talked about; transformation leaders change what can be talked about. Transactional leaders accept the rules and values; transformation leaders change them. Transactional leaders talk about payoffs; transformation leaders' talk about goals. Transactional leaders bargain; transformation leaders symbolise. At this critical junction, we need both the transactional and transformational leadership to pilot the continent through the rough seas of the rapidly changing global world of our time.

For now, Africa is caught between experience of deprivation and creativity. The new African leader must be submerged with creativity; creativity is essential. Life is constantly changing, but people always fear change. The leader is one who whose responsibility it is to help the people adapt and undertake something new and different. The new leaders should strive towards visible success that promotes cooperation, consensus than rivalry; that shows great concern for accountability and transparency not corruption. Effective leaders pass on these values not only through their performance, but mostly out of what they are as human beings. With the scaffolding of underdevelopment put aside, solitude should be the furnace of transformation of the new leadership need for Africa. Such leadership will never be satisfied to leave people on the same spot, but always willing to pulling them on. Without a unifying passion, progress can never come the way of the people. We all must gun for a shared future with prosperity.

The Paradox of Africa's Democracy and Good Governance

The basic tenets of democracy seem to have evaded the continent. Our governing elites have failed to anchor in democratic principles despite the lofty ideals enshrined in most of the constitutions of African States. The struggle for political emancipation which was eventually granted, apparently but failed to grant economic independence to the colonized states. In short, quasi political independence was extended but economic [power. Africa was given a cheque with insufficient rights to funds in improving the welfare of their citizens. Soon after independence, the new ruling elites started behaving as the departed colonial masters with a difference – the difference being their total allegiance to the colonial powers and this gave room for foreign interferences in derailing the rising aspirations of the people (Forje, 2015, Osita, 2016). Professor Steve Panford (2017) notes: *"From the 1950s on, the US supported the overthrow of Kwame Nkrumah of Ghana; it lent support to the French to suppress the independence struggle in Algeria; it conspired with Belgium to murder Patrice Lumumba of Congo; it supported UNITA in Angola and the apartheid regime in South Africa among other interventions in Africa".*

As democracy begins emerging on the African continent, it is only necessary that we exhibit open and single-mindedness with full support to its growth, implementation towards the perpetual liberation and development of the continent for the common good of all. It is imperative for the region to consolidate its democratic and good governance trajectories to make the changes Africa's golden age of sustainable transformation and quality livelihood. Change can only come through the active participation of the state and civil society including other stakeholders. Civil society has the greater role to play in changing the structure of the state for the common good of all. The African civil society must become more proactive than before to ensure that the struggle for self-determination creates a governance system and society we all want for the betterment of the people; or else the struggle for independence would have been in vein.

More than fifty years have elapsed since African countries gained independence. Civil society went into slumber no longer vibrant as during the pre-independence era. The attainment of self-rule gave birth to the notion of *'rising expectation'*. The failure of leaders to deliver gave birth to *'rising destructive frustration'* and society dropped into the bottom depth of underdevelopment, endemic poverty, mismanagement and corruption. With the attainment of self-rule 'rising expectation suddenly turned soar, civil society devastated and crippled, rising destructive frustration entered the political arena; with no one in total control. The exploitation spree became free for all or for those who walked the corridors of power in the capital. The development compass was lost.

Civil society has to regain its pre-independence momentum, fighting spirit, vigour and be more than ever proactive as the watch dog and custodian of society without which UN Agenda 2030, AU Agenda 2063 and National Agendas will fall on the wayside like the MDGs. The realization of AU Agenda 2063 and other comprehensive forward look development strategies rest on how proactive civil society rehabilitates itself in the right structural form and focus on the correct vision. Development requires every one stretching her/him to the limits of their abilities.

The SDGs could be seen as an attempt to establish 'correctness' in the way development has gone in Africa all this while. The AU Agenda 2063 could equally be seen in the same line after haven failed to implement Africa's most articulate plan – The Lagos Plan of Action (LPA). In all, the MDGs was the perfect storm to trigger SDGs and AU Agenda 2063 away from development path to a more focused vision of transforming current Africa into a more prosperous society. To a large extent, national governments are making efforts to change, introducing new forms of human capital development, attempts in reshaping the administrative and governance trajectories and other progressive requirements for the continent's industrial/developmental take-off.

As mentioned before, countries like Botswana, Ghana, Mauritius and an extent Rwanda are knocking at the doors of democratic governance and good management. All is not perfect, but these countries are exhibiting the will for constructive change. It is just proper that civil society joins the bandwagon rendering its proactive support and pushing government to continue in the right direction. Civil society should be the hawk watch at government and demanding nothing less than democratic governance and quality management. All in society must cultivate the stamina of serving in the development war zone while constantly trying to avoid the fatal bullets of corruption, inertia and bad management. Africa is in great demand of citizenry to serve in the *'development construction zone'* and prepared to carry with him/her the natural survival instinct of constructing the kind of society we want for present and future generations.

The Latecomer Advantage

Africa no longer needs to develop the wheel but take advantage of what exist in accelerating its development nexus. Unfortunately, colonial rule help to destroy the technological base of the continent, relegated science and technology to be the back ground of the development continuum. Even with the attainment of independence, science and technology were not given the attention it deserved in propelling the technological transformation of the region either by African governments. For over half-a-century, we have continued to ignore science, technology and innovation in the development nexus of the continent. Entrepreneurship has equally been relegated to the background. Africa risks being left behind and cannot benefit from the globalisation nexus or fever which has caught the world because the region is scientifically, technological and entrepreneurially underdeveloped.

Only countries with a good mastery of science, technology and innovation benefit from the magic wane of globalisation. Ankomah (2017:46-47) points out that Africa accounts for about 5%of global GDP, but is responsible for only 1.3% of global expenditure on R&D. As a result, Africa remains disadvantaged on overall STI efforts due to the low investment in STI capacity development. But if the continent should become competitive globally and close the development gap between Africa and the rest of the world, it will largely be the result of its governments plugging the STI investment gap".

The areas mentioned here are not exhaustive. They show the huge task awaiting the continent and why an intercourse between state, civil society and the private sector including the international community remain crucial. The ball is in the court of the government to reach out to the private sector and civil society to map out strong partnerships that can benefit the people of Africa. Notwithstanding our weaknesses, we should exploit various concepts within the cultural heritage to forge ahead the development of the continent. For example, Civil Rights activist, and iconic singer, Mama Africa, Miriam Makeba (Member of Parliament, South Africa) asserts: "Africa has her mysteries and even a wise man cannot understand them. But a wise man respects them". Let us respect and use our cultural heritage concepts in transforming the continent for the better. In addition, we should not be deceived that diversity is a liability. Rather ensure that our cultural or ethnic diversities constitute the greatest assets we have for the reconstruction, transformation and building of a strong Africa. Our strength, pride, security, self-esteem, defensive and offensive weapons is our diversity which must be treasured and respected at all cost. We should at all cost ensure that foreign cultural values and ideas do not destroy our cultural heritage values. It is our last defence line given the growing wave of the recolonisation saga of the continent.

These are just some of the selected cardinal areas for serious discourse requiring urgent attention. The continent is in turmoil. Imperialism feeds on it like a vulture; power hungry elite worsen it as they thoughtlessly implement their maters' military designs and economic schemes. The first-generation of African nationalist feared that left on their own African states would become pawns on the imperialist chessboard. A united continent is the only way in building a strong common defence barrier against foreign invasion. Therefore, the defence line must be strengthened and fortified to evade all attacking forces. Regional Economic Communities (RECs) provide such a defence line in promoting the economic integration, free movement of persons and goods across the continent. In addition,

RECs rank closest to each other on regional infrastructure and productive integration and furthest apart on free movement of people and financial and macroeconomic integration as depicted on the **Table on Closer Look.**

Closer look

By assigning scores on each dimension, the index allows regions to see exactly where they fall short.

(score on each dimension by regional economic community)

	Trade Integration	Regional Infrastructure	Productive Integration	Free Movement of People	Financial Integration
CEN-SAD	0.353	0.251	0.247	0.479	0.524
COMESA	0.572	0.439	0.452	0.268	0.343
EAC	0.780	0.496	0.553	0.715	0.156
ECCAS	0.526	0.451	0.293	0.400	0.599
ECOWAS	0.442	0.426	0.265	0.800	0.611
IGAD	0.505	0.630	0.434	0.454	0.211
SADC	0.508	0.502	0.350	0.530	0.397
UMA	0.631	0.491	0.481	0.493	0.199
Average	**0.540**	**0.461**	**0.384**	**0.517**	**0.381**

Sources: Economic Commission for Africa, African Union Commission, and African Development Bank (2016).

CEN-SAD = Community of Sahel-Saharan States, COMESA = Common Market for Eastern and Southern Africa, EAC = East African Community, ECCAS = Economic Community of Central African States, ECOWAS = Economic Community of West African States, IGAD = Intergovernmental Authority on Development, SADC = Southern African Development Community, and UMA = Arab Maghreb Union. Scores are calculated on a scale of 0 (low) to 1 (high).

Source: See also Lopes (2016). "Inching Toward Integration", Finance and Development, June 2016. Pp218-219

It is imperative, therefore, for African countries to focus on integration to better realize the Pan-African ideal not only as struggle for the liberation of the continent from the yoke of European ruled African territories but as an instrument for the development of the region. Unfortunately, African leaders have never succeeded in translating this noble ideal into political capital. Attempts towards integration have only yielded mixed and sometimes minimal results. Prof, Carlos Lopes (2016:18) asserts: "A series of initiative dating to 1980 – the Lagos Plan of Action (LPA), the Abuja Treaty, the New Partnership for Africa's Development (NEPAD), and the recent AU Agenda 2063 – were each heralded as the economic response to Africa's need for a new, more interconnected future. Why is it proving to be so painfully difficult to implement this vision of a truly integrated continent"? Unfortunately, in Africa, trade links to the rest of the world are more direct and efficient than trade between neighbouring countries.

Africa is at the cross-roads calling for close of ranks by all forces. Closing ranks after centuries of destruction will not automatically make us rich or powerful. But it will give us a sense of purpose and direction to forge ahead, and it will make it difficult for the people to be disregarded and humiliated. This generation is here challenged to articulate a new vision, and to examine their priorities and actions more critically to draw lessons to forge ahead. Vision inspires, practice teaches us leading to progress, development, sustainability and consolidated welfare for all. Our needs as separate countries are being ignored by the rich and powerful. The result is that the continent is marginalised, destroyed and exploited. For how long will we allow this to continue? Will Africa remain technologically unprogressive? Or will it embrace technological progress of our time?

The challenge the continent faces is finding the right solution between the greatest divide of our time - Afro-pessimism and Afro-Optimism. Following Lopes (1995:37), Afro-pessimisms stress the enormity of the problems confronting and dividing the continent rather than focusing on critical and fundamental issues that unite and builds the continent. Afro-pessimism enhances the notion of despair and rising destructive frustration, rather than building the strength, potentials of the continent that advances, enhances and consolidates the unity and building of a capable developmental state as prelude to attaining the status of a developed polity anew for the continent.

Fifty years after the shackle of colonial rule was cut, we have remained buried in the in the taste of power will all the fanfare it entails; the trappings of power; walking on a red carpet, the 21 gun salute, the guide-of-honour and other numerous benefits have and continue to derail the construction of a strong and united continent.

De-railing the unity and development of the continent implied a deliberate implanting of the shallowness of the democratic seed and failure in conducting free, fair, credible, accountable, transparent and clean elections to usher in a governance structure the people want. The ruling elites did not want to respond to the will of the people.

More than fifty years down the road, we find the old guards holding on to power. The only possible way of changing the guards or power is through violence with exception of in a few states; hence the consolidated resistance in providing formidable barriers to preparing a structure-functional level political ground for the emergence of democratic governance on the continent. To a large extent, this explains why the political and economic foundation for a strong, united and integrated Africa remains weak, shaky and unstable. In short, the continent is littered with failed and fragile democracies without the required clouts to bargain for its sovereignty and rights within the international community of nations.

"More worrying is the failure by most African states to deliver services, support industrial and agricultural production as well as improve the well-being and livelihood of the people. Failure of most African states to have the ability and the political will to engage in any meaningful radical social project for the benefits of the least advantage makes injustice and gross inequity to waste human resources. The state is more of a burden than a support to the population becoming itself a factor for the disintegration of the lives of the population. Another barrier is the endemic nature of conflict and violence in Africa turning virtually the continent into a security no-go area. Much of the security hazard is related to the prevailing economic ruin and poverty afflicting large sections of the population of Africa" (Muchie 2000:13). As a result of these armed conflicts often perpetuated by the developed polities and implemented by African leaders, the continent subjects its young population, even at the ages of seven or less to be child-soldiers in most of the conflicts and wars that have taken place and are ongoing in Angola, Burundi, Chad, Congo, Liberia, Rwanda, Sierra Leone, Sudan, Ivory Coast, Central African Republic, Uganda. (Nigeria, Biafran War) and others (see UNICEF 1999). These armed conflicts continue subjecting the continent into the worse scourge of poverty and exploitation. And poverty, as always, served to deny a people a voice. The poor and illiterate in Africa are usually and conveniently silent. Progress can never come the way of the continent with such prevailing situation.

Perhaps the views of US Assistant Secretary of State, Cohen, (Morrow, 1992:34); attempts an explanation of the chaos theory that bedevils the region. Cohen argues that African independence leaders were often close to European left-wingers, 'who implemented in Africa the biggest socialist fantasies that they weren't able to implement in their own countries – mainly government ownership of everything and government engineering of the economy at every level. Further, a collective Western guilt over colonialism meant African despots got their own airlines and shipping lines as well as similar prestige projects financed by indulgent governments that would never have condoned such extravagance at home. Here formed a destructive paradigm: the state came to own and manage 80% of the formal economy'. Senior executives were appointed for political reasons, not for competence; the enterprises, incompetently run, money lost. |Tribalism, provincialism and nepotism grew rank and led to over employment – along with resentment and low morale.'

Attempts have been made to present a holistic picture of the continent and how the people can move on from here. The conclusion is undogmatic and the message important. One can easily make the point that there is no best way to development and there is no close correspondence between development policy or development strategy on the one hand and the resulting political system on the other... Nonetheless, we have argued that the strategy of economic development pursued by a country can predispose it towards authoritarianism or democracy although it seldom is the sole determining factor. Africa needs development and democratic governance that caters for the interest of the people.

We need comprehensive strategic and prioritized policies and actions that are people oriented and focused in addressing issues such as (i) poverty and inequality; (ii) human capital formation; (iii) addressing issues of unemployment, job creation, investment, savings and growth; (iv) putting an end to endemic corruption and inertia; (v) ensuring the structural-functional role of the state; (vi) intensifying participation, democracy and freedom, and name the rest of concerted activities that improves, enhances and sustains the quality livelihood of all citizens. The publication argues very strong and vividly that the strategy of economic development pursued by countries of the continent can predispose it towards authoritarianism or democracy although it seldom is the sole determining factor (Forje, 2009). Africa is at the cross-road because it is suffering from the politics of surplus waste and the Babel of bad politics. Chaos is what characterizes the region. The book benefits from the last two quotes which should be the guiding factor moving forward:

> *"It is a bad habit to say another man's thoughts are bad and ours only are good and that those holding different views from ours are the enemies of the country"*
>
> *(Gandhi, 1944, on Indian Home Rule)*

> *"It is always possible to bind together a considerable number of people in love, so long as there other people lefty over to receive the manifestations of their aggressiveness"*
>
> *(Freud Sigmund, 1930)*

The continent of Africa exists within a period of sustained nastiness, as the politicians and their congeners methodically evade the golden rule, both in words and in deeds, they do to others what they surely do not want done to themselves. A new approach, mindset, behaviour and attitude are needed to arrest the growing disastrous situation. We need to constructively dig into the background of our past and present to find answers for moving majestically forward into a brighter future. It is harsh irony that we have failed to realize or look into the crystal ball of the vision of our erstwhile founding fathers but continue drifting apart towards our destruction. Our developmental attitude is characterized by chaos theories, articulate self-interest, hate, greed, trading of accusations and counter-accusations rather than pulling our forces together in the '*harambee, ubuntu and batho pele*' spirit which constitutes an inherent part of our cultural heritage and values. We must forge ahead with an open and functional attitude to provide quality livelihood to all.

Without which, the agony of Africa will continue unabated. Why must this generation continue threading on the path of Africa as infested with wars, hostile terrain and often impossible communications even in the age of great advances in science and technology? Unfortunately, we have made the region a genius for extremes, for the beginning and the end. There is always something new arising from the continent that often works against the progress of the people. It is time to activate a new jig-saw for the progress and veritable position of Africa in the global new world of our time.

References

Adams A. Nassau (1993), Worlds Apart. The North-South Divide and the International System. Zed Books, London and New Jersey.

Ankomah Baffour (2017). "We Ignore Science, Technology and Innovation at Our Peril: ACBF Calls for More Action from African Countries", New African, No. 570, March 2017, AN IC Publication, London, pp 46-47

Bass M. Bernard (1985). Leadership and Performance beyond Expectations. The Free Press, New York

Bessant, J. and S. Cole (1985), Stacking the Chips – Information Technology and the Distribution of Income, Frances Pinter, London

Derdzinski L. Joseph and Porreca Jackson (2017). "Measuring Security: Understanding State Capacity in Oil-Producing States", ASPJ Africa and Francophonie, 1st Quarter, Vol. 8, No. 1, 2017, pp55-74

Dodds Felix, David Donoghue and Jimena Leiva (2017) Negotiating the Sustainable Development Goals, Earthscan / Routledge, London and New York

Ford Leighton (1991) Jesus: The Transforming Leader. Hodder and Stoughton Publishing London

Forje W. John (2015). Perspectives on Democracy and Good Governance in Africa. Reorganising the State and Society for a Better Tomorrow. Lambert Academic Publishing, Germany.

Forje W. John (2009). Here the People Rule: Political Transition and Challenges for Democratic Consolidation in Africa. Nova Science Publishers Inc. New York.

Forje W. John (1989), Science and Technology in Africa. Tenth Volume, Longman Guide to World Science and Technology Series, Longman Publishing Group. Essex,

Freeman, C. (1989). 'New Technology and Catching Up' in C. Cooper and R. Kaplinsky (eds.) Technology and Development in the Third Industrial Revolution, Frank Cass, London and Portland OR, USA.

Freeman, C. (1994). 'The Economics of Technical Change', Cambridge Journal of Economics, Vol. 18. Pp.463-514

Gandhi M. K. (1944). Hind Swaraji or Indian Home Rule. Navajivan, Indian

Holslag Jonathan (2009) "China's New Security Strategy for Africa," Parameters, Summer 2009, 23-37. This article contains broad discussion of China's security policies toward Africa.

Levine Arthur (1981). When Dreams and Heroes Died, Jossey Bass |Publishers, San Francisco/London

Lopes L, (1995). "Enough Is Enough: For an Alternative Diagnosis of the African Crises," Discussion Paper No. 5, Scandinavian Institute of African Studies, Uppsala, Sweden

Lopes Carlos (2016). "Inching Toward Integration", Finance and Development, June 2016, Vol. 53. No. 2, International Monetary Fund (IMF) Washington, USA, pp 18-21

Meffe David (2017). "21st-Century Approach to Maintaining Peace in Africa." New African, No. 572, May 2017, AN IC Publication, London, pp30-33

Meffe David (2017). "A New Approach to Ending Africa's Wars", New African. No. 572, May 2017, AN IC Publication, London, pp34-36

Morrow Lance (1992). "Africa: The Scramble for Existence", Time Magazine International –The Agony of Africa, Vol. 140, N0.10, September 7, 1992, USA, pp30-34

Muchie Mammo (2000) Towards A New Theory for Reframing Pan-Africanism: An Idea Whose Time Has Come. Development Research Series, Research Centre on Development and International Relations (DIR), Working Paper No. 83, Aalborg University, Denmark

Muzawazi Tapiwa Kwame (2017). "Journey into the Heart of Africa," (Baffour Ankomah) (2017) New African, April 2017, No.571, an IC Publication, London, UK. Pp39-43

Ndiaye Michelle (2017) Africa Peace and Security Programme Director (IPSSS – Addis Ababa University) and Head of the Tana Forum Secretariat, New African, No.571 April 2017,

New African (2017). "Agenda 2063 – Key Projects" No. 569. February 2017, An IC Publication, London, pp30-31

Osita Agbu (2016). Elections And Governance in Nigeria's Fourth Republic, CODESRIA, Dakar, Senegal

Panford Steve (2017). "The Paradox of United States Democracy", New Africa, No. 571, April 2017, AN IC Publication, London, pp30-31

Sigmund Freud (1930 & 1961) Civilisation and Its Discontents. Trans. James Strachey. W. W. Norton: New York

Sirleaf Johnson Ellen and Obasanjo Olusegun (2017). "The Tana Forum 2017: Africa Rising", New African, April 2017, No.571, An IC Publication, London, pp34-35

Shivji G. Issa (2008). Pan-Africanism or Pragmatism? Mkuki na Nyota Publishers, Dar es Salaam, Tanzania

Africa's curse and blessings: The mineral resource and manufacturing paradigm: An analytical, developmental and comparative perspective approach within the context of FOCAC

Introduction: Annexation and Plundering or Power and Benefit-Sharing

China's engagement on the African continent has been on-going for a long time before it became the focal point of international attention. China's interest in Africa is not new.

Map1: Africa's Top Exporters To China.

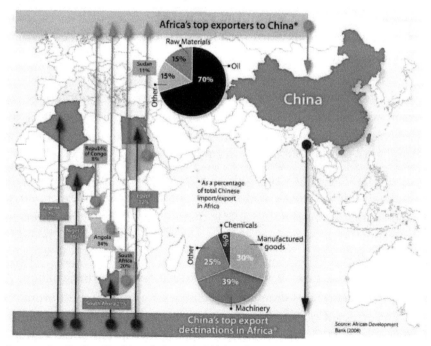

Source: Credit Conflict Trends Issue 1, 2014, p 3).

However, following its rapid rise as a global economic power it takes a new dimension China and Africa have historical relations dating as far back as 202 BC and AD 220. There were plans to import Chinese labour to work in German Plantations in the Coastal region of Cameroon before Zintgraff travelled inland to discover hard working people of the grassfields which put to rest the importation trajectory idea (Fowler and Zeitlin 1996; Chilver 1966).Only there was no Forum on Africa-China Cooperation (FOCAC) then. Experiences like this could be found across the continent. It equally challenges Africa's pattern of socio-economic transformation. This paper could be seen as China's role with a different appetiser under the canopy of globalisation. What is the impact of such cooperation?

Approaching the subject matter, three simple assertions are envisaged: (i) what exists can be divided into humankind and nature; (ii) human beings, as well as nature, have fundamental needs, the condition sine qua non of their continued interest and existence: and (iii) human beings depend on nature for the satisfaction of their needs, but not vice versa. The natural resources of the continent constitute dangerous tsunamis. Hence the chapter takes a critical and surgical analysis of the rhetorical of problems with the hopes of advancing new ideas specifically tackling the structural causes of underdevelopment. Does China's coming to Africa imply a 'silent tsunamis with a difference? Is it silent expansionist capitalism for exploitation or an expanding socialist movement for the common good? Africa's top exporters to China are appearing on **Map 1.**

In recent past years, Beijing singles Africa as an area of significant and valuable economic and strategic interest. Trade between China and Africa increased by 700% during the 1990s, and China is currently Africa's largest trading partner. In 2010, trade between Africa and China was worth US$114 billion and in 2011, US$166.3 billion. In the first 19 months of 2012 it was US$163.9 billion. A major aspect of this dramatic trade increase is due to the Forum on China-Africa Cooperation (FOCAC) created in 2000 (Gordon & Yang 2012; AISA Handout 2014: 7, Iwilade 2014; Tull 2006; Rotberg 2007; Padraig & Taylor, 2010; Anshan & April 2014) It should be noted that Chinese expansion into Africa is a natural extension of China's opening up to the world and its pursuit of capitalism –

policies that have been assiduously encouraged by all Western countries, some of whom now decry the results of this openness with China's expansion into Africa. (Lei 2005:487-514).

It can also be seen within the context of Den Xiaoping's speech at a Special Session of the United Nations General Assembly in 1974:

"If capitalism is restored in a big socialist country, it will inevitably become a superpower. If one day China should change her colour and turn into a superpower, if she too should play the tyrant in the world, and everywhere subject others to her bullying, aggression and exploitation, the people of the world should identify her as social-imperialism, expose it, oppose it and work together with the Chinese people to overthrow it" (See Manji /Marks 2007: ix).

The Forum on China-Africa Cooperation (FOCAC) is to institutionalise the new relations. How FOCAC will move beyond the *talking shop dichotomy* remains the challenging question for it to concretise its mission which should be structured within the premises of ***"win-win" not "win-lose"***?

However, it must be cautioned that currently, Beijing is an actor in Africa that does provide a discourse which effectively legitimises human-rights abuses and undemocratic practices under the guise of state sovereignty and 'non-interference'. Taylor (2007:24) notes that: "common sense about human rights and sovereignty is only one of the common values shared by China and Africa; there is no doubt that China's success in Africa has partly benefited from it (Wenping 2005).Has or is Africa benefiting from its resources? Is each African state responding responsibly to FOCAC? Is there a serious disconnect between the state, the people and resources use in the case of Africa?

Many factors point in the direction of China as a new favourable and welcome partner to the continent's economic transformation. Whether China will be a ***bully*** or a ***saint*** remains to be seen. It can also constitute a serious threat to the development of Africa if not properly manage. To begin with, China can be hailed as a sort of *economic miracle* or what could be described as compressing *Western 250 years of industrialisation into one generation*. China has come a long way from the humble beginnings of the *'long-march'* from underdevelopment into a service delivery society. This is a fate for Africa to draw valuable lessons as it begins its post-fifty years of independence. Africa has numerous advantages to accomplish such a developmental change. However, this calls for visionary leadership and strategically prioritising priorities for ultimate good of society. It also entails constructive mobilisation of human and natural resources, the peoples' involvement and determination to improve on their welfare and owning their development.

Khodeli (2009) analysing the paradoxical phenomenon known as *"resource curse"* explains how the abundance of natural resources often goes hand in hand with endemic poverty, corruption, a lack of institutional control and opacity in the management of resources, when it is not synonymous with the word *"war"*. Thus, despite the high price of raw materials on the world market, 60% of the world's poorest people live in resources-rich countries particularly in Africa. The quests for transparency and the obligation for States to be accountable to their citizens may well, reverse this paradoxical phenomenon transforming this *"curse"* into a *"blessing"*, in the interest of the people concerned.

China's interface with Africa is not all gold. There are dark spots which have to be patched and properly cleaned-up. The growing geo-political and economic strength of China in the world and Africa in particular sends mixed messages. China's growing importance in Africa and its presence in conflict zones, Chad, Democratic Republic of Congo, Sudan, among others to influence the strategic approach of *'look and accept China'*, and since leaders of African countries have a great deal of interest in Beijing's traditional investment approach that – unlike western donors – does not pay attention to political conditionality (Kabemba 2012). In addition, China has an eye towards a further market for its household goods, machinery and high-tech goods, which tend to be more affordable to African consumers. It is not surprising that China has gained impacted footholds and greater participation in the oil sector of African countries; for example, in Chad it has secured concessions for the China National Petroleum Company (CNPC) to the extent of building a refinery near N'Djamena (Jeune Afrique, 23 September 2007; Kopinski et al (eds.) 2010).

4

Take the case of an American Oil Executive which promised 5% royalties for Gambian oil, which implied that Gambia would receive USA$400 million a year; this was seen as too much for little Gambia. Giving 5% to Gambia was doing the country a favour while retaining 95% was the right thing to do. Or the case of Lissouba of the Congo who enacted the renegotiation of an oil contact contracted by a former military leader who demanded a 33% instead of the 15% royalties to Congo. Most of the oil companies where happy with the 33% increase royalties except a French company. The French President requested Lissouba to appoint an ex-military leader, Vice President and Minister of the Armed Forces. Lissouba did not react to the order. This resulted in his overthrow through a *'mini civil war'* in which the French Oil Company offered the rebels the use of the company boats and other logistics to chase Lissouba out of power. The new 'Military President' requested the Oil Company to pay 20% instead of the 33% royalties Lissouba was demanding (New African Magazine, No.536, February 2014).

Charles Taylor during his trial at The Hague stated how an American Oil Company offered Liberia 5 cents for every dollar of their oil, which he refused. The company was constantly pushing behind the scene for Taylor to be indicted. Interestingly, the company made a roundabout turn and offered to cause the charges to be dropped if Taylor accepted the offer of 5 cents for each dollar, which he still refused. Taylor was tried and found guilty of 'aiding and abetting rebels in Sierra Leone' and sentenced to 50 years in prison. One is not holding a brief for Taylor but unpacking the kind of double dealings characteristics of the West and in partnership with served African leaders. Is FOCAC going to be an instrument in influencing positive China/African interlude policies that leads to improved quality wellbeing of Africans? Or play a new role?

The histories of the defunct French Oil Company (ELF) Aquitaine and Loik Le Floch-Prigent, and people like Mobutu, Charles Taylor, Yahya Jammeh, Pascal Lissouba, and many others are edifying for those interested in the ways of the West in business and political dealings with Africa. The exploitation of Africa by the West is facilitated by Africa's colonial and postcolonial history, and the horrors of colonialism and slavery, which in the main, are responsible for the continent's lack of the requisite capital – human, financial, machinery and know-how – to exploit its own natural resources, and set up competitive companies/enterprises for the continent's development.

Indeed, it is possible that some Western experts or consultants usually advise African states that some procedures for adding value to their mineral resources are a bit to advance for black Africans. It is further revealed that when President Mahatma of Ghana came to power, more and more foreigners became involved in illegal mining in the informal mining sector. A review of the Mining Act which exclusively reserved small scale mining in the informal sector for Ghanaian citizen was immediately ordered; which provided for foreigners caught mining illegally to be fined USA$100.00 with the equipment used by the illegal mining operators confiscated. The scales of illegal mining and their cost in many African countries are yet to be unravelled (New African Magazine, No. 536, February 2014).

Cameroon's Newspapers 'Le Messager' No. 4046, 26 March 2014 on Mining Scandal in Cameroon; and 'La Nouvelle Expression', N0.3694, 25 March 2014) details accounts of 'mining scandals' orchestrated by barons of the Cameroon regime, including those at the highest level of the state, in collusion with foreign interests in GeoCam/Geovic (that got a mineral exploitation permit without feasibility studies and expertise); C & K Mining Inc.(which started mining operations before formal agreements were signed); Cam Iron(that lavished hundreds of millions in kickbacks to barons of the regime); SNH (with its opaque petrol transactions); SONARA (with flagrant influence peddling); and many others (Asonganyi 2014:11).

These events, constitute just a tip of the iceberg on the continent's mineral and exploitation spree, should drive a new message to African countries through the lenses of President Yahya Jammeh of Gambia; *"the solution for Africa is to be rough at the pre-exploitation negotiations, to get what it rightly deserves or the oil and other mineral resources should remain untapped until such a time that the foreign companies give Africa its due, or the continent develops its own capital, machinery and know-how to exploit the resources for itself".* Leadership role is crucial. For now

Africa seem to be suffering from leadership deficiency and determined political will to brave all odds.

Africa and FOCAC: The "Blame and Reality" Theories

China – Africa relationship has rapidly become a hot topic. The increase in trade and investments between the two continents since the establishment of FOCAC has been remarkable. This is expected to grow but not without some controversies. In some cases it is viewed with *suspicions*. Others see it as making a *'difference'* in the transformation of African countries. The *'blame and reality'* theories confidently can back claims made by either side. The 'blame' theory approach argues that societal conditions are the primary source of social problems, and that the key to understanding social problems understands the distribution of power in society. For example, Africa is underdeveloped because of colonialism (even fifty years after independence, underdevelopment is blamed on others).

The shortcomings of society are blamed on colonial rule. The 'reality' theory urges people too critically and objectively look at why things are the way they are? Why the continent is underdeveloped in the midst of plenty? Accepting the 'reality' theory provides objective critical assessment of why one is underdeveloped; and what should be done to get out of the existing predicament? For example, the reality is that Africa was colonised. But what has Africa done to show that colonialism was wrong? *FOCAC has to prove that it is the right institution at the right time for the right purpose.* As a result, either position begs for concrete answers to a number of very pertinent questions. Looking at both theories scientifically and objectively provides a constructive approach as a necessary precondition to restructuring society along more focused human needs. Fifty years on, Africa should avoid the blame approach to development.

FOCAC should focus on a structural-functional China and Africa interface on 'shared-values' in the context conceived in terms of the collective interests and aspirations of the stakeholders and in the overall interest of Africa. This chapter aims to contribute to a better understanding of the important role, relationship and aftermath in the new (FOCAC) concocted marriage between the two parties, especially with Africa. There are other related soul-searching questions needing concrete answers from China, Africa and FOCAC. Africa has to do must of the homework.

Table 1: Some Soul-Searching Questions for Africa – China (FOCAC) to Address	
What is the impact of China's role on the socio-economic transformation of the African continent?	What did Africa gain from decades of colonial rule?
	What gains have been attained in post-colonial era?
What would be the impact of FOCAC on the socioeconomic transformation of Africa?	What do they expect to harvest from the "Dragons" approach as new suitor?
What motivates China's sudden interest in Africa?	What type of critical stock-taking should be done to? streamline the past, present and to better map a new dawn for the continent?
What policy implications must African states develop to strengthen and benefit from the new accord?	How can the resources be properly developed to? improves the welfare of Africans?
Has China any hidden agenda – following the shift of power of power from the Atlantic to the Asia-Pacific region and that the continent must therefore position itself to take advantage of this development?	What is western's attitude towards Chinese courtship with Africa? Are Western interests challenged by China's aggressive entering into Africa which exposes Western exploitative agenda behind the colonisation of the continent?
Is China an aspirant great power that wants to challenge the existing status quo, or to reinforce it?	Who stands to benefit most from the new marriage and how must it be contracted?
Is China a 'rogue investor'?	What alternatives have Africa in place?
How prepared is Africa welcoming the new guest?	How prepared are African's for the marriage? How should Africa respond to China's shifting Growth model as well as craft its own development path?
What alternatives have the Chinese if the marriage collapses?	How constructively engaged, prepared and united is Africa in confronting the China's policy approaches encapsulated in the new offensive trajectory of the 'New China Dream' and in the wake of rising globalsation knowledge-based economy of the 21st century and beyond
Is China ready to alter or adjust its strategy?	
How prepared is FOCAC?	
Who controls FOCAC?	
Can FOCAC change anything?	
Where lays the balance of power?	

Source: Forje (2014)

No one can deny the fact that Africa was colonised. The challenge for FOCAC and the continent is to operate in a structural-functional way that proves 'colonial rule' or any form of invasion was and is wrong; and geared towards exploitation and not in harnessing the mineral wealth for the overall socio-economic transformation and benefit of the continent. The recent discovery of niobium, rare earth metals, titanium sands, ilmenite, zircon, coal, oil, gas, and rutile in Kenya for example, adds to the list of much needed resources from the continent. It is Africans bleeding their continent to death and not the departed colonial masters. Africans must assume responsibilities for their own circumstances take control of their development trajectories and create sustainable solutions to impediments confronting the continent. Existing lop-holes are systematically exploited by external bodies to enhance their development and domination over the continent.

8

The *"reality"* theory begins with a focus on the situation and needs of the people, by accepting that mistakes have been made in the past and with a strong determination to progressively forge ahead, constructively and scientifically responding to the challenges of the time. Therefore, China's entering into Africa provides the best possible opportunity to turn around the Euro-centric attitude adopted by African states. Is FOCAC designed to be part of the changing miracle factor for Africa's economic take-off? The particular emphasis should be on the social and wellbeing aspects of economic success encapsulated in the notion of an *African Dream* – by adopting an Afro-centric approach to the development construct. Africans should ask themselves why underdevelopment in the midst of plenty?

Africa has to develop and own its terms of development trajectory. Africa after years of western exploitation with no concrete infrastructural establishment to show must seek new ways for its socioeconomic transformation, which sends fears across the spine of powerful Western countries. China for now provides that positive avenue for change. A new *'game changer'* is emerging. The continent has to exploit its mineral wealth and other resources for the constructive development of the peoples' sustainable welfare. All these changes require strategic planning and positioning of Africa's relations with the new suitor, China in realistic perspective. Apparently, China needs Africa to sustain at least, 7-10% of its growth rates. What is Africa's optimum response vis-à-vis this new reality? Can FOCAC provide the basic nexus as a game-changing factor? Or will it slum into the old Western attitude?

It is imperative for African policy-makers to critically and objectively articulate policy strategies penetrating into the 'real' characteristics and 'reasoning' surrounding Africa-China relationships explore and deepen future partnerships based on the real needs of Africa and within the context of and as China's economy changes within the globalisation synergy context. Africa has to carefully read between the lines of the *'push and pull'* factors for partnership and within the canopy of globalisation as well as within the context of its own development goals and aspirations. Here we see a relationship between the *'blame and reality'* theory, and the *'pull and push'* factors impacting the construct of a new and brave continent. How does FOCAC fit into this construct?

Both the *"blame and reality"* theory are entangled with a number of characteristics and critiques of the Africa-China economic relations. The first as noted by (Mutambara 2013:54) is what can be termed Western-inspired criticisms: and the second, consists of genuine grievances levelled by Africans themselves. Given these challenges, there is need for a comprehensive and concerted African strategic response. Second and most importantly, Africa must not blame China as its offensive is cajoled in its interests and tailored to meet its needs and responsibility to the citizens of China. This is also the pattern adopted by the West. Third, Africa must take responsibility for her own problems and seek workable solutions – *African solutions to African problems*. Fourth, Africans must blame themselves for the current plight of the continent. For example, the exchange of African minerals and other products for Chinese manufactured and imported products are undermining Africa's own manufacturing businesses. This could be seen as the bad and ugly side of China as the suitor for the African maiden. Simply stated, Africa faces daunting socio-economic and techno-administrative challenges that have to be overcome (Forje 2009). East or West, Africa must seek its on endurable solutions to her problems.

We cannot dismiss lightly the issue of 'plunder and conflict' that the existence of mineral resources in Africa has become a curse rather than a blessing for Africa. The pernicious conflicts on the continent are increasingly being linked with the struggle over mineral resources with the result that these resources are being described as a curse afflicting the continent. The tragedy of the continent is that African elites should see these resources as a good basis for foreign interests to destabilise the continent and to act accordingly. The problem of 'blood diamonds' wars is linked with the issue of plundering resources and minerals in cohort with the global conglomerates and international mafias (Nabudere 2004;Lanning & Mueller 1979) for the interest of foreign countries.

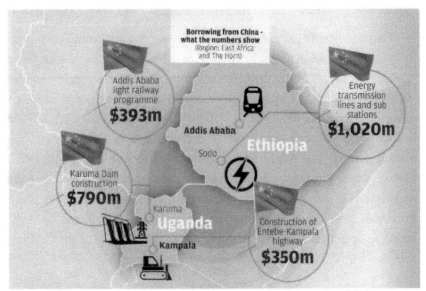

Source: New African, No.565, October 2016, An IC Publication, London United Kingdom p.51

Though China's trade with Africa has surged from USA$100billion in 2000 to USA$166 billion in 2011, it has mainly been in exchange of African minerals for Chinese manufactured goods. Essentially, there have been no signs in improving the manufacturing paradigm of African states. Importantly, there are no conditionalities for Chinese investments in Africa like those possessed by the West making Chinese stretched hand of friendship most welcome by many African countries. African policymakers must weight which alternative provides the breakthrough from underdevelopment to modernity. How best do they exploit the alternative Chinese pragmatism and experience or Western ideology? Whether to blame Africa for looking to China for ideas as the new *'game-changer'* or remain underdeveloped through the canopy of the *'double talk'* of the West? This constitute the ethical challenges facing policy-makers in Africa; challenges which are best met by educating citizens to be capable and willing to sharing the responsibility for their development and in creating a prosperous society.

China and FOCAC: The Dragon's Rapid Changing Structure

China's rapidly growing demand for energy and natural resources to meet its double digit growth rate as well as sustain its huge population increasingly necessitates important policy decisions and strategic partnership with African countries. The new dynamics of globalisation gives China new impetus to rebottle old wine in new bottles that perpetuates Africa's perspectives on the devastating impact of the slave trade and the continuation of Rodney's (1972) How Europe Underdeveloped Africa. That Africa develops Europe and Asia calls for serious debates within the continent to put in place measures that ensures new phenomenon and forward looking strategic approach on **"How Africa Can Develop It Self?"** What role can FOCAC play in developing the continent?

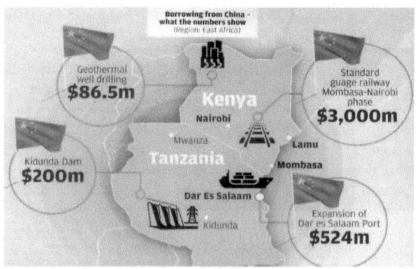

Source: New African, No.565, October 2016, An IC Publication, London United Kingdom p.51

On the other hand, blessed with a strong endowment of mineral fuels, ores and other resources, African countries can benefit immensely from Chinese demands driving commodity prices up and generates billions in infrastructure investment on the continent. Both sides need each other for varying reasons, and the exchange of essential natural resources for infrastructure to foster economic development and the welfare of citizens are more likely to benefit than paternalistic and failed aid strategies (Richardson 2010). The Chinese emerging track record is not an indicator of a new trajectory which would benefit the majority of the African people. It provides something new and significant.

Africa offers China resources. China in return offers Africa finances and technology that accelerates the social, economic and technological (SET) transformation of the continent. The Forum for China-Africa Cooperation (FOCAC) initiated in 2000 creates the requisite platform for both sides to hammer out from a constructive and critical mindset perspectives, and on equal basis, and in their best interests the much needed common grounds to meet the challenges and needs of both continents within the context of a fast changing global context of the 21st century and beyond. Whether China's entry into Africa is a new form of neo-colonialism or providing African nations with a tremendous opportunity to reconstruct itself, depends upon Africans capitalising and driving a hard bargain that provides greater benefits and dividends to the continent. What is the stand of FOCAC in championing developments in that direction?

Again, China for now, no doubt, is the dominant investor player in Africa. Its growing presence is likely to be more beneficial to the continent than Africa's experience with its existing traditional western allies. The reality of Africa's weak administrative systems, poor governance and the absence of the rule of law and total dependence on natural resources must be recognised and seriously addressed to give the continent the right leverage in its bargaining power and developmental process. The statement by President Jacob Zuma (South Africa) to Chinese and African dignitaries in 2012 is significant in this context: *"Africa's commitment to China's development has been demonstrated by supply of raw materials, other products and technology transfer. This trade pattern is unsustainable in the long term. Africa's past economic experience with Europe dictates a need to be cautious when entering into partnerships with other economies."* Such a statement like all others points towards Africa's weaknesses and strengths raising a number of fundamental issues and challenges requiring strategic planning and prioritising mechanisms for Africa to emerged into the status of a capable developmental state as the transition to a service delivery society.

In short, Africa's situation is compounded by the lack of adequate skilled human capital and technological expertise, all of which are necessary ingredients for transforming the continent's natural resources into avenues for comprehensive, endure-able and sustainable transformation of the people's welfare. Added value should be given to the continents vast abundance of natural resources. It is these acute weak*nesses that make Africa susceptible to what is commonly known as the* 'resource curse' and furthers de-industrialisation (Manji 2008). Can China-Africa accord through FOCAC turn around the *"resource curse"* into a veritable *"resource blessing"* like turning the *'brain-drain into a brain g*ain' for the good of the continent? China takes advantage of the continent's skilled manpower shortage to export labour and not technological skills into the region. Such issues should be properly hammered out within FOCAC; and for it to establish a positive and progressive agenda for the wellbeing of citizens of the two countries.

Currently there are well over 80 Chinese companies with over 300000 Chinese people in South Africa. China's role in Africa is a **'wake-up call'** for African leaders to sit-up and put the African continent in proper perspective and order to benefit from China's new rush into Africa. There are great expectations on China's role, but there are also risks of hollow outcome though far better than what the colonial masters have done to Africa. Africa's expectation must march expected China's expectation by advancing from the state of fragmented, misdirected and mismanagement attitude into serious and conscious development agenda for the welfare of African citizens. China's role in the new rush for segments of the sleeping elephant may seem to be dubious as it might currently be, if one measures it with the statement of Deng Xiaoping in 1974 - the dragon embracing capitalism and inevitably becoming a superpower. China's oil industry has experienced significant restructuring to meet the country's oil needs and in wearing the true coat of capitalism without a human face. Africa should avoid being a new punching bag.

FOCAC: A Conduit for Change!

What has characterised the Africa-China relationship since the creation of FOCAC is to critically pierce into the notion of the *'China Dream'* and juxtapose it in exploring the basis of future partnership in light of the changing circumstances as the Chinese economy changes with new entrants like India, Brazil, and others into Africa and in light of the unstoppable forces of globalisation. Africa's need are to be articulated responding to China's shifting growth model (Mutambara 2013:54-55). Presently, China is seen as an alternative to the West that the continent had already known, especially in the areas of imposed conditionality's. It is these conditionalities that most African countries are wary about. Many think of course, that China's mission is a better alternative, as they are *'problem-free'*. But what about the workers China's development projects injects into the continent with no traces of technology transfer or human skill-building left behind?

Source: Credit - New African, No.565, October 2016, An IC Publication, London United Kingdom p.53

By getting heavily involved economically in Africa, the Chinese have broken Western's hold on Africa-World trade. Historically, Europe and the USA have always considered Africa their undisputed hegemonic area of political and economic influence for exploitation.

Or what is known in African parlance as *"Chop Farm"*. China and FOCAC now presents a new competitive dynamics that does not go down well in Europe and the United States which have been supporting dictators in Africa; plundering Africa's natural resources in a new era; not adding value to African commodities and engaging in unfair and poor labour practices. The hypocrisy development paradigm campaign generated by the West comes as no surprise. The wide spread accusation of China not supporting the democratisation bandwagon is strongly wedged against what equally repossesses western *'double talk'* attitude presenting China as a 'devil' with Africa selling its soul to the devil by entering into economic and not democratic and human rights deals.

The West supports dictators in Africa as long as it is in their overall interests. The issue of *'permanent interests and not permanent friends'* come to play here. This explains why China's message and strategy resonates so strongly with many African nations and leaders, the appeal of their principle of non-interference in the affairs of sovereign states. *"One can safely state that the behaviour of the Western powers on the African continent has and continues to be double-faced and hypocritical, as they have supported regimes just as corrupt if not more than those have propped up dictators, finance conflicts, turned a blind eye to genocide and knowingly gone about business practices that used militias and child soldiers as a means to extract natural resources"* (Richardson, 2010).

Apparently, the underlining argument against China's penetration into Africa is that by supporting internationally-ostracised regimes, corruption, economic mismanagement and instability will proliferate. Many harbours the belief that the growing influence of China, call it a ('Beijing Consensus' of state-led development paradigm) throughout the continent is challenging the *'Washington Consensus'* of economic liberalism and democracy which places premium on human rights and freedoms without improved quality livelihood for the people. Western approach through the imposed financial conglomerate of the World Bank/IMF strategy of *'one size fits all'* is not the same as the pragmatism of Chinese approach. Comparatively, Western presence in Africa for centuries has been destructive and has been compressed by the progressive development advantage for the continent during the short span of FOCAC – China relationship.

This does not mean that FOCAC-China accord is friction free. Far from that as there is no smoke without a fire. No doubt, Africa is embedded with many and varied problems as well as suffering from every conceivable kind of derivate, yet there is no gainsaying that the image of Africa projected to the international community is much worse than the reality. The Sino-Africa accord should critically and objectively be addressed from the perspectives of 'a blame and reality theory' (with more emphasis on the reality theory) as well as from an 'Afro-centric – Euro-Centric - Sino-centric' angle.

Courting the Beautiful Maiden – Setting the Scene

The beautiful African maiden has many suitors. She is the envy of the entire world. What is required of her is to keep her Africanness and not to pollute it with unwanted creams and unnecessary hair mesh that distorts her beauty. African leaders must identify and uphold the continent's strength, opportunities as well as weaknesses and threats impeding or advancing its transition process. Black has always been beautiful and will remain so: hence Africa holds the future of the world. But because of her current underdeveloped status, she is treated with scorn, neglect and spitefulness the world over. The African identity is in its people, their dreams, ambitions and goals. Why is Africa the gateway to the future of the world; and why must the continent seriously invest in building its stock of skilled human capital to improve on the negative label attached to it? The newly emerged China – Africa (FOCAC) relation could be the new gateway to Africa's emancipation from the doldrums of underdevelopment to affluence. Can we talk of beauty and the beast? Or is it *beauty and beauty 'and 'beast and the beast'? Which is which - FOCAC? Concrete answers and results are imperatively needed.*

A look into the past shows that the new but aggressive courtship, to state the least, with Chinese President Jian Zemin declaration on the five cornerstones of China's Africa policy and six pillars of Sino-African relations are based on issues depicted on Table 2 – China's Africa Policy Nexus. How does these relate to improving the mining and manufacturing sectors of African countries? How can these be deployed to castigate the West? What must Africa do to ensure that it derives the best out of its given natural resources potentials in improving the wellbeing of its citizens. China has laid out its policy nexus. What is the position of Africa's leadership and policy nexus? How does FOCAC intend to function within the known and unknown agendas of China and Africa? This alone insinuate a one-way traffic; but too early to throw out the child with the bath-water. On the other hand, it could stimulate progressive policy actions on the part of those lacking behind – Africa in this case. How FOCAC will be able to manage this nexus of development remains to be seen. This may spark fear among the least developed partner member countries. Will FOCAC be an equal partnership body or constituting a hidden destructive agenda organ? Will FOCAC adopt a non-interference role (Richard 2008; Large 2008)? Will it be a peace building and a developmental constructing body in line with China's Africa's policy nexus as expounded by President Jian Zemin?

Table 2	China's Africa Policy Nexus		
	Friendship	}	Non-interference
==============➔	Equality	}	African Ownership in Dealing with its Problems
China's Africa Policy	Unity and Cooperation	}	Mutual Trust and Co-operation
And Pillars of Sino- African Relationship	Common development	}	Increase of economic assistance with limited Political conditions;
==============➔	Looking to the Future	}	Lobbying for the international community to pay more attention to Africa;
		}	Promotion of an international environment more conducive to Africa's development.
What is Africa's Response - And how does FOCAC intend to address them?			

Source; Forje 2014

Such awaited pragmatic policy orientation and focus of China on the realities of Africa's transition to a service delivery society has not been welcome by western countries with the strong belief of holding a centralised hegemonic control over the continent. Africa-China relations should therefore evolve in tandem with global political and economic developments and with respect to the sovereign rights of the people and the states within the continent (Ampiah & Naidu 2008). Chinese vision on Africa challenges African leaders is not only to develop a national and continental strategic visionary approach, but also build sufficient developmental capability and regulatory frameworks to prevent China from behaving like the exploitative western imperialists did during the colonial period which has not abated in post-colonial Africa.

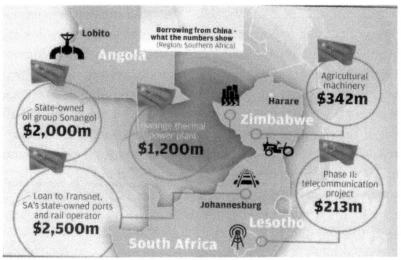

Source: Credit - New African, No.565, October 2016, An IC Publication, London United Kingdom p.55

The foregoing provides the backdrop for this paper which constructs a framework of new beginnings, undertakes an overview of vital socioeconomic and political developments in many states and a prognosis of likely futures for Africa. So far the continent has been riddle with conflicts and instability. Thus, conflict, stability and opportunity (CSO) define the frame. Africa must move from conflict to stability and opportunity. Africa is constantly being exploited because the many years of instability/conflicts made attempts at meaningful state-building difficult if not impossible, especially as every succeeding government legitimated its claims to power on the basis of undoing the wrongs of previous governments. The absence of democracy complicates the problem as it denies the continent the necessary freedoms for dynamic politics of empowerment and participation of the ordinary citizen. The continent needs stability and peaceful transition from one elected government to another. The significance of electoral stability increases when the corruption, violence and disputations characterising the conduct and outcomes of elections are taken into consideration.

The stability of the democratic regime and the country as a whole is badly rocked looking at developments in Nigeria, Central African Republic, Sudan, Southern Sudan, DRC, Burkina Faso, Somalia, and Egypt among others. Africa needs a new beginning. FOCAC should focus in that direction. Only stability can offer the right avenue and framework for its opportunity and progress towards a new society. "Democratic stability by itself enables the creation, expansion and deepening opportunities for participation, citizen engagement, bargaining, consensus-building, institution-building, and strengthening economic reforms. It is not as if opportunities did not exist in the past, but they were too restrictive, exclusionary, short-lived and discontinuous and experimental to address the major issues on any sustainable basis and scale. Another strand of opportunity consists of functional political and economic institutions which should play key roles expected of them in the reconstitution of the state" (Osaghae 2014:14).

Africa and FOCAC must leverage its new relationship with China in the best interest of its own economic transformation as well as emulate China's Peaceful Development Miracle (CPDM). The vision posed by China should be used as a new historic opportunity to capture capital in order to diversify Africa's economies and reduce aid dependency. This goes as a warning to African countries to judiciously use the monies obtain from China's interest in the continent's oil and mineral wealth should not be squandered. Loans should be used to develop local economies and escape the trappings of being dependent on external commodities markets for foreign income. It goes without saying that the new relationship should provide major potentials to break pre-existing and failed development paradigms by focusing on trade and investment in human capital development, institutional building and infrastructure development. China with a cash-rich position (USA$2.5 trillion in currency reserves) is certainly not short of funds if Africa wants or needs more. The projects they fund are indicative of their intentions often directed towards projects for infrastructure for key suppliers of oil and minerals. A breakdown of these shows 54% geared towards public works; 28, 5% to the extraction or production of natural resources and 2.5% to humanitarian activities with the remaining 15% unspecified. Their intentions are clear. FOCAC should be vigilant to ensure its independence as a just broker for both sides.

Table 3:	Mineral Resources Potential of Sub-Saharan Africa	
Commodity	Africa Relative to the World (%)	Notable Sub-Saharan Producers % of African Production
Platinum Group Metals	89	South Africa 97%
Coltan	80	Congo 100%
Diamonds	55	Botswana 35%; Congo 34%; South Africa 17%; Angola 8%
Chromite	50	South Africa 98%
Cobalt	49	Congo 75%; Zambia 22%
Manganese	33	South Africa 56%; Gabon 32%
Gold	20	South Africa 56%; Ghana 13%; Tanzania 10%; Mali 8%
Uranium	17	Namibia 46%; Niger 44%
Petroleum	12	Angola; Equatorial Guinea, Nigeria, Gabon, Gongo-Bra. Ghana, Cameroon, Sudan etc
Bauxite	9	Guinea 95%; Ghana 5%
Copper	5	Zambia 60%; Congo 17%; South Africa 14%
Aluminium Metal	4	South Africa 48%; Mozambique 32%
Iron	3	South Africa 73%; Mauritania 20%

Source: Compiled from USA Geological Survey's Mineral Year Book 2007

Africa's wealth is legendary as Ogbunwezeh (2007) and others note: "40 percent of the world's potential hydro-electric power supply; the bulk of the world's diamond and chromium; 30 percent of the uranium; 50 percent of the world's gold; 90 percent of its cobalt; 50 percent of its phosphates; 40 percent of its platinum; 7.5 percent of its coal; 8 percent of its known petroleum reserves: 12 percent of its natural gas; 3 percent of its iron ore; 64 percent of the world's manganese; 13 percent of its copper; vast bauxite, nickel and land resources and millions of untilled farmlands". These outstanding statistics have not improved the wellbeing of the African population. It goes without saying that the success of failure of every nation is a reflection on leadership. Nweke (2010:12) is explicit in expressing his disappointment with Africa's leadership, and asks: "how can people so hungry for self-rule become so dispassionate about a future they had fought and lost so much to have? How can a people destroy the very thing they love so much with the same hands that they used in building it? Why should it be that Africa keeps going round in circles instead of moving forward?" This issue is echoed in Forje (2002; 41-60): "The Disappointment of Independence" which outlines Africa's pockets of democracy and development that leaves the continent most vulnerable to exploitation more than ever before.

The continent has 40-50% of the world's mineral resources and only 10% of its population; but is still the poorest and most underdeveloped continent. Africa's poverty is not caused by lack of money. It is a mindset issue; a mentality structure – the average child born in our environment inherits. The leader who can introduce a wealth creating mindset is crucial to Africa's prosperity and the people's welfare. This should be the vision and operational dynamics for FOCAC. Therefore, the continent needs leaders who will help Africa to use people and time as critical resources. Table 3 – The Mineral Resources Potential of Sub-Saharan Africa – provides in nutshell some of the answers to the plethora of problems confronting the continent. A critical and objective look at this from the continent's perspectives provides valuable answers and the way forward to rebuilding the continent as a veritable player in global politics and development .See how rich Africa is but wallowing in endemic poverty in the age of human scientific accomplishment. With modern scientific survey, the resources of the continent could even be much larger than presented on Table 3. Cameroon for example, will soon start a geological survey of its mineral and natural resources endowment in seven of its ten regions. It is imperative for all African countries to undertake a country-wide geological survey of the mineral, gas, oil and other natural resources potentials of the country.

In addition, the continent is endowed with massive deposits of rare earth metals that are crucial for global commerce such as; titanium sands; ilmenite; zircon, coal; gas and rutile and others yet to be discovered and exploited across the continent.. South Africa alone has 80% of the world's high-grade manganese deposits, and South Africa and Zimbabwe have 80% of the platinum-group metals. Guinea has the largest iron ore products today. South Africa and Mauritania, together account for about 2% of the world reserve. For gold, South Africa and Ghana together account for about 15% of

2012 world reserves. For copper, the Democratic Republic of Congo and Zambia together have about 6% of the world reserves, and for cobalt the Democratic Republic Congo has about 45% of the world reserves. Africa's unknown reserves are likely to be many times more (African Transformation Report 2014). The demand for these resources converts the continent into a conflict prone zone; making resources a curse rather than a blessing to the people. How well armed is FOCAC to ensure that resources remain blessings to the region and used in transforming the quality well-being of the population?

Witness the recent discoveries of oil in Ghana, high-grade iron ore in Guinea; oil and gas in East Africa, gas and coal in Mozambique notes the report. Thanks to the high demand, Africa's share of global production is significant for many minerals: South Africa at 77% for platinum and 46% for chromate, Democratic Republic of Congo at 53% for cobalt and 21% for industrial diamonds and Namibia and Niger at 16% for uranium. With the discovery of new mineral deposits, African countries are challenged to make maximum returns from its fledgling extractive industries; diversify the process of exports, from raw materials to process products. African countries are now discovering the power and wealth of extractive minerals should draw valuable lessons from other countries that long discovered these resources for the development of the country). The demand for these resources makes the continent a conflict prone zone; making resources a curse rather than a blessing to the people.

Based on this statistical data, Africa is blessed with a strong endowment of not only mineral fuels and ores, but other resources, and therefore, courted by many financially, military and technologically powerful nations, China for example. Seen within this perspective, China has strategic economic interests in Africa and is increasingly in need of certain strategic natural resources, crude oil for example. In 2005, Nigeria, Angola, Equatorial Guinea, Gabon, Congo Brazzaville, Sudan and Chad supplied almost 30 per cent of China's crude oil imports, compared to nine per cent from Nigeria, Angola and Gabon in 1995. Comparatively, the Middle East supplied 45 per cent of China's crude oil in 1995, and 47 percent in 2005. Crude oil import from East Asia was 41 per cent in 2005 and 7 per cent in 1995; while Russia's supply was within the range of 0 per cent in 2005 and 10 per cent in 1995. As a result of China's increased dependence on Africa for crude oil, trade between Beijing and Africa has been on the steady increase. Who is benefiting from the increased trade phenomenon? How many large scale industries have the Chinese created in Africa? What is the level of technology-transfer to the continent compared to the resources being milked from Africa? What is FOCAC's stand on this pertinent issue? Tangible proves and answers are needed.

Many of Africa' resource-rich countries simply lack the institutional capacity to fully assess and collect the governments' share of the profits. "The number of ministries and agencies responsible for assessing the different income streams to government can also impair the ability to collect revenues, as can the weak government accounting systems. Countries have to put in place systems to ensure that they are earning a fair share from their resources – and to promote local content and linkages to the rest of the economy. Governments should not allow the revenues from the resources extraction to lead to uncontrolled public spending that contributes to high inflation, wage hikes, and exchange rate appreciations, discouraging other exports. Prudent macroeconomic and exchange rate management is thus critical in avoiding the resources curse. The various agencies that collect revenues for the country need the skills and resources to create a clear, comprehensive tax and fiscal regime that can be managed to collect revenue for the state. Where skills are not available domestically countries should engage qualified international audit, legal, and commercial consultants – and twin their support to develop local capability" (ACET, African Transformation Report 2014). Corrupt practices and behaviour eliminated.

Apparently, some African countries have started to be foresighted in addressing the situation. Apart from South Africa with long experience in mining, Tanzania's response to minerals and gas discovery takes the bold step at the Mzumbe University in collaboration with Stellenbosch University (South Africa) in preparing Masters Degrees programmes in managing huge projects in mining, gas and oil. And as a response to the nation's development needs. In addition, the Tanzania Commission for Universities has authorised a new master's degree course in leadership and management, business administration and social entrepreneurship. It is imperative for African governments, civil society and the private sector to empower more people with oil and gas exploration expertise and to encourage more and more students to enrol in these fields of studies. By building the necessary human and institutional capacity, can Africa build, control and improve on the status of manufacturing and trade as a prelude to improving the quality well-being of citizens. What does it mean to FOCAC in engaging in the human resources development initiatives of African countries (Ashan and April, 2013)?

Resources, Investment and Trade: The Pull and Push Factors

Apparently, the extraordinary developments ongoing within the Sino-African new found love is partly China's spectacular ascendancy and impact on the world economy. It should be noted that trade links between the two continents in 2005 barely represented 25 per cent of China's foreign trade. Accordingly, many of the resources imported from Africa are strategic for China's rise to superpower status. China is now Africa's third-ranked trade partner (after the US and France), from a much lower base 25 years ago, passing Britain, Portugal, Japan, India, Italy, and Germany on the continents global trade list. It is therefore with some trepidation that these external powers view China's perceived infringement on traditional Western spheres of courtship, influence, coupled with further perceptions that China's focus on *'government-business'* is weakening international efforts to isolate autocratic governments, strengthen democratic governance, and promote human rights (CCR 2007:14; Zweig & Jianhai (2005:32). The policy context is an important factor influencing the China- Africa accord.

The resources potential and state of underdevelopment and other factors constitute some of the pull factors. With globalisation, the economy restructuring towards industrial production and services, African countries are attracting large numbers of labourers from rural areas as well as from other countries. With increasing unemployment hitting hard on the unemployed youths in Africa, social tensions and xenophobic tendencies become imperative, as well as the control over mineral resources and institutions. Thus social movements, trade unions, and Diasporas communities, respectively, find political leverage by using transnational networks for support, enabling them to exert increased pressure on governments and corporations. The influx of migrant workers influences local politics, pushing norms and policies towards greater protection for example human rights.

Japan shows new investment interest by providing USA$32billon to resource-rich African nations for investment in infrastructure and mineral resource development. In addition, the country will fund education, health-care and human resources development, and cement relations with Africa. Japan's new assistance package for Africa is the starting point of the supply chain for the minerals the country requires for its automotive and electronic industries. Will a new East – West or West-Asian conflict emerged on the African continent on the race for resources? How prepared are African countries to confront such and emerging resources conflict predicament? Without security of supply for these metals, it stands to lose large parts of its global market share in these sectors Seen here, Africa's resources holds the key for the economic growth and success of many of today's economic giants. African countries have to indigenise and this calls for visionary leadership and for the continent to own its resources and development path.

Africa provides a perfect courtship of an ideal match in meeting China's growing demand for energy and natural resources as well as important strategic partnership with African nations. China's fuel imports from Africa increased from US$10.1 billion in 2004 to US$38.5 billion in 2008 an increase of 280%. Africa's exports of non-fuel minerals rose from US$1.4 billion in 2004 to US$7.2 billion in 2008, an increase of 402.7%. During the same period, exports of precious stones and metals (mainly platinum and diamonds) increased from US$742 million to US$1.77 billion in 2008, indicating a percentage increase of 138.8%. Apparently, the demand by Beijing for raw materials has helped to increase world prices for commodities, favouring African countries and, of course, increasing revenues. It could be observed that Sino-Africa trade increased from about USA$10 million in 1950 to USA$100 million in 1960. This trade took another 20 years to increase from USA$100 million to USA$1 billion, and required yet another two decades to rise from USA$1 billion to USA$10 billion. However, it took only four years for this trade to grow from USA$10 billion in 2000 to USA$30 billion in 2004. Remarkably, the total trade between Africa and China reached USA$55.5 billion in 2006: a 40 per cent increase over 2005. Consequently, at the FOCAC meeting of November 2006, the Chinese Premier, Wen Jiabao, proposed that Beijing and African governments should increase their cooperation and aim to boost bilateral trade to USA$1000 by 2010 (CCR, 2007:14; see also Briefings on Preferential Tariff Policy 2005).

China's trade with Africa has surged from US$10 billion in 2000 to US$16 billion in 2011 For example; South Africa's manufacturing barely contributes 15% of Gross Domestic Product (GDP); Kenya 11% and Nigeria 10%. Trade between South Africa and China increased from USA$15 billion to about USA$9 billion, making South Africa (with about 20 per cent of Chinese trade in Africa) Beijing's second largest trading partner in Africa after Angola today. This is mostly in the exchange of African minerals for Chinese manufactured goods. While China exports manufactured and agricultural goods, electronics and textiles to South Africa, it imports manganese, gold, tobacco, aluminium, car parts and chrome ore from South Africa. China is also exporting electronic goods to ten other mostly Southern African countries from South African brand-names such as SAB Miller, Anglo-Gold Ashanti, Anglo-American, Standard Bank, and Spur all have a presence in China (Centre for Conflict Resolution (CCR) 2007:7).

On the other hand, the world has advanced and is advancing while the continent seemingly is falling behind making it a continent described as 'poverty in wealth'. It is challenge to which the universities of Africa, African think-tanks, policy-makers in Africa should rise, doing so in partnership and synergy with independent networks (FOCAC, for example) and free-thinking individual minds. In a way Chinese imports are undermining Africa's own manufacturing businesses. Chinese involvement in crisis-ridden Zimbabwe could be seen to be of strategic importance to both parties. Beijing obtained an advantage in securing mining concessions as well as provides commodity-based loans at an extraordinary value to Zimbabwe's economic situation. However, a major aspect of trade relations are supposed to consist of textile, clothing and leader goods exports from Zimbabwe to China; but cheap Chinese goods have contributed to job losses in many African countries. The influx of Chinese goods contributes to the weakening of Zimbabwe's already 'bankrupt' economy. China's exports of about 74 per cent of imports of garments contributes to serious job losses estimated at between 23.000 and 85.000 in South Africa in 2006.

According to the Ghana Investment Promotion Council (GIPC), 2011 saw 79 Chinese investment projects registered with a total value of USA$145m, while in 2012, China registered 56 projects, making it the top investor in the country in terms of a number of registered projects, . Other figures show that more than 30 Chinese companies were engaged in project contracting in Ghana by the end of 2011. The value of the newly signed contracts totalled USA$1.57bn. China has also been on a spending spree in Ghana and in other African countries supporting the construction of infrastructure. The Ghana Development Bank, for instance, has committed to providing aid assistance to the government of Ghana to the tune of USA$3bn in commercial loans to cover 12 projects, including oil and gas, irrigation of the Accra plains, rehabilitation of the western corridor railway infrastructure, And retrofitting of the Takoradi port, among others. (Gyasi 2014:75). Like in most African countries, Chinese investment areas are mainly in construction, mining, steel, industry, building materials, chemical industry, the pharmaceutical sector, food processing, fisheries, agriculture, slate production and power plants among others. Following the Fitch rating, China's Export-Import (Exim) Bank lent USA$67.2bn to Sub-Saharan Africa between 2001 and 2010, overtaking the World Bank's lending of USA$54.7bn. China also handed out USA$7bn in grants to more than 30 African countries as its quest for natural resources has come in exchange for building roads and railways, and nurturing a market for Chinese products.

Within the past decade more than 800.000 Chinese businesses (mostly in the retail sector) were established across Africa. Trade between the two continents was valued at about USA$166bn in 2011, from a mere USA$10.5bn in 2000. China is now Africa's largest trading partner having surpassed the United States of America in 2009. Such astronomic growth is due thanks to China's policy of based on the principles of non-interference in the internal affairs of African countries, and partly due to its quick approach to did delivery. China provides aid in the form of hard cash or investment in physical infrastructure, like assisting to build schools, hospital, roads, railways, dams, agribusiness, and sending out doctors to helping poor countries. With these and many developments going on across the continent, some experts contend that Africa is chewing too quickly at the juicy carrot being dangled by Chinas, and in the process getting short-changed by importing cheap Chinese goods while exporting valuable commodities like oil and timber (Gyas 2014).

With such developments, Africa risks entering a new and unsustainable 'colonial relations' in the 21st century by continuously exporting raw materials while improving Chinese manufactured sector and destabilising its own economic take-off. African countries should be genuinely concern with this kind of development – the extractive trade in raw materials without added value, understating the value of unexploited natural resources; bringing labour from China with low employment of locals; little or no skills or technology transfer; buying primary goods and selling African manufactured goods; creates unfair local labour practices; and cheap Chinese goods (sometimes low quality) undercutting African products. The main economic mainstay of Zambia is the mining sector. As leading producer of copper, and to a lesser extent, the country produces zinc, lead, silver and cobalt as well as possessing large nickel and iron-ore deposits. Zambia is dependent on external investment to develop its mining sector. China's increasing need for raw materials and minerals is therefore viewed as a strategic opportunity for Zambia's economic take-off. Like other African countries, the major concern, however, is how external demand for Africa's mineral wealth can translate into revenue that can be used for the continent's economic development.

Many African countries have difficulties in attracting foreign capital. Attracting foreign investments, they have to develop their infrastructure with particular emphasis on transportation (railways, good roads, etc.) and energy. While Africa needs capital in order to build its infrastructure, it needs its infrastructure to attract foreign investment to better take full advantage of its raw materials. For many countries, Zimbabwe for example, China's involvement has been strategic. China has gained advantage in securing mining concessions; providing commodity-based loans at an extraordinary good value because of Zimbabwe's economic crisis. Furthermore, a major aspect of trade relations consists of textile, clothing and leather goods export from Zimbabwe to China. Yet, cheap Chinese goods contribute to large-scale job losses not only in Zimbabwe but also in other country's fledging manufacturing and textile industries (Ndulo 2007; Sachikonye 2007). China's relations with African countries cannot be assessed in a vacuum; and the effects of globalisation are indeed an important consideration as well as in meeting the growing needs of its population when examining the new found accord.

Growing instability in the Middle East and uncertainty in other regions of the world, makes some countries within the Central African sub-region a fertile place for China especially as these countries are endowed with mineral resources much needed by China (Curtis, 2007: Yates 2007). Nigeria, Africa's most populous country, and a major oil exporter (ranked sixth world oil exporter and still unable to provide reliable and predictable supplies of petroleum to its over 150 million citizens), with a focus to becoming a major economic player by 2020, envisage a number of increasingly attractiveness to foreign investors may be reshaping the relationship. The same applies to South Africa to redouble efforts in meeting the basic needs of its population. Enhanced basic infrastructure is crucial first step in the direction of attracting more investors. These are some of the issues FOCAC should be addressing.

Therefore, a focused strategic well-calculated policy approach will benefit corporations in favour of Africa and China provides a proper calling for. The cooperation should oscillate on the orientation and strong emphasis on development and moral values - the idea of economics as a moral science; a science of human beings in communities, not of interacting robots that benefits China. Africa needs partners that foster growth; with growth fostering employment; and employment contributing to improved and sustainable wellbeing of citizens. In short, growth might sensibly be pursued as a means to one or more basic goods – health requires decent food and medicine. Leisure requires time away from toil. Personality requires a place to withdraw, a 'room behind the shop'. Populations too poor to afford these goods have every reason to seek to become richer. Here in an affluent world, however, the material prerequisite of health, leisure and personality have long since been achieved; our difficulty is making proper use of them" (Skidelsky and Skidelsky 2012) and ensuring that the most vulnerable in Africa part-take in the process of shared-prosperity.

We need to understand the *'balancing act'* of China's Africa Policy. Africa provides the crucible in which China's *'soft power'* is tested. For example, Sudan-China bilateral relations, in particular, illustrates the complexity and nuanced nature of Beijing's relationship with African countries (Wenping 2007; Srinivasan 2007). Most African countries are still in the stage of transitional and fragile-post independence and post-conflict stage. Entrenched predatory economic relations have torn apart most of the continent's resource-rich country and control over these resources is not yet fully consolidated by these countries. As most governments are weak and fragile emerging either from a protracted civil war conflict, (DRC, Sudan, Chad, South Sudan, etc.) and autocratic rule for decades, the political economy of these nations are mostly maintained and run by Western patronage of the former colonial powers.

The return to democratic governance has seen little changes. China however does not promote democratisation as a pre-requisite for economic development in African countries. She is more interested and focused in obtaining needed resources for the rotation of its industrial structure and welfare. Apparently, there are no simple cut and paste solutions. But Africa has to be cautious in signing a new pact of prolonged colonial rule and exploitation. Western Europe has to listen to Easterly (2006) call for a more constructive approach to foreign aid, in which researchers concentrate on implementing targeted, piecemeal improvements that are tailored to each given situation, instead of focusing on one-size-fits all plan.

Africa can be prosperous without following the democracy model of the West; while embracing such a model does not guarantee economic success. The contrived and tenuous links between democracy and economic development should be rejected with the contempt that they deserve. Democracy must be embraced as a public good in itself, not as a pre-condition for something else. A democratic tradition, respect for human rights, and good governance disposition allow our people to express themselves and determine their destiny as fully empowered citizens. African states must internally, without depending on the benevolence or conditionalities of external players strive to creatively and simultaneously achieve both democracy and economic prosperity (Mutambara op cit). While democracy is necessary, ensuring bread and butter on the table daily and sleeping with two eyes close is equally important. At the same time, what is most important, and what intrigues African policymakers about China, is that it can provide a personal level of expertise that Western experts cannot. Without the resources potentials of Africa, China is able to feed its huge population. Africa is not. Something is wrong somewhere which must be adequately looked into. Can FOCAC provide such an entry point, not only looking at mineral and oil resources?

The pattern and manner in which China-Africa accord oscillates does not show any form of human capital development and proper technology transfer to Africa. The Chinese come with their financial capital, human capital and finished products leaving no room for building the human capital and industrial capability of African countries. Technology transfer fails taking place in African countries, also the non- development of manufactured products. In short, it is a *"win-lose"* situation for Africa. It is not directed towards improving on the manufacturing sector of the continent either. Nor is China-Africa connection directed towards building the continent's human capital to give added value to its resources. The Wealth of Nations (Adam Smith), Rodney's (1972) Underdevelopment of Africa; the Stages of Economic Growth (Rostow 1960) and the Late-comer Advantage (Gerschenkron 1962) including other similar publications highlight the importance of human capital development and technology in the process of transformation from a backward economy to a quality service delivery polity. The real problem is that of the continent always being evasive, mealy-mouthed and blaming others. Things have to change for the continent to harvest the best out of its resources.

Africa's underdevelopment is rooted in an ill-will and the ineptitude of the continent's leaders to articulate and implement forward looking people-oriented policies for the sustainable transformation of the continent. The truth is, all those who can and dare voice the grievances are stifled, ignored and downgraded. Such attitude fails in providing African solutions to African problems. Without which, the continent emerges as the best losers in the China-Africa (FOCAC) accord. Many argue that Africa is being short-changed by importing cheap Chinese goods while exporting valuable commodities. Because of Africa's state of endemic poverty, citizens are mesmerised with the availability of affordable cheap quality Chinese products. Can FOCAC help improve the quality of exported Chinese goods into the continent as well as ensure fair trade between the continents? Africa has to improve on its import quality control mechanisms.

In terms of manufacture, cheap and poor quality Chinese goods continue to flood the continent pushing locally produced products to the background. Often Chinese goods sent to Africa are characterised as *"buy, use, throw and come tomorrow"* only to repeat the scenario each time. Such trade invasion is detrimental to the industrialisation of Africa. The importation of poor quality goods should be blamed on the type of *'quality control mechanism system'* put in place by African governments for imported goods. Though price-sensitive markets across the continent are receptive to the easy availability of low-priced Chinese goods, however, a cautionary tale can be narrated as Africa must be vigilant to ensure Chinese products do not flood the market to the detriment of any chance of starting domestic production in non-natural resource sectors. Nesi (2013) lamenting how Chinese competition devastated the Italian industry should be a lesson to African countries to step-up their quality control mechanism system to better safeguard local products. Nesi opines: that the biggest problem was the dismantling of the international clothing regime, which allowed cheap Chinese textiles to flood into Europe. At the time, economists predicted that Italian firms would in return be able to sell their high-priced textiles to

China. But this promise proved a chimera, except for a few firms with famous names. This highlights why a progressive people focused Afro-centric approach is imperative.

The pull and push factors in the FOCAC marriage exists for both sides. These push and pull factors make for the *'good, bad, and ugly'* relationship. Both sides from their vantage points have to shifter the good from the bad and ugly to achieve the kind of development that best suit their short, medium and long-term interests. How can Chinese 'soft power' help in accelerating the activities of FCAC? (Ashan & April 2013). For Africa, first, is how to encourage Chinese investment of finances boosting local manufacturing capacity; second, for Africa to diversify with strong emphasis on manufacturing; curbing the inflow of poor quality goods; and corrupt practices among officials; and third, for the continent to own its development path. It means sharpening its policy and implementation mechanisms. African governments, desperate for some financial relief, are willing to make whatever changers are necessary to bring capital into their countries. The multinationals are setting the terms: harmonisation of free trade, and protection of private industrial products and investments. The hidden agenda of Africa and China must no longer remain secret; and for Africa to move forward in attracting and encouraging corporate investment in the continent. Such investments would mean bringing back a factory to Africa and increasing the employment opportunities for the fast growing youth population. African products should be promoted as well.

More factories, more employment will reduce poverty as well as increase the possibilities for attaining 'basic goods' and meeting 'basic needs'. The 'basic goods and needs' constitute living well. The 'basic goods' are health, security, respect, harmony with nature, friendship, leisure and personality – which can be defined as *'the ability to frame and execute a plan of life reflective of one's tastes, temperament and conception of the good that often entail 'autonomy'* (Skidelsky and Skidelsky 2012). The Chinese have framed their invasion strategy within the context of seven basic needs (*health, security, and respect, harmony with nature, friendship, leisure and 'personality'*) which constitutes the living paradigm for their citizens. Within this frame of mind, the ability to frame and execute their invasion strategic plan of continuous development and progress must be reflective of their citizen's wellbeing. Is Africa operating on the same wave length to realise 'basic needs' for the people of the continent?

To unlock Africa's deficiencies in the mineral and manufacturing sectors like in other areas requires comprehensive and quality education for Africans to be in a key positions to address the demands and challenges of this century and to prepare future generations to be well equipped to withstand impeding future challenges without which this generation has failed in its obligations and responsibility presently and in the future. The challenge for this generation of leaders is to bear in mind that education constitutes the critical and solid foundation for the reconstruction and development of Africa. No doubt as noted by Mwamwenda and Lukhele-Olorunju (2013:2).

> *"education is investing in economic development, given that sustainable development calls for adequate and ever-increasing skills and knowledge bases, which are inherently products of education. Moreover, education not only contributes to economic development, but also to a sustainable democratic society, as its graduates positively contribute to and participates in the governance of their society."*

In short, "education transforms lives and contributes to success and prosperity in society" opines First Woman Vice President of South Africa (Phumile Mlambo-Ngcuka). The continent should not only gun for education but quality education as well as to ensure increasing quantity to meet the challenges and prospects of the region.

China – Africa interlude for now looks like a one way traffic: it still has to evolve on the structure of a *'win-win'* situation or from the perspective of *'equity-benefit or prosperity-sharing'*. China has a clearly formulated long-term agenda strategy in terms of its objectives for engaging with Africa. Apparently, Africa is still uncertain as to what it wants to achieve from a reinforced relationship with China. Without a focused long-term prioritised strategic agenda; and in the absence of a constructive control mechanism to monitor China's pledges the relationship will oscillate on the basis of a 'win-lose' relationship for Africa.

The resources of the continent will be continuously exploited in return for peanuts investments (compared with what China benefits from the continent) designed to deepen the dependency of Africa on China (see Shinn and Eisenman 2012; Rotberg 2013; The Economic Commission on Africa 2013). Africa is a rich continent and does not deserve to be where it is. Africa must unite; come together, speak with one voice; have one destiny: and the African Union as the continent's umbrella organisation must sit down and sensibly deliberate on the continent's economy as its way forward to enhancing the welfare of the people. The continent must avoid the situation where (Ankomah in an interview with the Zimbabwe Minister for Youth Development, Indigenisation and Economic Empowerment 2013: 48-55) speaks of "Milking the Cow Without Feeding it is unacceptable". Will FOCAC present a different image?

Unlocking Africa's Mineral and Manufacturing Debacles

Unlocking the continent's mineral and manufacturing debacles requires new development strategies and attitude toward entrepreneurship. Fostering African entrepreneurship will accelerate the manufacturing debacle the continent is wrongly plunged into. Africa's entrepreneurs face a monumental challenge which has to be overcome to grapple with as millions of unemployed youths remain with an uncertain future. There are jobs to be created in a myriad of small and micro enterprises. Apparently, there is no shortage of entrepreneurs in Africa. What they need most is new orientation, skill or capacity building and financial backing. The private sector, especially the informal sector has proved its worth, as during the years of economic crisis small firms in the informal sector provided and continue to provide a growing share of jobs and output services to the nation. Contextualised within this premises there is need for FOCAC to (i) improve the business environment; (ii) expand access to credit facilities especially to women; (iii) encourage self-sustaining services; (iv) stimulating local markets; (v) creating friendly policies in respect of taxation, access to credits and scaling down all forms of administrative red-tapes that hinder the growth of the sector as well as impedes the quality of welfare of the people.

These and other positive measures will have a trickle effects in the manufacturing sector as well as it will encourage greater investments in the continent's untapped mineral wealth exploitation. Other policy measures for FOCAC should include;-

- developing the energy sector and improving on road, transport, railway infrastructure; (note that the expanding mineral sector requires sustained energy supply and road transportation) ;
- sustainable funding for development;
- mobilising domestic private saving and investment;
- creating an enabling friendly investment environment – one that fosters private investment – domestic and foreign;
- closer ties among African countries – regional integration and coordination should be encouraged – facilitating the free movements of people and goods;
- overcoming the nexus of weaknesses in the agricultural sector; and
- human capacity building among others.

The challenge facing Africa's mineral resources and manufacturing is exceptional. But the cost of failure and not acting rightly is appalling. The focus for the continent should be long-term strategic planning of not less than 50 years ahead, drawing experiences from the past fifty years of deepening crisis, poor terms of trade, weak growth in the productive sectors; uncontrolled population growth and less quality services delivery to citizens. It is crucial for each country to get its equation right and for the African union to ensure proper coordination and continental execution.

Africa's underdevelopment problems cannot be solved quickly or through a single focus on capital accumulation or economic adjustment. The political aspects need to be looked into. The continent's production structures need to be transformed and policies need to be reoriented radically. While national policies are needed as each country is unique, there is equally a need for broad based continental approach. Many inter-related factors stand on the way of progress for the continent – the pace of technological advance, the weakening market for primary products and the rapidly changing structure of world production impact on the sustainable transformation of the continent putting pressure on policymakers to look far-into-the-future. Thus a long-term perspective is imperative. For now Africa lacks a long-term comprehensive strategy for its transition from a backward to modern economic structure.

The silent tsunamis are the existence of *trade inequality'* in the world. Africa has the resources and not the vision to eradicate its state of poverty and underdevelopment. Trade justice is called for as leverage towards sustainable development. The challenge here is to enable the poorest regions to benefit from international manufacturing and trade where appropriate and yet allow them the special and differential treatment necessary so that African countries can develop strategic sectors of their own – so that they are not solely dependent upon producing primary products such as basic foodstuffs, That sad, the approach should be supported by technology transfer, human capital development, entrepreneurship, innovation, development and proper utilisation of local resources. China-Africa accord should be a house that unites resources, development and sustainability. For now, China's entry into the continent is impacting positively and negatively, and it is left to African countries to make the right choices and ensure that negative consequences are converted into positive and beneficial impacts to the continent. Globalisation as it is now, is affecting indigenous crafts and trade. Can the Chinese help African countries to turn around existing negative or impeding factors holding back Africa's progress?

The Afro-Centric, Euro-Centric or Sino-Centric" Approach

The formation of FOCAC constitute an attempt by both countries to build stronger ties of partnership demonstrates Africa's persistent aspiration and desire to reduce its dependency on the West. Africa's mineral resources and the West-China invasion of Africa could be classified as an axis of evil. It is like the people of Southern Cameroons in 1961 had to make a choice of two evils (Forje 1981: Sobseh 2012; Awasom 2011). Africa is called upon to choose between the 'one size fits all, aid, and dependency prone approach' and the 'pragmatism of China's state-led business development agenda'. The choice is Africa's. Emulating or accepting the Chinese approach is not an inherently bad thing if only it works to improved and sustained the wellbeing of the citizens. Despite its vast oil wealth, Central Africa still struggles to sustain strong inclusive economic growth. (Akitoby and Coorey 2012). Africa should note that Western countries trade with and invest in China, and yet China is certainly not a Western-type democracy. If the West does not present democracy or human rights preconditions to China before investing or dealing with the country, why should China place such conditionalities on African regimes before engagement?

Therefore, an Afro-centric approach first is the start of objectively seeking 'African Solutions to African Problems'; by emulating the Sino-centric strategy, it enhances Africa's strive towards owning its development agenda. FOCAC operate and prioritise an Afro-centric approach. But a successful Afro-centric agenda requires a combination of input factors - (i) servant and served leadership; (ii) a committed pro-active citizenry that is responsive to ideas of a visionary servant leadership; (iii) a risk-taking productive and competitive private sector capable of adding value to the natural resources potential of the continent; and (iv) an international community equally responsive to the constructive, progressive desires and aspirations of the exploited people of Africa. Western approach which goes under the 'aid' syndrome or handouts, of course, is that they do nothing to address the root causes of the continent's poverty. The food insecurity crisis and the Arab Spring constitute a wake-up call to African leaders to focus attention on creating the requisite environment for the employment of the continent's population. The key to that is diversifying the continent's economy. If the manufacturing sector (and trade) is to be improved, strong emphasis should be directed towards human capital, incentives to entrepreneurial activities, research and development and tax heavens to the private sector. African countries must invest heavily in education reform and vocational training. A new business ethics and approach should emerge (Kelsall 2013).

There is much more in common with the Afro-centric and Sino-centric ideals that can catapult the continent's mineral and other resources to the greater advantage of the African people as compared to the Euro-centric approach which has been the dominant development agenda for ages past but only contribute to the impoverishment of the continent. This does not excaudate the fact that certain weaknesses exist in the 'Afro-centric – Sino-centric' development trajectory. The scramble for Africa is on. Investors size up opportunities in the new Africa of post-1990, even as it struggles to implement political and economic reforms. But as Africa boasts uncommon potentials, it also faces substantial challenges. Africa should draw lessons from China's experiences (Hutton 2006). The good news for Africa is that it is still an untutored 'research desert' waiting for serious investors. FOCAC should think seriously in that direction. The bad and ugly news is that it lacks nearly everything needed to develop its natural resources potentials and to run a business: stable electricity, ample paved roads, logistics, middle managers, an operational tax system, normal bank loans and laws governing industries attractive to foreign and domestic investors linking the mining and other areas in holistic developmental approach. There is a compelling quest for integrating sub-Saharan Africa into the global economic system (Moss 2007) as well as for diversification of its products and being competitive.

Africa does not differ from other frontier markets struggling to overhaul problem economics and general underdevelopment status. Africa host some of the world's longest-running ethnic insurgencies, precisely in the borderlands that possess so many natural resources; the Democratic Republic of Congo; Somalia, Central Africa Republic, to list but a few. China through FOCAC should see ethnicity and democratic governance as assets not liabilities in the developmental process. Therefore, the idea of non-interference in State's activities needs a second thought. What distinguishes it is the fact that it has only now embarked on political and economic reforms simultaneously. Africa needs ethnic and political stability if she wants lasting economic development. It needs to develop its human capital. It needs an aggressive and risk-taking, entrepreneurial private sector to give added value to its mineral potentials and other resources. Some valuable lessons can be learned from Zimbabwe's 'indigenisation policy strategy'. Indeed Africa has no way out. Africa has to transform its relations with the rest of the world by ensuring that the true value of the country's resources is taken into account in investment transactions.

For now, most countries are stifling people, leaving them to wallow in abject poverty while our resources enrich others abroad. It is now time for Africans to realise that they must negotiate the true value of their resources. Africa cannot escape this. Negotiating the true value of their resources has no colour – whether Europe, China, Russia or America - the resources of the continent must be used to improve the welfare of the people, first, by asserting the rights of the people and second, by ensuring their ownership. The African balance sheet is weak because the continent's resources are not captured on the balance sheets of the multinational companies and are not used to benefit the people. Something is wrong somewhere which needs urgent ratification for the people to benefit from their natural endowment.

The SWOT "Ubuntu and Harambee" Spirit – Lessons for FOCAC

The take-home message or lessons is simple and straight forward. China's metamorphosis into an emerging global economic force over the past few decades presents the continent of Africa with a model worth emulating. To begin with, the Chinese stated out by imitation and innovation of consumer goods and exporting to frontier markets that are resource-rich, but lack the technical expertise and technology to manufacture. Knowledge, entrepreneurial and skills-sharing should be of the utmost priority to Africa. The 'Ubuntu mindset' provides a pre-requisite for public sector leadership, excellence and as pathfinder for creativity, innovation, entrepreneurship, productivity and growth. Africa needs to understand the 'Ubuntu ideology' and the 'Ubuntu mindset' in transforming the continent as a service delivery society and world player. Africa should inject into the mindset of FOCAC the "Ubuntu Spirit". Of course, there is nothing as 'free lunch', but 'hard work and cooperation' on both parties.

Good leadership and a proactive citizenry are urgently needed. Africa has to make the final decision which development path to highlight given the prevailing global paradigm. The intriguing thing about the Sino-African relationship, however, is it going beyond a relationship simply based on trade to a boom in investment that is challenging the classic development paradigms established by Western Financial Conglomerates under the canopy of The World Bank and International Monetary Fund? There is hardly a month that passes without China signing a multimillion-dollar bilateral agreement with an African country for the construction of roads, railways, ports, dams, football stadiums, hotels, offices block and name the rest. It is no longer the search for minerals and other resources but the attempt to implant a new structure of developmental approach that touches on the lives of the people in a way. Land acquisition has also entered the jig-saw.

Despite the fragile state of the continent's underdevelopment, it is blessed with vast natural riches opportunities to turn around its predicament. Using the SWOT approach (strength, weakness, opportunities and threats) the continent can better formulate its development strategies. The continent's strength and opportunities are its vast resources and untapped research desert; a rapidly growing youthful population and many more things in its favour. The weaknesses and threats (weak human capital development, fragile institutions, poor governance, poverty, corruption, and unemployment) are as many but can be overcome through a good combination of 'strength, opportunities, leadership and the ubuntu spirit'.

The dialectics of Africa-China (FOCAC) accord is in the court of the people premised within the ideological orientation of 'growth with depth' if Africa is to transform. Both sides must be guided by the *"Ubuntu Spirit"* – the act of sharing and avoiding the greedy construct of might or riches being right. Developing a sense of shared belonging and dialogue would lead groups to avoid conflict and share common interests, build trust, lessen conflicts, prejudice and stereotypes, improves the chances of making progress on key issues and build strong relationships essential for reconstructing or reconstituting solid and peaceful communities. Mutual dialogue and encounter can help people understand each other. The new China-Africa relationship should build on these principles - sharing for the common good for both parties. Understanding this African cultural trait empowers people to build new bridges and contacts between individuals and communities to form new patterns of relationships.

New modes of political, economic and social interaction as well as acceptance of a culture of dialogue and other supporting levels of society will contribute positively to the China-Africa accord and help diffuse any form of confrontation, for example the rising xenophobic tendency due to inequalities in society. To transform requires growth in conjunction with other inputs. These are issues which FOCAC should pay greater attention to as depicted in Table 4. New Vision for FOCAC / Africa's Growth with Depth: requires a number of interrelated issues and actions. To list just a few necessary actions; we have good governance, good education, entrepreneurial skills, innovation, creativity, infrastructure, trade, productivity, good management, cooperation, unity, integration and peaceful co-existence.

The Africa of today and tomorrow needs strong and focused leadership. Leadership is a function of power; power must be appropriately used to yield good results. Without power there is no leadership at all. The continent needs focused, powerful leadership with the people's interest at heart. Not absentee leaders totally disinterested in the welfare of the people, but rallying people to sign songs of praises in the glorification of his tenure in office. It is time we begin to show red card to such leaders. The need for strong and functional institutions is imperative if progress is to be made. The nuts and bolts must be tightened as the governance and participating instrument for sustainable development and equity in the distribution of the continent's resources.

The mineral resource and manufacturing paradigm – *curse or blessings* – should pay greater attention to managing oil, gas and minerals as a veritable inputs transforming the economic and development take-off in Africa by ensuring that extractive industries in African countries is highly concentrated on extraction upstream, so that exports are also limited to the raw primary product, not semi-processed or processed versions. The upstream part of the value chain is often in an enclave with few links to the rest of the economy. Similarly, the concentration on unprocessed products misses opportunities to develop links with the economy to increase incomes and employment.

Table 4:   New Vision for FOCAC / Africa's Growth with Depth

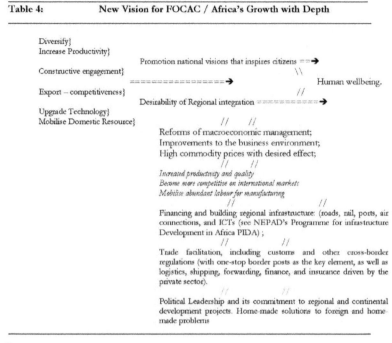

Source: Forje 2014

Moreover, the exports of raw commodities expose a country to volatile prices and thus volatile revenues. All this, coupled with the fact that extractive resources tend to be exhaustible and non-renewable, makes sustainable development particularly challenging for countries highly dependent on them (ACET 2014).Importantly, African countries should work towards sustainable development construed around the following critical dimensions of sustainable development, namely, *longevity, education and command over resources* at national, regional, and continental levels.

It requires constructive relationships between the state and the private sector. Private companies will lead in the production and distribution of goods and services, as well as in upgrading technologies and production processes, and in expanding employment. The private sector need a state that has strong capabilities in setting an overall economic vision and strategy, efficiently providing supportive infrastructure and services, maintaining a regulatory environment conducive to entrepreneurial activity, and making it easier to acquire new technology and enter new economic activities and markets. As Africa drifts from the *"White Man's Burden"* to the *"Chinese or Asian Burden"* should bear in mind the historical past of the continent in shaping a better tomorrow.

Under the colonial regimes, Africans were discriminated against socially, economically and politically; and extrajudicial methods were used to further entrench the system of black servitude to ensure that there was a correlation between race and wealth. By design, the colonial socio-economic and political system was geared to serve the interests of the colonial powers and its colonial metropolis at the expense of the indigenous black population. Is the new Chinese invasion going to repeat the old scenario or usher a new game changer attitude? The new relationship should be used to intensify and improve on the "New Indigenisation Programme of African States" that returns power and ownership of the resources to the people.

Empowerment policies continue to ratchet up the livelihoods of Africans. Only the indigenisation and people's empowerment reform programme can meet the goals of the people. The Millennium Development Goals provides the compass to address Africa's telescopic view of the demographic and socioeconomic impact of the state of underdevelopment and the consequences of HIV/AIDS epidemic with deepening poverty putting a brake on the quality wellbeing of the citizens. China is able to feed its population. Africa is not but spends a mouth-watering USA$40billion annually to import food (Jere 2014:8-16); yet has the potential to do and even go beyond the continent in terms of food supply and security. Inadequate African government institutions that have been weakened by social and political instability and conflicts often lack the capacity to produce and implement effective economic plans.

Such institutions are also prone to widespread corruption (Owoye 2012), which siphons off an estimated 20-30 percent of funding from basic services provision on the continent (Transparency International 2010).Good management is needed to ensure that resources are blessings not a curse to the people. In short, African leaders should not allow a situation where the children end up hungry and suffering because they were and are irresponsible, because they gave away the natural wealth of the continent, our God-given resources for zero-dollars. That is unacceptable.

The new China-Africa partnership must operate from the basis of zero tolerance to corruption, exploitation and undermining the African position. Therefore, strong, accountable and participatory institutions and processes are required to manage diversity in African states constructively, and to chart an economic path to nationally and continentally inclusive development (Jinadu 2013).Relationship between China – Africa should not only focus on minerals, oil and other extractive items but extended to improve on agricultural production, education, manufacturing and the health sector. Education and employment policies need to shift their focus from production of primary resources, to creating more training and opportunities further up the economic value chain in food process and related services. African states must also take greater control of their own resources in order to foster development, and should adopt new technologies to counter the climate of endemic poverty. Unfair terms of trade can reverse gains made by Africa states.

There is no other alternative for the China-African relationship to reward the people. It is the obligation of African states to unapologetically intensify the implementation of an 'indigenisation programme' in its dealings with the new found partner in order to meet the goals of the people - quality welfare through owning the natural resources for the benefit of the continent's current and future generations. To capitalise on these benefits, though, one must meet an important precondition. The determination of the masses to be masters and owners of their development path is vital. Only then can we establish the true ownership of the continent's resources as well as equity in prosperity-sharing. Potentially, the most effective way involves developing and taping into the human capital as the most valuable and reliable resources for the continent's solutions to its predicaments.

The accord between China and Africa (FOCAC) should not be a one-way traffic – extracting Africa's resources with nothing in return.

It should be a two-way process of China ploughing back something relevant that Africa can hold, for example, the kick-starting of agro-processing value chains. Agriculture is embedded with the potential to contribute greatly to economic transformation, just as it did earlier in many developed countries. Agriculture has the enviable potential of increasing incomes in the rural areas. It can increase exports and the foreign exchange needed to import machinery and other inputs for industrial and manufacturing related activities. Establishing manufacturing plants in Africa is an imperative to improve on its service delivery status. The transfer of technology and building the human capacity in African countries to ensure continuity and sustainability is vital and FOCAC should be thinking in that direction.

China and Africa may never share a common vision of ends and means in politics and economics, but they can all be committed to a process that allows everyone to share in defining how those differences are reconciled. There is permanent interest and never permanent friends as far as the foreign policies of States are concerned. That is the meaning and in essence of the marriage of partnership and reason. Making this partnership function will require the two parties to practice critical friendship – living but forceful encounter between equals who journey together. It is the combination of those two qualities – love and forcefulness, rigour and reason – that defines the relationships that are central to the democratic revolution of social problems. It is hope the discourse creates the structural basis for inter-societal relationship and critical true friendship to satisfy the scholars or the politicians as well as it does represent a challenge for all to understand and respond to in very practical ways for the common good.

Preventive Precautionary Measures: Is Indigenisation the Answer?

Is Africa-China (FOCAC partnership) a *'match made in heaven'* or what? Even if accepted as a 'match made in heaven' it must be to the advantage of the people, Africa in particular. Even if, concocted in heaven, certain precautionary measures should be taken based on the SWOT approach. Some of the measures include: as depicted in Table 4: Some Precautionary Measures. The China-Africa accord should be premised on the growth of the continent's economies with depth under the canopy of diversification of production, competitiveness in exports, and productivity of the private sector, building the human and infrastructural capacity, expanding its technological base with the immanent desire to improve and sustain the well-being of citizens. Former South African President, Thabo Mbeki, (New African February 2014:13) rightly notes: "we must as indigenous people make sure we have control of our resources. And so indigenisation is correct."

Powers suspicious of China also tend to exaggerate the likelihood that she will successfully export her revolutionary model or condone to supporting authoritarian regimes in Africa. This in turn breeds hostility. Peking's view of the world requires intense polarisation, the division of the world between friends and foes, acknowledgement and celebration of hostility and struggle Polarisation is sharpened by policy makers in other states who perceive China's hostility and proceed to assert that things Chinese – whether Chinese interests, Chinese ideas, Chinese style of organisations and tactics, or even Chinese aid – are in themselves a threat to other governments and people (Larkin 1971; Adie 1964). What Africa ants is genuine development that puts food on the table and by deploying, rightly the resources potentials of the continent to the greatest benefit of improving the quality livelihood of the people. Is FOCAC operating in that direction, making significant impact on the lives of the people? Africa should not continue making 'catastrophic miscalculations' about its resources potentials fifty years after independence. The new Africa-China interlude under FOCAC should be such that the destructive political interests of each side are not achieved. What should be achieved is improving the well-being of the lives of the people.

The proceeding discussion establishes that many forms of Chinese activities should be tolerable. Still, some Chinese capabilities will prompt precautions and some Chinese initiatives may spark countermeasures. But two questions must be answered in each case: Who is to judge whether countermeasures are desirable? Who is to parry a Chinese initiative or development related activities? The easy answer may be correct: only African governments can choose and implement counter measures. To be effective, actions must be deftly chosen and aptly undertaken. An African government's decision that it is necessary to dull the cutting edge of a Chinese penetration into Africa should be based on a judgement of both China's intentions and the likelihood that she would achieve her intentions and for African governments to ensure that they are not exploited. These are pertinent issues needing the attention of FOCAC.

Does 'indigenisation' provide the answer? Admittedly, estimates show that the majority of the world's natural resources are in Africa and yet most Africans are poor. Former South African President provides a comprehensive answer to the question "So when the Africans say "indigenisation', why is this strange notion? And yet when we talk about solutions to Africa's development, one of the issues that we have to address is exactly this indigenisation. How are we utilising our resources to impact positively on African development? I am saying this because I can see that there is a cloud that is building up somewhere on the horizon when Zimbabweans say 'indigenisation'. But we have to, as intellectuals and though leaders, address that and say: 'Yes, indeed as Africans we are concerned about our own renaissance, our own development, and we must as indigenous people make sure that we have control of our development, our future, and that includes our resources. And therefore indigenisation is correct" (Ankomah, 2014:13). Is FOCAC's thinking in that direction? For it to have a lasting impact on the continent, it has to articulate a new mindset and direction. Africa is sitting on the platinum of strategic minerals of our earth and good use must be made for the wellbeing of the people. Zimbabwean radical definition of mineral resources and this goes for the continent include: any landscape, scenery or site having aesthetic appeal of scene value or historic or archaeological interest (New African No. 536, February 2014, p13).

A number of interwoven factors ensure some form of communality between China and Africa which FOCAC must be serious attention to. First, the relationship should oscillate within the principles of 'morality and benefit' for the common good. Second, Africa and China re actively committed to promoting the welfare of their citizens – they are coming from the common background of underdevelopment in search of modernity. Third, the two continents should perceive their cooperation from their own ideological and philosophical trajectories. Here they share similar values – the *'Ubuntu Spirit'* and the *'Confucianism'* ideological orientation. The two are bridged by friendship and shared-values based on mutual respect and benefits for mutual gains. Fourth, Africa and China should attach greater value to promoting a bottom-up development approach as compared to Western top-down development strategy. In short, this leads to African solutions to African Problems by permitting local problems to be adequately addressed by the local people. Such a strategic orientation allows Africa to remain in charge of its own fate and to craft policy measures that enhances its socio-eco-techno-politico transformation.

The outcome of China's marriage with Africa (FOCAC), upon which the future turns, is a function of the imagination and will. Do the continent resources make it a sick patient of Europe? Are capitalism and sustainability mutually exclusive (Porritt 2005:58)? Since the start of the 19th century and following the work of David Ricardo, trade between nations has been considered an essential aspect of capitalism. Economic growth and free trade remain the two driving forces behind the spread of capitalism to every corner of the World, and the benefit of free trade is still the central ideological tenet of key institutions such as the International Monetary Fund (IMF), and the World Trade Organisation (WTO).

Profitability has quite simply become the key measure of corporate success in a capitalist system ensuring frequent and rapid shifts in the productive base of any economy. And it is these profits that provide the dividends of millions of people now depend in terms of their pensions and other investments. The swing of capitalism's pendulum ensures China to follow that tract in the ultimate interest of the people of Africa. In areas of economic production that are not geographically bounded, capital now tends to flow to countries with an 'absolute' advantage in these areas leading to a standards-lowering competition between nations.

Therefore a proper balance from a sustainability perspective, in terms of China-Africa interlude, what is best done locally, regionally, nationally, internationally and globally is an extremely complex one.

Both parties (Africa and China) must look at the trade-offs between the environment, social and economic benefits for the better wellbeing of their citizens. The underlying concern is whether there is some dynamics at the heart of capitalism and China's interests that kind of balanced approach, which mandates 'getting bigger' as a condition of getting richer, and which unavoidably crushes human scale, diverse cultures and local differentiation. Both parties, especially Africa must transform their *consciousness;* for Africa, a progressive new mindset is imperative *reaching out* to all segment of society to ensure change, progress, development and sustainability.

Hope and optimism remains the guiding principles for the future is now as Africa is on the verge of industrialising and urbanising very rapidly, and her populations are beginning to demand continues quality lifestyles comparable with Europe, Japan and the United Sates. Africa can learn from the achievements of the past as well as mistakes made. The proper utilisation of its resources is a continuous circular system will make a good living by supplying goods without depleting natural resources and the ecosystems. Africa has the golden opportunity of a beacon to dispel the gloom of underdevelopment and external exploitation. As such it has to rethink the development of self-reflection as a holistic approach to the continent's future. The challenge is for the two countries to enhance and harness their relations and potential advantages as a marriage of love, reason and wellbeing.

Writing on the Wall – Which Script and Way?

The current discourse in the West about China's penetration into Africa is very much a reminiscent of the Cold War era with the western thought acting and behaving as the continent was its exclusive preserve for exploitation and domination. It is nothing short of a vulture scaring off other vultures from its perch. The world has change and Africa has to change too. In a way, there is a writing on the wall; a message which the West is attempting to convey to Africa. This should be seen as the sounding of an alarm bell related to China. There is the age-old adage; send a thief to catch a thief. And the two will tend to out play the other. Therefore, the continent must bear in mind a number of intertwined activities in order to articulate a new path bearing strategy in mind: The ball is thrown into the penalty areas of FOCAC, China and African countries – and for the continent to draw the strategic defence line for soul search questions needing comprehensive answers (Chris 2007; Giles & Marcus 2008). These are some of the challenges facing Africa, China and the newly created FOCAC Forum (See Table 5).

Table 5	Some Challenges Facing Africa, China and FOCAC
China (like the West) is after Africa's energy and other resources which it badly needs for it's growing economy;	Does Africa need the West to tell people about these when the continent's physical body and body politics are still suffering from similar forced encounters with
China does not respect human rights at home and therefore will not be interested about human-rights in Africa	How can Western blackened pot call the Chinese pot-clean kettle black;
China careless about the cost to the environment If only its energy needs and growth are assured and sustained	Are they no legitimate issues that should concern and even be liked in Africa and China's deepening engagement with Africa
From the perspectives of international affairs, China (like the West) seeks only the protection of Chinese interests no matter whose ox is gored There could be no other reasons why the West thinks Africa should be wary of China.	Is the West not part of a racket of offender when it comes to exploiting and dominating the continent; Has Africa not got the inherent right to choose its Africa is in the plethoras of development after years centuries of western neglect and exploitation and should articulate and aggregate policies that protect its interests

Africa should thread cautiously and in its ultimate interests like the East or West does

The challenge is Africa's and the solution is Africa's. And how Africa can engage with FOCAC, to construct a new platform for Africa / China interface and the rest of the world without degrading its integrity and sovereignty? How to accelerate the development and ensure quality living standards of the people and for Africa to claim its rightful place within the community of nations? It is time for the sleeping giant to awake and claim its own territory within the global construct of nations. FOCAC should be a focal point in promoting the awakening of the sleeping continent.

Conclusion: The Absence and Search for a Holistic Compass

Africa-China relations have major potential to break pre-existing and failed development paradigms by focusing on trade and investment and promoting sustainable development throughout the continent. It challenges African leaders to rethink their policy strategies from a more proactive perspective reflecting the over-all welfare of the people. Only time will tell the long-term effects of

China's venture into Africa. The author's assumption is that China's entry into Africa can be converted to a positive deal for both sides provide African countries do their home-work from the perspectives of the common 'welfare' of the people. The exchange of essential needs such as natural resources and infrastructure to sustain or foster economic development is much more likely to achieve great things than paternalistic and failed aid strategies (Moss 2007; Hutton 2006). The growth of the manufacturing sector depends to a large extent on the creativity, innovative, entrepreneurial, risk-taking and productive skills of Africans. For now, Africans are lacking in most of these areas, especially the risk taking aspect. Time to embrace it is now or the continent will never develop.

The economies of China and Africa must grow enormously every year in order to maintain political stability, and that cannot happen without the massive quantities of natural resources needed by China and financial, infrastructural and human capital greatly need by African countries. Both sides must evolve on the structural and reality basis of 'win-win' and not 'win-loss' for Africa. China needs Africa much as Africa needs China. The financial prowess, technology and cooperation will are there with China; but Africa must articulate forward oriented people-focused policy strategic approach to obtain the maximum best gains from the relationship. Zambian economist, Dambisa Moyo (2010) is categorical on this, stating that: "China's African role is wider, more sophisticated and more business-like than any other country's at any time in post-war period'. Therefore, both parties (China and Africa) at every level must take reasonable measures to ensure that relationship brings potential benefits to the people and in particular the African continent supplying the much needed resources, build the human capital of the people, as well as create afforded opportunities for employment and other avenues to economic empowerment.

It is imperative for Africa to develop a new mindset, realise its worth and importance to China and to the world, to unify, and re-invest prudently in its people and in developing its human capital as well as mobilising and utilising its resources for the good of its people. It is hardly to sufficiently underline just how quickly China-Africa accord is transforming the continent. Africa's three biggest concerns today are the gross-underdevelopment of its human capital, unemployment and deficient leadership which breeds poverty and exploitation. How does FOCAC intend to address these burning issues? Dependence on oil, or extractive minerals without seriously addressing these issues spell catastrophe for the future of the continent. Some of the mineral rich nations seek keeping the dark side of the country's extraordinary oil or mineral wealth under wraps and presenting a wrong picture of the reality of the continent. We have to admit that Africa is underdeveloped and doing the right things for its proper transformation.

Africa is the richest continents in the world – but millions of Africans wallow in endemic poverty. There is need for shared-responsibility between the region and the world to ensure that the former is able to take advantage of global economic opportunities Underdevelopment and injustice anywhere is a threat to development and justice everywhere. The ongoing outflow of African youths (risking their lives) to Europe presents a good case in point. Africa finds itself in precarious position of exporting both its human capital and natural resources, which is not healthy for the economic development of Africa. FOCAC should not only be looking at trade but how Africa influences China's attitude towards Africa.

Unemployment and poverty are widest among the continent's population; for instance, the case of Africa's economic giants, Nigeria and South Africa with the following statistics of unemployed in South Africa: Whites 4%; Coloured 11%; Asians 29%; and Blacks 62% (Ochieno, 2014:37). These figures portray a continent with true challenges that must be confronted with all zeal if a brave New Africa is to be constructed. China-Africa accord should lead to a genuine structural adjustment with functional African institutions responding to the urgent needs of the people. For now Africa remains underperforming and yet in possession of and not in control of valuable resources that capital seeks for profitable purposes, which when properly deployed should improve greatly on the welfare of the citizens. The challenge is for Africa to walk the talk of its impediment and not just to talk the talk of underdevelopment and exploitation.

This is what China / Africa interface through FOCAC needs to brave the dilemma of underdevelopment and dependency and become a continent of entrepreneurs and self-reliance development to better exploit, harness and use its natural potentials in improving and sustaining the livelihood of the people. The Sino-African relations should provide more support and training for the rise of enterprises and to improve African Economic Empowerment (AEE) as well as improve in infrastructure development. This challenges every African to wear the winning spirit of progress and development from the Africanness in us; 'embrace' Africa, and embrace who we are as 'Africans" (Mafikizolo 2014:49). Table 6 attempts further explanation of what is required of us.

Table 6: Some Precautionary Measures to Be Taken By Africa

- Bearing in mind that the socio-economic, politico-techno transformation of the continent rests foremost in the hands of Africans;
- There should not be a disparity in the size of the trading partners, potentially allowing China to dominate the relationship and impose terms;
- Chinese deals should not exclude African workers and firms from the bulk of the work in large projects by bringing their own workforces from China. This idea also implies to African firms getting a share in development contracts. Experts from the Diaspora should be involved in building the human and infrastructural capacity of the continent; that is pat of African solutions to African problems;
- The Dutch disease and over-dependence on natural-resources exports should be voided.
- Africa should diversify and expand its sphere of product ivy, competitiveness as well as improved its technological capability;
- Competition over African resources, allowing Africans more leverage and say in the negotiation process and to haggle for terms. China's arrival as an alternative source of trade, aid and investment has created a competitive environment where African states are no longer exclusively dependent on Western nations;
- The failure to improve governance and political institutions will prevent the money going to the right places instead of enriching corrupt officials;
- Cheap Chinese products should not flood African markets, putting local African goods at huge disadvantage, further hampering the diversification away from natural-resources sectors into textiles or manufacturing and distorting the building and manufacturing capabilities of the continent
- The need of good leadership at the highest levels to make things move remains imperative and this should be backed by a responsive citizenry to construct a capable developmental state.

Policy Recommendations

Given that transformation is long-term process, it requires constructive relationships between China and Africa on one the one hand, and on the other, between the state and private sector. Seen in this regard, obtaining maximum benefits requires articulate policy formulation and implementation phases. This is the time for Africa to realise its importance to the world, to unity and re-invest prudently in its people, institutes and infrastructure and developing its human capital. Some of the policy measures that need to be emphasised here include among others, the following: The list is not exhaustive; as the policy recommendations emerged from the issues discussed in the paper. Importantly, Africa should re-draw its development strategy and approaches to using its resources: there the following policy recommendations;

➤ Building the human capital and infrastructural base should be given top priority in the China-Africa accord; this will determine the sincerity and committed attitude of African leadership in their endeavour to develop the continent. This should be the top priority of FOCAC;

➤ Formulation of strategic policies that gives added value to the resources potentials of the continent; and importantly, taking into consideration the desire of the people to move from an backward and underdeveloped economy to a quality service delivery one;

➤ Shifting of some labour and energy intensive industries to Africa as Chinese firms move up the value chain. This could be a potential solution to reducing the dependency on extractive industries and revenues from natural-resources export. Presently, China is more interested in helping to create low-cost manufacturing bases in Africa, with no substantial transfer of technology which is not good for the continent.

➤ .The creation of special economic zones across the continent as a means of boosting non-natural resource industries and trade. The building of special trade and economic cooperation zones focusing on boosting manufactured exports can help overcome the Dutch disease; What are the measures put in place by FOCAC and other partners bodies, e.g. NEPAD; ECOWAS; CEMAC; SADC and others.

➢ The fear of Chinese's- Japanese-Asian invasion into the continent could bread a kind of war-fare among African countries – the transfer of East-West conflict into Africa leading to greater fragmentation of the continent. Resources could divide the continent – paving the way for the politics of "divide and rule" which could be very disastrous for the unity and development of the continent. FOCACV should establish necessary bench marks in addressing these problems;

➢ China can offer its own experience of growth as an example and model for other developing countries to consider and learn from, something the USA, as the doyen of developed countries, cannot.

➢ African countries should take advantage of Gerschenkron "Later Comer Advantage" by building on it to enhance its transformation from a backward to service delivery society; FOCAC has a significant role to play here;

➢ China has driven up both demand and prices for global commodities, making the supply of natural resources more lucrative than ever before.

➢ FOCAC / Africa should seek to reduce dependence on external financing by strengthening mobilisation of domestic resources through better collection of tax revenues, curbing illicit financial flows; and fostering intra-African trade, which represents a mere ten percent of total imports and exports. Judicious use of these taxes must be maintained;

➢ The unity of the continent is important. African countries must constitute a united front at global political and economic for a to promote the continent's interests more effectively and efficiently; and to create more beneficial international partnerships to socio-economic development;

➢ USA$2.5 trillion in currency reserves available for financing needs. The IMF possesses US$257 billion in usable resources, while China has USA$2.5 trillion in currency reserves. This makes Chinese currency reserves roughly 10 times bigger than all the funds at the IMF's disposal.

➢ The challenge is Africa's to emerge out gaining from the relationship; by knowing what it wants for the African people (present and future generations) and to stand by its priority needs and interests;

➢ Can China-Africa interface break Africa's triple evils of poverty, unemployment and inequality?

➢ Finally and unquestionably, Africa is relevant again on the global scene as everybody seems to be talking about it a lot more since China has been around; providing a golden opportunity for the continent to take-off to a quality service delivery society if only they get their calculus right.

References

Adie, W.A.C. (1964)."Chinese Policy towards Africa," in Hamrell, S. and Widstrand, S.G. (eds.) The Soviet Bloc, China and Africa. The Scandinavian Institute of African Affairs, Uppsala, Sweden.

Africa Institute of South Africa (2014) "Handouts: Strategizing FOCAC 2015 and Beyond" .Pretoria, South Africa.

African Centre for Economic Transformation (ACET). African Transformation Report (2014). See also (http:://acetforafrica.org) March 2014.

Akitoby Bernardin and Coorey Sharmini (2012). Oil wealth in Central Africa: Policies for Inclusive Growth, International Monetary Fund, Washington.

Alden, Chris (2008) China in Africa. Zed Books, London.

Ampiah Kweku and Naidu Sanusha (eds.) (2008). Crouching Tiger, Hidden Dragon? Africa and China. (Scottsville; University of KwaZulu-Natal Press, 2008) South Africa.

Anshan Li and Yazini April (2014).Forum on China – Africa Cooperation: The Politics of Human Resources Development. Africa institute of South Africa, Pretoria, South Africa.

Ankomah Baffour (2013) "Milking the Cow without Feeding It is Unacceptable", New Africa – Special Report – Zimbabwe the Second Coming", An IC Publication, July 2013, London, pp48-55.

Ankomah Baffour (2014). "Solving The Great Conundrum: How Africa Can Own Its Own Resources", New African No.536, February 2014, AN IC Publication, London, pp8-14.

Asonganyi Tazoacha (2014). "Massi Gams. Lobbying & Foreign Corruption Networks', The Guardian Post, No.0597, Wednesday, 30 April, 2014, Yaoundé-Cameroon, p11.

Awasom Fru Nicodemus (2011). "Towards Understanding the Anglophone-Francophone Conundrum in Postcolonial Cameroon and The Bakassi (Nigeria) Addendum", in Abdalla Bujra (ed.) (2011,) Political Culture Governance and the State in Africa. Development Policy Management Forum (DPMF), Nairobi – Kenya, pp63-92.

"Briefings on Preferential Tariff on Part of Imported Commodities from Africa Held", 5 February 2005 (Available at http://english.mofcom.gov.cn/article/newsrelease/significantn ews/20).

Centre for Conflict Resolution (CCR) (2007). Crouching Tiger, Hidden Dragon? China and Africa: Engaging The World's Next Superpower. Policy Statement report, 17-18 September 2007, Cape Town, South Africa.

Centre for Conflict Resolution (2007). Seminar Concept Note, September 2007. Cape Town, South Africa.

Chilver, E. M. (1966). Zintgraff's Exploration in Bamenda, Adamawa and the Benue Lands 1889-1892. Buea, Cameroon; Government Printer.

Curtis Devon (2007). "China and the Democratic Republic of the Congo (DRC) Paper presented at the CCR Seminar; Crouching Tiger; Hidden Dragon? China and Africa: Engaging the World's Next Superpower, Cape Town, South Africa, 17-18 September 2007.

Easterly William (2006). The White Man's Burden: Why the West's Efforts to Aid the Rest Have Done So Much ill And So Little Good. Penguin Press HC.

Economic Commission for Africa (2013). Economic Report on Africa 2013: Making the Most of Africa's Commodities-Industrialising for Growth, Jobs and Economic Transformation. (The Economic Commission on Africa, Addis Ababa, Ethiopia.

Firoz, Manji and Stephen Marks (eds.) (2007). African Perspectives on China in Africa, Fahamu Publishers, Oxford.

Forje W. John (1981). The One and Indivisible Cameroon: Political and Economic Integration in a Fragmented Polity, University of Lund Printing Press, Lund Political Studies Series 35 (Lund-Sweden).

Forje W. John (2002). "The Disappointment of Independence", Future Research Quarterly, fall 2002, Vol. 18, Number 3, World Future Society, Bethesda, Maryland, USA.

Fowler Ian & Zeitlyn (Eds.) (1996) African Crossroads. Intersections between History and Anthropology in Cameroon. Cameroon Studies – Vol.2, Berghahn Books, Providence – Oxford, United Kingdom.

Gerschenkron Alexander (1962). Economic Backwardness in Historical Perspective. The Belknap Press of Harvard University Press, Cambridge, USA.

Giles, Mohan & Marcus Power (2008)."New African Choices? The Politics of Chinese Engagement." The Politics of Chinese Engagement, Review of African Political Economy, 35 (115), pp23-42.

Gyasi Stephen Jnr. (2014). Ghana and China, Friends for Life?" New African, Issue 537, March 2014, IC Publications, London, pp74-75.

Holslag, Jonathan (2007). Friendly Giant? China's Evolving Policy? Asia Paper, Vol. 2 (5) 24 August 2007.

Holslag Jonathan (2006). "China's New Mercantilism in Central Africa", African and Asian Studies, 5(2), 2006, p.145.

Hutton Will (2007) The Writing on the Wall. Why we Must Embrace China as a Partner or Face it as an Enemy. Simon & Schuster trade, New York.

Iwilade Akin (2014), "Has The Rise Of China in Africa Made Democratisation Less Likely?" Conflict Trends, Issue 1, 2014, pp3-10 (ACCORD, South Africa.

Jere Jane Gina (2014). "How Africa Can Feed itself…Beyond Food Ad and Corporate Greed", New Africa African, No. 537, March 2014, IC Publication, London, pp8-16.

Joseph, Richard (2008). "Progress and Retreat in Africa: Challenges for a 'Frontier 'Region" Journal of Democracy, 19 (2).

Jinadu L. Adele (2013). "Governance and Development in Africa", paper prepared for the CCR Policy Research Seminar, 'Achieving the Millennium Development Goals in Africa', Cape Town, South Africa, 13-14 May 2013.

Kabemba Claude (2012). Chinese Involvement in the Democratic Republic of Congo, 4th October 2012 (www.osisa.org).

Kelsall Tim (2013). Business, Politics and the state in Africa: Challenge the Orthodoxies on growth and Transformation. Zed Books, London.

Khodeli Iraki (2009). From Curse to Blessing? Using Natural Resources to Fuel Sustainable Development. UNESCO/Willey-Blackwell Publishers.

Kopinski, Dominik, Polus, Andrzej and Taylor, Ian (eds.) (2012). China's Rise in Africa: Perspectives on a Developing Connection. Routledge, London.

Larkin D. Bruce (1971) China and Africa 1949 – 1970: The Foreign Policy of The People's Republic of China, University of California Press, Los Angeles, USA.

La Nouvelle Expression (2014) No. 3694, 25 March 2014, Yaoundé-Cameroon.

Lanning, G. & Mueller, M. (1979) Africa Undermined: A History of the Mining Companies and the Underdevelopment of Africa. Penguin Books, London.

Large Daniel (2008). China and the Contradictions of Non-interference" in Sudan. Review of African Political Economy, 35 (115), pp93-106.

Lei Guang (2005). "Realpolitik Nationalism: International Sources of Chinese Nationalism", Modern China, Vol. 31. No.4, pp.487-514

Le Messager (2014) "The Mineral scandal in Cameroon", No.4046, 26 March 2014, Yaoundé-Cameroon.

Mafikizolo (2014) New African, No 545, December 2014, AN IPC Publication, London.

Manji Firoze & Stephen arks (eds.) (2007). African Perspectives on China in Africa. Nairobi and London, Fahamu Publishers.

Manji Firoze (2008) China's New Role in Africa and the South: A Search for a New Perspective. Pambazuka Press.

Mathews, Gordon and Yang Yang (2012). "How Africans Pursue Low-End Globalisation in Hong Kong and Mainland China", Journal of Current Chinese Affairs.

Mlambo-Ngcuka Phumzile (2007). Address to the Conference of Ministers of Education of the African-Union. Sandton, Johannesburg,-South Africa.

Moss J. Todd (2007). African development. Making sense of the Issues and Actors. Lynne Rienner Publishers, Inc. Boulder, Colorado, USA.

Moyo, Dambisa. (2009)."Did Aid: Why Aid Is Not Working and How There Is a Better Way for Africa, Straus and Giroux, New York.

Mutambara Arthur (2013). "How African States Need to Respond to China's Shifting Growth Model", New African, No.529, June 2013, London, pp54-55.

Mwamwenda Tuntufye & Lukhele-Olorunju Phindile (eds.) (2013), "Introduction: The Triumph and Prosperity of Education in Africa", Africa Institute of South Africa, Pretoria-South Africa., pp1-41.

Nabudere W. Dani (2004) Africa's First World War: Mineral Wealth, Conflicts and War in the Great Lakes Region, AAPS Occasional Paper Series, Vol.8. No.1 2004, Pretoria, South Africa.

Ndulo Muna (2007). "Chinese Investments in Zambia", Paper presented at the CCR Seminar, Crouching Tiger, Hidden Dragon? China and Africa: Engaging in the World's Next Superpower. Cape Town, South Africa, 17 – 18 September 2007.

Nesi Edoardo (2013). Story of My People. Random House, New York.

New African Magazine (2014). "Solving the Great Conundrum. How Africa Own Its Resources: New African Magazine, No.536, February 2014, AN IC Publications, London.

Nweke, O. (2010)."The Failure of African Leadership." (http://talkafricagh.wordpress.com).

Obi, Cyril (2008). "Enter the Dragon? Chinese Companies and Resistance in the Niger Delta", Review of African Political Economy, 35 (3).pp417-434.

Ochieno Joseph (2014). "South Africa: Equality Delayed", New African, No.538, April 2014. An IC Publication, London. (www.newafricanmagazine.com).

Ogbunwezeh, F. (2006). African Poverty as a Failure of Leadership. (www.glopbalpolitician.com assessed 20 September 2010).

Osaghae Eghosa (2014), "The Decolonisation Challenge And Matters Arising...", The Thinker, Quarter 2, Vol. 60, 2014,, South Africa, pp12-18.

Owoye Oluwole (2012). "Bad Governance and Corruption in Africa: Symptoms of Leadership and International Failure", paper presented at International Conference on Democratic Governance: Challenges in Africa and Asia. University of Pennsylvania, United States, 7 August 2012.

Porritt Jonathon (2005). Capitalism as If the World Matters. Earthscan, London.

Padraig, Carmody and Taylor Ian (2010) Fleigemony and Force in China's Resource Diplomacy in Africa: Sudan and Zambia Compared. Geopolitics, 15 (3), pp.496-515.

Power Marcus and Ana Alves (eds.) (2013). China and Angola: A Marriage of Convenience. Fahamu Books, Oxford, UK.

Richardson Gonzalez Patricio (2010). "China and Africa: A Mutually Opportunistic Partnership? (ARI/99/2010).

Rodney Walter (1972), How Europe Underdeveloped Africa. Dar es Salaam, Tanzania Publishing House & London, Bogle L'Ouverture Publications.

Rotberg Robert (ed.) (2007) China into Africa: Trade Aid and Influence. Brookings Institute Press, Washington, D.C.

Rotberg Robert (2013). Africa Emerges: Consummate Challenges, Abundant Opportunities. Policy, Cambridge, UK.

Rostow Walter (1960). The Stages of Economic Growth. London.

Sachikonye Lloyd (2007). "China and Zimbabwe" Paper presented at the CCR Seminar. Crouching Tiger, Hidden Dragon? China and Africa: Engaging The World's Superpower. Cape Town, South Africa, 17-18 September 2007.

Shinn H. David and Joshua Eisenman (2012). China and Africa: A Century of Engagement. University of Pennsylvania Press, Philadelphia, USA.

Skidelsky Robert and Edward Skidelsky (2012). How Much Is Enough? Money and the Good Life. Other Press, New York, USA.

Smith Adam (1776). The Wealth of Nations. London.

Sobseh Y. Emmanuel (2011). Rethinking Citizenship, Politics and Governance in Cameroon: Towards A Better Future. Global Pres, Cameroon.

Taylor Ian (2007). "Unpacking China's Resource Diplomacy in Africa", in Melber Henning et al (2007).

China in Africa, Current African Issues No.35, Nordiska Afrikainstitute 2007, Uppsala Sweden, pp10-25

Transparency International (2010) "Africa Corruption Hampers MDGs – Transparency International", All African com, 27 October 2010. (http://allafrica.com/stones/20101027133htm).

Tull, Denis (2008) China's Engagement in Africa: Scope, Significance and Consequences", Journal of Modern African Studies, 44 (3), pp.459-479.

Wenping He (2007). "The Balancing Act of China's Africa Policy", in China Security, 3(3):23-40 (2007).

Wenping He (2005). Chinese Academy of Social Sciences, Beijing, China.

Yates Douglas (2007). "China and Gabon", Paper presented at the CCR Seminar: Crouching Tiger: Hidden Dragon? China and Africa: Engaging the World's Next Superpower." Cape Town, South Africa, 17-18 September 2007.

Zweig David & Jianhai Bi (2005). "China's Global Hunt for Energy", Foreign Affairs, Vol. 84, No. 5, September/October 2005, p32.

Chapter Two

Wrong education reinforces exploitation, inequality and underdevelopment: What Africa must do

Abstract

Africa's sustainable development rests on its human capacity (human capital development) and a strong structural-functional institutional construct to propel, and manage the transformation processes and challenges. Weak human capital development and fragile institutions are recipes for disaster and underdevelopment. The paper argues that without a pool of skilled human capital value cannot be added to existing vast natural resources as the ingredient for transforming the welfare of the people. Jamshed Tata, an Indian industrialist noted way back in 1876 that, 'priority list of preconditions for industrialisation: is knowledge and skills and experience. Then in addition some iron and steel; plus cheap domestically produced electricity.' This tells us of a skill mismatch and with organisations seeking graduates to employ. The education system is not tailored to the actual needs of the continent. The paper argues that Africa has to create and fulfil real structural transformation needs by redesigning African education with creativity, innovation and entrepreneurship (Muchie 2015; Lema Catherine Forje). Inappropriate education only fans underdevelopment, divisive tendencies, marginalisation, inferiority complex and inequality.

Education creates unprecedented opportunities with important implications for Africa's ability to identify and exploit opportunities of transforming its economies and for the employability of its rapidly growing youth population. With education, the continent can leapfrog the industrialisation stage and bridge technological divides as well as adding value to its vast natural resources potentials. The paper examines the narratives (both positive and negative) Africa's search for owning its development trajectories and being a veritable player in global politics and improving the wellbeing of its citizens. Centuries of colonial rule destroyed indigenous knowledge and cultural values forcing an inferiority complex and dependency syndrome on the people which has helped in retarding the progress of the continent. The paper concludes by advocating for new impetus into the education curricula ensuring that education is home grown without losing the universally accepted scientific norms, inquiries, objectivity and credibility. Why more African scientists, engineers and medical doctors are working in the United States than in the whole of Africa it is questioned?

The current curricula is tailored to meet the needs of the developed world and not to address the continent's wants and aspirations Curriculum should be construed with a progressive Afrocentric orientation in mind without sacrificing academic excellence. How do we reconcile Eurocentric and Afrocentric ideologies (i.e. marrying the world of scientific research and indigenous peoples cultural heritage ad values) for the good of humankind. The two worlds cannot be isolated or separated but bridges built across. Building bridges across the two worlds entails 'talking back to' and 'talking up to' thereby building up an institution of knowledge for a better world construct. Decolonising the curriculum is a thing that must be done to lead Africa on the right path of development.

Keywords: curriculum development, human capital building, The Africa We Want, indigenous knowledge, dependency

Introduction

Facing the Realities – Time to Act

Since the colonisation of Africa, external bodies have and continue to have the upper strata in the continent's transformation nexus. To begin with, the colonial powers laid down the modalities for the education, political and economic structures of African states. Cecil Rhodes outlining the case for colonialism in the1890s noted: *"we must find lands from which we can easily obtain raw materials and at the same time exploit the cheap slave labour that is available from the natives of the colonies. The colonies will also provide a dumping ground for the surplus goods produced in our factories."*(Ellwood, 2001:13). A new development concept - the Eurocentric Agenda - was established under the nexus of destroying everything in use empowering the people and making them susceptible as slaves to foreign cultures and values. The cultural heritage, values and indigenous knowledge system of the people were destroyed. This destructive agenda was undertaken under the notion of civilising the uncivilised and designed to render the people poor and dependent on the metropolis.

The education structure was specifically designed like the economic structure to benefit metropolitan countries. "This was irrespective of whether the resource base of a given African country was mineral resources, agriculture, and land to be populated by colonial settlers or a combination of any of these resources. The result was the same; i.e. an African economy that was outward oriented to suit the needs of metropolitan countries" at large" (Bjura, 2004:21). What rationale underlies our interests for the topic? What are the fundamental arguments advanced for a new approach to human capital development? It cannot be denied that with education, "people's quality of life is greatly enhanced, as it contributes to their capacity and ability to achieve; people become better at identifying and solving their problems, creating jobs and increasing income, thus contributing to quality of life. Education is liberating, both for a given individual and the society (Asmal 2004).

Education creates unprecedented opportunities with important implications for Africa's ability to identify and exploit opportunities of transforming its economies and for the employability of its rapidly growing youth population. With education, the continent can leapfrog the industrialisation stage and bridge technological divides as well as adding value to its vast natural resources potentials. The paper examines the narratives (both positive and negative) Africa's search for owning its development trajectories and being a veritable player in global politics and improving the wellbeing of its citizens. Centuries of colonial rule destroyed indigenous knowledge and cultural values forcing an inferiority complex and dependency syndrome on the people which has helped in retarding the progress of the continent. Priority must be given to meeting the basic needs of the people, hence there be strong emphasis health, education, employment and food security are essential for enhancing human capacities to meet the challenge of sustained development.

Wrong education means a development strategy designed to imitate the life-styles of the consumption patterns of affluent industrial societies is clearly inconsistent with the Afrocentric vision of the development African wants. Eurocentric development without a human-face is a replica of capitalism which accentuates inequalities as the high consumption levels would be possible to secure for only a small minority of the population in each African country. Concern for social justice is an integral part of genuine development that unfortunately has bypassed Africa. A fairer distribution of income and productive assets like land remains essential as the means for speeding up development and making it sustainable. A people-oriented development strategy (Afrocentric) will have to pay much greater note to women; a nation cannot genuinely develop so long as half its population remains marginalised and suffers discrimination.

The result of Africa's education curriculum should be seen within the lenses of imperialism perpetuated through the ways in which knowledge about indigenous peoples was collected, classified and assessed and then represented in various ways back to the West, and then through the eyes of the West, back to those who have been colonised and accepted by the colonised. The paper argues that the significance of indigenous curriculum and perspectives of a progressive Afrocentric human capital development should account for how, and why, such perspectives must form the corner stone for the sustainable transformation of Africa – developing Africa through the lenses of Africans for Africans. Our unfortunate illiterate brothers and sisters should not be left behind. Progressive adult education training should be extended, bearing in mind that a literate population is more productive than an illiterate one. Therefore, revamping and expanding primary education to reach all is imperative. The quality of primary education, the first step in the long-chain in human capital development plays a key role in determining the quality of all higher levels of education, as well as improving the productivity of other economic and social programmes, health for example.

Colonial education was used as a mechanism for creating new indigenous elites. Religion (indigenous or exogenous) contributed either positively or negatively in advancing or negating the wellbeing of the people. Religion is one element of human culture which embodies the knowledge systems (epistemologies, ontologies (metaphysics), axiologies (social, political, ethical and aesthetic), educational, filial, culinary, sexual, entertainment, sporting and other traditions and values of peoples. We see how religion prevents the female child from acquiring the necessary human capital development. Thus the overarching nature of religion, even in apparently secular aspects of cultural values, remains in the way it underwrites virtually all aspects of social existence. Exogenous religion was deployed to rob the people of their land and cultural heritage. At the same time, it was these religious bodies that established the first educational institutions for human knowledge acquisition (Adelowo 2014). Indigenous African religions have become extinct, succumbing to the centuries of concerted exogenous efforts from both east, west and within to destroy them, leading to the demise of indigenous ways of understanding, interpreting and manipulating reality in such societies. Religion to a large extent impacted negatively as the most effective tools used throughout the continent to dispossess Africans of their religious heritage, indigenous knowledge systems, scientific heritage, cultural identity and value systems. What is at stake is the preservation of indigenous knowledge and cultures they encapsulate, thereby making an Afrocentric connection to the natural world in a sustainable way possible.

Education and religion were not the only mechanism for producing elite groups who converted to the Eurocentric ideology to continue the hegemony and domination. The challenge always is to demystify, to decolonise and to constitute a new mindset for developing the underdeveloped continent. Africa should not develop through imperial or Eurocentric eyes. Africa needs African strategies. School knowledge systems must be informed by a much more comprehensive system of knowledge which links universities, scholarly societies and indigenous cultural heritage and value systems to the evolving views of development in the ultimate interest of Africa. An Afrocentric curriculum should be one trading with other knowledge systems, putting an end to the old system and starting a new road or agenda of another on its own right. The equalisation of opportunities required new processes through which the various systems of society such as services are delivered. Gifford (2015) argues that the enchanted religious imagination militates against development by encouraging fear and distrust, and diminishi9ng human responsibility and agency. The prosperity gospel of 'covenant wealth from tithes and offerings' is antithesis of Weber's Protestant ethic; and to magnify the person of the pastor is to perpetuate the curse of the 'Big Man'.

The words of former Executive Secretary of the Economic Commission for Africa (ECA), Prof. Adebayo Adediji (1982) should sink deep into the policy orientations of African policy makers; "...African countries cannot continue to pursue economic policies and strategies as if all they want to be is a poor imitation of America, France, England, USSR, or China....the time has come for us to think seriously about evolving a genuinely authentic strategy for development – a strategy for development that is not externally oriented, that is not based on copying other societies hook, line and sinker, and that does not lead to acculturative modernisation." It is extremely wrong for the continent's efforts towards development to be structured primarily on inherited theories of transformation with dismal developmental prospect for the future of Africa.

There is more to growth than capital accumulation, the introduction of new processes and products and the expansion of the employed labour force. The quality of the labour force as reflected in its health and nutrition, skills and education also is important. Indeed they are important for four reasons; First, a healthy and educated population is an end in itself; it is one of the goals of development; Second, human capital is a direct input into the production process. For example, a high incidence of morbidity lowers the productivity of labour and reduces the number of days worked. Skilled labour is likely to be able to work faster with less supervision, with fewer errors and to produce goods and services of higher quality; Third, human capital is complementary to physical capital, Machines require skilled workers to operate them and mechanics to repair them. A country that emphasizes physical capital formation while neglecting its human capital will soon discover that the returns on physical capital are low. Forth, human capital formation is necessary for technical change. It is difficult to introduce improved methods of production, new ways of doing things and more complex and sophisticated products unless the labour force (and indeed the buyers and consumers) have sufficient training and education to enable them to understand what is being asked of them (or offered to them). Investment, human capital and technical change are closely interlinked (Griffin, 1989:233). Without the requisite human capital, participation within the international community is greatly restrained.

Our current standing within the global economic context calls for a redefinition of the development approaches, priorities and strategies for the continent. Why must Africa, after more than half-a-century of political independence, continue to sustain the wrong aspects of colonial policy, particularly the raw material export, non-industrialisation and dependency syndromes, which was and is encouraged, nourished, sustained and even enshrined in the constitution by the departing colonial powers for their own articulate interests? The importance of imposed or inherited structures, whether the global capitalist system of which Africa is a subordinate part, or the artificial and often inappropriate state borders, political and educational systems set up by colonial powers, is examined in the light of the exercise of agency and urgency by African peoples desire to construct the continent they want through a progressive Afrocentric ideological orientation. We need an orientation envisioning changing failed or crippling democracies into winning nations.

Conceptual Construct −The Overarching Purpose
Facing the Perils of Education Underdevelopment

Why is Africa poor in the midst of vast natural resources endowment? What role can human capital development play in transforming the poor image of the country? Why has democratic governance failed on the continent? What can be done to reverse the current poor imagine of the continent as well as ensure sustainable welfare to the vast majority of the population? These and many cross cutting-edge questions need soul-searching answers in addressing the plight of the people. Based on the adage the *'knowledge is power'*, so also it can be stated that *'education is development,* and *'development is power'.* Africa has no education, and therefore cannot develop, but exploited by those with requisite know-how; and without development, the welfare of the people is seriously compromised as the continent is undermined by those with the know-how.

The Eurocentric curriculum is identified and idealised as the *'saviours of the African people'.* But Fanon (1990:193) argues that the problem of creating and legitimating a national culture represents a

71

special battlefield and intellectuals are important to this battle in a number different ways (Smith 2012:73). First, African intellectuals were assimilated into the culture of the occupying power; (the emergence of the 'negritude' orientation); second, the struggle for independence instigated into the minds of some of these assimilated Africans, or created the stage of a period of disturbance and the urgent need for the intellectuals to remember who they actually are, a time for remembering the past. And thirdly, the consequences of assimilation and era of remembering who they are constitute the new stage producing a revolutionary and realignment – progressive Afrocentric orientation which should put an end to the idea of *'they came, they saw, they named, they claimed and they owned'*.

The orientation through a progressive Afrocentric education curriculum should be *'we were, we are, we will progress, develop and own our development trajectories' for our wellbeing.* Building on our key history that encompasses colonial violence, post-colonial domination, and internal and externally generated underdevelopment, we have the capacity to discuss our development and security in a far more holistic and nuanced ways. We must empower our institutions at the national, regional and continental levels to handle the new development challenges. The people must be mobilised to ensure they partner with the state to ensure a holistic front in addressing the development challenges. Partnerships and cooperation with each other and the rest of the world should arise from internal cohesion. They must rise out of poverty, inequality, corruption and low productivity to embrace the rapidly changing circumstance imposed by the world construct. But they must not destroy their cultural heritage value system which must be used as input factors to the development and sustainable transformation of the African continent.

Confronted by such complex issues, it is argued for radical departures from existing development paradigms and policies that retard the progress of the continent – an urgent but radical changes in attitudes, mindset, political will and approaches to development as well as the restructuring of the pattern of production, distribution and lifestyles – leading to individual and collective self-reliance and self-sustainability provides the way Africa can claim its place in a growing complexed, hostile and complicated world structure. Africa once was the space setter in education – the first university in the world was in Timbuktu – Mali, long before the establishment of the Universities of Oxford, Sorbonne and others. Not many African universities are ranked as centres of excellence in the world. Two of the five oldest universities in the world are in Africa – Morocco, University of al-Karaounine founded in 859; and Egypt – al-Ashar University, founded in 970-972.

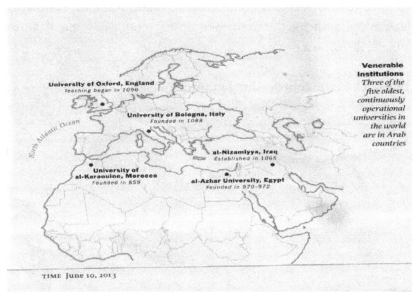

Source: Vick & Khalil (2013) "Faith and the Campus. Islamists, Secularists, Democrats and Generals all want to shape Cairo's al-Azhar University, Time, Vol.181, No.22, 2013,pp22-27

We can only but agree with the views of Swaniker (2017:42-45) and others. "For the first time in our history, we are poised to build institutions of higher learning that are uniquely Africa, informed by the needs of our economies and, most importantly, within reach for many of our youth. In order to do this, we must return to first principles. Our universities can still be critical drivers of local development, as was originally espoused at their formation." We need a common vision in articulating the kind of education we want without destroying the fundamental basis of excellence, knowledge acquisition as well as contributing to knowledge. We should bear in mind that education is central to the construction of thriving communities. Young people – regardless of race, ethnic construct, nationality, or degree of material means – long to translate high ideals into practical realities and aspire to make a meaningful contribution to the fortunes of humanity. We must not deny this vast opportunity for the African youth in playing a meaningful role to the betterment of society; education needs to enable young people to think critically and deeply about the purpose of their lives and the aims toward which their talents should be directed. And it should empower them to take constructive action, fostering qualities such as ethical leadership, principled action, and moral courage (One Country. Vol.23, 2016)

Fig.1. The Afrocentric Curriculum Agenda

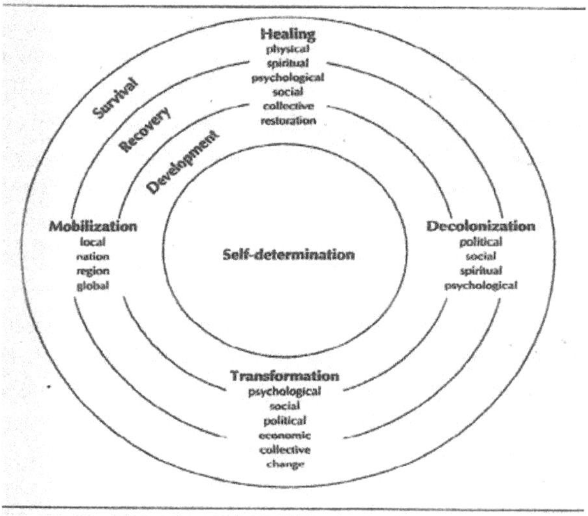

Source: Credit Smith Linda (2012:121) – The Indigenous Research Agenda
(Note: Afrocentric Curriculum Agenda, my conversion)

It is interesting to note that Africa has more academics with foreign degrees and more graduates with study abroad experience, and has imported more knowledge and concepts from abroad than any other continent, making it probably the most internationalized higher education system in the world. Hence innovation and change in internationalization should come from Africa (de Wit 2012). At the same time, Africa keeps copying western concepts, strategies and policies developed by their western counterparts without developing their own innovative ideas about how to internalize their education systems. It is evident that Africa needs to rally around a unified and amplified voice if it is to assert its own interests in national, continental and global development. The Afrocentric education curriculum setup should dig deep into an agenda that puts into its true perspectives four cardinal issues of; (i) *'survival,(ii) recovery, (iii)development and(iv) self-determination'* as illustrated in **Figure 1: An Afrocentric Curriculum**. Expounding on these four cardinal tides, Smith (2012:121) notes that 'survival of peoples as physical beings, of languages, of social and spiritual practices, of social relations; recovery of territories, of indigenous rights, and histories; recovery is a selective process, often responding to immediate crises rather than a planned approach.

Self-determination is the right of the people to define the shape of their destiny and own it. Self-determination in a research agenda becomes something more than a political goal. It becomes a goal of social justice expressed through and across a wide range of psychological, social justice which is expressed across a wide range of psychological, social, cultural and economic terrains. These four major areas are backed by for cardinal points, namely, *'healing, mobilisation, decolonisation, and transformation'* represent processes, not goals or ends in themselves. They are processes which connect, inform and clarify the tensions in society as well as give visions and directions at the national, continental and global levels for constructive changes to occur.

Africa's new education curriculum needs (a) Healing: physical, spiritual, psychological, social, collective, restoration etc.; (b) Mobilisation requiring; local, nation, region, continent and global; (c) Decolonisation: political, social, spiritual and psychological; and (d) Transformation: psychological, social, political, economic, collective, change. In short, the new curriculum calls for a new mindset, comprehensive political will towards a new era for the development of Africa. This provides the way for a winning Africa in the battle against underdevelopment, exclusion, marginalisation, exploitation and undermining of the sovereignty of the African people. Undermining results from Africa's encounter with Euro-colonialism, a reflection of the nexus between indigenous knowledge, culture and development, and indeed a call for the revival and reinstitution of indigenous knowledge, not as a challenge to Western science, but a complementary form of knowledge necessary to steer and promote sustainable development in Africa and beyond'(Mawere, 2014). Hammering on the role of indigenous knowledge, Awuah-Nyamekye (2015) notes that Eurocentric scholars even viewed indigenous knowledge as superstitious, irrational and anti-development. He goes on to discuss an interesting and insightful discourse on the state and role that indigenous knowledge can play in addressing a tapestry of problems of the world and challenges connected with the application of indigenous knowledge n enlightenment science-dominated contexts.

Zeleza (1997) asserts western writings on Africa clearly demonstrates the regimes of representation are suffused with Africa's implacable 'otherness' and pathology....Africa remains a deeply contested intellectual and ideological terrain, a continent that is perhaps still as misrepresented and misunderstood as it was at the beginning of the century. Muchie (2015:36) asserts that regardless of the different phases African universities have passed through, what is clear is that higher education institutions in Africa have not been home-grown. Universities in Africa still do not include the rich sources of indigenous knowledge. Just as the post-colonial state became largely a legacy of colonialism, the universities also became part of the institutions where the varieties of knowledge that originated in Africa from time immemorial have been bypassed, ignore, and suppressed rather than being used to serve as building blocks for developing Africa's own authentic African higher education systems. But alas, research, knowledge, higher education and learning rooted in African values and philosophies have routinely been discontinued.'

Michelle Romo et al (2011) looking at the university in African democratic citizens notes that higher education in Africa contributes to democratisation, beyond producing the professionals that are necessary for developing and sustaining a modern political system, remains an unresolved question. ...the potential of a university to act as a training ground for democratic citizenship is best realised by supporting students' exercise of democratic leadership on campus. This in turn, develops and fosters democratic leadership in civil society. In boundaries of the education imagination, Hugo Wayne (2011) puts out that explorations of the limits of education reveal what education is, what it does, and how it works, providing the reader with an overarching vision of individual and collective development as well as systematic principles to recognise what is specifically educational in these processes. While Mouton et al (2015) writes about a resurgence of interest in training programmes for higher education leaders and management (HELM) at African universities.

Lema (2016) posits that "human capital education is central to economic development of a nation". While Mwamwenda and Lukkele-Olorunju (2013:1) notes; "only through education will Africans be in a position to address the demands and challenges of this century." The Deputy Chair of the African Union Commission, (Erastus Mwench, in Lukkele-Olorunji) states that Africa has for some time now, decided to anchor its development of education." Do we anchor the right kind of human capital development to enhance our welfare? Cloete et al (2014) posit that "the dominant global discourse in higher education now focuses on 'world-class' universities – inevitably located in North America, Europe and, increasingly, East Asia. The rest of the world, including Africa, is left to play 'catch-up'. But that discourse should focus rather on the tensions, even contradictions, between 'excellence' and 'engagement' with which all universities must grapple. Here the African experience has much to offer the high-participation and generously resourced systems of the so-called 'developed' world."

True the continent has made great strides in the field of education since independence. Nigeria for example, which had three universities at the time today boost of over 120 such institutions. The same can be traced throughout the continent. For a country or a continent, there is no greater wealth than well-trained human resources. Former South Africa's Minister of Education (Asmal Kadar) argues that education is not only critical, but also a solid foundation for both the reconstruction and development of Africa, adding that providing education is investing in economic development, given that sustainable development calls for adequate and ever-increasing skills and knowledge base, which are inherently products of education. While Langa (2014) looks at the landscape and dynamics of change in the higher education system by describing the attest developments of trends of expansion, financing, governance and policy reforms closely linked to the development of higher education in Portuguese speaking African countries.

Speaking on developing human resources, Margaret Joan Anstee (Director General of UN Office at Vienna and as Under Secretary-General responsible for UN activities relating to social policy and development in Africa) notes: "...The challenge to planners and practitioners is to maintain wherever possible the vitality of this cultural legacy and of traditional support systems during this period of social change... Redressing the social ills of African society and improving the distribution of social services can be achieved in the context of social planning...The ultimate purpose of development, it should not be forgotten, is to improve the well-being of people...all people...."

Africa developing and owning its own development trajectories requires a new *development thinking and a comprehensive and progressive education curriculum;* one construed within the contextual frame of an encompassing Afrocentric science-techno-entrepreneurial developmental approach premised under the umbrella of a *'people-first or people-centred'* development. The education curriculum left behind by the colonial masters with its hidden and even exposed agenda of furthering the underdevelopment and dependency of Africa has to be given a new face lift and test of life making the continent productive and competitive within the global based-knowledge economy of our time. Why must Africa be at the bottom step of the development ladder? That has to change and challenges African academics to spearhead the drive towards a new development episode and epoch for the continent (Adedeji, 1989). What this entails, points in the direction of the continent's education system tailored (a) producing a modern African responding to the material, cultural, social, spiritual and human needs of the people; (b) meeting the challenges of the African people within the global community where science and technology has attained a level of profundity and within a conducive environment that ensures quality services delivery and welfare to all citizens.

The new development thinking of Africa articulated in AU Agenda 2063 – *Building the Africa We Want,* cannot evolve on the colonial imposed form of education curriculum that focused on the liberal arts relegating technical and entrepreneurial education to the background. Africa of today and tomorrow needs a progressive and well-articulated curriculum with a strong orientation on science, technology and entrepreneurial education without which the anvil for industrialisation neither can be structured nor sustainable welfare attained for the population. Taking advantage of Gerschenkron's (1962) *"the late-comer advantage",* and with the vast opportunities offered in the global world, Africa has to streamline and tailor its human capital development in a way that its educational system graduates students who are *job-creators'* and not *job-seekers'* in the public sector.

Forje (2013:149) posits that human capital development faces serious challenges, ranging from the absence of an enabling environment, poor infrastructure, inadequate teaching staff, political interference and financial problems to the centralised nature of the administrative establishment that must be holistically and comprehensively addressed to yield credibility, functionality and quality service delivery. Only a new curriculum teaching methods and management styles adapted to the needs of the society is urgently required. Articulating and implementing a comprehensive progressive Afrocentric education curriculum should evolve within the premises of scientific excellence and academic objectivity and credibility that restores the region back into the heydays of when *"Africa civilised Europe"* (Ankomah, 2015:72-77).

Currently, the education system in practice reduces the African into a 'neo-Europe' minus economic development and sustainable welfare for the vast majority of citizens. Entrepreneurship education and the innovation journey which Africa needs involves educating, motivating and coordinating people to develop and implement ideas by engaging in transactions with others while making the adaptations needed to achieve desired outcomes within changing global context. Skilled manpower in all discipline and spheres of activities are needed to move the continent from its current to a higher status of welfare.

The African challenge is failures of 'development' and failures in the management of the continents human environment. The gap between the rich and poor nations is widening – not shrinking – and there is little prospect, given present trends and institutional arrangements that this process will be reversed. Therefore, African countries need to re-examine the critical role of education in the development process and to formulate realistic policy measures to dealing with them – a new education curricula is needed; to ensure that the appropriate institutions, equipment, infrastructures are in place to facilitate the new curriculum in place; and to raise the level of those working in the sector to perform well.

Wrong education reinforces poverty and inequality as it equally intensifies under-development and poor resources utilisation. Africa with vast natural resources benefits very little since added value is not given to these resources. Most state spending in Africa is wasteful, low priority being accorded to those sectors as education and health which provide the necessary inputs for the building up of human capital, improving productive and creating the basis for an industrial society. The solution to Africa's predicament lies in the development and improvement of indigenous managerial skills (a not in) selling off state enterprises into private hands. By denuding the existence of meagre stocks of human capital the continent has, it acts as a long-term constraint on development. Improving its human capital base is prelude to building and entrepreneurial and an industrial base.

The Khartoum Declaration presented a clear perspective of investments in health and education; regrettably, over the past decade human conditions of most Africans have deteriorated calamitously; the unemployment and underemployment situation has worsened markedly". The development of human resources is seen not as the hoped-for product of measures of economic development, but as the very means of development. The disastrous effect of structural adjustment programmes in Africa in the last couple of decades has been that they have been implemented at human cost and sacrifices' to the point that they have been 'rending the fabric of African society', weakening the very capacity of the people to engage in socio-economic recovery and development (Brown, 1995:264-5). Why is Africa underdeveloped in spite of being the centre of academic excellence following the establishment of the first university in the world in 859 BC? We have to dispel the fact or thinking that "the curious idea that a great white race has been responsible for all the great civilisations of the past is nothing more than a crude superstition propagated mainly by European-oriented racist historians. Apparently for 781 years, between 711 AD and 1492, Africans from ancient Northwest and West Africa, together with their Islamic fellows from Arabia, had put Southern Europe to the sword, conquered it, governed it, and brought civilisation, education, and general enlightenment to Europe as a whole" (Ankomah, 2015:72).

Tabaro (2015:82) writing on tracing African civilisation "...Count Volney remarked that although the black people were slave of the Europeans, they were the source of science, philosophy, technology, astronomy, medicine, mathematics, the arts, etc. that were so beneficial to Europe at the time. The African origin of civilisation in Europe, Asia and America is beyond contention. I hope following Cheikh Anta Diop (1923-1986), Chancellor Williams (1893-1992), from his book, Destruction of Black Civilisation) and Martin Bernal (1937-2013, in Black Athena). George James in *'Stolen Legacy'*, it is possible to demonstrate how Africa lost its civilisation and why Europeans denied and continue to do so that Africans enjoyed advanced human culture and civilisation" (Ubuntu). Adding his voice, Pheko Motsoko (2014 – New African July) made an important commentary; "how can the Ubuntu philosophy be restored for the benefit of humanity in general, and not just for Africans alone"?

Africa has to explore its past in building a new society through a genuine Afrocentric curriculum centred education development strategic approach. The African Development Goals (ADGs) requires resources mobilisation and utilisation and building a solid human capital base that covert and gives added value to its vast natural resources base. Former World Bank President, Barber Conable (1988), asserts: "Without education, development will not occur. Only an educated people can command skills necessary for sustainable economic growth and for a better quality of life." To move forward Africa needs education or a critical mass backed by the political will to develop.

Many reasons can be advanced highlighting the cardinal role of education in the continent's development. It goes without saying that human capital development means helping to meet other basic needs, and helps sustain and accelerates overall development. In addition, the important role of education lies in the fact that it helps to determine the distribution of employment and income for both present and future generations. No doubt, education influences social welfare through its indirect effects of health, fertility and life expectancy. The only way to empower the rapidly increasing youth population is through education so that they meet the challenges of and fit well in demands of the job market.

Therefore, education creates unprecedented opportunities with important implications for Africa's ability to identify and exploit opportunities of transforming its economies and for the employability of its rapidly growing youth population. With education, the continent can leapfrog the industrialisation stage and bridge technological divides as well as adding value to its vast natural resources potentials. The paper examines the narratives (both positive and negative) Africa's search for owning its development trajectories and being a veritable player in global politics and improving the wellbeing of its citizens. It strongly emphasises that the creation, mastery, and utilisation of modern science and technology are basic achievements that distinguishes the developed from the developing polities. The widening gap in overall development and wealth between the African nations and the developed countries is to a large extent the science and technology gap. Africa's future development policies will need to address with greater vigour the closing of the knowledge gap with the North.

Knowledge is vital to the future of the continent, for development depends more and more on the benefits derived from the advances of science and technology. Progress here calls for the overhaul of education systems, so that greater attention is given to education in science and technology and to training in engineering and technical skills. It therefore, requires a comprehensive science and technology policies with clear sectoral priorities, integrating science and technology in national plans, as well as provide adequate resources for strengthening scientific and technological capability (Forje 1989; Skorov, G. E. 1978; OAU 1980).

Centuries of colonial rule destroyed indigenous knowledge and cultural values forcing an inferiority complex and dependency syndrome on the people which has helped in retarding the progress of the continent. The new centres of power have not fared better either than the departed colonial masters. It is business as usual. Rather, the belief is that existing status-quo should not undergo change but consolidated through false promises – the West and African ruling elites as the sole provider of the welfare of the people. Colonial curriculum established the positional superiority of western knowledge. An Afrocentric curriculum should focus on the individual and society with capacity to reason, on a society which promotes collective autonomy and collective-interests, and in constructing a state that is built on the rational rule of law and justice regulating the public sphere of life for all citizens.

Africa's new education curriculum should strongly focus on the following critical issues; (i) education must provide to the younger segments of the African society as fast as human and financial resources permit with the ultimate goal of developing a comprehensive system of human capital development for all age groups – free education for all; (ii) placing strong emphasis on a more equitable distribution of education opportunities and on the reduction of existing inequalities based on economic status, geographic location, and sex; (iii) the attainment of greater internal efficiency of the education system and priority reduction to the misuse of resources (students dropping out, corruption, poor infrastructures, etc.); (iv) education focused or directed to greater internal efficiency and tailored to the needs of the society, to the job market and ensuring that the students are properly equipped with the necessary skills that qualify them for the employment or embarking on the road of entrepreneurial related activities; and (v) develop the capacity of maintenance of an institutional capacity to formulate and carry out education policy, as well as to plan, analyse, manage and evaluate education and training programmes and projects at all levels. In line with this, Africa's future is inescapably linked to its ability to create an effective marriage between culture and science and technology – a challenge in which education plays a decisive part. Therefore, suitable education innovation for the continent calls for political and cultural authenticity, not a pale imitation of ex-colonial models, with specific country situations designed, implemented and owned by African countries themselves (World Bank, 1989; Akilu et al. eds. 1983).

Breaking out of the current downward spiral of the Eurocentric education partly requires drawing up a progressive Afrocentric education curriculum and turning swords into ploughshares by making proper us of the 'conversion of the *'brain-drain into brain gain'* (Glaser, 1978; Adams, 1968; Kannappan, 1968; Seers 1969; UNITAR, 1971; Henderson, 1968; Castells 2016) for the sustainable transformation of Africa. It is interesting, but ironically to note that Africa which lacks the human capital for its development continue to export this valuable scare resources to the developed North. Any country exporting both its raw materials and human resources is doomed to perpetual underdevelopment, exploitation and dependency. Here is where Africa is facing serious underdevelopment/development dichotomy problems. A new education curriculum should provide the requisite game changer for the development of the region.

One can question rightly who is developing who? Is the introduction of the USA *"Green Card"* for example, not a deliberate attempt to drain the continent of its valuable human capital and render the region permanently underdeveloped? Are the inappropriate policies and implementation strategies of African countries that lead to poor utilisation of its human capital, creating jobs and employment opportunities for the bustling youth population not a deliberate strategy of the Eurocentric underdevelopment agenda for the continent? Whilst imperialism is often thought of as a system which drew everything back into the centre, it was also a system which distributed materials and ideas outwards. With its developed human capital Europe developed a 'positional superiority' as a useful tool in which knowledge and culture were as much part of imperialism as raw materials and military strength. Knowledge was also there to be discovered, extracted, appropriated and distributed. There is an escalating spectacle of an unholy alliance between the governing elites and the West to underdevelop the continent.

The 'brain drain' phenomena cannot be stopped; but it can be usefully converted into a *'brain gain'* factor accelerating the development of Africa. This of course requires African governments creating the necessary enabling environment attracting its exported human capital back home. The existence of failed states (Asonganyi 2015, Ghani & Lockhart, 2008) on the continent does not create the attractive pull factors for the *'brain gained'* return dichotomy. There is an urgent need for policy articulation and implementation strategies of bringing back our Diasporas as the engine of growth for the sustainable transformation of Africa. If the AU Agenda 2063 - *'Building the Africa We Want'*- is to be realised, the African diasporas must be encouraged to return and invest home. Tapping into the vast potentials and prowess of the Diasporas as the *'connectors'* is what could be the vital game changer for Africa's progress. The Diaspora is the termite accelerating the underdevelopment as it equally provides the much needed fertilise for fuelling economic growth and the way forward for closing the development gap, stimulating entrepreneurship, innovation, creativity and industrialisation as stimulants to growth and sustainable livelihood.

Human capital development is crying for change, for without change there can be no development. Can anyone hear and listen to the voices of the poor, the illiterate and disadvantaged? Education is a much-needed wake-up call for the development of the continent. Economic development can accelerate social development by providing opportunities for underprivileged groups or by spreading education more rapidly. Africa is caught up in a series of downward spirals, particularly poverty and lack of education for example. These have to be addressed and done so correctly through new technology and knowledge and properly used for the good of the people. The seriousness of the African crisis and human capital development cannot be overemphasised. Something is rotten in the continent of Africa. Without a thorough decolonisation of the education curriculum there can be movement towards capable developmental states in Africa.

What is emphasised is comprehensive proactive actions to righting the wrongs of the current education system. Developing a new political will through which change can be brought is important. This should begin with critical self-reflection directed by knowing ourselves, understanding ourselves, interrogating where our focus should be, and developing cognizance of the need to change, how to change and to move forward. Without understanding what we want, constructive changes cannot be undertaken that benefits the people. Importantly, we should develop solidarity with the struggles to be the game changer in developing a new education curriculum from a realistic perspective considering important debates that are unfolded within them.

In respect of higher education, efforts should be directed towards improving academic standards of the universities. Presently, no African university is within the barometer of the first 100 universities in the world; there is need to increase their efficiency and quantity; change their output mix by controlling enrolments in certain fields of study and increasing them in others; and to reduce the serious burden on public resources through sharing of costs between the beneficiaries and users, on the one hand, and the governments on the other (Kwapong, op cit.187). Priority of science and technology, entrepreneurial education must be strengthened. With the private sector encouraged to invest in research and development geared towards the development and transformation of the continent's resources for the industrialisation and wellbeing of the people.

Fighting corruption in the education sector is important in improving quality and efficiency. Here Cameroon has to make extra efforts in streamlining the way degrees and certificates are issued which has and continues to be a great source of confusion and sources of corruption national and international. Within the past couple of years great confusion has infiltrated the education sector of Cameroon, especially higher education. The current political impasse in the country throws dark clouds on the education status of the country. On the other hand positive progress can be seen from South Africa where nine of its 23 universities rank in the top 4% of the 20,000 registered universities worldwide, and 11 in the top 8%. From the Department of Basic education, we discover that the

University of South Africa (UNISA) is a pioneer of tertiary distance education and is the largest correspondence university in the world with approximately 300,000 students. Student to teach ratio was 1:29 in 2012. This has improved from 1:50 in 1994. Efforts in building the human capital are ongoing. What is important is making use of such trained capital and to avoid the export of the most needed resources for development to developed countries.

Unlocking the human-resources potential: strategy, innovation and change

In 2000, over 160 countries committed to vastly expand education opportunities for children, youth, and adults by 2015. The Millennium Development Goals MDGs has come and gone with not much achieved. In 2013, the African Union advanced the AU 2063 Agenda - *The Africa We Want,* and in 2015, the United Nations propagated its Sustainable Development Goals (SDGs 2030) following the non-achievement of the Millennium Development Goals (MDGs). The success or failure of these development agenda pivots on *'leadership'; 'political will'* and the kind of *'citizen's responses'* towards human capital development and of its usage in the transformation process. In Africa, one of its greatest deficits has been that of 'leadership'.

Leadership we are told is always necessary in any endeavour, applying equally to politics, business, economics, society and culture. In today's global context and national development the perception of effective leadership is fast changing calling for participatory and consensual servant leadership as the inspiration for effective development attainment. The older model of a heroic, authoritarian, served leader-picture the hard charging demanding and worship is outdated. The new conventional wisdom, though, tells us that this model has given way to the *'servant, soft'* leader ideal, where leaders inspire their followers and avoid acting like dictators or semi-gods (Nye 2008; Mouton et al (2015; Jowl James et al; 2015).

Any society must ask three interrelated questions in order to develop its strategy: *where are we, where do we want to be, and how will we get there?* While the questions do not change over time, the realities

87

and environments that countries face do. Given today's realities, how should African countries answer these questions? What form of education curriculum is needed for the continent to get out of its current doldrums of a developing and dependent continent and to improve the quality of livelihood of the people? To get to where Africa wants to be, requires that the education sector (primary, secondary and tertiary) institutions and curriculum in Africa have to be home-grown addressing the critical needs of the continent. From time immemorial, education on the continent has failed to include the rich sources of indigenous knowledge, culture and value systems.

Knowledge and skills are critical ingredients of economic development and societal transformation. If only Africans could be educated to a higher level and their skills developed, the productive potential of the continent - and its strength in the global economy - would be vastly enhanced. Though many countries have acquired impressive educational capabilities in the past many decades, serious deficiencies in human capital development exist in particularly in science and technology related disciplines throughout the continent. Educational policies place wrong emphasis on disciplines that do not accelerate the socio-economic transformation of the region. In many cases, indigenous knowledge is related to the background. The foundation for development is (i) building national consciousness and awareness; (ii) development of human resources; and (iii) the proper utilisation of human and natural resources in effecting appropriate changes in society.

What role has concepts like *(Ubuntu, Harambee, Batho Pele, Ujamaa, etc.,)* played in the epistemology of the educational curriculum and transformation process of the continent? As noted by Muchie (2015:36-37) "universities became institutions where the varieties of knowledge that originated in Africa have been bypassed, ignored and suppressed rather than being used to serve as building blocks for developing Africa's own authentic African higher education systems. But alas, research, knowledge, higher education and learning rooted in African values and philosophies have routinely been disconnected." Sad enough, the education construct of Africa evolves on the lines set in the past by colonial masters, and has been too academic and unsuited to the scientific, vocational, and others needs of societies in the process of modernisation. This is not a call for inculcating purely materialistic values; education should focus at producing young people who are not alienated from their own culture and community but are equipped to contribute to, and benefit from, the progress of their societies.

Lessons can be drawn from Japan and other countries of the Asian region that are technologising and not losing their cultural roots. Africa is fast losing its cultural heritage or has even lost this crucial ingredient in the transformation process. It is now the most unculturalised continent in the world; neither knowing whether it is African nor European. A society without its cultural roots is easily derailed by the penetration of external cultural values as Africa has become. This compromises its development orientation. Apparently, this is the pattern of education the current curriculum imparts on the people. We do not need to go further to see why Africa is underdeveloped. African education system is in a gross state of despair lacking substance in its cultural heritage and value system. It is necessary to look into the role of local knowledge and its effects and contribution on the adoption of technologies. New technologies like other innovations face resistance prior to their adoption. What is important is to put the blame game aside and assume responsibility for our future. Individual Africans must take initiatives and commit ourselves to engaging in activities that changes us and the continent, for the better. What is important is the proper usage of the continent's resources to impact on the welfare of the people.

Statistically, 33 million children did not attend school in 2012, 56% of whom were girls. This includes 5.5 million in Nigeria and more than one million in Ethiopia. The realisation of MDG 2 – Achieve universal primary education - shows that in 2012, 10 countries, including Rwanda, Benin, Algeria, Cameroon, Cape Verde, Congo, Mauritius South Africa, Tunisia and Zambia, were able to get more than 90% of their school-age children into classrooms (Africa MDG Report). Rwanda for example, made remarkable progress with 97% school enrolment on the continent in 2012. Girl's enrolment (98%) exceeding boys (95%), while the percentage of children completing their primary school cycle stood at 73% - 'a dramatic increase from 53% in 2008'. Chad, Cote d'Ivoire and Niger were the only African countries in 2012 with youth literacy rate below 50% (Kuwonu, 2015:23). Due to a combination of many interrelated factors, Africa remains the only continent where more than half of parents are not able to help their children with homework. The illiteracy population rate on the continent needs to be radically brought down.

African universities are open to a sort of *"Scramble for Africa"* as these institutions are starved of funds, research equipment, infrastructures etc. and become beggars robbed off their research opportunities and results. To a large extent, research results gather dust on the shelves and drawers of researchers, with no avenues for innovation, entrepreneurship, production and transformation of these results to the benefit of society. For now, "we study what we do not need, and need what we do not study. After inheriting an educational system from the colonial-powers who wanted not more than paper-pushers and lots of messengers and cooks, the newly independent African countries just carried on with the inherited educational system as if no independence had come at all, and as if the agendas and aspirations of the colonial governments and the African governments were one and the same" (Ankomah, 2013:25). All these impede the successful transformation of the continent. Investing in human capital development is turning opportunities into reality; making the long and difficult road shorter and easier for the continent suffering abject poverty in the midst of plenty.

Unlocking the continent's human resource potentials gives added value to its huge natural resources exploited by the developed countries. African governments should seize all available opportunity to improve the on its human capital development. The focus is on Africa. If you are down, there is nowhere else to move but up. The process of acceleration has started and there is no turning back. Poor education or human capital development is holding the continent back and our leaders are poised to take action. The people are gradually graduating from their current status of ignorance and getting to know their inherent rights. Just as they are demanding probity and accountability, the people will demand good education for all as a right. African countries must organise themselves and push with a common voice and purpose for the support they need to address the state of poor human capital development. Addressing poor human capital development must be positioned as a regional and national agenda, protected by national constitutions and to be pursued irrespective of which political party is in power. This is critical to ensuring that the momentum is not lost as a result of changes in government. Finally, we owe it to ourselves and future generations to ensure political and economic stability on the continent.

Breaking this vicious circle requires a committed effort to improve education and other essential basic needs - health, water supplies, sanitation etc.; particularly in poverty stricken areas. Expanding educational opportunities means enrolling many children in primary schools, limiting the number of children dropping out of school; and getting more females on the education bandwagon. Through large-scale literacy programmes several African countries; and parental literacy has in turn helped the increase in literacy rate. There has been significant expansion in secondary and higher education. Today, focus is being directed to technical and vocation training including entrepreneurship. This gradual shift is important as prelude to industrialisation. A shift in the pattern of production and exports from raw materials to manufactures and, within the latter, to products with high and medium R&D intensity, is required to counteract the adverse consequences of the decline in prices of Africa's commodities including *'the black gold'* – oil (The South Commission 1990:109).

The greatest obstacle to development is ignorance. Education curriculum should break that barrier and build consciousness, awareness and erase the growing state of ignorance that bedevils the region. Acceptance of an Afrocentric developmental approach as a strategic objective should be promoted and actively inculcated among policy-makers political leaders, civil servants, business people, academics and all other groups in society. The support of the people and participation in the development process are an essential part of the foundation in building a quality services delivery society. Therefore promoting the 'Afrocentric consciousness and awareness' among the people and across the continent, strengthens their belief, mutual trust, confidence building and commitment towards constructing a brave continent within the global-knowledge-based economic context. Developing a new mindset and consciousness is the fundamental game changer in transforming Africa from a so-called backward into a developed polity. The progress and achievements of the developed countries rest on their degree of awareness and consciousness of society. This is the miracle or medicine for the sustainable transformation of a society. Africa has to cultivate that spirit or else perish in the wallows of exploitation and underdevelopment.

However, African countries need to raise the quality and quantity of primary, secondary and tertiary education and to adapt it to its development needs. It has already been alluded to the issue of insufficient attention given to the importance of science and technology culture through the education system. Most importantly getting the female gender interested in science related disciplines is crucial. University education of a higher standard constitutes an important instrument of modernisation and development. The research and development (R&D) component, innovation, creativity, productivity and entrepreneurship should be emphasised in the education curriculum as these constitute the structural basis for industrialisation. Strengthening the educational systems is essential for narrowing the knowledge gap between Africa and the rest of the world as well as building the needed consciousness and awareness needed in transforming the society. Building the right critical mass is crucial for the transformation of the continent.

Therefore, the reform of curricula, particularly fostering technical and scientific skills, the development of entrepreneurship and management capacities at all levels of education must be adapted to the cultural, economic and developmental requirements of African countries. They must seek a new era of economic growth by investing into the areas mentioned by ensuring that the level of spending on weapons or arsenals of human destruction is greatly diminished. Such constructive changes should be geared towards enhancing the welfare of citizen's rests on political will, consciousness, change in mindset and commitments of leaders and civil society towards making the vital changes required.

It is time African nations turn away from the destructive Eurocentric developmental agenda and approach so entrenched within the mindset of African countries and focus instead on their common future through an Afrocentric agenda. African countries must not become prisoners of their own making – policy articulation and implementation strategies. They must face the common challenge of providing for sustainable development and act in concert to remove all factors constraining the progress of the region. By beating ignorance through building the necessary human capitals they can successful achieve AU Agenda 2063. Therefore with quality human sciences development, problems of underdevelopment can be addressed through the following channels;

- Getting at the sources;
- Dealing with the effects;
- Assessing national and continental risk;
- Making informed choices;
- Providing the necessary financial means, infrastructure, equipment, institutional and legal frame works; and
- Investing in the continent's future.

Together these priorities provide the gateway to building the Africa We Want. Concerted holistic actions are needed to achieve envisaged goals. Wrong education generates poverty, tensions and conflicts nationally and across the continent. The people are still awaiting concrete solutions for their problems; which can best come through a people-focused development approach; erasing their state of ignorance, enhancing their status of consciousness and awareness remains imperative. The severity of the crises of development hanging over the continent can be attributed to a variety of factors including articulated self-interests of those on the corridors of power who strongly belief in military power solutions to socio-eco-politico problems. Yet they fail to understand as noted by President Eisenhower (1953) "that every gun that is made, every warship launched, every rocket fired represents, in the final analysis, a theft from those who hunger and are not fed, who are cold and not clothed." We find both national and global military expenditure well in excess of expenditure on human capital development; agricultural technologies among others. Without substantial increased investments on education, research and development they can be no economic growth and sustainable welfare. Africa is in great need of a new education curriculum focusing on the following areas;-

- *Human capital development in the basic sciences, engineering. Medicine and public health;*
- *Technical and vocational training, including the development of entrepreneurship and management skills, and industrial apprenticeships;*
- *Taking advantage of the 'late-comer advantage' in promoting distance-education programmes within and across borders*

There is a failure on the part of African governments in tapping from the existing human capital potentials found within and beyond the frontiers of the continent. How do we bring the wealth of talents outside to accelerate the transformation process in the African region? The brain drain needs to be converted in a brain gain phenomenon. But to benefit from the Diasporas requires the establishment of an enabling environment for all to operate without harassment. Striving for good governance is a prerequisite for the sustainable transformation of the continent. The knowledge of the Diasporas wealth lost, just as the failure to give added value to existing natural resources. Once a system of good governance is put in place, the Diasporas will respond positively in the reconstruction of the continent. For now, much as they try to be active and serious participants in the transformation, poor administrative system and corruption stands as rock towards their active and positive engagement.

Quality versus Quantity

The challenge to emerging generation of African leaders is to put in place a functional and democratic governance system that assures among others, openness and transparency; efficiency and effectiveness, separation of powers, and the rule of law etc. (Forje 2004) to effectively and efficiently utilise its human and natural resources for the common good of the people. Development is a process of profound structural transformation. It cannot simply be imported. By now, there is ample evidence that successful development is vitally linked to education and the resilience of the economy, polity, and civil society, all functioning in a spirit of harmony to promote shared goals and objectives. Thus the success of Africa's struggle against underdevelopment, exploitation, marginalisation and poverty depends on the ability of the continent to reform and regenerate its economies, polities, and societies in 1 tone with its basic development goals. The AU Agenda 2063 provides such a guide line backed by the global UN Agenda 2030 (SDGs) and the national development objectives of each of the 54 member countries of the African Union. Africa should develop one voice, goal and work towards common objectives from a strong and united clear position, using the AU 2063 agenda as the road map.

Infrastructure deficit is a major drawback on the continent. There is general acceptance that economic infrastructure is critical for economic growth and poverty reduction, given its pivotal role in improving competiveness, facilitating both domestic and international trade and integration of the continent of Africa to the global economy. However, in Africa there is large infrastructure deficit in terms of access and quality, to be filled in the sector of education, energy, transport, information and communication technology (ICT) (Anyanwu and Erhijakpor 2009; Ncube 2013-72-80). Africa is in urgent need of both quality and quantity. We also need to develop self-understanding and to decolonise the mind (Ngugi wa Thiong'o, 1986) to get free of the effects of Eurocentric assault on the 'African mind'. We need collective and pubic political action aimed at addressing structural changes on the development of this emerging continent.

"We cannot emphasise enough the fact Africa's underdevelopment is the price of the development of Europe which is based on historical realities gyrating around Europe's criminal past wherein slavery and colonialism enable Europe to spawn its future capital and invest"(Mhango, 2018).

It is most critical as imperative that each African country takes a critical self-examination to ensure its institutional health is sufficiently sound to be able to respond to the vigorous demands presented by contemporary world construct. One of these challenges which underscore this paper is that of overcoming the knowledge gap. And in the words of Prime Minister Hailemariam Desalegn (Ethiopia): "today in our globalised world, no country can achieve development in isolation" *(Speech at the 2016, Africa Forum in Sharm-el-Sheikh, Egypt)* Structural transformation in the education sector is needed to develop the requisite human capital the continent needs in addressing what The President of the African Development Bank, Akinwumi Adesina (2016) sees as High 5s – five major priorities for the continent; (i) light up and power Africa: (ii) Feed Africa; (iii) Industrialise Africa: (iv) Integrate Africa; and (v) improve the quality of life for Africans *(Speech at Africa Forum, February 2016 Forum, Sharm el-Sheikh, Egypt)*. Hence this publication prescribes a progressive Afrocentric restorative recompense as the only way forward for Africa in the world construct. We must ask ourselves, why is the continent abundantly rich in terms of resources and culture, yet waxing in abject poverty, squalor, misery and underdevelopment? What measures has the continent put in place as a constructive and comprehensive strategic answer(s) resulting from the perpetual plunderage of the region with worst impunity and insensitivity launched on the people by European treasure-hunting adventures?

Increase in the number of educational institutions of learning is important to give access to education to the widest number of the continent's fast growing population. Equally important in this direction is the *'issue of quality of education'* to drive up the continent's expertise, productive and competitivity in the global market. Undeniably, the education architecture of the continent is extricable linked to the political/governance culture of the 54 countries making up the continent. Given the need of the continent, there is the desire to pursue both quantity and quality without sacrificing the essence of quality and scientific objectivity. Scholars find it difficult to agree on the exact meaning of quality in education. If the continent is to compete, the issue of quality cannot be relegated to the back ground. The multiplicity of institutions of learning shows also a high degree of falling quality of education in virtually all levels. The challenge for human capital development in Africa is to improve on quality and quantity as well as to ensure proper utilisation. Paradoxically, Africa remains the most resources endowed continent, but remains less developed economically compared to other parts of world, thanks to its historical past of slavery, colonialism and neo-colonialism.

The recent students' protests that have erupted across South Africa's university campuses demanding an end to colonialist education curriculum and mentalities should ring a bell into the minds and souls of policymakers across the continent for an urgent change in the education curriculum of the continent. African countries north of the Limpopo and South of the Sahara need to sharpen their tools and act in concert in creating functional units of educational technology knowledge for their development break through as well as engagement with which all universities must grapple. African universities should in concert begin discoursing and addressing the tensions, even contradictions, between Eurocentric and Afrocentric curriculum, between 'excellence' and 'engagement' to better place the continent on the right path of human capital development in the development of Africa and of the world at large. We have to reshape the debate on development in the global information economy for years to come.

A random sample indicates the following increase, for example, Botswana during 2000-04 academic year had a record of 11,121 university students, and in 2008/9 the number increased to 15,000; South Africa should the following increase 2000 with 670000 increased to 834000 in 2009; Kenya with 53 state and private universities in 2010 with an enrolment that increased from 118,230 (2007) to 142,356 in 208/2010; Rwanda tertiary education increased from 1 to 30 (2010) with a student enrolment of 60,000; Uganda with one higher institution in 1922, now has over 100 tertiary institutions; Zimbabwe with the creation of the University of Zimbabwe (1980) to having nine public and three church-based universities with 12 institutes of technology colleges and over 400 private vocational institutions. Since 1980, Tanzania can pride itself with 40 public universities; Nigeria had three universities at independence in 1960, and by 2010 boosts of 110 universities, 183 polytechnics, and 86 colleges of education; in 1961 Ethiopia with a single university now has 22 public universities and this number is expected to increase to 33. Cameroon that had a lone State university in 1963 today boosts of 8 state universities and a growing number of higher institutes of Learning with over 25 private universities and technical institutes (Forje 2013, MINSUP,2017). Obanya (2014) in "Educationeering" defines as directing the triple academic functions of research, teaching, and responsive social engagement towards the education challenges of society. Research and development is imperative for Africa's entrepreneurial take-off. Our development plans will never be realized without the quantity and quality skilled manpower. Our development nexus must touch on all human, cultural, politico-economic sequels of our transformation to enhanced and harness our quality livelihood.

A number of reasons can be attributed to existing falling standards. These include drastic increase in enrolment and inadequacy of teachers, less classrooms, inadequate equipment/ infrastructures, poor teaching environment poor pay-packets, among others; the rapid increase in educational establishments contributes to the use of under-qualified or unprofessional academics. In addition, the issue of curriculum is crucial to quality in education. Many of the private institutions are *profit-making focus*ed'. Proprietors of these institutions are more focused on money-making rather than producing quality teaching standards. Government should put a strict control over these institutions and also formulate country centred excellence curricula that meets national needs and universal standards. Even though in some countries these private universities are monitored by state universities, the state universities are not properly equipped either. Finally, the quality of education has much to do with the competence or incompetence of the administrators and managers of education institutions. How some of these private institutions receive their accreditations is questionable. There is also the issue of poor financial investments in the sector. Financial sustainability is crucial in ensuring quality and quantity. In all, most countries have not been aggressive or pro-Afrocentric in character in giving a broad spectrum of the needs of the continent in the education sector and in meeting national needs and the job market.

The good news in the continent's education is the rapid increase of the female gender obtaining education and doing extremely well in nearly all disciplines. The science, maths, physics, engineering and other disciplines; vocation and technical education once the exclusive domain of the male gender, has been invaded successfully and rightly by women. Rwanda is making great strides here, and was a good performer towards achieving the MDGs and education for all by 2015. This falls in line with the government's focus on education which among others is on *educating citizens who are liberated from all kinds of discrimination, including gender-based discrimination, exclusion and favouritism; transform the Rwandan population into human capital for development through the acquisition of skills development; develop the Rwandan citizen an autonomy of thought, patriotic spirit, sense of civic pride, love of work well done and awareness.* This could be contrasted with the position of Nigeria as the country is confronted with issues such as (i) low levels of political will and commitment of some state governments on basic education issues; (ii) low and poor motivations/attitude of the trainees ...with no intention of working as teachers in the future; (iii) a high rate of unqualified teachers in the system; (iv) dearth of institutional materials and teaching aids; (Yazani and Magwanda 2014:117). So a progressively construed and implemented Afrocentric curriculum is a rallying call and cry for a more just and sustainable future for the continent.

Apparently, any definition of development is incomplete if it fails to comprehend the role and contribution of women in development and the consequences of development for the lives of women and society. Women should be encouraged and engaged in opportunities for creative work and economic development. Empowering women is very crucial in the process of change. Development in Africa depends on women; policy articulation and implementation on development objectives have added values and benefits when women's interest and role are taken into account. Progress on gender equality has been unacceptably slow and uneven. Widespread and persistent gender inequalities are holding back progress for all. To achieve full gender parity in Africa, African countries need to address structural barriers that discriminate against women and girls in accessing education, employment and finance, as well as restrictions on the right of women to use or own land. Early marriages, female genital mutilation (FGM) and violence against women are some of the cultural impediments that hold back progress and the gender front in Africa today (Musau, 2015:24).

The African Capacity Building Foundation (ACBF: celebrating its 25th anniversary this year) as one of Africa's most effective Pan-African organisation should intensify its training capacity to positively impact on building human capital and critical skills most needed to support government policy articulation and policy implementation as well as strengthen the voice of civil society and the relationship between civil society and the government for the sustainable transformation of the continent. Developing the capacity of the continent and its major institution is imperative for promoting and consolidating the development of the continent. Going forward means a relentless effort of upholding the virtues of productivity, efficiency and effectiveness, harnessing knowledge and developing skills, ensuring cost-effectiveness and focusing on the welfare of all citizens.

The scourge of unemployment: An avenue for migration

The *'brain drain –gain phenomenon'* is triggered by the considerable scourge of unemployment. Only with considerable increase in human capital development that can substantially lead to increases in vestment; and with more effective employment creating putting incomes in the hands of the poor, can African countries hope to increase the desperately slow pace of improvement of the livelihood of the population. Therefore there is in urgent need of restructuring not only the educational sector but the job creation sector and the entire government structure. Restructuring is a continuous process in all economies through which more productive activities replace less productive ones; or through which archaic ideas are replaced with new and progressive ones. In short, restructuring is always needed as nations change their competiveness, but equally required for domestic economic efficiency.

Bariagaber Assefaw (2014) analysis the nature and type of South-South migration, focusing on issues, such as brain gain and/or brain drain, remittance flows, technical know-how transfer, violations of the right of Africa migrants and gender dimensions of migration. He further shows the dynamics of migration from Eastern and Southern Africa to the Arab Gulf States as well as to developed countries, focusing on the skills of migrants, brain gain and/or drain, remittance flows, technical know-how transfer, violations of the rights of African migrants and gender dimension of migrants; and assesses the successes, impediments and challenges of African international migrants from Easter and Southern Africa and to formulate policy recommendations to maximize the gains and minimise the cost associated with international migration in Africa.

Restructuring and Renewal should be a positive progressive process. The North depends on the South and vice versa. Therefore, common grounds of mutual interest and benefit to both parties must be established to create a just, stable, peaceful and secured world. Without such a common understanding in the interest of the people, the poorest in Africa will for an unforeseeable future remain outside the realm of quality living standards. United Nations Sustainable Development Goals (UN SDG 2030) goal (Four) calls for inclusive and equitable education and learning opportunities for all' and goal (Nine) 'calls for building resilient infrastructure, promote inclusive and sustainable industrialisation and foster innovation'.

Converting the *'brain drain'* into a *'brain gain'* will help keep at bay most of the skilled human potentials on the continent. There are a number of countries on the continent having more medical personnel - doctors, pharmacists, nurses and other health workers abroad than at home, the case of Botswana. Gambia, Liberia speaks for themselves (Dugger 2003; McKaiser 2016; Maassen, 2011). Williams (2016) points out that there are more African engineers and scientists in the US than on the continent, and studies are suggesting that Africa will need 2.5 million engineers to sustain its current level of economic growth, for infrastructure development, for technological innovation etc. In a number of countries the cost of 'brain drain' is high, for example, in Uganda the replacement of departing Ugandans costs USA\$4 billion on an annual basis expatriate have to be contracted to carry out the work left behind. On the other hand remittances from the Diaspora far outweigh what is given as foreign aid assistance to African countries. But we should bear mind that it takes years to train a medical doctor or a civil engineer. Why should Africa lose this human capital through a twinkle of second as a result of the poor policy? In a society that is already bifurcated by inequality, the ever-growing youth unemployment statistics represent a poisoned chalice and this contributes seriously for the youths fleeing the continent to greener pastures in other parts of the world. Not even the emerging petro-developmental state in Africa (Ovadia 2016) is able to haut the flight saga. Many African countries are confronted with the ever-growing unemployment curse, and government failures to address this would eventually lead inexorably to disaster (Mills and Herbst, 2016). For now there are no signs of curbing the unemployment rate and averting the brain drain saga.

The reality is that Africa will need their citizens – whether educated at home or abroad – who will serve their society. Africa is not well served by emigrants who remit no benefits from abroad. On the other hand professionals working overseas could become more valuable resources for the home country as they might provide higher remittances or loans for development related activities back home. What is important is creating the enabling environment as the attracting pull factor for the Diasporas to develop interest of actively involved in the process of development in the home country. Africa cannot afford to lose or waste is human capital. Every African country needs skilled human power intimate with its own needs. Educational and manpower planning should coordinate more closely with the job market providers to ensure the employment prospects in the country.

Conclusion: Decolonising and truimphically moving forward

It is argued that poor education is underdeveloping the continent. Notwithstanding the remarkable achievements of higher education, it can be concluded that Africa as a continent is confronted with serious challenges of attaining the education goals it has set itself and the international community, (Mwamwenda 2013, 42; UN MDGs 2015; Thomas 2010). The issue of poor curriculum has been stressed as well as the neglect of indigenous knowledge systems and concepts in enhancing the transformation agenda of the continent.

Smith (2012) is categorical in showing the relationship between knowledge research and imperialism and the ways in which it has come to structure our own ways of knowing, though the development of academic disciplines and through the education of colonial elites and of indigenous or 'native' intellectuals. Western knowledge and science are 'beneficiaries' of the colonisation of indigenous peoples. The knowledge gained through our colonisation has been used, in turn, to colonise us in what Ngugi wa Thiong'o calls the colonisation 'of the mind'. A new curriculum conceived and executed under the umbrella of progressive Afrocentric ideology should put that to rest once and for ever.

Even with its meagre human capital, Africa has become the continent exporting its scarce human capital. The brain drain is draining the region of its skilled human power, just as it can be a blessing to the transformation of the region and improving the welfare of its citizens. In terms of remittances, the Diaspora is a fundamental funder to improving the living conditions of many fellows back home. Africa cannot develop on remittances. The diasporas or 'returners are often portrayed as agents of development who bring with them economic capital, knowledge and skills as well as social connections and experience gained in the 'developed North' (Akesson & Baaz, 2015). The continent needs vital human capital to ensure sustainable development. A progressive Afrocentric education curriculum constitutes the greatest arsenal in changing everything and transforming the continent's failed economic and political systems. On this should the continent build the future it wants.

The views expounded by Kwapong (1995:193) should be seriously taken by all states; 'to meet the challenge of capacity building that will enable the African nations to move confidently into the 21st century and beyond and to better share in the benefits of the information and biological revolutions, African nations must give pride of place to a total overhaul of their education systems. Education must, therefore, be brought back to centre stage and given the highest priority in the current programmes of economic and social reform and reconstruction. Nothing short of a high quality, cost-effective, efficient and equitable education available to the populations of the African nations will ensure this transition from the present state of distress and malaise into a prosperous and confident 21st century. For all of this, leadership, democratic participatory institutions and processes and, above all, good governance will ensure a bright and prosperous future for an educated Africa."

By way of conclusion, the paper has only scratched the surface of the problem and the need for change. It addresses a number of important issues. First it explains why a new education curriculum is necessary. Second, it outlines some of the key ways in which the politics for education curriculum is needed. By discussing the politics of change the importance for the continent's sustainable transformation is highlighted and streamlined. Africa is not an island or cannot develop in isolation. Interaction with other communities and solidarity within and across national frontiers is imperative. The paper cannot claim to have covered the entire structural categories undermining the current curriculum. We need a critical education curriculum renewal for an emerging Africa. An Africa that bids not farewell to Eurocentrism but fare forward voyagers to Afrocentrism in the 21st century.

References

Adams Walter (ed.) (1968). The Brain Drain. The Macmillan Publishing Company, United Kingdom.

Adedeji Adebayo (1989). "The African University and the Engineering of Structural Change and Transformation", National University of Lesotho 1989 Convocation Lecture, 27 September 1989, Roma.

Adedeji Adebayo (1982). "Development and Economic Growth in Africa to the Year 2000: Alternative Projections and Policies", in Timothy M. Shaw (ed.) (1982) Alternative Future for Africa, Westview Press, Boulder, Colorado, USA.

Adelowo E. Dada (2014) Perspectives in Religious Studies, Vols. 1, 2, & 3. HERN Publishers, Nigeria.

Africa Millennium Development Gap Report (2015), United Nations, New York.

Akesson Lisa & Maria Eriksson Baaz (eds.) (2015). Africa's Return Migrants. The New Developers? Zed Books, London, UK.

Akilu Lemma, M. S. Swaminathan, E. W.von Weizsacker (eds.) (1983). New Frontiers in Technology Development: Integration of Emerging and Traditional Technologies. United Nations, Tycooly International Publishing, Dublin, p.ixv.

Ankomah Baffour (2015)"When Africa Civilised Europe", New African, No.554, October 2015, IC Publication, London, pp72-77.

Ankomah Baffour (2013)."What Africa Can Learn from Singapore (Part 1), New African No. 526, March 2013, IC Publication, London, pp24-28.

Anstee Joan Margaret (1990). Social Development in Africa: Perspective, Reality and Promise", in James Pickett & Hans Singer, (1990). Towards Economic Recovery in Sub-Saharan Africa: Essays in Honour of Robert Gardiner, Routledge Publishers, UK.

Anyanwu, J. C. & Erhijakpor, A. E. O. (2009) "The Impact of Road Infrastructure on Poverty Reduction in Africa', in Thomas W. Beasley (ed.) Poverty in Africa, Nova Science Publishers, Inc. Pp1-40.

Asonganyi Tazoacha (2015) Cameroon: Difficult Choices in a Failed Democracy, - A Memoir, NGT Publishing, Madison, USA.

Awuah-Nyameke Samuel & Munyaradzi Mawere (eds.) (2015). Between Rhetoric and Reality: The State and Use of Indigenous Knowledge in Post-Colonial Africa. Langaa RPCIG, Bamenda, Cameron Republic.

Bariagaber Assefaw (ed.) (2014). International Migration and Development in Eastern and Southern Africa. OSSREA Publishers, Addis Ababa, Ethiopia.

Bjura Abdalla (2004). Pan-African Political and Economic Visions of Development. From the OAU to the AU: From the Lagos Plan of Action (LPA) to the New Partnership for African

Development (NEPAD)), Development Policy Management Forum (DPMF) Occasional Paper, No.13, Addis Ababa, Ethiopia.

Brown Barratt Michael (1995) Africa Choices – After Thirty Years of the World Bank, Penguin Books, Wright Lane, London, United Kingdom.

Castells Manuel (2016). Higher Education and Development. African Minds Publishers, Cape Town, Republic of South Africa.

Cloete Nico, Peter Massen and Tracy Bailey (eds.) (2014) Knowledge Production and Contradictory Functions in African Higher Education. African Minds Publishers, South Africa.

Conable Barber (1988) Education in Sub-Saharan Africa: Policies for Adjustment, Revitalisation and Expansion, World Bank, Washington D.C. p.5.

Dugger, C. W. (2003) Botswana's Brain Drain Cripples War on AIDS. New York Times.
(Available at:
http:www.nytimes.com/2003/11/13/world/Botswana).

Ellwood Wayne (2001).The No-Nonsense Guide to Globalisation. Verso Publishers and New International Publications Ltd, London.

De Wit Hanis (2012). Africa Must Lead in Innovation in Internationalisation, University World News, Issue 0239, 16 September 2012 – World Blog.

Fanon Frantz (1990). The Wretched of the Earth. Penguin Books, London.

Forje W. John (2013) "The Triumph and Prosperity of Education in Cameroon" in Mwamwend & Lukhele-Olorunju (eds.) (2013). The Triumph And Prosperity of Education in Africa, Africa Institute of South Africa, Pretoria, South Africa, pp98-157.

Forje W. John (2004) The Wind of Change: A Journey through Africa's Political Landscape and a Search for An Alternative. The Archie Mafeje Lectures, 19 October 2004, Africa Institute of South Africa, Pretoria, South Africa.

Forje W. John (1989). Science and Technology in Africa. Longman World Series on Science and Technology, Vol. 10, Longman Publishing Group, Essex, United Kingdom.

Gerschenkron Alexander (1962) Economic Backwardness in Historical Perspectives, Cambridge, MA. The Belknap Press, Harvard University Press, USA.

Ghani Ashraf & Clare Lockhart (2008) Fixing Failed States. Oxford University Press, United States of America and Oxford, UK.

Gifford Paul (2015). Christianity, Development and Modernity in Africa. Hurst Publishers, London, United Kingdom.

Glaser A. William & G. Christopher Habers (1978).The Brain Drain – Emigration and Return. Pergamon Press, London, United Kingdom (Findings of a UNITAR multinational comparative survey of professional personnel of developing countries who study abroad).

Griffin Keith (1989). Alternative Strategies for Economic Development. Economic Choices before the Developing Countries, the MacMillan Press Ltd, Hampshire, United Kingdom.

Henderson Gregory (1970). Emigration of Highly-Skilled Manpower from the Developing Countries, UNITAR, Research Report No.3, 1970.

Jowi James, Manya Klemencic & Thierry Lueschr-Mamashela (2015). Student Politics in Africa: Representation and Activism. African Higher Education Dynamics Series Vol.2, African Minds Publishers, Cape Town. South Africa.

Kannappan Subbiah (1968). "The Brain Drain and Developing countries," International Labour Review, Vol. 98. No. 1, July 1968, pp.1-26.

Kuwonu Franck (2015). "MDG2: Achieve Universal Primary Education. More Students in Schools But Still Not All", Africa Renewal, Vol. 29, No. 3, December 2015, New York, pp 23.

Kwapong A. Alexander (1995). "Meeting the Challenge of Education in Africa", in Bade Onimode & Richard Synge (eds.) (1995) Issues in African Development: Essays in Honour of Adebayo Adedeji at 65. Heinemann Education Books (Nigeria) PLC, Ibadan, Nigeria, pp181-193.

Langa Victorino Patricio (2014). Higher Education in Portuguese Speaking Africa Countries. African Minds African Minds Publishers, South Africa.

Lema Catherine Forje "Entrepreneurship Education Human Capital Development And Quality Livelihood" (2016) in Forje W. John (ed.) Shaping Africa's Future: Transforming African and Global Relations for A Just and Stable World. Centre for Action-Oriented Research on Africa's Development (CARAD), Bali-Nyonga, Cameroon (Forthcoming).

Maassen Peter, Ian Bunting, Pundy Pillay, Bailey Tracy & Cloete Nico (2011). Universities and Economic Development in Africa. African Minds Publishers, Cape Town, South Africa.

Mawere Munyaradzi (2014). Culture, Indigenous Knowledge and Development in Africa. Reviving Interconnections for Sustainable Development. Langaa RPCIG, Bamenda, Cameroon Republic.

McKaiser Eusebius (2016). Run Racist Run. Journeys into the Heart of Racism, Bookstorm (SA).

Mhango Nkuzi Nkwazi (2018). How Africa Developed Europe. Deconstructing the History of Africa, Excavating Untold Truth and What Ought to Be Done and Known. Langaa RPCIG, Cameroon.

Mills Greg & Herbst Jeffrey (2016) How South Africa Works: And Must Do Better, McMillan Publishers, South Africa.

MINISUP (Ministry of Higher Education) (2017). La Tutelle Académique Des Universités D'Etat Sur Les Institutions Privées D'Enseignement Supérieur Au Cameroun. Evaluation de la mise en Œuvre, Yaoundé – Cameroon.

Mouton Johann & Lauren Wildschut (2015). Leadership and Management. Case Studies in Training in Higher Education in Africa. African Minds Publishers, cape Town, South Africa.

Muchie Mammo (2015). "Time for Universities Made in the Image of Africa", New African, No.554, October 2015, London, pp36-7.

Musau Zipporah (2015). "MDG 3: Promote Gender Equality And Empower Women: Closing Africa's 'Elusive' Gender Gap', Africa Renewal, Vol.29, No.3, December 2015, United Nations, New York, United States of America, pp24.

Mwamwenda Tuntufye & Phindile Lukhele-Olorunju (eds.) (2013). The Triumph and Prosperity of Education in Africa, Africa Institute of South Africa (AISA), Pretoria, South Africa.

Mwamwenda S. Tuntufye (2013). "Some Important Aspects of Triumph and Prosperity of Education in Africa" in Mwamwenda et al. (2013), pp42-59.

Ncube Mthuli (2013). "Infrastructure Deficit, Financing Needs and the Post-2015 MDG Framework in Africa", Institute of Development Studies (IDS), Vol. 44, No.5-6, September 2013, John Wiley & Sons, UK, pp72-80.

Myezwa Hellen, Lilian Mariga & Roy McConkey (2014). Inclusive Education in Low-Income Countries. A Resource Book for Teachers educators, parent's trainers and Community Development. Disability Innovations Africa, South Africa.

Ngugi Wa Thiong'o (1986) Decolonising the Mind: The Politics of Language in African Literature, James Curry Publishers, London.

Nye Joseph (2008). The Powers to Lead: Soft, Hard, and Smart. Oxford University Press, United States of America.

Obanya Pai (2014). Educationeering. HEBN Publishers, Nigeria

One Country (2016). "New Patterns of Community Life in an Urbanising World", Vol.23, Issue 4, January 2016- December 2016, pp2-3.

Organisation of African Unity (OAU) (1980). The Lagos Plan of Action for the Socio-economic Development of Africa 1980-2000. Addis Ababa, Ethiopian.

Ovadia Salah Jesse (2016). The Petro-Developmental State in Africa: Making Oil Work in Angola, Nigeria and the Gulf of Guinea. Hurst Publishers, United Kingdom.

President Eisenhower (April 1953): Quote taken from his final valedictory speech to the American Society of Newspaper Editors, Washington DC. Eisenhower is remembered for his catch reference to the 'military-industrial complex' concept).

Room Michelle, Thiery M. Luescher-Mamashella, Robert Mattes, Angolwisye Mwollo-ntallima & Njuguna Ng'ethe (2011). The University in Africa and Democratic Citizenship: Hothouse or Training Ground? African Minds Publishers, Cape Town, South Africa.

Seers Dudley (1969). "The Brain Drain from the Developing Countries," (Brighton: Institute of Development Studies, University of Sussex, 1969, Britain, UK.

Skorov G. E. (1978). Science, Technology and Economic Growth in Developing Countries. Pergamon Press,, United Kingdom.

Smith Tuhiwai Linda (1212). Decolonising Methodologies: Research and Indigenous Peoples. (2nd edition), Zed Books, London and Otago University Press, Dunedin.

Swaniker Fred (2017). "Start of a New Golden Age?" New African, No. 572, May 2017, AN IC Publication, London, UK. Pp.42-45.

Tabaro Patrick Justice (2015). "Civilisation: Tracing African Civilisation", New African, No.554, October 2015, AN IPC Publication, London, pp82.

The South Commission (1990).The Challenge to The South – The Report of the South Commission, under the chairmanship of President Julius Nyerere Oxford University Press, United States of America.

Thomas C. (2010) Higher Education in Africa. Time to Pull Out the Steps.
See (http://allafrica.com/stories/201004300680.html)

United Nations (2010). United Nations University Revitalising Higher Education in Sub- Saharan Africa.
(see http.//www.edu/Africa/files/UNU-RevitalisingHigherEducation-pdf)

United Nations Institute for Training and Research (UNITAR) (1971). The Brain Drain from Five Developing Countries: Cameroon, Colombia, Lebanon, the Philippines, Trinidad and Tobago, UNITAR Research Report No.5, 1971.

Williams Stephen (2015) "Next Einstein Forum", New African, No. 561, May 2016, IC Publication, London pp12-13

World Bank (1989). A Joint Statement on Africa's Long-term Development, May 1989, Washington D.C. USA, para.8.

Wayne Hugo (2015). Boundaries of the Educational Imagination. African Minds Publishers, Cape Town, South Africa.

Yazani F. April & Janelle Mangwanda (2014)" A Snapshot View of Consolidated Democracy in South Africa and Nigeria", in Africa

Insight, Vol. 44(2) September 2014, Pretoria, South Africa, p108-124.

Zeleza T. Paul (1997) Manufacturing African Studies and Crises. CODESRIA Book Series, Antony Rowe Ltd, Codesria, Dakar, Senegal.

Chapter Three

Debunking Africa's golden age of scientific evolution: Exploiting the latecomer advantage in building the Africa we want: Opportunities, challenges and prospects

Abstract

Africa finds itself entangled with the old developmental myths and needs new ideas, new thinking and new development paths which must be home grown, owned and adequately utilised for the sustainable transformation and welfare of the people. Africa of the past was the centre of learning with the first university of the world established in 859 AD in Timbuktu (Mali) with Europe following almost centuries after. Africa should be the citadel of knowledge because no continent has so many of its citizens who studied around the world like. Unfortunately, it is has emerged as the citadel of the highest confusion. Today the continent remains at the bottom of the development ladder the so-called 'science desert' of the world but holding vital potentials for development. However, the 'science desert' status is a clarion call for African policy-makers to convert the notion of a 'science desert' into an 'oasis of development' and not condone to the dictates of what outsiders think African should do and be. As a 'science desert', there is much to be gained and learned – making the 'continent the place to be' as the centre for global transformation. The paper examines critically the development myths surrounding the transformation of the continent by adopting a progressive Afrocentric developmental approach by which science, technology and innovation aptly changes society and significantly contributing to the improvement of the quality livelihood of all citizens. It further postulate that the 'golden age' of the continent's scientific prowess can be regained by making proper use of the late-come advantage (Gerschenkron 1962); backed by developing and using properly its human capital. It is envisioned the continent cannot change without developing a new mindset, attitude and political will transforming from a backward into a modern polity. In the face of scourge of poverty, underdevelopment, exploitation, the continent must be committed to reducing its underdevelopment vulnerability through the application of science and technology and the fortification of indigenous knowledge and cultural value systems aimed at improving the welfare of the people. Conclusion points in the direction of science and technology as society 'game changer' which should be positively placed at the disposal for improving the quality of welfare of all citizens. The role of science and technology in Africa's development remains a significant imperative in the transformation of the continent that should not be played with. A new wind of change is called for to move Africa from its current underdeveloped to a new and well-conceived developmental status restoring and upholding the dignity and quality livelihood of the people. Three inter-locking factors 'three 'Es' – 'empower, educate and engage' - society is imperative in moving the continent forward.

Keywords: blame and reality theories, human capital development, science and technology, myths, change, policy

Introduction: General overview – looking back to moving forward

The golden age of Africa's scientific excellence could be structured in the Swahili words of **'kukopa ni harusi, kulipa matanga'**, meaning **'the party is over'**. In spite of this setback, Africa is still rising. A new era and attitude towards the development and use of science and technology in the transformation of the continent in this age of a global knowledge based economy is imperative. Africa's golden age of science and technology was lost due to the dehumanising impact of slavery and colonial governance. What Africa lost, Europe benefited and Africa can now equally benefit from its lost human knowledge base. The two continents are challenge in developing the habit and attitude of sharing and working together – the spirit of 'Harambee and Bathe Pelo' being the guiding star.

'TSHUMISANO' a Venda (South African word) meaning "Cooperation or Partnership"; in that spirit, indigenous knowledge and modern science should cohabit and science and technology should provide support for the continent's enterprise or small and medium size enterprises (SMME)| as the structural basis to leap frog the industrial awakening of the region and the anvil on which to build, improve and sustain quality wellbeing for the people of Africa. Sustainable quality wellbeing for the continent's population can be attained only empowerment through technology and by unlocking human potential through technology and capacity building. For now there is a serious disconnect between indigenous knowledge and modern science which renders Africa very vulnerable in the process of development. A paradigm shift or dichotomy – "Tshumisano" - should emerge between the two thereby placing the continent on the right rail for the continent's scientific and technological take-off.

Many factors contribute to the falling status of the continent's state of science and technology prowess, ranging from slavery, colonialism to poor policy articulation and implementation since independence. A new capable developmental attitude for the continent is most needed by taking advantage of the evolutionary impetus of advances in science and technology. The continent is obliged to learn, have openness, with a critical thinking mindset: the ability to choose, analyse and with confidence to be able to take a decision different from those of others. Critical thinking leads to innovation rather than learning to imitate the wrong way. The continent as a result of its so-called underdevelopment is challenged to seek and provide comprehensive solutions for complex problems.

It means Africa learning and mastering how to drive on the fast lane of the globalisation highway. Doing that calls for the development or revision of existing policy formulation, attitude and behaviour as part and parcel of structured reformulation process. To achieve such a goal requires a process development and improvement, problem-solving, and training which entails, capacity building, empowerment, technology transfer, entrepreneurial development, incorporation of indigenous knowledge, innovative, competitive and investments to enhance the transformation process of the continent. Africa needs a new 'techno-social system' to sustain its transformation process. Africa need to dialogue with the developed societies about development and use the dialogue as a learning process in doing things differently and avoiding getting deeper into problems confronting and constraining their development agenda. Sometimes that will mean thinking of solutions not necessarily discovered yet. For now, Africa should not be thinking about exploring the solar system, (even though there is no harm doing so) but how to build public transport, educational and health facilities and other basic infrastructures for quality livelihood.

Table 1: Myths and Scenarios Surrounding Africa's Transformation.

Africa being underdeveloped due to colonial rule	Europe owes Africa its redevelopment of the continent
Africa has fabulous wealth of minerals needing	Land owned by foreign investors should be seized and used
Development aid from Europe is not forthcoming	No Marshall Plan for Africa's transformation
Africa waiting-for-aid breeds complacency	Africa needs investors to engage with Africa equitably
Development needs pragmatism and partnership	Africans doing the thinking, Europe providing finances
Africa given the freedom to own is policies	African civil society stop supporting leaders who plunder
Quality human capital needed for Africa's development	The West will never develop Africa
Failure to empower citizenry training in STI	Playing the 'gate keeping' of protecting failed leaders
Civil servants failing telling truth – fear for their safety	Capacity utilisation, retention, harmonisation, sustainability
Africa infested with unskilled labour	Technology + innovation enabling Africa to develop faster

//_____//

//

Where is Africa's Science and Technology?
What should be done about it?
What are the missing gaps?
How can it develop Africa | and improve in the quality of livelihood?
Why was the continent largely bypassed by previous industrial revolutions?
How can Africa use the opportunities provided by the fourth industrial revolution
to transform itself into a veritable player in the knowledge-based global world?

//

Why African universities are not educating Africans to solve Africa\s problems |?

//

Africa should not still be playing catch-up when the fifth revolution comes around

//

Addressing longstanding challenges such as lack of capacity and infrastructure but because these
Trends will change almost every part of peoples' lives – jobs, relationships, economies, industries,
throughout the continent Public-Private Partnership (PPP) needed in accelerating and taking
ownership of its development nexus

African 'waiting-for-help' approach breeds complacency leading to an absence of thought about the
industrialisation of the continent. The continent needs investors to engage with Africa

creating joint venture and encouraging the transfer of technology, skills and innovation to
Africa

STI = science, technology and innovation	Source: Forje, Bali, 16 June 2016

The continent must develop a different way of looking at knowledge, learning and decision-making in the ultimate interest and wellbeing of the people. Current education teaches us there is one solution for everything. But what is valid for you is not necessarily valid for me or not in a particular context. Differences have to be understood and lived with. Sustainability solutions are very often locale specific (Sarabhai, 2012:2). It is from our differences and diversity that knowledge is improved. In other words diversities and differences should be perceived as assets not liabilities in the development process. Unfortunately scientific and technological activities in Africa have not been systematically linked to the productive sector, thereby making the impact of science and technology to be insignificant (Ibukun, 1995:166). For science and technology to be of services to the people, it must evolve within the premises of capacity building, technology transfer, empowerment, and incorporating indigenous knowledge among others. One of the areas for science and technology is to improve on the current energy deficit in many African countries. The continent cannot industrialize with form of erratic energy supply. The lack of electricity constrains the economy and inhibits growth. How can science and technology resolve the current state of poor energy supply? And yet the continent is blessed with an enormous pool of power generating opportunities ranging from solar energy, hydro-power, gas, wind mills and others.

Some of these arguments are situated as indicative in Table 1: Myths and Scenarios Surrounding Africa's Transformation. There is need to x-ray the historical past to better understand the present and in order to construct a sustainable future. Looking into the historical past is taking cognizance of indigenous knowledge systems and cultural values and relating this to modern science and technology for the overall welfare of the people. Indigenous knowledge and modern science and technology should be developed and placed at the services of humanity and not for destructive purposes. New and emerging technologies are changing the context and mode of industrial production and communalisations, and as a result, new international patterns of industrialisation and connectivity among people and nations are emerging. These new technologies present certain challenges as well as offer vast opportunities to African countries to jump start their developmental journeys, as well as draw valuable lessons from the failures or blunders of the developed countries.

These and other myths or scenarios highlight issues of leadership, capacity and infrastructure development as the serious missing link in Africa's development. The continent has the resources but not the capacity to give added value and enhance its rising potentials in the world. The current world economic situation and declining economic growth rates in many countries does not signal the end of 'Africa's Rising Role (ARR) provides the opportunity for African countries to 'regroup, refocus and make themselves more resilient to external shocks' as noted by President Uhuru Kenyatta (Kenya) at the 26th World Economic Forum on Africa, in Rwanda 2016. For the continent moving ahead requires science and technology and the imminent digital revolution receiving serious attention by African governments. It is common because human capital and digital development including research and innovation remain critical to the continent's future and improving the welfare of citizens. As such the emergence of new technologies is accompanied by increased entry barriers requiring trained critical human mass, high capital investment and infrastructures. The implications of new technologies are entire not negative. It is evidently clear that through well-articulated and executed policies, new and emerging technologies can be harnessed for the benefit of the continent and humanity in general (Bhalla et al.1988; Forje, 1987;UNIDO 1989: ICPSA 1980).

For now, the continent is embedded with a young and growing population, vast resources and largely untapped markets providing the foundation for a continent-wide renewal that should be driven by the transformative power of technological innovation and entrepreneurship. Apparently, technology is not a 'magic bullet' but a tool for widely tackling the challenges faced by Africa (Graham, 2016:62-3). What Africa most need is a science and technology subculture anvil positively transforming not destroying society. There is the urgency for creating a democratic governance system and a scientific and technological base that in unionism constructs the underlying structural base a better future for a rapidly increasing population.

This requires a process of: (i) reinvigorating; (ii) engaging, (iii) educating; and (iv) empowering all citizens against underdevelopment, poverty, exploitation and inequality among other ills without which the continent we want cannot be. Empowering citizens entails changing lives and opening minds towards sustainable development. Equally this poses serious challenges to African universities and universalities – that of educating young Africans to solve Africa's problems. A new education curriculum specific to the needs and aspirations of the continent, will motivate the educated ones to utilise their acquired skills at home rather than risking their lives in search of greener pastures elsewhere. Reducing vulnerability should focus on stimulating economic policies that lead to prolonged growth and low inflation; invest in science and technology related activities leading to an industrial foundation for the continent. Government needs to undertake structural reforms to improve productivity and raise potential growth, promote entrepreneurship, innovation and raise potential growth and to increase spending to boost demand, which will promote economic growth.

So far many African leaders have not exhibited renewed commitment towards building a capable democratic developmental state. It is necessary to strengthen the capacity of society to respond accordingly to the emerging challenges. Second, there is the need to develop the scientific, technological, innovative and entrepreneurial base of the people and to protect them from the wrong deployment of scientific and technological achievements. By and large, popular sentiment long holds that authoritarian regimes are technologically-challenged dinosaurs ready to inappropriately deploy scientific and technological progress in achieving selfish ends. Thirdly, there is the need for civil society to be better prepared in helping protecting fragile new democracies against the danger of backsliding into authoritarian regime construct and extremist movements derailing the progress of African countries. The fourth issue entails a process of positive response from the West towards the set aspirations and desires of African countries in constructing the continent they want.

Apparently, growing inequality and the failure to invest in the development of human capital and social infrastructure leads to a crisis of political dysfunctional, conflicts and destabilisation within the global environment with the consequences of derailing or slowing down the transformation process of the continent. There is much to be gained from indigenous knowledge and cultural values (currently undervalue) which must be promoted or incorporated in modern science and technology knowledge.

Science and technology transforming the emerging African society must focus and contribute to the improvement of the quality of living for all citizens while ensuring that science-technology driven development is equitable and sustainable contributing to a just, peaceful and stable global environment. Africa must develop a continental action plan to renew science and technology policies for its transformation – rethinking the Lagos Plan of Action (LPA) that never was implemented), NEPAD Vision and AU Agenda 2063 provides ways forward for the Africa we want. The people of Africa since the start of the fifties decided to break the chains of painful historical past from colonial era to liberation and attaining quality livelihood achievable through the conscious development and deployment of science and technology.

There has to be a progressive African movement for the renewal of the continent's lost golden era of scientific and technological heritage and the development of contemporary science and technology for the its progress. Society cannot progress without human capacity and infrastructure building, and proper utilisation, capacity retention, capacity harmonisation, including the sustainability of capacity projects (Nnadozie 2016:50). There is much strength in indigenous knowledge and cultures but there are also specific problems beaconing Africans to sharpen their ideas into profitable developmental activities for the overall welfare of the people. Debunking ongoing process to the scientific and technological uplift of Africa means creating strong institutions and functional infrastructures so that Africa emerges as a region to be 'heard, not as a problem to be solved.' Genuine autonomy or independence will have been attained by African countries when they have, quantitatively and qualitatively, acquired the same technology as the most developed countries. It is only then that globalisation will bring potential benefits to African countries.

Taking advantage of the 'latecomer' concept means new technologies presenting both threats and opportunities which together constitute the major challenging factor for the continent's science and technology system. Failure of African countries responding positively, comprehensively and constructively to these challenges will further marginalise them from world economic and social progress. It is imperative that strategic policy responses be articulated and implemented to take advantage of the benefits and to moderate the negative effects of underdevelopment and dependency. It is for these reasons that the strength, weakness, opportunities and threats (SWOT|) approach constitutes a cardinal factor in the conceptual approach of the paper.

Conceptual and analytical premises

The conceptual premises of departure are construed within the 'blame' and 'reality theories' with the SWOT approach used as the analytical tool to situate and advance the science technology and innovation of the continent. Both theories should blend into a common synergy to produce the Africa we want through an Agenda of 'here and now'. The continent remains underdeveloped for continuously hanging on the 'blame theory'. Africa can develop by taking advantage of Gerschenkron's idea of a 'latecomer advantage' not needing with the aid of science and technology to go through Rostow's stages of development. It is easy to condemn a theory by considering only its caricature. The Rostow's stages of development have its significance. The contemporary African situation, calls an urgent process to changing the lives of the people taking advantage of what is available in the 21st century in accelerating the transformation process.

Bear in mind that science and technology is not the alpha and omega – something more is needed to give greater impetus to the development and deployment of S&T in transforming the society and welfare of the population. Therefore the 'reality and blame theories' backed by the SWOT analytical approach, provides the frame work for Africa building a new scientific and technological age as well as constructing Miracle Development for Africa (MDA). Rostow (1962|) prescribes five stages - the traditional society; the pre take-off stage; take-off; the road to maturity and the society of mass communication - through which African countries must transverse from backwardness to maturity. Africa in no way needs to subject itself through these various stages. The process of development can with the help of science and technology cut-short these stages. The proper use of science and technology changes the developmental status quo of a country. Why not take advantage of and properly utilise existing opportunities?

Fforde Adam (2009) argues that development is a predictable process with knowable solutions. As well as providing a penetrating critique and coping strategies for evaluating contending solutions to problems of development. Subramanian and Pisupati (2010) emphasis the role of traditional knowledge contributing immensely to shaping development and human well-being through a variety of sectors, including agriculture, health, education and governance Traditional knowledge, (TK) or Indigenous knowledge (IK), Fforde points out is increasingly underrepresented or under-utilised. Unfortunately, the applicability of traditional knowledge to human and environmental welfare though well-recognised, but collated information on how TK contributes to different sectors is not easily accessible. Here Oqubay (2015) demonstrates that industrial policies work better when they are designed to be sector-specific, i.e., policies that work in one area or sector may not necessarily work in another. Therefore, the politics of policy independence which enables a developmental state to learn by doing, by copying and making mistakes and learning from failure provides the better alternative or way forward. Government policy learning as well as 'collective learning' of government and the key stakeholders in the economy is seen as critical for effective policy formulation and implementation. A well-articulated and implement science and technology policy and development plan, means no one should be left behind would be left behind.

However, a strict distinction must be established between the 'adequacy' of technology in general, in relation to the socio-cultural and institutional conditions to the geo-climatically/environmental conditions of the same country, If African countries could make wide use of the latest achievements of contemporary science and technology, it would significantly promote their economic growth and the liquidation of poverty, hunger, and disease. Therefore, the all-round application of new technology makes it possible to solve the problem of industrialisation and sharply increase the efficiency of agricultural production in a historically short period of time. On the eve of an African Union Summit in 2007, Calestous Juma told African leaders that their biggest challenge 'is not scarcity of science and technology knowledge, but how to harness the technology and to improve of the welfare of the people. What Africa needs is more engineers to allow it to leapfrog industrialised and emerging economies knowledge ... that latecomers grow faster than frontrunners. Which should give Africa hope to grow as fast as China, if not faster?'(Nording, 2007:22-23).

The developing countries' struggle against the political diktat of imperialism, the rapacious exploitation of human and natural resources, and, especially, 'technological neo-colonialism' is constantly taking on new forms and methods. However, the goals of this struggle do not change: the regulation of transnational corporations' activities and the achievement of technological independence. Therefore, African countries acting in concerted and uniform way, and setting up lists of common regional demands which must be met in the import of foreign technology, have begun to play an important role in the struggle against transnational corporations' dominance of the technology market.

Apparently TK or IK can be effectively integrated with conventional science and technology policy articulation in accelerating the transformation of the continent. Presently, the distance separating a less-developed country (for example, Burundi, Cameroon, Chad, Central African Republic) from a developed country, (for example, South Korea, Malaysia, United Kingdom etc.) precisely in terms of the satisfaction of social needs is infinitely greater than that which separates the semi-developed from any developed country, whatever the latter's social relations. Being a latecomer provides vast opportunities in accelerating the transformation of the continent in a sustainable way. As latecomer, and with the aid of technology, we do not need to go through Rostow's stages of development like the West did.

Broadening scientific and technological revolution creates great opportunities for the modernisation of the economies of African states for these countries to overcome their underdevelopment predicaments. African countries need two variables: accumulated funds (investments) and technological knowledge: and the two must circulate with the same freedom and fluidity. The two are complementary and not competitive. Technological knowledge cannot become production of goods without accumulated funds being available. Table 2 attempts streamlining some of the inherent factors underscoring the 'blame and reality' theories.

Table 2: Looking at Some of the 'Blame and Reality' Theoretical Approach for Africa.

The Blame Theory	The Reality Theory
Africa's underdevelopment is due to colonial Rule;	Fifty years after independence Africa should take responsibility of its rule;
Capitalism and imperialism are contributors to Africa's technological underdevelopment	Indigenous knowledge is not well used in the transformation of Africa
Bad governance contributes to underdevelopment	Good leadership and policies
The developed states continue exploiting developing countries.	contribute to development
One is as dependent as one is under-developed	Dependency can't be the cause of economic backwardness
Impossible to assimilate imported techno-technique	One is not as underdeveloped as one logy / is dependent.
Technology appropriate for third World countries is an underdeveloped technology	Technology is not neutral: it is the 'carrier' of social progress
Dependency is the cause of the continent's underdevelopment	The West perpetuates the underdevelopment of African countries
Poor leadership contributes to under-development and exploitation	Level of national education determines the progress of technology
Undermining our cultural values is under-mining Africa's development	Transfer of technology puts serious obstacles on the path to the formation of viable national economic
Copying wrong external values is a recipe for underdevelopment and exploitation	complexes in African countries, keeping these countries at the periphery of the world capitalist system as well
Africa has it self to blame for its current status	maintaining the unequal status of these countries in the international capitalist division of labour in the field of science and technology
	African countries making wide use of the latest achievements of modern science and technology would significantly promote their economic growth and the liquidation of poverty
Forje (June, 28, 2016)	

The two theoretical approach leads to deploying the SWOT analysis for a clearer view of the prospects and predicaments of the continent. The blame and reality views have their strength and weaknesses, and should be used to strengthen as well as mapping a way forward for Africa owing its development nexus. The systematic application of scientific or other organised knowledge to practical tasks – developments which are deeply rooted in an important innovation leads to improved sustained citizen's welfare currently lacking in many African countries. This gives credence to the SWOT approach and deepens our understanding of the 'blame and reality' theories to development; and why it is imperative for the continent to make the right choice for its transformation.

Table 3: Some Pertinent Factors - underscores the importance why African leaders must act holistically for the good of the continent. While shining a light on the needs is an important first step, only actions taken holistically to implement high-level decisions will determine success of failures of moving or not Africa into the club of quality livelihood for all citizens. It is therefore imperative for African countries to adhere to the orientation of advocated by the New Partnership for African Development (NEPAD) Consolidated Plan of Action on promoting Science and Technology for the development of Africa. It challenges African countries to promote the development of skilled human capital, competitive environment, and supporting institutions – universities, technical and vocational schools, research laboratories, standards bodies, and information and communication infrastructure to list but a few – that make and enhance this enterprise innovation possible.

Interface between Indigenous Knowledge & Science, Technology and Innovation

The reality theory indicates Africa taking the bull by the horn, meeting its obligations and responsibilities in ensuring the sustainable transformation of the continent. The real challenge is ensuring that advancements in science and technology is combined with relevance to African indigenous knowledge and cultural heritage as well as meeting social reality of mass rural and urban poverty. The challenging task therefore is to harness ongoing advances in the new frontiers of science and technology in upgrading traditional skills and occupations. Wieizsacker et al (1983) asserted that there are unusual opportunities for developing countries, especially those bypassed by the great benefits of science and technology, to improve the quality of life of their rural and urban poor through the integration of traditional and emerging technologies.

Table 3: Some Pertinent Factors Underscoring the SWOT Analytical Approach

Strength:

- Africa's resources are vast and much needed by the developed polities
- A rapidly growing youth population;
- Vast market for western produced goods
- Virgin area still to be researched and tapped
- Provides vast development opportunities for other continents
- Valuing Africa and African people;
- Africa holds the future of the world

Weakness

- Fragmentation resulting from colonial rule which created alien political, economic and social entities;
- Intensive exploitation of labour and resources;
- Poor human capital development;
- Weak institutions and poor infrastructures;
- Underdeveloped private sector;
- Weak and corrupt administrative/bureaucratic setup; Weak leadership, poor governance and system;
- Colonial legacies constraining the development process;
- Inadequate human development, poor financial mobilisation and utilisation;
- Inequality in shared-prosperity leading to widening gaps between the rich and poor;
- Absence of a vibrant and committed media industry in educating the people about their rights and active involvement in the development process and moving forward;
- The developed countries using their prowess in scientific and technological advancement in p[promoting its agenda and defending its interests;

Opportunities

- Making proper use of the 'latecomer' advantaged;
- Africa does not need to develop the wheel;
- Vast untapped natural resources and human capital;
- Provides as bases for the future of the world;
- Diversity as 'assets' not as liability in state construction;
- Bright future for Africa provided it does its hone work properly and in the ultimate interest of the people
- Using the diasporas as channels in the sustainable transformation of the region;
- Promoting technical entrepreneurship and technological innovation

Threats;

- Negative trends on economic, social, political, humanitarian science leads to the international community perceiving Africa through dark lenses; with nothing good emerged for the continent;
- The international community faltering in their commitments towards the continent;
- Declining external resources flow;
- Weak scientific and technological base;
- Poor usage of indigenous knowledge and cultural heritage values as weapons for development;
- Poor state construction;
- Gross negligence of the female gender in the development process;
- Poor regional integration impacting negatively on the free movements of people and goods within the continent;
- The forces of post-modernism imperialism and the new colonising powers;
- Hostile international environment;
- Rising religious fundamentalism, and xenophobic attitude;
- Globalisation as a 'curse' but can be converted into a 'blessing';
- Poor governance leads to the exclusion of citizens' participation in the development process;
- Re-colonisation of Africa in the age of scientific and technological awakening;
- Self articulate interests of leaders/ruling elites;
- Politics and forces of globalisation should be critically scrutinised

Forje (2016)

Interface between indigenous knowledge, science and technology and development and underdevelopment is intrinsically linked to the proponents of the dependency school which argues strongly on the ideas that;

126

	Underdevelopment is intimately connected with the expansion of the industrialised capitalist countries;
	Underdevelopment cannot be considered as the original condition in an evolutionary process;
Africa's Under- ==➜	The problems of underdevelopment does not significantly differ from
development	the prevailing 19th Century evolutionism; Africa rested peacefully and
	Unsuspectingly like a sleeping beauty, awaiting a western prince charming to
	awaken the continent's process of chronic development, if not by a kiss, then
	by the sword (Blomstrom and Hettne, 1985:28)
	Dependency is, however, not only an external phenomenon but also manifested in different ways in the (internal, ideological and political structure)

Unsuspectingly like a sleeping beauty, awaiting a western prince charming to awaken the continent's process of chronic development, if not by a kiss, then by the sword (Blomstrom and Hettne, 1985:28)

Dependency is, however, not only an external phenomenon but also manifested in different ways in the (internal, ideological and political structure)

These underlying ideas act as wake-up calls for African countries sitting up and facing the realities of their current predicaments. A social revolution is the inevitable result for the continent in meeting its social obligations and responsibilities to the people. These responsibilities to citizen's means building capacity and creating jobs and promoting equitable social development with advancement towards certain well-defined objectives corresponding to conditions of humans found in the modern world. Africa will progress towards this model as soon as they are able to eliminate certain social, political, cultural and institutional obstacles. It goes without saying that these conceptual approaches provide an analytical process of development in various historical and concrete manifestations.

Meeting that challenge requires new ethical, moral and social contract in remedying the shortcomings as well as failures of narrow conception of development. We cannot run from the reality that the continent's future is inescapably linked to its ability to create an effective marriage between indigenous knowledge and science and technology - a challenge in which education plays a decisive part. Current African education curriculum needs a sharpen therapy and innovation to inject progressive political and cultural authenticity, not a pale imitation of ex-colonial models (Kwapong 1995:191). By all imagination, a key requirement for the success of all economic and social policy reforms is that they should not only be relevant to specific country situations, but 'they must be designed, implemented and owned by African countries themselves' (World Bank 1989; AU 2013;) Africa must thread on the path of a comprehensive strategic opportunities for capacity building and proper utilisation of its human and natural resources for the overall good of the people.

Currently, the continent is faced with the overwhelming issue of improper utilisation of human and natural resources – the *'brain drain'*- *'brain gain'* phenomenon and the wrongfully exploitation or depletion of natural resources. The *'brain drain'* phenomenon is making Africa to lose its critical human mass. What is required is to convert the *'brain drain'* phenomenon (the loss of critical human skills in developing countries to the developed West or its higher-paying, more prestigious jobs in developed countries into a *'brain gain'* asset factor for the development of Africa. Some now interpret this trend as *'brain circulation'*, the flows of human resources in both directions. Note that returning skilled humans capital not only add talent to the labour market, but play a key role in explaining and promoting the benefits of science, technology and innovation (STI) capacity for meeting social and economic goals.

The Diaspora should be encouraged to play a more meaningful role in the development of the continent. Countries of the East Asian region provide good examples of proper utilisation of the skills of the Diasporas in giving a new human-look and transforming the society. Creating an enabling environment for the Diasporas through prestige and opportunities for cutting-edge S&T related activities plays a crucial role in determining the willingness of scientist's engineers and other skilled workers to stay at home or return. Articulating and implementing a comprehensive/holistic policy can enable latecomer nations use science, technology and innovation to turn the challenges of underdevelopment into an opportunity for a strategic process of linkage, leverage, learning and delivering quality services to the people.

This imply Africa having a critical mass of scientists, technologist, entrepreneurs, skilled labour force and scholars who are capable of effectively operating the requisite institutional framework such as universities, scientific research and development institutions and enterprises. It goes without saying that the urgent need of creating

128

and operating appropriate national and multidisciplinary network of institutions, enterprises co-operating on a national and regional basis to develop the research capabilities and productive capacity of the continent. This has to be the overriding challenge for African nations, regional groupings, the African Union and enterprises should focus in addressing, and urgently too. The challenge of building a critical human mass and institutional capacity is essentially is essentially, (i) to produce a modern African responding to the material, spiritual and human needs; and (ii) meeting the exigencies of the people like the Japan, Korea and the Asian Tiger's nations have done for their citizens.

The African society can only be transformed when there is concerted synergy between the various actors working in the common interest and focusing on the people and continent, otherwise AU Agenda 2063 or any national agenda has no meaning to the welfare of African citizens. The vast natural resources of the continent cannot be of use to the people without the comprehensive utilisation of science and technology. Failure in articulating and implementing a holistic developmental policy strategy and using science and technology for improving the welfare of the people makes Africa 'poor in the midst of plenty'. The continent's quest for science and technology should leave no one behind, Therefore, it is the obligation and responsibility of the policymakers to make science and technology an integral part of the development nexus with the total involvement of all citizens.

Developing a new mindset remain essential in meeting the challenges of the continent beyond the 21st century calls for a new structural-functional relationship or social contract between the various actors, state, people, educational / research institutions and the private sector as the important instrument for the sustainable transformation of the continent. It is strongly believed that a progressive Afrocentric basic strategy of development will increase national self-reliance. By all standards, this means self-confidence, reliance primary on one's own resources, human and natural, and the capacity for autonomous goal-setting and decision-making (in short, Africa directing and claiming ownership of its development path). Of course, the continent cannot develop in isolation given today's political and economic construct. Cooperation within and across national and continental frontiers is vital to ignite and ensure that science and technology are placed at the services of humankind.

Imperative of African Co-operation – *"TSHUMISANO"*

If the *Africa We Want* and if we are to take advantage of the latecomer advantage through science and technology, African cooperation becomes a sine qua non in forging ahead the sustainable development of the continent. 'Such cooperation, while strengthening the various national and collective capabilities should also bring about an active and self-sustaining capacity to participate on any ultimate basis of equality in the present post-industrial and information revolution. The agenda for capacity building is comprehensive and long-term, but there must be prioritisation in sustained implementation on a modular,' (Kwapong op cit.190). Regional Economic Community (RECs) and universities research institutions across the continent must intensify research and exchange ideas to benefit from advances in science and technology for improving the people's standard of livelihood.

Unfortunately, Africa is falling behind in the funding of science and technology. The result is falling numbers of research findings or findings gathering dust in the drawers and on the shelves of researchers. There is very little link between the researchers and private sectors to convert research results into products. Thus University - private sector interface can help build capacity, mobilise valuable human and financial resources and encourage scientific cooperation between and among countries.

We live in an interconnected world despite our economic and scientific differences – evidence by rapid movement of people, goods and information at ever increasing speed which has resulted in an era of unprecedented global economic growth. However, not all are sharing in these advances. For example, while the economies of the Asian countries are accelerating at breakneck speed, Africa, by almost all measures, is being left behind. Even though the past couple of years a number of African countries continue to register as fastest growing economies in the world, results still does not trigger down to improve the quality of livelihood of ordinary citizens.

Cooperation between African countries is very important for its economic transformation. So also the relationship between science and security is important. Science investment is critical for promoting entrepreneurship and increasing innovation and economic growth – a key element for promoting security. While economic growth does not guarantee security, it does provide an incentive for citizens to demand that their leaders pursue policies that maintain both domestic and regional stability (Forje, 1978; Turekian, 2007). Economic growth equally catalyses investments into technologies helping improve the basic needs of the people Scientific and technological breakthroughs no doubt can advance many sustainable development goals, - improving agricultural output; providing clean portable water, enhancing, low sources of energy, improving health facilities among many others). Thus scientific cooperation between countries will foster relationships and enables mutually beneficial economic growth. It is necessary to establish joint ventures and other forms of cooperation within and across national frontiers among research institutions, universities and other bodies. Cooperation, notes Thabo Mbeki (former President of South Africa, 'is of material relevance to the West; not so much that they have suddenly fallen in love with the Africans or the developing world, but because there is a shared interest between the developed and developing countries to deal with this matter' (Ighobor, 2016:18). We have to jointly deal with the issue of science, technology and innovation for the common good of humankind.

We can draw a good example from the World's-Leading Project, based in South Africa – the world's largest telescope and also the world's largest science instrument. Its importance to Africa is that it is radically changing perception of what Africa can do. When Africa first expressed interest in the Square Kilometre Array (SKA), people in Europe and America were very sceptical. They said you cannot do science and technology in Africa. Today SKA has a crucial role in building Africa's capacity to deal with its own problems. One of SKA's spin-offs is the creation of an African research cloud (Williams, 2016:56-7). Former Director of the project, Prof. Bernie

Fanaroff points out how he SKA project is not just for astronomy but also attracting scientists – reverse brain drain, attracting best young researchers coming back to Africa to work. That has been exciting as six research chairs in South Africa as well as starting research chairs in other countries. More than 818 bursaries have been awarded in the last decade, and graduated over 16 PhD's. With about 140 of these bursaries going to young students from African partner countries... (Williams op cit.) This is an example of cooperation that can be duplicated in other areas to develop the continent's capacity for the long-term livelihood improvement of citizens.

Cooperation will further strengthen mutual trust and confidence between people and countries as well as build peace and stability in the world. It can equally lead to both the developed and developing countries taking their share of responsibility, individually and collectively, to promote and sustain conditions which will enable developing countries to follow a self-reliant strategy in science and technology. For African countries, this calls for the establishment of effective interaction on a durable basis between the science and technology, the educational system, the productive system, and the political system – links which are badly missing in African countries. "We can build capacity in Africa, mobilise valuable human and financial resources and encourage scientific cooperation between and among nations. Such action will be critical for breaking a vicious cycle of falling scientific/economic output. Debt dependency and violence" notes Turekian (2007:21). A paradigm change is necessary to move Africa forward in all aspects of transformation, comprehensively, constructively and inclusively.

This paper is written from a progressive Afrocentric perspective, which means an emphasis on African social scientists taking a longer view on how, where, when and by what means change should come the way of Africa transforming itself by constructing the Africa the people want. The role of science and technology cannot be bypassed in constructing the Africa we want – and this entails strengthening national institutions or agencies for scientific and technological development; as well as reorientating our mindset of making our institutions to be more responsive to the goals of basic needs and social equity.

For now, the continent is blessed with vast natural resources abundance, requiring skilled human capital in giving added value to these resources as well as improving on the quality livelihood of the citizens. All that is required is not developing the wheel but taking advantage of the developed wheel. Africa must now create a national system of economic learning and development, putting in place the basic elements of infrastructures and providing the necessary sustainable financial incentives and not to waste its demographic dividend. For now and a long time to come, the continent holds the highest proportion of youth in its demographic make-up which should enhance the productive segment of the continent's transformation, Africa is creating more than 250000 jobs every year, but every year there are millions of young people entering the employment markets of African countries which becomes a breeding ground for all forms of destructive forces – Jihadists, and Boko Haram for example.

Chart 1

Gauging progress

The African Regional Integration Index measures 16 different indicators across five broad dimensions.

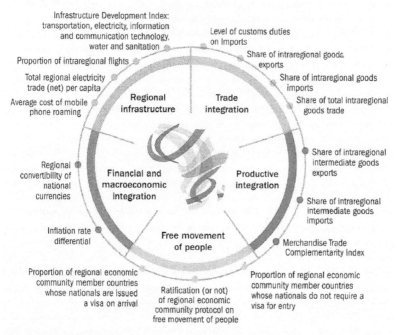

Sources: Economic Commission for Africa, African Union Commission, and African Development Bank (2016).

Chart 1 illustrates the progress and status of the continent's regional integration index measurements in six different countries; while Chart 2 – The Measuring Up of some existing Regional Economic Communities (RECs). The progress of some existing organisations appears on Chart 2 – Measuring Up. Such a performance should equally be extended to the science, technology, innovation, and research and development nexus to enhance the sustainable development of the continent. As sub-Saharan Africa has emerged as the world's second fastest-growing region in recent years, economic integration has become an increasingly important driver of growth. At the same time, by 2035, the number of sub-Saharan Africans joining the working-age population (ages 15-64) will exceed that from the rest of the world combined. These two development trends call for policy challenge: creating jobs and being competitive the global market economy. Sustained human capital development, science and technology remain imperative in meeting the needs of the region. The world economy also stands to benefit if sub-Saharan Africa's labour force is trained and well equipped and integrated into the global supply chains in an era of declining working-age populations elsewhere. Science and technology should promote Africa's development. The wonders that information and communication technology (ICT) can do towards promoting development can no longer be emphasised. 'The transition to a competitive-based development cooperation strategy for Africa will entail a clear recognition of the role of infrastructure in Africa's development and focused investment in the associated engineering fields' (Juma 2007:7).

Regional Economic Communities as well as all institutions should strengthen their science and technology components to ensure they derive the greatest opportunities offered by science and technology in improving the welfare of their citizens. The failure of science transforming the African society is the result of three interlinked structural criteria, namely: (i) unevenness of productivity as between sectors; (ii) disarticulation of the economic system and poor governance construct; and (iii) domination from outside – giving birth to the continent's status of an underdevelopment part of the world. The poor performance of science and technology transforming Africa could be seen as the result of the fact the accumulation in the periphery being patterned to the advantage of the centre.

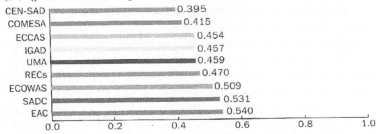

Chart 2

Measuring up
Well-established organizations—such as the East African Community—with close economic, political, and social ties score better overall on the integration index.
(average overall scores on regional integration by regional economic community)

CEN-SAD	0.395
COMESA	0.415
ECCAS	0.454
IGAD	0.457
UMA	0.459
RECs	0.470
ECOWAS	0.509
SADC	0.531
EAC	0.540

0.0   0.2   0.4   0.6   0.8   1.0

Sources: Economic Commission for Africa, African Union Commission, and African Development Bank (2016).
    Note: CEN-SAD = Community of Sahel-Saharan States, COMESA = Common Market for Eastern and Southern Africa, EAC = East African Community, ECCAS = Economic Community of Central African States, ECOWAS = Economic Community of West African States, IGAD = Intergovernmental Authority on Development, RECs = average of all regional economic communities, SADC = Southern African Development Community, and UMA = Arab Maghreb Union. Scores are calculated on a scale of 0 (low) to 1 (high).

Africa must pull itself together socially, ideologically and politically to identify the differences between a self-centred or collective developmental approach. We live in a world where of (i) an autocratic, dynamic capitalism in the centre, and (ii) a blocked capitalism in the periphery with no human facing. The crumps of progress fail to trickle down to the unfortunate masses. The politically dominating centre creates an export sector in the periphery according to its own needs, leaving the centre of the periphery to barely hold and to move around with a begging pan in hand cementing the state and art of dependency. This to a large extent this explains why the development process of African countries is often thwarted.

So far the structural-functional-political base of the continent is incapable of transforming society to the benefit and welfare of the citizens. Science transforming society in Africa needs a convergence of domestic resource use and domestic demand as the first iron law of transformation. Africa's strategy of convergence should lead to a shift towards production for basic needs and also the rationalisation of the agricultural sector through the spread of industrialisation techniques and the shift of balance in favour of entrepreneurship and industry. The continent is in daring need of a strategy of comprehensive planning that sees the rapid emergence of an indigenously oriented technology in partnership with the fast growing role of modern technology. The continent has but one choice – to move away from underdevelopment to industrialisation with a human face – the wellbeing of the citizens as the outstanding vision and goal in mind.

Science transforming the African society must be engraved and harnessed with the touch and smile of a *'human face'* bringing wealth, prosperity and sustainable quality livelihood to all. It has to have the 'golden touch' of the peoples' welfare and wellbeing. Let Africa give science and technology a new image in changing the future and fortune of the continent. Africa should no longer be seen as continent rich in poverty but one that is rich in richness and the richness translating into quality livelihood for present and future generations. Therefore, science and technology should be the new instrument of basic human needs and the force of improved social priorities, of alleviating poverty and inequality; of ensuring peace, security and stability; of accelerating the industrialisation of the continent and giving it a voice in global politics and as strategy of delinking for achieving greater autonomy and giving the capacity as the goal of developing Africa not destroying and further enslaving the continent.

With science and technology, Africa can move from poverty to power by breaking the cycle of poverty, ignorance, inequality and exploitation to giving the people power over their own destinies a radical redistribution of power, opportunities and assets through the driving forces and transformation of creating active citizens and effective states. Africa needs to harmonise its science and technology development policy and integration process across its various regional blocs. By building local science, technology and innovation (STI) capacity, African countries can not only better absorb and adapt foreign technologies, but also develop local solutions to local problems. For example, educational systems must be designed to be responsive to the research and human capital and social needs of the private sector, rather than having course offerings, curriculum, and research programmes imposed on them by government planners or from outside and serving external interests.

Africa today has the opportunities for articulating '*latecomer strategies*' for catching up and owning its development trajectories; and shaping the course of the African people to improve their quality of life and to uplift the people in a sustainable way of living. These obligations and responsibilities current leaders owe present and future generations. Achieving this vision entails putting the collective interest and good of the citizens before their articulate self-interests. With this in mind, the continent can be counted and respected.

By way of conclusion – The road ahead

So far, Africa has had some two decades of progress. First there has been some marked improvement in governance in a number of countries, with the number of electoral democracies jumping from just four in 1990 to 23 today. Apparently, with democracy comes better governance, greater adherence to the rule of law, stronger public institutions, a better business environment and less corruption. Second, there are more skilled leaders and policymakers. A new generation of entrepreneurs, technicians and manager is rising to the top of government agencies, civil society organisations and within the private business sector. Third, and related, economic and social policies have improved significantly and will do more with the proper utilisation of science, technology and innovation. Many countries are experiencing less state control, less red tape, and a lower cost of doing business (Radelet 2016:7-8). Rwanda has taken great strides in this area.

Chart 3 – Two Decades of Development Progress – illustrates Africa's gradual and steady efforts to progress with the eventual goals of meeting UN Sustainable Development Goals (SDGs) and African Union (AU) visionary Agenda 2063, building the *Africa We Want*. The newly adopted UN (SDGs) 25 September 2015, plus AU Agenda 2065 (2013) well implemented could transform the continent.

African leaders in partnership with world leaders should listen to the voice of Pope Francis to the UN General Assembly: "A selfish and boundless thirst for power and material prosperity leads both to the misuse of available natural resources and to the exclusion of the weak and the disadvantaged" (Ighobor, 2015:4). It is a question of aligning interests to place the continent on the brink of a transformation for the common good of humanity.

Chart 3: Two Decades of Development Progress

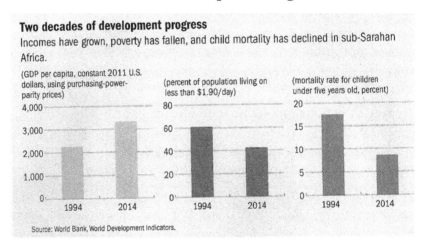

Two decades of development progress
Incomes have grown, poverty has fallen, and child mortality has declined in sub-Sarahan Africa.

Source: World Bank, World Development Indicators.

However, global circumstance will not remain favourable, but may change significantly making many countries to confront some of their difficult challenges. It is such conveyor belts that the continent should strongly but significantly guide against and prepare itself to better offer quality services delivery to citizens. Here lies the challenges testing the skills of Africa's new generations of leaders and how science, technology and innovation related activities are critically deployed to bear in the *'game changing'* nexus. Therefore, continued long-term progress through these challenging era calls for comprehensive and holistic action plans which should include; (i) the continent's surge for progress cannot persist without strong education and health systems. Getting as many people to undergo human capital development is vital. So far many countries have significantly made progress in school enrolment and in getting the girl child into the classrooms. There has been marked improvement

138

in the health care sector, with low rates of infant mortality, and robust efforts are needed to improve the healthcare sector, bolster the delivery of basic health services as well as strengthen health systems more broadly. Any society with a healthy population is on the right track of development; (ii) African countries must move aggressively to diversify their economies from dependence especially on single commodity exports. The continent's natural resources should be given an industrial touch. Exporting raw materials will not develop the continent. These raw resources need to be given added value. Science and technology provides the leverage for aggressively diversify the continent's economy; (iii) continued long-term progress requires building institutions of governance and deepening democracy as well as empowering the female gender who constitutes in some countries more than 52 percent of the population; (iv) strong emphasis on macroeconomic management, reducing trade deficit, controlling budget deficits. This is a tall list of expectations requiring coordinated activities as well as political will, participation and equity in benefit-sharing to usher change, social justice and balanced development in society. These developments require difficult but right choices. At the bottom is how to mobilise domestic resources and its proper usage; and (v) last but not the least, the positive and responsive support from the international community supporting Africa's surge of progress and continued assistance to help mitigate the impacts of any eventual slowdown. These developments set the time for a policy reset, courageous leadership and a proactive citizenry looking ahead over a longer-term horizon as well as actively participating in capacity building, improve governance as well as expand prosperity. The road ahead is both bright as it equally holds slippery aspects.

African countries face complex problems of effectively using natural, financial, and human resources in transforming the region from a backward to a modern society with a difference. It is clear from the discourse that the scientific and technological revolution has given rise to new trends in the development of African and the world economic and political solution and has led to changes in the developed countries' strategy in African countries. Thus the ever broadening scientific and technological revolution creates great opportunities for the modernisation of the economies of African states, for them to overcome their backwardness – hunger, disease, poverty, illiteracy, and other urgent problems underpinning their development process. As such, the continent is urgent need of excellent science, technology and innovation that creates and enhances the structural base for competitive industries for building a better society.

In short African countries can circumvent the Rostow's theory of the *stages of development* with the progressive deployment of advances in science and technology, and learning from best practices around the world. These requires articulating and implementing comprehensive policies to development that enhances the welfare of citizens by; *(i) creating a learning economy; (ii) stimulating entrepreneurship; (iii) promoting competition, openness and partnership; and (iv) building strong and effective institutions* The road ahead is grown will challenges making the continent not to be immune to the multiple transitions afoot in the global economy. Importantly, Africa must be well-armed and ready top confronting pending challenges. AU Agenda 2063 which holds a set of seven aspirations properly married with the UN SDGs (2030) provides a way forward to sustainable development and quality livelihood.

Development is about improving people's living standard, especially African lives (who currently trail at the bottom of quality livelihood in the world) through economic, social, political and technological change. It is a transformation that certainly requires growing wealth but it is also about reducing poverty and inequality, building individual skills, having access to social services, and raising the quality of life. Economic growth and development both depend on distributive politics – how society deals with vested interest and conflicts as demonstrated in the 'blame and reality' theories. New priorities are emerging for African countries to take their obligations and responsibilities in creating the Africa they want.

Africans must either start constructing a solid foundation for its scientific and technological training capacity base or forever remain an impoverished appendage to the developed countries and a slave in global economy. There is an urgent need with a well-structured national science, technology and innovation policy and strategy as well as the political will to implement policies. The productive capacities of modern economies are not based merely on capital, land and labour. They are equally dependent on progressive scientific knowledge and sustained technological construct. The caveat here is for African countries to stimulate and mobilise domestic resources. The link between SDGs and Agenda 2063 is to galvanise the continent in particular and the world in general into taking progressive action to achieve set goals.

Africa's pressing needs are numerous ranging from inadequacy in food security, poor water supply, erratic energy supply, poor healthcare system, antiquated educational system failing to meet today's society needs, poor road infrastructure among many others. This brief snapshot on the current science and technology nexus of Africa calls for immediate short-term, medium-term and long-term proactive critical thinking, benchmarking and serious implementation solutions and strategies that should rightly move the continent forward. Experience of recent years shows that relations based on equality, respect for sovereignty and mutual benefit are very effective in strengthening scientific and technological cooperation among transitional states and between them and the developed economies. Cooperation among developing states remain important for developing countries' liberation from scientific and technological dependence.

Attempts have been made in this paper highlighting some fundamental issues on the role of science and technology as a serious *'game changer'* in providing basic human needs, Seen in these perspectives, science and technology plays an essential role as the engine of economic growth and societal transformation. It remains the catalytic converter with human capital development travelling the process. Therefore centres of excellence have to be established to create a new generation of African Lions to regain the lost historical scientific and technological past of the continent. There is no reason why the *'African Lions'* cannot overcome the *'Asian Tigers'*. This is the million dollar question confronting the continent requiring consolidated African solutions in constructing the *Africa We Want*. With concerted actions, courageous leadership and a progressive proactive civil society Africa can make substantial developmental strides towards a modern society. We must 'ensure that ethical considerations are addressed, while ensuring science-driven development is equitable and sustainable' (SFSA 2016).

The paper shows how broadening scientific and technological revolution and other changes creates great opportunities for the modernisation process of the economies of African countries for them to overcome their backwardness / underdevelopment – hunger, disease, poverty, illiteracy as well as other urgent problems constraining their quality livelihood. The continent should fight its way out of the periphery of world capitalist system, and avoid maintaining the unequal status of the continent in the international capitalist division of labour in the field of science and technology and other development areas. The heat is on and is time for Africa to deliver basic needs to the people. Taking advantage of the *'latecomer advantage'* Africa is opportune to accelerate its developmental process and this requires visionary leadership, democratic governance, partnership, cooperation among African countries and between the developed economies Africa must seek new path ways to development by exploiting all available ways and means and engaging science and technologies in monitoring and correcting government failures. Africa is now challenged to *walk the talk* in a well comprehensive and consolidated manner.

Recommendations

> ➤ African countries must discard the *'blame theory'* and holistically embrace the 'reality theory' to accelerate, reinforce and consolidate their developmental approach;
> ➤ Creating the solid foundation for a comprehensive and consolidated socio-economic transformation of Africa for welfare of all citizens
> ➤ African countries must holistically bear responsibilities and obligations for their economic development and social progress;
> ➤ The states have full and sovereign rights to freely dispose of their natural resources;
> ➤ Priority attention should be devoted to national enterprises and capital in the economic development of the continent;

➢ A new and progressive education curriculum with stronger emphasis on science related disciplines, physics, mathematics, chemistry, engineering akin to the developmental needs of the continent is an imperative;

➢ Positive contributions to the continent's economic development requires foreign capital investments and the import of foreign technology

➢ Identifying the problems and obstacles limiting the transfer of technical expertise to African countries as well as making conscious efforts in building up its critical mass and capacity in the domain of science and technology; innovation and entrepreneurship;

➢ Determining other factors affecting the choice of specific ways and means of the transfer of existing technology by countries providing and receiving such technology;

➢ Ensue that technologies imported meet local conditions and needs of the society; with the significant impact of creating less dependency on the developed polities;

➢ The urgent need to promote African and international science and technology partnerships geared towards the holistic transformation of the continent for the benefit of its citizens.

➢ The urgent need to articulate and to reset policies addressing current challenges, as well as ensure the resumption of the continent's strong rising path remains an urgent task to accomplish

References

African Union (2013) AU Agenda 2063: The Africa We Want, Third Edition, January 2015, Addis Ababa, Ethiopia.

Awotwi Nicholas & Herman Musahara (2016) Implementation of the Millennium Development Goals. Progress and Challenges in Some African Countries, OSSREA Publishers, Ethiopia.

Bhalla, A.S, James, D. (1988) New Technologies and Development Experiences in Technology Blending. Lynne Publishers, London, United Kingdom.

Cornwall Andrea & Deborah Eade (eds.) (2011) Reconstructing Development Discourse: Buzzwords and Fuzz words. Practical Action Press.

Conable Barber (1988) Education in Sub-Saharan Africa: Policies for Adjustment, Revitalisation and Expansion, World Bank, Washington, D.C.

Economic Commission for Africa (ECA) (2016) (Economic Commission for Africa, The African Union Commission and the Africa, and the African Development Bank (2016) African Regional integration Index Database (Addis Ababa).

Economic Commission for Africa (2012), Assessing Regional Integration in Africa V: Towards an African Continental Free Trade (Addis Ababa.

Fengler Wolfgang & Homi Khara (eds.) (2010) Delivering and Differently: Lesson from the Field. Brookings Institution Press, US.

Fforde Adam (2009) Coping with Facts – A Sceptic's Guide to the Problems of Development. Kumarian Press.

Forje W., John (1978) |"Science And Technology: The African Search For A Third Way To Development" in Ward Morehouse (ed.) (1978) Science, Technology and The Social Order, Transaction Books, New Brunswick, New Jersey., USA, pp355-360.

Forje W. John (1987) Science and Technology in Africa. Longman Guide to World Science and Technology, Vol. 10, Longman House. Essex, United Kingdom.

Gerschenkron, Alexander (1962) Economic Backwardness in Historical Perspectives, Cambridge, M.A. The Belknap Press, Harvard University Press, USA.

Ibukun Olu (1995) "Reorienting Science and Technology in Africa" in Onimode and Synge (eds.) Issues in African Development, Heinemann, Ibadan Nigeria, pp163-180.

ICPS (1990)"Science and Technology in Developing Countries: Strategies for the 90s", Report to the Division of Science and Technology Policies, UNESCO, Paris, France.

Ighobor Kingsley (2016). "Mbeki Panel ramps Up War against Illicit Financial Flows" in African Renewal, Vol.30. No.1, April 2016, United Nations Plaza, United, pp18-19.

Ighobor Kingsley (2015) "Sustainable Development Goals Are in sync with Africa's Priorities", African Renewal, Vol. 29, No.3, December 2015, United Nations, pp3-5.

Juma Calestous (2007)"Engineering in International Development: Linking With Infrastructure Investments in Africa", Development Outreach, Special Report on Science and Technology: Building Capacity for Development, Vol. Nine. No.1, January 2007. The World Bank, Washington, pp6-9.

Kwapong A. Alexander (1995)"Meeting the Challenge of Education in Africa|", in Bade Onimode & Richard Synge (4eds.) (1995) Issues in African Development, Heinemann Educational Books (Nigeria) PLC and African Centre for Development and Strategic Studies (ACDESS) Nigeria, pp181-193.

Lopes Carlos (2016) "Inching Toward Integration", Finance and Development, Vol. 53, No.2, June 2016, Finance and Development, International Monetary Fund, Washington, pp18-21.

Lynne Graham (2016)"Rwanda Hosts WEF Africa and presents the Benefits of Good Governance - Is Africa Still Rising?" New Africa No.562, June 2016, IC Publication, London. Pp 60-63.

Nnadozie Emmanuel (2016). Highlights of Capacity Development Forum (CDF3), New African, No.562, June 2016, IC Publication, London, pp50-51.

Nording Linda (2007): AU Summit – The Subtle Shift" Research Africa, 20 February 2007, Cape Town, South Africa.

Oqubay Arkebe (2015) Made in Africa: Industrial Policy in Ethiopia. Oxford University Press, United Kingdom.

Radelet Steven (2016) "Africa's Rise – Interrupted" in Finance And Development, Vol. 53, Number 2, June 2016 –Africa Growths Ups and Downs, International Monetary Fund, Washington, DC, pp7-11.

Rostow W. (1962) The Stages of Economic Development. Cambridge University Press, Cambridge, United Kingdom.

Science Forum South Africa (2016) Handout – Call for Thematic Session Proposals, for Science Forum South Africa, Pretoria December 2016. (info@sfsa.co.za).

The New Partnership for African Development's (NEPAD) S&T Consolidation Pan of Action, available at: http://www.nepadst.org/doclibray/pdfs/ast_plan_of_action.pdf.

Turekian Vaughan (2007) "Comments: Can Science Foster Peace in Africa? In, Research Africa, 23 January 2007, Cape Town, pp 20.

Sarabhai Kartikeya (2012). "Learning to Open our Minds", Soka Gakkai International, (SGI Quarterly Magazine) April 2012, pp2-4.

Subramanian M. Sneetha & Balakrishna Pisupati (eds.) (2010) Traditional Knowledge in Policy and Practice: Approaches to Development and Human Well-being, United Nations University Press.

United Nations (UN) United Nations Statistical Division (UNSD), (2016). UNdata, United Nations, New York, USA.

UNIDO (1989)"New and Industrialisation Prospects for Developing Countries☺ Main Policy Issues". Background paper for Expert Group Meeting on Prospects for Industrialisation Policies in Developing Countries Taking into Account the Impact of development in the Field of New and High Technologies, 4-7 April, 1989, Vienna, Austria.

Von Weizsacker, E.W., Swaminathan, M.S., Lemma, Akilu (eds.) (1983), New Frontiers in Technology Development: Integration of Emerging and Traditional Technologies. United Nations, Tycooly International Publishing, Dublin, p.ixv.

Williams Stephen (2016) "A World Leading Project", New African, No.562, June 2016, An IC Publication, London, pp56-57.

World Bank (1989). A Joint Statement on Africa's Long-term Development, May 1989, World Bank, Washington D.C.p.2 para.8.

Chapter Four

Articulating a new public sector reform: Towards enhancing governance and services delivery in Africa. Challenges and prospects

Abstract

The African Public Service Charter streamlines a new way forward in improving public administration in Africa. This paper based on the views in this and other related documents goes further to add its opinion on how to improve this vital institution as a veritable body in meeting the social contract between the State and the People. The focus is on agenda setting to policy decision-making, implementation and evaluation as an important denominator through the political administrative interface. The link between dysfunctional political/administrative relations constitutes a malfunctioning administration and stagnation in economic and social development has become increasingly acknowledge. The exploration of factors that impeded and those that catalyse the interface between politician and bureaucratic leaders for effective and efficient policy articulation, implementation and evaluation therefore present a fertile prospect for a robust discourse in this dicey yet useful area of public administration Conceptually and theoretically, the paper is premised within the framework and confines of 'self-reliance', 'participation', 'partnership', 'collaboration', 'and 'shared-prosperity' in putting into proper perspectives the search for African Solutions to African Problems (ASAP)and for the continent owing its development trajectories. It is argued and proposed that Africa's New Public Service Policy (ANPS) trajectory should incorporate constructive elements of an interface between the politicians and bureaucrats, distinct from the centralised authoritarian structure-functional systems practised in China or Russia for example. The bureaucracy as the provider of impartial and professional expertise to elected politicians should ideally serve as a 'bridge' between politics and society. The paper maintains that such a constructive act of partnership and participation within the confines of the rule of law and separation of powers provides the best condition (a sine-qua-non) for the development of democratic systems of governance and service delivery in improving the quality of livelihood of citizens. Africa is on the move and should craft its development trajectories that improves policy articulation, implementation and evaluation in fostering public services delivery as a veritable output functions of government in improving and sustaining the quality wellbeing of citizens. Hence, a political/administrative interface clearly articulated provides the way forward in seeking African Solutions to African Problems (ASAP). An analytical and comparative approach is adopted. In conclusion, Africa can only move forward by claiming ownership of its development and by adapting best practices that brings greater dividends to citizens.

Keywords: Political, administrative, policy, service delivery, innovation, shared-prosperity; reform

Introduction: The search for a new way

The field of public administration is a vast area with many tons of articles, books, and monographs produced every year. During the past couple of decades, the civil service has taken centre stage in the governance dichotomy. As the output function of government, it is constantly under the microscope for critical analysis and evaluation. In the United States, the central preoccupations of this field are directed towards "managerial", whereas in Europe it is largely judicial. It is hardly surprising; therefore, we know so little about the role of bureaucracy in a political system. It can make or mar government activities.

Two views concerning the role of the bureaucracy in different political systems have gained especially wide currency. The first mostly applicable to the Anglo-Saxon countries holds that the bureaucracy is totally subordinate to the political institutions. Rephrased differently, the bureaucracy is not recognised as having any degree of autonomy, All the literature on the British civil service has accepted this point of view (Kingsley 1944) recently begun to receive attention. This is in large part because the Federal bureaucracy has usually been regarded as unquestionably subordinate and obedient to the directives of the political.

In the United States, the bureaucracy's role in society and in the political process has only begun to receive attention. This is in large part because the Federal bureaucracy has usually been regarded as unquestionably subordinate and obedient to the directives of political elites (Sisson 1959). The development of the administrative system

148

in the US displays a paradoxical mixture of continued political selection and control at higher levels and commitment to merit and de-politicisation at lower levels. On the one hand, almost all the top positions in government – at present over 4000 positions – are held by political appointees; on the other hand, the remaining public employees are selected by a rigorously enforced merit system. The two versions of public employment have existed side by side for years in the United States but there has been pressure on that co-existence since the 1980s resulting from the debate as to what extent the political appointments should be expanded or contracted (Peters and Pierre, 2004). The Canadian situation is one displaying a high degree of politicisation of the county's civil service. For a very long time, (since 1935, the country operated virtually as a one party state. Domination of the Liberal Party forged a special relationship between politicians and career officials. The account of the situation in Canada is somewhat depressing as the civil service is riddled with low morale, loss of confidence in its leaders and themselves, and dissatisfaction with managerial practices (Peters and Pierre, 2004).

The bureaucracy in France is generally regarded as an all-powerful institution (Sharp 1931). The French higher civil service is seen as an integral part of the politico-administrative system as is practiced in former French colonial territories. In Britain, the civil service is seen as an impartial body ready to render services to which ever political party that assumes governance stewardship. The tradition for its political neutrality is well respected. Therefore, adherence to the merit principle for selection, promotion and decision-making and objectivity in tendering of advice to political masters well respected (Peters and Pierre, 2004). The former Soviet Union and its Satellites states see no difference between the political party and the public service – for these states, the two are one and indivisible.

In Greece for example, the civil service has always been heavily politicised, probably to a greater extent than any other Western European country. Over politicisation of the Greek civil service is often manifested in the many in which personnel are hired and promoted. While officially all relevant procedures are standardised and meritocratic, unofficially it is widely admitted that politicisation is quite extensive. While the seniority and professional capacities play an important role, their political opinions are personal contacts as matter as much, if not more. The Greek situation shows how polarised political system and political culture have been conducive to the penetration of the civil service by successive incoming governments (top-down politicisation) and the involvement of civil servants in politics (bottom-up politicisation) Thus in the Greek case, politicisation 'from above' is promoted through the duplication of administrative structures, efforts to change the behaviour of civil servants, waves of new appointments in the civil service and politicisation of promotions to the top positions in the hierarchy . What makes politicisation in Greece different from elsewhere is its pervasiveness, persistence, and strength of clientelistic practices, combined with an egalitarian spirit, which make the country somewhat different from other core western democracies (Sharma 2007:82).

Therefore, the distinction between politics and administration, or between politicians and administrators, was effaced under the Fifth Republic of General de Gaulle's appointment of civil servants (Couve de Murville, Chenot, Pisani, Charic, Giscard d'Estaing etc.) to key ministerial posts. A pattern copied in Cameroon, from Mbida through Ahidjo to Biya (see Ridley and Blondel 1965; Vedel (ed.) 1962). In a way such appointments creates contradictory atmospheres. First, it brings in technocrats with a better understanding of the field. Second, it creates a kind of elitism and exclusion of the masses from being participants in the governance process which is not healthy for services delivery. Third, the technocrats hold allegiance to whoever appoints them. This creates a centralised top-down administrative approach.

In a country with a centralised authoritarian dominant monolithic political party construct, (Cameroon) for example, does aggravates ethnic, regional and class difference; and politicisation of the public service by the ruling elites. Constructive decentralisation, we must admit is inhibited with success and failures to which each state gives continent it deems appropriate to its national contingencies; and as the process of power and responsibility sharing between the state and its constituencies; and decentralisation as a learning instrument for the promotion and strengthening of democracy at various levels, i.e. promoting a 'bottom-up' or an all-inclusive decision-making processes and involvement of the vast majority of the population.

It is argued that the post-independent African state because of the colonial legacy developed a centralised hegemonic power state. The state, civil society and private sector were not critical partners in the political, economic and service delivery trajectory. Throughout Africa 'the public sector initially grew relatively fast because the post-colonial state was under enormous pressure to Africanise or indigenises and expand the civil service. For the masses 'uhuru' meant more social services and jobs. It was in the interest of the new political class to satisfy this hunger for social and economic development and to contain the swelling ranks of the unemployed. And it also served their accumulative interests to expand the state apparatuses' (Zeleza 1997:333). The state dominated everything and yet was not fully equipped in undertaking the necessary changes (Forje 2006; 2009; 2011) thereby creating negatives impacting on service delivery in three aspects; namely;

- *failure of the existing state institutional structure to provide dynamism for an inclusive society;*
- *the need to care and nurture democracy engaging communities and citizens, accountability, equity and inclusiveness; and*
- *the need for institutions that command respect, legitimacy, accountability and could instil confidence and trust within society on state institutions*

Within this context, one could argue that due to the centralised nature of the state construct and of its *'top-down'* policy approach, the strategy of decentralisation created opportunities to improve efficiency in governance and service delivery, required the politics and policies of decentralisation as such approach creates opportunities by;

- *enhancing effectiveness through de-bureaucratisation and serious reduction in the number of interacting mechanisms of forces involved in service delivery;*

- *empowering stakeholder to be active partners in the process of quality service delivery, to ensure a social contract between the state, civil society and private sector*

The nature and training of these top public civil servants equally matters as to how they relate to society. Public administration within the Anglo-Saxon world falls as a university discipline, in contrast to the French-speaking world carried out in specialised schools – Ecole Nationale d'Administration (ENA); for example, in Cameroon the main and dominant elite body is Ecole Nationale d'Administration et Magistracy (ENAM) National Advanced School of Administration and Magistracy, which creates an administrative elite corps (Suleiman (1974) that significantly widens the social basis of the higher civil service and the rest of the people.

In Africa for example, a situation existed with the coming of independence where development economics shared the policy optimism of emerging generation of African political leaders. It also shared with them the respect of using the state to redress economic and social imbalances caused by colonial policy. The situation where the indigenous private sector was very weak, it makes perfect political sense to embrace the notion that the state ought to serve as the catalyst of the development process. While the political agenda was shaped by nationalist leaders of Africa, economic policies were fashioned by external advisors. The extensive role of the state in development posed a special challenge to the public service especially in Africa where capacities were low. The cadre of trained and experience public servants was very small in these countries and it was necessary to make the best use of scarce human resources.

A call was made for a new style of administration that met the development needs of the new style of administration that met the development needs of the new states better than conventional public administration. This 'development administration' refers to the administration of development programmes, the method used by large-scale organisations, notably governments, to implement policies and plans designed to meet developmental objectives, (Hyden, 1995:73: Fred, 1970:6-7).Development administration which is control-oriented and stresses regularity. The new development style of administration is viewed as placing emphasis on flexibility and innovativeness (Gant 1979; Schaffer 1969).

Here higher civil servants in general, assume roles that are at once administrative and political. The concept, 'politique' in French covers both 'politics' and 'policy' and to the extent that higher civil servants formulate policies, with all the social and political implications that this entails. Their functions are interlinked with administrative and political activities (Chapman 1959). The Cameroon system encourages and involves higher civil servants to be engaged in party politics; thereby making the public service to be highly politicised and influenced by political party and ethnic affiliations and ideologies. One cannot avoid posing questions about 'the right kind of society;' the purpose of the state, the basis and justification of government business and of its responsibility to the people. British top civil servants do not abandon their official duties and join the political party campaign bandwagon like in Cameroon. It is assumed once appointed to high public bureaucratic post to become a member of the ruling party.

Importantly, Africa countries must fashion their own public service construct that comprehensively addresses their needs without compromising the ideals of equality and service delivery to every citizen. Here a 'bottom-up' approach provides the ways and means of inclusion, participation and equity in benefit-sharing. The public bureaucracy remains the key instrument in the national development process of the continent. Underlining the characteristics hindering the public service to deliver effectively and efficiently and the relationship between the service and other actors and the impact on the State's ability to formulate and deliver on its development agenda.

Failure to deliver increases the number of poor; and growing poverty and inequality can also be attributed to the dysfunctional and poorly developed bureaucracies throughout the continent. Breaking existing barriers requires states to be supported by a highly competent, professional and meritocratic public administration similar to those of the East Asian countries. The African public service needs constructive reforms aimed at transforming the bureaucracy and positioning it to be the lead actor in the development agenda. The public service should be constructed and operated on the principles of accountability, openness, transparency and good governance.

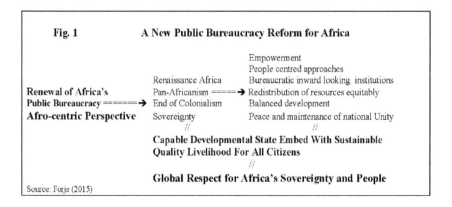

Fig. 1   A New Public Bureaucracy Reform for Africa

Source: Forje (2015)

A properly structure-functional public service is a veritable system / development changer. This is what the continent most need for its articulating a new public service reform that should be construed from the perspectives of a progressive Afro-centric orientation. In short, Africa is not cursed but blessed with poor leadership. Africa needs a new public bureaucracy and leadership as depicted in Fig 1: A New Public Bureaucracy Reform for Africa.

There are numerous challenges the continent faces in the process of reforming and building a healthy apolitical, professional bureaucracy at the services of the people. Achieving such a reform requires visionary leadership and a proactive citizenry. What are the challenges; What capacities do the people need to develop? What should the people do to develop the needed capacity of its bureaucratic set-up? An Afro-centric approach is required to address the numerous challenges. The leadership and bureaucracy that Africa need is one which must work with people to develop a path that development should take requiring a genuine vision and action plan focused on African solutions for African problems.

- human capital development.
- democratic and good governance
- empowerment of the people
- proper utilisation of resources
- exploiting the late-comer advantage (Gerschenkron 1962)

- putting in place corrective measures addressing past mistakes
- mobilising the masses to engage in development of indigenous policies;
- drastic movements from the 'blame' to the 'reality' factors inhibiting the development of the continent;
- putting in a place a free, objective, mass media out to inform, and educate the people on the problems of societal socio-economic-politico transformation
- promoting innovation, entrepreneurship, science and technology for an improved service delivery
- building necessary institutions and infrastructures
- building links with the diasporas and ensuring African unity

Indeed, the determination of ends, the choice of means, the balance of social forces, are the stuff of politics. In these terms it is clear that some civil servants are engaged in politics. This partly explains why a number of members of parliament and senate are retired civil servants. Very often, the relations between the political and administrative leadership tend to be conflictual and tense. As a result, the policy-making and policy-implementation processes became problematic and ineffective, making the state of affairs not healthy which requires that both sides of the leadership divide find ways and means of minimising conflicts and tensions to ensure smooth administrative procedures.

The continent needs strong state institutions as well as creating systems to enhance service delivery. Strategic objectives and action plans are required for building strong state institutions and creating systems to enhance service delivery requiring actions as indicated in Fig 2: Building Strong State Institutions. It also needs a proactive intellectual community to advance the discourse on good governance and improved quality livelihood. The role of the public intellectual is to raise the level of public discourse so that it might better grapple with the complex issues of the day. To a large extent, African intellectuals seem to shy away from such obligations and responsibilities due to the nature of political construct in the country. What is clear as noted by Skwati (2014): "The commitment by the public sector to embrace innovation as a new way of thinking around possible solutions to service delivery challenges is inarguably on the rise" and by no means improved service delivery improvement can change a country's fortunes to the better.

Fig. 2: Building Strong State Institutions	
Strategic Objectives	**Actions**
Creating Systems to enhance service delivery	Establish centres of good practice t support improvement of public administration institutions Strong state institutions central to constructing and s strengthen capacity and management of a capable Developmental state Reengineer services processes
Building State capacity Requires Sound systems	Develop sound financial management services Human resources information systems Information Technology Management systems e-Government Supply chain management systems
Public Service Reconstruction Restructure and Reorganise the state	Public service census establishes legitimate public Servants Redefine missions of ministries to pave the way for reorganisation and reconstruction of the state

Forje (2013) Emerging Perspectives on Capacity Building, Lambert Academic Publishing, Germany, pp41-42

A critical interface between State and the rest of society is necessary to hammer out differences and create the much needed enabling environment for a functional public bureaucracy capable of addressing the socio-economic crisis, incarceration, the wealth gap or any of the urgent political and administrative issues plaguing the sustainable transformation of the continent from a backward to a service delivery polity. There are also important arguments about the intellectual and his/her relationship to the polity.

The South African initiative is an attempt of blending the divergent views expressed here to better create a unique response and process crafting a public service that is accountable, transparent, responsible and delivering services much needed by society. This unique approach is possible and yield more dividends because more Africans are now living under democratic rule compared to the situation in the late 1970s and 1980s when only a handful of African countries were considered democratic. The politician is thus one who can fight, plead and convince; but, above all, (s)he is guided by an ethic responsibility' which Weber opposed to the 'ethic of ultimate ends." The civil servant who replaces the politician is a specialist, guided by rational standards and hence oblivious to the political implications. The replacement of the politician by the civil servant gives rise, it is argued, to a technocracy, which is seen 'as the rise to power of those who possess technical knowledge or ability, to the detriment of the traditional type of politician. According to Meynaud (1965), it is technical competence that determines influence. Technocracy is the combined result of the competence and infiltration of the technocrat at an appropriate point or sector of the deliberation machine. It is this combination of circumstances which favours and permits the technologists' penetration into the political sector.

Another, arising from the first, is the vital factor responsible for attacks on the administration is the ubiquity of civil servants not only in the State apparatus, where they are naturally to be found, but in the parastatal and in the private sector. The large part of attacks on the administration could be regarded as emanating from these factors where a clique of few, and all the charges of nepotism, personal gain or articulate self-interests, collusion etc., brings into sharp focus the class divisions and distinctions in service delivery in African societies; in addition pointing to the undemocratic recruitment of for example, Cameroon ethnic ruling elites and to the undemocratic of the (African) or Cameroon society. Still another important reason for the persistent questioning of the administrator's traditional authority has to do with the decline of representative institutions, particularly the political parties and parliament.

The importance of parliament and of the political parties is in sharp contrast to the dominant features of the single-party State, and especially where the State is in some measures associated with the ruling party. In the case of Cameroon, the authoritarian nature of the administration is mirrored in the authoritarian disposition of the ruling government. In attacking the government and the administration, one is actually attacking the State. The State's influence on the Cameroon society has not changed much over the past couple of decades, i.e. since the return to multi-party pluralism. The marriage between the politician and the administrator is seen by the centralised governance structure of creating a kind of stability of political and administrative personnel which reflects the authoritarian disposition of the regime.

The initiative by the African Association for Public Administration and Management (AAPAM) introducing at its annual Roundtable Conference a Ministerial Panel Platform to engage Ministers and Cabinet Secretaries in continental issue affecting the continent's administration and development by delving into navigating the conundrum that is the political/administrative interface by infusing a Ministerial perspective to conference deliberations is welcome and this could be extended to the participation of political parties It is necessary for African countries to adhere to the African Charter on the Values and Principles of Public Service and administration especially in the areas of leadership and management development; performance management and measurement; and human resources development, planning and policy architecture.

In the case of Cameroon, it is probably the stability or longevity of the presidency and the authoritarian disposition of the holder of that office for more than three decades that reflects a greater administrative and political stability than actually exists. To a large extent, it has harnessed, enhanced and influenced the institutionalisation of 'centralised ethnic hegemonic authoritarian governance structure and seriously contributed to the flourishing of malpractices and corruption. Focus on a strong executive leads to reduction in parliament's powers with reduced powers and role of the administration (Neustadt 1964:53). No one will deny that the technicians, whatever their differences, share with other groups, justified in the African society a commitment to the existing political and social system. To the degree that such differences do affect the shape of public, however, it is difficult to call them merely differences of tactics.

These divergent views, 'subordinate' and autonomous' of the role of the bureaucracy in a political system have adverse an unfortunate consequence.- - they have hindered the study of the bureaucracy as an integral, and dynamic part of the political system In other words, the bureaucracy has seldom been seen as an institution that operates within the higher politico-administrative framework. If the bureaucracy is seen as an institution that interacts with other institutions in a society, it becomes easier to understand why a governmental bureaucracy cannot be characterised as either totally subservient or totally autonomous.

Far-reaching administrative reforms are urgently needed in many African countries today is a matter that hardly anyone questions. The Conference of African Ministers of the Pubic Service and Administration has injected new blood to improve the structure and output functions and service delivery of the sector. Two key factors here relate to (i) institutional capacity and (ii) overall strategic orientation. At the level of strategy there is always the tension between application of shared-values and particularities and specificities of each member state. Hence there are always constraints and established parameters on what can be done in governance and democracy.

Cardinal in the objectives of the Conference of African Minister of the Public Service and Administration is the need to move forward as a collective, compliance to adopted shared-values is not a choice but a necessity. More often than not, states aspirations and indeed to manage strategic tension that exists between the collective and individual interests largely depends on the available capacity – i.e. the capacity and resources made available have never matched expectations. Added to this, is the *implementation* question or challenges on a-day-to-day basis. Generally, one can state that institutional transformation is on track, the foundations are being laid for more effective, efficient and responsive delivery to improve on the quality wellbeing of citizens. Therefore institutions should be at the services of its people. These institutions should be manned by competent, professional, citizens to deliver effective and efficient services. These institutions at all levels of government must be people-oriented, developmental, democratic, responsible, accountable and merit-based.

This ultimately imply a new public service trajectory conceived within the framework of improving the living standards of the people, without *denying, delaying and perverting* services delivery to anyone. This credo fits into the framework or motto of the Association of African Public Administration and Management

(AAPAM) and should be the catechism of every African citizen to advance the role of the civil service in providing the needed services for the peoples' well-being. The challenging question for the African public service is how to reconcile the highly centralised authoritarian system with a people-oriented and focused decentralised structure that ensures quality services delivery to all. The people are challenged, that with highly centralised or highly decentralised system split into multitudinous groups, each of which pursues its own interests to reconcile differences to ensure that social justice prevails. The living inequality (of various sectors of the administration), which is fundamentality in an administrative system as differentiated as that of the African continent and which alone maintains it as a system, forbids that the standard of measure be reduced to simple calculation.

In the case of Cameroon and other African countries, best described as *'a stalemate society'*, this is generally thought sufficient to point to its centralised authoritarian administrative structure, hence the call for decentralisation and democratic governance. The justification and need for decentralisation and good governance is premised on a priori grounds that centralisation and authoritarian governance system has failed to deliver the services much needed by the people to have a sustainable quality of livelihood.

Ultimately there is a fundamental, perhaps irreconcilable, contradiction between the search for objective, rational policies, contradiction between the search for objective, rational policies, and the widespread practice of basing public policies on the compromises that are affected between the various administrations. For if public policy is the lowest common denominator of conflicts among opposing groups (politicians and administrators) for example, within the administration, is this not the surest negation of objectivity and rationality? It could even be said that administrators fear rationality because of its possible adverse effects on the autonomy of their institutions. (Suleiman 1974:383; Bertucci 2001; Forje2012).

It is true that old habits or methods and ideas die slowing in African countries. But if progress entails 'mobility, competition and negotiation' – i.e. modernisation and democratisation – then it is not difficult to conclude that Africa is catching up. The undemocratic recruitment of the administrative elite may be equally deplorable.

There are a number of paradoxes of the African political community and administrative system that have to be understood to better draw meaningful conclusions. Administrative inefficiency and poor governance constitute other perpetual themes of the proponents of the 'stalemate society' thesis, a theme very closely related to the pleas for decentralisation, democratisation and good governance as the gateway (Africa's New Public Service) trajectory for quality services delivery.

We can see that interest groups play a very important role in the policy-making process and greater consolidation among these groups is occurring, with the encouragement of the administration (the South Africa experience or new initiative of partnership between the political and administrative bodies) should receive greater attention. The behaviour of the administrative corps in a society must be seen in the context of the larger social and political framework of which it is part. Administration is not an activity that is separate from politics. It becomes all the more difficult to argue, that the reasons for Africa's resistance to change are to be found in the colonial heritage and character and to equally argue at the same time that the centralised authoritarian administration constitutes the chief obstacle to change in the society.

Of course, the administration is part of the society; it shares the values of the society; it reflects and sometimes exaggerates some of society's defects. In the same vein, the rising level of centralised authoritarian power of the Executive is paralleled by the rapid descent of the powers of Parliament, backed by a corrupt Judiciary contradictions between wanting a weak Executive (in the sense of power-sharing with the other branches of government – judiciary and legislative) which strengthens the role of the bureaucracy as an independent and impartial institution ready to serve which ever shade of political party that assumes government office. This is the only way of having merit-based public institutions providing the most conducive enabling environment for its citizens to exploit, flourish and attain their full potentials. The continent failed in attaining MDGs 2015. We should not fail on the post-2015 Development Agenda in lifting huge sections of the population out of the scourges of poverty and misery. A well-structured and functional public service can radically transform, using the varied opportunities as springboards to ensure its transformation from a backward to quality service delivery society. Currently, there is inadequate engagement of citizens in governance and development making the social welfare gap between the bottom-up and top-down divide to widen. The rich are getting richer as the poor get poorer for each passing day.

People's Governance as Prelude to Quality Services

One of the most crucial challenges ahead of the continent relates to the issue of democratic governance from the community level through the divisional, national, and regional up to the continental and global level. At the nation-state level, the challenge is to deepen systems of democratic governance within and between countries, to reduce the power and influence of bureaucracies, to improve public and service delivery systems, among others. But these tasks of internal democratisation must go hand in hand with the democratisation of the institutions of global governance, particularly the international and regional financial institutions.

Accountability is the necessary counterpart to voice. When accountable authorities answer to engaged communities, social justice is served, service delivery improved and human welfare enhanced, and citizens will develop trust and confidence in the State and its institutions. Participation and voice grow stronger when political, economic and social power is widely dispersed. Locally determined solutions are usually more sustainable than top-down decisions. Public administration must be widely dispersed to ensure that people to people build alliances that actively intervene in the existing institutions of power and decision-making the local, divisional, provincial, and national levels.

Such empowered intervention should have as its goal the reorientation and making transparent and democratic the functioning of processes and institutions of power and decision-making. The South African approach of building linkages between the politician and administrator provides a way of building trust between the two blocks and forging constructive new alternatives between the various stakeholders. The growing number of credible elections compared to

162

the 1980s *(The African Charter on democratic Elections and Governance, The African Public Service Charter and the African Peer Review Mechanism (of NEPAD))* are pointers in the direction of tangible testimony of the gradual movements towards a consolidated partnership between politicians and administrators for the common welfare of society.

Only by understanding the differences that separate the two and seeking common solutions and common grounds can the quality of services delivery be improved to enhance and sustain the living standards of citizens. The centrality here is the quality wellbeing of citizens. This centrality should be rooted in our daily lives and in steering our ways through the chaotic currents stirred up in the dominant centralised authoritarian ethnic hegemonic system of governance widely spread across the continent.

Peoples' government incorporates decentralisation, public-private partnership participation; and creating vast opportunities for improving and enhancing service delivery. It also empowers the different stakeholders to be active partners in the governance process; as it introduces as well as challenges the different actors to cultivate a sense of leadership, moral, ethical and good sense of citizenship.

Africa is rising. Change must occur. Africa is not an Island. Africa cannot remain static. Change is the message of this paper. A progressive Afro-centric vision is great need. It appeals to the African Public Service Sector to gear up towards the vital implementation of a 'Service-Oriented Architecture Strategy (SOAS) to confront the challenges of the 21st century and beyond. The public bureaucracy is the engine of government and pivotal to all sectors of society. The centrality of the public service in bringing about good governance and development can no longer be emphasised. Thus a new millennium dawns on Africa, challenging the people and leaders in particular to be constantly reminded of certain traits making up for good leadership and collective progress of society. Fig. 3: Attributes of Leadership in Crafting a new Society takes up some of the issues involved.

Fig. 3: Attributes of Leadership in Crafting a New Society
• Self-confidence =➔ the ability to overcome fear and failure and inspire confidence in their followers; • Persistence ====➔ remaining inwardly optimistic and not being shattered by frequent turndowns; • Resilience =====➔ the inner strength that enables leaders to bounce back after suffering frequent defeats; • Independence ==➔ getting satisfaction from being responsible to oneself • Daring =======➔ Not gambling, but calmly evaluating risks and not being afraid of risk-taking
Source: Forje (2015) Compiled from D'Souza, 2008

One should at this juncture emphasise that leadership is cause, everything else is effect. Thus urging for competence, effectiveness, and efficiency, visionary and pro-active leaders in their respective domains or constituencies. The significance of democratic and good governance principles is vital in piloting the continent out of its current mess. No doubt, the popular and effective participation of citizens in public policy processes, transparency, and accountability of government in all its undertakings, particularly in the management of the extractive sector are critical for sustainable socio-economic development.

One of the most serious factors plaguing the sustainable transformation of the continent is that of corruption. The status of the continent as a weak capable developmental and democratic region has roots in decades past with corruption playing a critical role. Aside from corruption characterising the colonial and post-colonial governments in Africa, the menace, unfortunately continues unabated. For example, in a 2009 Report of the African Union (AU) and the African Development Bank (AfDB), corruption cost Africa USA$159 billion a year. And this was estimated to be more than the entire international development aid to Africa that year. Objectively and critically, the continent does not really need aid from the international development partners if only corruption is tackled to its roots on the continent. Even though corruption is a world-wide phenomenon, for example, it is estimated that the act costs the European Union (EU) economy EUR120 billion per year, which is just a little less than the annual budget of the Union. Apparently, this finding is mind-boggling and underscores the urgent need for Africa countries to seriously address the issue. It is not fictitious claiming that the continent's public service through the Conference of African Ministers for Public Service and Administrative together with other organisations like the African Association for Public administration and management (AAPAM) enormously bought into the idea of thinking and working innovatively. However, there is a serious concern and constraint to effective implementation of national and continental visions by African countries being the inadequate engagement of citizens in governance and development through decentralisation of powers, resources, functions and responsibilities to autonomous local government (Scot & Wallis 2013). Inadequate engagement of citizens in governance and development constitutes a major constraint to effective implementation of national visions by African countries.

Fashioning an Afro-centric approach

Africa's positive way foreword is fashioning and building bridges across existing divide. It means fostering collaboration for sustainable governance for Africa to move forward. Answers to the social, economic and political development problems facing Africa are not self-evident. However, what is clear, is first, the incontestable reality that Africa itself must have a major role in the decisions that affect its future; solutions cannot be imposed unilaterally from outside. Second, important as it may be to respond to immediate problems (for example, famine and drought, poverty eradication, employment) or find ways to deal with balance of payments deficits and debt obligations in the short run, much responses do not represent permanent or long-term solutions. Even if the immediate and short-term problems are being dealt with, a long-term strategy must be developed and acted upon. If not, the short-terms problems are likely to repeat themselves (Kwapong & Lesser 1990: ix; in Forje 2013:61).

The Afro-centric should be able to address fundamental problems plaguing the region within the context of Africa Power and Politics Programme (APPP) of what works, and pursuing the idea of good governance and development for the collective good of the citizens. The African Charter on the Values and Principles of the Public Service and Administration backed the African Peer Review mechanism (of NEPAD) among other such documents like the African Charter on Democracy, Elections and Governance provide new guides for the renewal and implementation of a functional public service sector geared towards meeting the aspirations and needs of the people. Since independence one notices the symptoms of gradual system's collapse. Across the African continent we notice the 'decay and decline of the public bureaucracy, the total politicisation of the public service all contributing to poor services delivery, with things getting worse during the decades of the World Bank imposed Structural Adjustment Programme (SAP) of the 1980s.

A progressive Afro-centric approach will require A New Public Service Policy (ANPS) focused on constructively addressing the underdevelopment/development problematique of the continent. Some of critical issues involved are expressed on Fig 4 Towards A Renewal Bureaucracy for Africa. The fragilities of the continent's current Public Service sector have to be addressed from within every nation state and collectively at the African Union to work in unionism. Building strong institutions is very necessary. The African economy is rife with imbalances that cannot be fixed under the inherited bureaucracy. An efficient and effective public bureaucracy is imperative if the continent want to be part of an emerging economy. Education, migration, employment and redistribution are key elements of a long-term solution to quality services delivery in Africa. In addition, African businesses must produce more jobs to fulfil the continent's promises and of claiming the future.

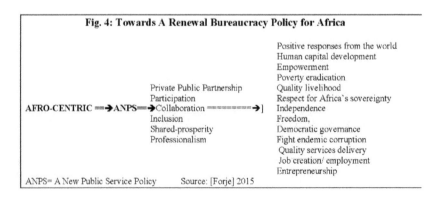

Fig. 4: Towards A Renewal Bureaucracy Policy for Africa

		Positive responses from the world
		Human capital development
		Empowerment
		Poverty eradication
	Private Public Partnership	Quality livelihood
	Participation	Respect for Africa's sovereignty
AFRO-CENTRIC ==➔ANPS==➔	Collaboration ========➔]	Independence
	Inclusion	Freedom,
	Shared-prosperity	Democratic governance
	Professionalism	Fight endemic corruption
		Quality services delivery
		Job creation/ employment
		Entrepreneurship

ANPS= A New Public Service Policy   Source: [Forje] 2015

During this period at least two key public administration values which suffered unconscionable assault included issues of transparency and accountability'. Many African countries are currently paying dearly for the collapse of transparency and accountability in the civil service and public life in general (Olaopa 2008). It is not surprising that many African countries are consistently rated very low by Transparency International as corrupt polities. This decay and decline leads to the bureaucracy becoming an institutionalised 'maze of inaction' rather than an institutional pathway for development.

While the wave of Africanisation of the bureaucracy (Cameroonisation, Nigerianisation, Gabonisation, Ethiopianisation etc.) ushered the civil service into a dawn of glory, the decay and decline of bureaucracy became most noticeable in authoritarian civilian governments or in military administered states. Africa's lost decade the 1980s to mid-1990s saw the gradual systems collapse necessitating a renewal when the continent gradually stated returning to the values of democratic governance in the 1990s. With the economic recover of most African countries in the 1990s the state of decay and decline emphasised desire to reengineering managerial revolution in the public service with a strong focus on re-professionalisation, which emerged as a 'management challenge and a panacea' to the state of decay and decline within the sector.

Afro-centric renewal strategic approach requires further strengthening the development of discipline with the goal to improve the capacity and institutional and infrastructure throughout the continent. To begin with, what was the existing infrastructure for human capital development? What was and is the strength of the existing manpower in the sector? Given that there were few institutions of higher learning.

The continent depended for its modern public administration on institution inherited from the (i) era of colonial tutelage; (ii) the beginning of colonial administration; and (iii) the introduction of central administration to the era of institutional transfer and home rule. With independence the few existing institutions played pioneer role as training institutions, in the case of Nigeria, the Institute of Public Administrations at the University of Ife and the University of

Zaria, which today are full faculties; and the Administrative Staff College of Nigeria (ASCON); in Ghana, the University of Legion (Olaopa 2008), Institutions like the Ghana Institute of Management and Public Administration (GIMPA), Kenya Institute of Administration (KIA); Uganda Management Institute (UMI) among other institutions now scattered around the continent. Other bodies responsible for training include The African association for Public Administration and Management (AAPAM); the Commonwealth Association for Public Administration and Management (CAPAM) among others in promoting professional and scholarly development of the discipline.

The Africa of tomorrow needs answers that are effective and lasting. That is why building the continent's human capital and functional bureaucratic public service and other logistics now remains imperative. A new mindset demystifying Africa as a failed or rouge continent can only be corrected through visionary servant leadership, a proactive civil society and a functional service delivery bureaucratic setup. A new Africa has to be constructed capable of utilising its natural endowment for the collective good of the people. The Conference of African Minsters for Public/Civil Service (CAMPS) through its African Charter on the Values and Principles of Public Service and Administration must redouble efforts in ensuring that African countries adhere strictly to the Charter.

The Renewal of the continent's bureaucracy should facilitate the emergence of a new type of Public Service, more capable of solving contemporary African problems as well as comply with a certain number of principles, for example the equality of clients of the Public Service and Administration, the prohibition of discrimination; impartiality, equity and respect for the law in Public Services delivery; the continuity of the Public service in all circumstance; adaptation to the needs of the users; professionalism and ethics in Public Service and Administration; the promotion and the protection of the users and Public Service Agents' rights; accountability, integrity and transparency in Public Service and Administration equality between men and women in the Public Service and Administration; reinforcement of international co-operation for the improvement of Public Service and the sharing of good practices and experiences among Member States and the effective and efficient use of resources.

The continental body Africa Union (AU) stepped in to fashion a continental approach directed towards the eradication of abuses or distortions in the existing system with a focus on restructuring, reorganising and renovating the system. It is not just an issue of investing more resources, but building institutional capacity and human capability in the public bureaucracy to better manage diversities in the public service, mobilise, and manage available resources to ensure increased investments in services delivery and improved outcomes. It is time for concrete actions. African countries face a stark choice between underdevelopment and development, between ad hoc, cosmetic short-term entrenched policies and resolute pursuit of long-term reforms needed to secure their future economic prosperity. Ad hoc cosmetic policies forsakes important economic adjustments needed to strengthen inclusive growth and democratize the state and modernize the private sectors to properly set the region on the path of progressive development. A democratic and good governance state construct in partnership with a healthy global economy provides a welcome opportunity to accelerate the pace of reform Countries in the region must strive to ensure political stability, economic growth, employment and job creation to keep pace with a rapidly expanding population. Economic growth has not been favourable in addressing the level of unemployment. Fig 5: An Afrocentric Renewal Approach to Confronting the Challenges of Poor Service delivery and underdevelopment provides a way forward to tackling the problems.

The African Charter on the Values and the Principles of the Public Service and Administration provides the guidelines to attaining a bureaucracy that cares and protects the welfare of citizens through the delivery of innovating and quality services, the modernisation and reinforcement of the Public Administration's capacities, the participation of the users in the administrative processes, the promotion of moral values in the Public Service, the improvement of working conditions of the Public Service Agents and the protection of their rights, the harmonisation of public policies and procedures of African Union Member States relating to Public

Service, the equality between men and women in the Public Service and Administration, the reinforcement of international co-operation for the improvement of Public Service and the sharing of good practices and experiences amongst Member States. Thus the African Charter on the Values and the Principles of the Public Service and Administration is geared towards an effective public service delivery towards a capable developmental state (CDS) in Africa. As such, member state of the African Union are urgently called upon to align their public service practices with the provision of the Charter and take the anti-corruption fight extremely serious and in line with the AU Convention on Preventing and Combating Corruption.

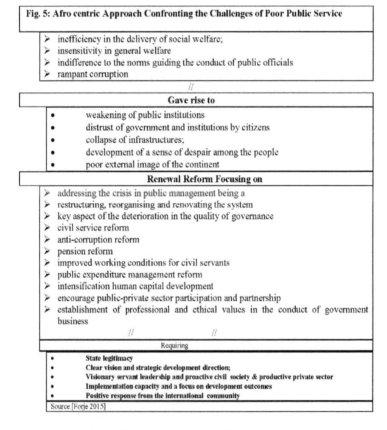

Fig. 5: Afro centric Approach Confronting the Challenges of Poor Public Service

> inefficiency in the delivery of social welfare;
> insensitivity in general welfare
> indifference to the norms guiding the conduct of public officials
> rampant corruption

//

Gave rise to

- weakening of public institutions
- distrust of government and institutions by citizens
- collapse of infrastructures;
- development of a sense of despair among the people
- poor external image of the continent

Renewal Reform Focusing on

> addressing the crisis in public management being a
> restructuring, reorganising and renovating the system
> key aspect of the deterioration in the quality of governance
> civil service reform
> anti-corruption reform
> pension reform
> improved working conditions for civil servants
> public expenditure management reform
> intensification human capital development
> encourage public-private sector participation and partnership
> establishment of professional and ethical values in the conduct of government business

// //

Requiring

- **State legitimacy**
- **Clear vision and strategic development direction;**
- **Visionary servant leadership and proactive civil society & productive private sector**
- **Implementation capacity and a focus on development outcomes**
- **Positive response from the international community**

Source [Forje 2015]

African countries are entrenched with problems because representation through the choice of the people and voices of the people are constantly thwarted. Society today is 'knowledge-driven' requiring skilled human resources potential, sense of direction, quality and style of leadership, accountability, transparency, productivity, far competition, and equity in the distribution of national wealth. (Forje 2007). The need for creating a civil service (like in Britain known traditionally) for its political neutrality; impartiality; adherence to merit principles for selection, promotion and decision-making; objectivity in tendering of advice to political masters, should at least be a point of reference. The cause and consequences of the politicisation of the public service in developed countries (Peters and Pierre, 2004) provides an appropriate launching-pad for understanding the developments elsewhere in the world, Africa in particular.

We cannot ignore, therefore, that politicisation can negate the merit principle in the organisation and functioning of the public services. T can undermine the morale and legitimacy of public bureaucracy and public confidence in it. Apparently, de-politicising the public service promotes merit, stability, continuity, professionalism and rationality; it persists despite political and social upheavals and violent swings in the political pendulum; and the public receives uniform and impartial treatment. However, some potentially positive features of politicisation of the public service could be recognised. Greater political commitment, for instance, may energise the public service in a way that may not be possible with a more neutral public service (Sharma, 2007:85).

To ensure good governance and reduce poverty and corruption, ensure proper service delivery, it is crucial to promote a harmonious state—civil society-private sector partnership and participation, as well as it is imperative to reduce existing opportunities for discretionary intervention by state authorities that use these mechanisms for their own benefits. Keeping the public service as much as possible clear from political ethnic and religious interferences and influences is a plus to effective and efficient services delivery.

Conclusions: Shaping our future and celebrating diversity

As we share the diversity of our struggles and celebrate the plurality of our resistance, our hopes and our aspirations, we are strengthened through comprehensive policies and the will to succeed. African countries share the diversity of their struggles; it is time to celebrate the plurality of its diversity as asset in the transformation process. This can only be done through good policies (input and output) functions of the state and the people. The end result is for the people and state to have trust in one another. Such developments show that administrative efficiency will increase with increased human capital development and with increases in specialisation (Simon 1976; Bertucci 2001). Our diversity is equally our strength and must be positively exploited.

The argument has been on developing a progressive Afro-centric approach. To attain this, the people must commit themselves to build people to people alliances (The Ubuntu, Batho Pele, and Harambe Spirit) to actively intervene in the existing institutions of power and decision-making, at the local, national and continental levels. Such empowered intervention will have as its goal the reorientation and building of a one and indivisible society, nation and continent. This is the foundations of African solutions to African problems. It creates the pathway for Africa articulating and owning its development for the benefit and good of the people. Seen within this perspective, Africa will celebrate its perseverance and struggle against large destructive development projects that dispossess and displace the people, making them refugees in their own continent.

Successes towards such an envisioned goal require commitments and resolve to overcome all hurdles. Therefore the political and administrative construct of the continent should be one that will not, and need not, wait only for our elected representatives and political leaders to address and resolve the multifarious economic, political, cultural, social and ecological crises that he continent faces. The emerging relationship between the *politician and administrator* should not be limited to a dialogue between the ruling party and administrators but extended to all political parties to better have an inside perspective of the structure and functioning of state apparatus. Where quality leadership exists, political leadership looms highest in the minds of many for a number of very important reasons, namely that of shaping the national vision and overseeing priority strategic policies for change and development for the collective good of society.

After all, the opposition parties constitute a *"government in waiting"* and should equally be schooled to properly understand and take-over the reigns of governance when the opportunity offers itself. This is what makes the *'bureaucracy'* an *impartial and independent institution* ready to serve whichever political party that takes over the reign of governance. The relationship should be an ongoing process of *renewal, reconciliation, reconstructing and the constant* search for best practices that improves the political and administrative apparatus to attain greater heights of efficiency and effectiveness in quality services delivery. The continent's institutions of higher learning plays an important role in this aspect of 'training' the political parties and society.

The challenge is of such magnitude that Africans must begin first to acknowledge inherent weaknesses and failures as actors of social change. It entails accepting the reality of the evolving situation and to accept the reality of consistent honest, humble and self-reflecting, and never be stooges to national and international institutions and structures of power out to destroy the continent. It is, therefore, necessary to develop appropriate mechanisms for de-emphasising the negative aspects of centralisation and hierarchy. The challenge that Africa has to restructure itself into a capable development state as prelude to transcending into a service delivery polity is now The need to reinforce the effectiveness of government and encourage the development of the rule of law, justice, legal reforms and other measures to move the continent forward cannot be overemphasised.

Africa must now start envisioning the possible; by recognising that it is only through continuous efforts in building alliances and movements through active linking and resisting that can sustain and further the development of the continent. Apparently it is from such a dynamic vision that the continent must assess, confront and transform the dominant political, economic, social and cultural systems that impoverishes the people of Africa. African leaders have expressed the desire for continental unity and have equally affirmed on many occasions that the continent has a common destiny.

Now is the time to ensure the realisation of those aspirations that Africa no longer can be on the valley of the death but on the avenue of the living. African states are challenged to recreate and re-design their states and make them development focused. Excellent and pragmatic development agenda has never been in want on the continent, the challenge has always been the political will for implementation and ensuring proper management of resources, creating more wealth and eliminating social inequalities and ethnic diversities. The journey for a New Africa starts here and now. On this basis, we advance the following recommendations.

Recommendations

Articulating a new good governance trajectory for service delivery in Africa does require among others the following policy recommendations;

- Human capital development (education) and creating awareness of the roles of stake holders in quality service delivery;
- Empowering stakeholders to be active partners in the process of service delivery as well as ensure a social contract between the state, civil society and the private sector;
- Lack of visionary leadership and a proactive citizenry – cultivating a new mindset – attitude, behaviour and concern;
- Developing new curricular for human capital development from a progressive Afrocentric perspectives and within the context of global scientific knowledge;
- Over-centralisation and authoritarian governance decision-making system is also demodulating; decentralisation and participatory promotes motivations as it encourages effectiveness and efficiency
- Cultivating a new mindset for honesty, trustworthiness and seeking positive proactive forward looking solutions to the plethora of African problems;
- Weakness of both leadership and citizens in the following; vision, transparency, ethics, goal orientation, team building leads to poor delivery of services;;

- The future of public service rest upon innovation, creativity change and doing things differently through taking calculated risks in the overall interests of the people
- Create a professional, non-apolitical bureaucracy ready to serve which ever political party that assumes office;
- Challenges facing public service can be solved through home grown solutions;
- Encourage efforts in mainstreaming gender empowerment and other concerns;
- Failure to mobilise the people to engage in development of indigenous policies, instead leaders impose policies which have been copied from the developed world which are not adaptable to local people;
- Eradicating poverty, unemployment, endemic diseases, promoting and sustaining the welfare of citizens – people first before profit.

References

African Association for Public Administration and Management (AAPAM) (2007). Proceedings of the 29th Roundtable Conference of the African Association for public Administration and Management Proceedings on the Them Political and Managerial Leadership for Change and Development in Africa, 3-7 September 2007, Mbabane – Swaziland.

African Association for Public Administration and Management (AAPAM) (2008), Proceeding of the 30th Roundtable Conference (AAPAM) on the Theme, Enhancing the Performance of the Public Service in a Developmental State, 6-10 October 2008, Accra-Ghana.

African Public Service: New Challenges, Professionalism and Ethics in cooperation with the Africa Training and Research Centre in Administration for Development (CAFRAD). ST/ESA/PAD/SER.E/20. New York (in English and French).

African Union (2008) African Charter on democracy, Elections and Governance. Addis Ababa, Ethiopia.

Bertucci Guido (2001) Managing Diversity in the Civil Service: UDESA-IIAS Joint Publication, IOS Press, Oxford, Washington, Tokyo.

Chapman Brain (1959) The Profession of Government, Unwin University Books, London.

D'Souza A. Anthony (2008) Leaders for Today: Hope for Tomorrow. Pauline Publications Africa, Nairobi – Kenya.

Forje W. John (2006) "Rethinking Decentralisation and Devolution of Power Within the African Context: Challenges and Opportunities", Paper presented at the 28th Roundtable Conference of the Africa Association for Public Administration and Management (AAPAM), Arusha, Tanzania 4-8 December 2006, on the Theme: Towards and Effective Delivery of Public Services in Africa.

Forje W. John (2007) "Enhancing Sustainable Governance and Development in Africa – A Reassessment of Current Challenges and Future Prospects", African Journal of Public Administration and Management, Vol. XV111, No. 1, January 2007, pp43-54.

Forje W. John (2009) The Challenges of Administrative Political and Developmental Renewal in Africa – Essays on Rethinking Government and Reorganisation, Nova Science Publishers, Inc., New York, USA.

Forje W. John (2011) State Building and Democracy in Africa. A Comparative and Developmental Approach. Nova Science Publishers, Inc. New York.

Forje W. John (2012). Emerging Perspectives on Capacity-Building and Quality Public Services Delivery in Africa; Challenges, Prospects and Opportunities for the Future Lambert Academic Publishing, Germany.

Forje W. John (2015) Cameroon without Corruption. The Search for a New Vision. Lambert Academic Publishing, Germany (Forthcoming).

Gant, G. (1979) Development Administration: Concepts, Goals, Methods. The University of Wisconsin Press, Madison, WI.

Gerschenkron Alexander (1962) Economic Backwardness in Historical Perspectives. The Belknap Press, Harvard University Press, Cambridge, MA.

Hyden Goran (1995) "The Changing Nature of the State and Public Management in Africa" in Bade Onimode & Richard Synge (eds.) (1995). Issues in African Development. Essays in Honour of Adebayo Adedeji at 65. Heinemann Educational Books (Nigeria) Plc, pp69-85.

Kingsley J. Donald (1944) Representative Bureaucracy. The Antioch Press, Yellow Springs, Ohio, United States of America.

Mills Wright (1857). The Power Elite. Oxford University Press, p237

Meynaud Jean (1965) Technocracy, Faber and Faber, London.

Neustadt, Richard (1964). Presidential Power: The Politics of Leadership. Signet Books, New York.

Olaopa Tunji (2008) Theory and Practice of Public Administration and Civil Service Reforms in Nigeria. Spectrum Books Limited, Ibadan – Nigeria.

Peters Guy & Pierre Jon (2004) Politicisation of the Public Service in Comparative Perspective: The Quest for Control, Routledge Taylor and Francis Group, London and New York.

Riggs, Fred (1970) Frontiers of Development Administration. Duke University Press, Durham, NC. United States of America.

Ridley, F. and Blondel, J. (1965) Public Administration in France, Barnes and Noble Publishers, New York New.

Schaffer, B. Bernhard (1969). "The Deadlock in Development Administration", in: Politics and Change in Developing Countries, in Ley Colin (ed.) (1969), Cambridge University Press, Cambridge.

Scott K. George & Malcolm Wallis (eds.) (2014) Citizen Engagement, Decentralisation and Service Delivery in Africa, AAPAM Book Series, Nairobi – Kenya.

Sharma C. Keshav (2007) "Trends in the Politicisation of the Public Service', African Journal of Public Administration and Management, Vol. XV111, No.1, January 2007, pp78-86.

Sharp R. Walter (1931). The French Civil Service: Bureaucracy in Transition, Macmillan, New York, United States of America.

Simon A. Herbert (1976) Administrative Behaviour – A Study of Decision-Making Processes in Administrative Organisation. The Free Press, London.

Sisson C. H. (1959). The Spirit of British Administration, Faber and Faber, London.

Suleiman N. Ezra (1974) Politics, Power, Ad Bureaucracy in France. The Administrative Elite. Princeton University Press, USA.

Vedel Georges (ed.) (1962) La Dépolarisation, Mythe ou Réalité, Armand Colins, Paris.

Weber Max, (1958) "Politics as a Vocation," in H. H. Gerth and C. Wright Mills (eds.) From Max Weber: Essays n Sociology, Oxford University Press, New York.

Zeleza Tiyambe Paul (1997). Manufacturing African Studies and Crises. Codesria Book Series, Dakar – Senegal.

Chapter Five

Repositioning Africa's public administration within the context of achieving UN Sustainable Development Goals (SDGs) 2030 & African Union (AU) Agenda 2063. Challenges and prospects for constructing the Africa we want.

Abstract: Building the Africa we want

*Africa finds itself within the confines of decay or development. The Millennium Development Goals (MDGs) have come and gone with extremely few countries attaining the set objectives. Post-2015 is coined within the context of Sustainable Development Goals (SDGs) and African Union (AU) Agenda 2063. The success of these two inter-related developmental objectives is to usher quality services and livelihood to the population. The paper argues that the success of attaining envisaged goals depends on three fundamentals – (i) leadership, (ii) a trained and committed public service sector; and (iii) an engaging citizenry. A proper mix or interface with a government focus on what people need and what has not been done. The conceptual frame of departure builds on a progressive Afrocentric-responsiveness to transform pubic administration, management and good governance nexus as the unavoidable prerequisite to realising developmental goals to better enable the sustainable attainment of AU Agenda 2063 and national visions. It should be noted that deficits in governance (in form of weak institutions, unaccountable leadership, constricted political spaces and non-inclusive democratic processes) are common features of many African countries since independence constraining quality welfare and livelihood of the people. Without structural changes in mentality, attitude and behaviour (MAB) the goals of AU Agenda 2063 within the context of the UN Sustainable Development Goals (SDGs) will equally face serious setbacks. Conceptually, analytically and methodologically, the paper is construed within the perspectives of Africa owning its resources and development path. Africa must be inventive in its approach to avoid economic stagnation and ease the attainment of the SDGs, but importantly for Africa to have and own its Agenda (2063) and not to have SDGs as the main strategy to give the people what they want. It strongly stress on the role of the **public service** as the output function of the government and as instrument for achieving Agenda 2063 in partnership with the people and private sector. This is expressed in (UNGA:225/96) which advocates and 'recognises that* *the there is a need for public administration systems to be sound, efficient and well equipped with the appropriate capacities and capabilities through inter alia, capacity-building, promotion of transfer, access and utilisation of technology, establishment or improvement of training programmes for public services, strengthening of partnership of the public sector with the private sector, as well as providing an enabling environment for private sector activities...." Thus implementing the African Charter on Values and Principles of Public Service and Administration (2011) and AU Agenda 2063, The Africa We Want will come our way with a functional public sector that delivers. The paper concludes that the public service sector must be well equipped and to demonstrate potentials in delivering quality service in a challenging context. Weak institutions lack of public accountability; and economic and social tensions underlain by sharp ethno-regional divisions and pervasive regional violence make development progress in Africa particularly challenging. Of course challenging does not mean impossible; and a veritable public service makes a great difference in turning the tide for a better Africa.*

Keywords: quality services delivery, accountability, responsibility, public-service private sector partnership

Introduction: An inspired public administration at the service of the people

There is an urgent need for an inspired public service sector if Africa is to achieve the SDG's and Africa's Agenda 2063. This equally highlights the important role the public service sector plays in national transformation and enhancing international cooperation. For it to play that role constructively and comprehensively the institution has to be properly equipped with the requisite human capital and infrastructure. Whether a foreign imposed or home grown developmental policies agenda the public sector must be well armed in all developmental facets, as well as ensure the realisation of government policy objectives which must be people-oriented, focused and making proper resources utilisation for the common good of society.

Only a competent, professional and neutral public Administration and management sector based on merit and embedded with visionary servant leadership, committed citizenry, and an enterprising and productive private sector can alter the face of the continent without which, the UN 2030 SDGs and AUs Agenda 2063 cannot be realised. Transforming public administration and management nexus in creating the Africa we want must now take centre-stage in all activities. The need to transform and capacitate the public administration and management is judiciously captured in a number of related documents; for example UNGA Resolution 50/225/96' AU Heads of State and Government Summit (Kampala, Uganda July 2010; the African Public Service Charter on Principles and Values (2011) among others come in handy. For Africa to achieve the lofty goals of Agenda 2063, SDGs 2030 and national visions, it is compelled to craft a solid base for a constructive and solid transformation of the national and continental public administration and management. The continent needs the commitment of responsible governors, legislators, investors, administrators, business people and partners of all kinds to see that development is inclusive and quality well-being improved, sustained and consolidated.

Without a capable structural-functional state bureaucracy, development efforts will come to nought. It is strongly argued that without robust governance, public administration and management the continent will continue to wallow in a sustained state of underdevelopment, entrenched marginalisation and exploitation. The people should *'dream and hope'* of an Africa whose institutions at all levels of government will have the capacity to prioritise, design, implement, monitor development activities and deliver quality services to the people in an accountable manner, and with full participation of the people. This is in line with Goal 16 of UN (SDGs) of 2030 which in essence is a plan of action for people, planet and prosperity as well as it seeks to strengthen universal peace and partnerships and AU Agenda 2063 envisioning a continent where the institutions are at the service of its citizens.

Administration is the handmaiden of policy in Government. And policy in government is best executed by the administration in partnership with the people. This highlights the need for striving for good governance, since 'a core element of good governance is a capable democratic state – a state embedded in the public will, relying on legitimacy through the democratic process, with strong institutions promoting the public interest' (ECA 2005:26). Apparently, a key task for Africa is to build the capacity and accountability of strong and efficient state institutions and human capital. That is the challenge for the New African Public Administration and Management (NAPAM).

Theoretical and Conceptual Frame

The theoretical and conceptual frame departs from an interface of many thoughts. For example, Kettl's (2002) assertion that public administration has long been based on the notions of hierarchy and authority – the way managers actually manage is increasingly at odds with the theory; and that the growing gap between theory and practice poses enormous challenges for managers in determining how best to work. Cruikshank (1999) argues that the will to help others and one-self is neither a bad nor a good thing. It is political; the will to empower contains the twin possibilities of domination and freedom and that even the most democratic modes of government entail power relations that are both voluntary and coercive. The great difficulty with any government administered by men over men, lies within the contextual framework of the government's capability first to enable it control the governed; and in the next phase obliged it to control itself. Kaufman (2001:24); points out that the ideal public service was portrayed as a neutral instrument (where) policy-making was envisioned as a universe apart of administration, the so-called 'politics/administration dichotomy.'

Contemporary, public administration consists of several dimensions, including political, legal, bureaucratic and managerial, and much of the day-to-day responsibility for making public policy falls in the hands of professional public administrators. In short, it is the professional public servant who determines the standards and regulations of public law and who make interpretive decisions involving a myriad of public policy areas. Thus governments come and go and the administration remains to serve which ever party that is elected into office. Transforming the African public administration

182

means creating a service delivery institution that promotes cooperation rather rivalry and show great concern for transparency and accountability.

Apparently, without an effective state, sustainable economic and social development remains almost impossible so also the attainment of quality livelihood for the citizens. The AU (2063) Agenda envisions an Africa where the institutions are at the service of its people – effective, accountable and inclusive institutions to enhance citizens' participation in development and in economic governance management; where the rule of law is fully respected; where authority and participation go-hand-in-hand for the common good of the people. The combination of factors (multiple policy imperatives, shifts in the global socio-economic and trade configurations contributing to the entrenchment of a marginalised continent); an existing imperatives to govern effectively and efficiently, creates an urgency to improve the African state's capacity and capability. Today Africa is under scrutiny and pressure to demonstrate practical action to divest itself from the scourge of under-development and stagnation into a path of sustained development. African states are obliged to be well-armed with abilities to flexibly and proactively make definitive choices that are in the interests of its long-term and sustained development (AAPAM 2015:3).

Transform Public Administration and Management to better contribute towards the attainment of Agenda 2063 within the context of UN Sustainable Development Goals requires a thorough analytical understanding and restructuring of the relationship between bureaucracy and politicians as depicted in Fig.1: Politicians and Bureaucrats Relationship. The main goal of transforming public administration is like the challenge of nation-building proceeding independence for many African countries to integrate diverse cultural, social and political groups into national unity. The African public administrative sector must transform and integrate diverse interest groups into a common sense of development goals and quality welfare for the people.

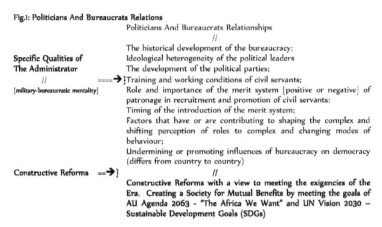

Fig.1: Politicians And Bureaucrats Relations

	Politicians And Bureaucrats Relationships
	//
	The historical development of the bureaucracy;
Specific Qualities of	Ideological heterogeneity of the political leaders
The Administrator	The development of the political parties;
// ====➔	}Training and working conditions of civil servants;
[military-bureaucratic mentality]	Role and importance of the merit system [positive or negative] of patronage in recruitment and promotion of civil servants;
	Timing of the introduction of the merit system;
	Factors that have or are contributing to shaping the complex and shifting perception of roles to complex and changing modes of behaviour;
	Undermining or promoting influences of bureaucracy on democracy (differs from country to country)
Constructive Reforms ==➔}	//
	Constructive Reforms with a view to meeting the exigencies of the Era. Creating a Society for Mutual Benefits by meeting the goals of AU Agenda 2063 - "The Africa We Want" and UN Vision 2030 – Sustainable Development Goals (SDGs)

[Note that the relationship between the civil servants and politicians raises the crucial question of the implementation of government policy and the influence of nonelected official's o that policy. Long-range policies are often the works of administrative officials rather than politicians. It could also be stated that government's willingness to consider changes in the Civil Service does not imply any intention on its part to alter the basic relationship between ministers and civil servants] (Source: Forje, 2015).

Transforming the public bureaucracy for the wellbeing of the people is an interface of state (the liberal, representative, electoral, administrative, legislative, and judicial institutions and practices articulated within the confines of a liberal constitutional framework)' governance is 'the conduct of conduct' or 'governmentality,' forms of action and relations of power that aim to guide and shape (rather than force, control, or dominate) the actions of others. The private sector compliments the public sector in services delivery. In this regards the interface helps people to help themselves; and creates a situation or manner of governing that relies on institutions, and the participatory role of the people. This makes sense to speak of *'the political,' 'the social,' 'the private,' and 'the public' domains* working in unionism for the common good of all. This position underscores the notion of transforming global relations for a just world (WSSF 2015) i.e. speaking of inequality at local, national and global levels that threatens world peace and peaceful coexistence., but appeals to policymakers, the state, civil society, private sector and how inequalities relates to governance, patterns of production and consumption.

In nutshell, the public service sector emerges as the coordinator that can make or mar the entire spectrum of the developmental process. Governance without effective implementation renders nugatory the intent of policy in as much as unaccounted for investment into government projects is a scar on the democratic edifice. Effective implementation is therefore no incident but rather a function of governance gone right. The central thrust of this contribution is to say that effective public administration machinery is an imperative requisite for good governance. Good governance also implies accountability, transparency, participation, openness and the rule of law. Since governance is the quality and level of the process by which decisions are implemented, it suffices to posit that the transformation of Africa's public administration and management augurs well for good governance and good governance points the way to quality livelihood. Africa needs sustainable quality livelihood. Now, the challenge of governance, is to design legitimate institutions and societal mechanisms to manage diversity by securing a sense of identity and sense of belonging that respects tolerance of the 'other' and at the same time embracing the rights and liberties of all citizens to cohabit peacefully within the same environment.

Quality livelihood for all can only be attained, accompanied and consolidated by a gradual reinvention of the African state, which must become increasingly, more tolerant and acceptable of the involvement of other actors in the continent's development endeavours, including civil society and the private sector (AU Agenda 2063:2014; UN Agenda 2030:2015) focused on ending poverty and hunger and to achieve sustainable development by promoting inclusive economic growth, protecting the environment and promoting social inclusion. Without social inclusion, the Mediterranean Sea will continue to be the main graveyard for fleeing Africa's youth with harrowing images of people risking, often losing their lives in an attempt to escape what is conceived to be a continent racked by conflict and poverty. Yet Africa has 11 of the 20 fastest-growing economies in the world, with enormous resources, and almost half of the world's uncultivated land that is suitable for growing food crops (Nwanze 2015:21).

Therefore, the public service has to restructure to perform better and be transformed to fulfil the objectives of a capable developmental state and equally to play the role required in the social and economic transformation of the continent. The transformation process requires overcoming a number of important challenges and constraints; some of the constraints emanate from the legacy of colonialism and apartheid which created a hierarchal strait-jacket; while others are the results of ongoing developmental dynamics generated by articulate self-interests to an extent that the public administration is overdue restructuring to enhance performance. Africa has been suffering from a scourge of *'deficient administrative and leadership syndrome'* accounting why development activities are often stalled. Over the past decade great strides have been made to establish order and bring sanity through a fundamental transformation of the African public administration and management as well as infuse good governance as relevant tools for development and inclusive social justice.

A transformed public administration: Facing the challenges of the good, bad and ugly

It is argued that without a transformed public service sector, proper management and visionary leadership the transition to achieving UN Agenda 2030 and AU 2063 will be difficult. The calibre of the public administration and leadership in tandem with committed sense of direction and engaged citizenry constitutes fundamental factors underscoring the needed change in attaining visions 2030 and 2063. The role and importance of the public administration sector is such that instead of *'bouncing-back'* it should be embedded with new vision and strength to *'bouncing forward'* with greater resilience for constructive change. The concept *'resilience' is marked by a forward-looking* orientation, instead of retreating into darker days of non-performance and non-delivery. There UN Agenda 2030 and AU Agenda 2063 challenge the continent's public administration to be performing – the symbol of quality services delivery, accountability and transparency. The distinction between politics and administration corresponds neatly to the distinction between formulation (the domain of politics) and execution (the domain of administration). The ulcer of present day administration is poor leadership, bad governance and corruption which must be properly addressed otherwise set goals can hardly be realised. The pressure and urgency for African countries to appreciate transforming the public administration and management system will continue to mount as issues of the bad and ugly nexus of the administration persist.

The forward-looking orientation and quality delivery should be seen more of a process whose implementation follows a holistic approach. In the words of Dodman et al (2009:153-154) public administration should be a process taking into account the economic, social, psychological, physical, cultural and environmental factors that are necessary for human survive and thrive. As a continent plagued with numerous ills, the public/civil service as the in/output functions of government comes under serious spotlight. How has the public service sector impacted positively or negatively to the inability or ability of the countries to address challenges and shake-off the entrenched title of underdevelopment and endemic poverty? Of course, the African Public Administration cannot be said to be a total failure. It has demonstrated some *'good'* in the face of extreme *'odds'* to propel Africa to where it is today.

Unfortunately, the bad and ugly sides override the good perspectives of this institution. Much more is yet to be done to restore respect, hope and confidence in the continent's public administration and management system. The unholy marriage between political party interests and the continent's public administration and management needs serious surgical attention so as to significantly improve on political accountability, public service delivery and administration, devolution of power to the local governance structures and the institutionalisation of a culture of regular competitive, free and fair elections as encapsulated in the realisation of African Agenda 2063 vision as well as in UN 2030 Agenda for Sustainable Development.

Just as the African Public Administration can be held accountable for the failures in transforming the continent to a capable developmental state; it has done some tremendous services in keeping many an African states afloat especially in crisis periods. Although the continent is still struggling to get to grips with major problems some significant trends do give grounds for optimism. Perhaps a most positive and visible sign include (i) The New

Partnership for Africa's Economic Development (NEPAD); (ii) Africa Peer Review Mechanism (APRM), (iii) Africa's Good Governance Charter; (iv) The Africa Charter on the Values and Principles of Public Service And Administration; (v) The Regional Economic Communities (RECs); (vi) the transformation of the Organisation of African Unity (OAU) into the Africa Union (AU) to mention but a few indicates that the continent is on the road to reform and becoming a potential world player. The activities of these institutions and Charter need reinforcement and implementation with a focus geared towards achieving the ideals of AU Agenda 2063 and UN Vision 2030.

It is on these positive grounds that the continent should navigate, build-on and transforms the region in attaining UN Agenda 2030 and AU Agenda 2063 as well as any set national objectives. However it calls for a holistic paradigm shift, political will, commitment, mentality, attitude and behavioural changes and partnership with other progressive forces, visionary leadership and an entrepreneurial productive and innovative private sector. Africa cannot achieve the ideals envision in UN Agenda 2030 and AU Agenda 2063 if the public administration continues to be ravaged by inertia, bad governance, corruption, poor productivity. At the same time, the public administration must be empowered to meet the exigencies and challenges of the 21st century and beyond. This calls for creating a public service which is apolitical capable of enhancing the continent's viable and competitive edge in the unstoppable world of globalisation and knowledge-based economy driven by rapid changes in information and communication technologies (ICTs). Rapidity in technological changes calls for intensive human capacity and institutional building of the continent's public administration.

As Africa struggles on the road of reform for greater social justice, and ownership of its development path, for present and future generations, the public administrative sector as the output functions of government, must equally be empowered to effectively and efficiently deliver the goods for quality livelihood for all citizens. Empowerment entails building and constantly updating its human capital, infrastructures, institutions and creating the necessary enabling working environment for the sector to keep abreast with the rapidly increasing human demands and changes in technological development. Importantly, leadership role is crucial in infusing a sense of direction. Leadership is a call to serve. A blend of the three – *government, society and the private sector* creates the foundation for constructing a capable developmental state, which Africa needs to ensure the realisation of UN Agenda 2030 and AU Agenda 2063.

Pahad (2015) notes that alternative and progressive voices are especially important for Africa, given the reality that the continent remains marginalised in terms of helping to fashion these relations, despite their direct impact on the lives and destiny of the one billion Africans. Discourse on African leadership in shaping the mind in Africa's socio-economic, political and cultural life since independence and in light of globalisation occupies the thoughts of Kondlo (2014). African states should rethink the place of public administration in the transformation of the continent; and to ensure the crafting and implementing people-centred policies necessary for economic growth and contributing to citizens' well-being. Mamadou (1996) argues strongly that the most promising way to overcome the shortcomings of the State system and its alien formal institutions in Africa is to recognise 'the structural and functional disconnect between the informal, indigenous institutions rooted in the region's history and culture, and formal institutions mostly transplanted from outside'

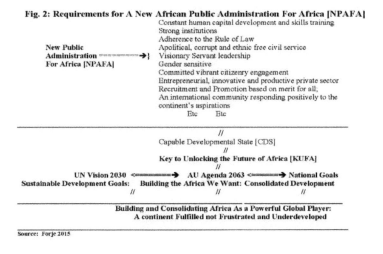

Fig. 2: Requirements for A New African Public Administration For Africa [NPAFA]

New Public Administration For Africa [NPAFA] ===========➔}
Constant human capital development and skills training
Strong institutions
Adherence to the Rule of Law
Apolitical, corrupt and ethnic free civil service
Visionary Servant leadership
Gender sensitive
Committed vibrant citizenry engagement
Entrepreneurial, innovative and productive private sector
Recruitment and Promotion based on merit for all;
An international community responding positively to the continent's aspirations
Etc   Etc

//
Capable Developmental State [CDS]
//
Key to Unlocking the Future of Africa [KUFA]
//
UN Vision 2030 ⟵=======➔ AU Agenda 2063 ⟵=======➔ National Goals
Sustainable Development Goals: Building the Africa We Want: Consolidated Development
//   //   //

Building and Consolidating Africa As a Powerful Global Player:
A continent Fulfilled not Frustrated and Underdeveloped

Source: Forje 2015

The continent's public administration must be tailored to meeting the needs of the people as well as be well equipped with the necessary human skills, institutional capacity and enabling working environment and conditions to ensure the accomplishment of envisaged goals.. New requirements are needed for the continent's public administration if UN visions 2030, AU Agenda 2063 and National Goals are to be realised. Fig 2: Requirements for A New African Public Administration (NPAFA) attempts a brief description of what is needed to ensure that Africa's Public Administration is adequately transformed to better contribute towards the attainment of AU Agenda 2063 within the context of UN Sustainable Development Goals (SDGs) 2030.

The absence of these requirements contributes to the diabolic fate of the continent inhibiting the proper utilisation of resources for the benefit of society. Far reaching structural changes are needed in transforming the African Public Administration and Management into a veritable player with strong emphasis on *building effective, accountable and inclusive institutions at all levels* rendering quality services for the attainment of sustainable development goals as envisaged by the United Nations, African Union and National Governments. A number of African states have designed certain goals to be achieved, for example, Cameroon 2035 vision, Kenya Vision of 2030 and so forth requiring a functional, effective, efficient and a productive public administration as well as a vibrant private sector (functioning in unionism) to ensure the realisation of these visions.

But the NPAFA can only achieve its goals when the practice of political appointments or the *'open spoils system'* is reduced or eliminated within the structural-functioning of the administration. Genuine administration or an apolitical public administration should not engage in party politics but rather be engaged in impartial administration (Sisson 1959). The ugly side of African Public Administration is the unholy marriage of party politics with the administrator. The institutionalisation of monolithic party system destroyed the genuine role of the administrator as the responsible output service delivery arm of the State. Even though there is a gradual return to plural democracy (good governance) today in a number of African states, the virus created with the monolithic governance structure lingers on.

Africa needs an impartial, responsible public administration that honestly delivers services whichever political party that assumes office. Kingsley (1944) pointed out that the essence of responsibility is psychological rather than mechanical and should be sought in an identity of aim and point of view, in a common background of social prejudice, which leads the agent to act as though (s)he were the principal. The administration is truly responsible (and in this sense impartial) when the Ministers and Civil Servants share the same background and hold similar social views, in other words, when the *bureaucracy is representative* with a *people-focused* ideological orientation of sustained quality livelihood for all.

To ensure *'a reconnect between state and civil society'*, and to identify the opportunities within indigenous institutions for building a more pluralistic and participatory form of governance and development, the need for *'partnership'* and interface between the various stakeholders (state, civil society, private sector and worldwide community) is imperative if the envisioned goals of 2030 and 2063 are to be achieved. The ugly face of the continent's administrative structure is its pollution with party politics and ethnic diversity that equally breeds corruption, inertia and non-productivity. That is why *'good governance'* and transforming *'public administration'* stands tall as perhaps the single most important factor in eradicating poverty and promoting development in attaining envision goals. An educated apolitical public administration creates a friendly and consolidated relation where the politician *leans* on the administrator and expects to be advised objectively, scientifically and impartially in the overall mutual benefit of society. This is what makes bureaucracy to be representative and exhibiting a common and uniform mode of behaviour for the ultimate good of society.

Thus a harmonious relationship should develop between politicians and civil servants which ensures the theory of a *'representative bureaucracy'* (as in Britain) creates a society of *'mutual benefits'* and *'mutual understanding'* and in a situation of *'unstable political system'* or *'frequent changes in governments'* policy-making power passes into the hands of the permanent bureaucracy. Politicians lean on their officials – (bureaucracy) – as it relieves the politicians of a difficult and chancy search for *'loyal'* advisers and administrators. Continuity is assured leading to the attainment of goals. Policy-making and execution falls into the hands of a permanent bureaucracy that is *apolitical, non-ethnic and non-religiously* constituted. A properly constituted or rightly transformed public administration system ensures that the basic tenets of administration continue even in the wake of a new government. Discontinuity, disharmony or instability among the stakeholders is a thing which every state structure should avoid as this helps in derailing the achievement of set objectives for example, Agendas UN 2030 and AU 2063 respectively.

Good working relations between the politicians of all political parties and public administrators provide the structural framework as provider of key services to the people. Deficit in governance, in the form of weak institutions, poor leadership, unskilled public administrators, constricted political spaces and non-inclusive democratic process accounts for the failures of governments in achieving set goals (MDGs) for example. The stability of the political system and the competence of the public administration create a better atmosphere or environment as well as this permits free flow of information greater coordination and connectivity among the different stakeholders in pursuit of common goals.

Evidently the golden age of the separation of administrative and political party functions is now to achieve the *"Africa We Want"* and in realisation of *UN Sustainable Development Goals.* The transformation of Africa's public administration and management augurs well for good governance and servant visionary leadership. Apparently, good visionary leadership challenges public administration and management to assume greater ownership for their work to ensure quality welfare for all. Furthermore understanding appreciating the strength and weaknesses of this institution, opportunities should be exploited to enhance its functioning capabilities in the process of development.

Conclusion and recommendations: The transformation and change we need

The chosen theme the 37th AAPAM Round Table Conference, 2016, "Transforming Public Administration and Management" puts Africa on the right path for change. This is coming within the backdrop of UN Agenda 2063 (SDGs 2015), and AU Agenda 2063 (2014) and with strong roots in the efforts deployed by the Conference of African Ministers of Public Service and Administration to promote and implement the African Union Vision on Public Service in the Continent. The African Public Service Charter on the Principles and Values (AU 2011) constitutes a handy tool in waging the war for transformation. `The genuine execution of the Charter i line with other Charters adopted by the continental body gives signs of hope for the concomitant implementation of UN Agenda 2030 and AU Agenda 2063 and the eventual transformation of the continent.

Charters are human construct; as Ketti (2002) famous dictum, notes; "if men were angels, no Government would be necessary. If angels were to govern men neither external nor internal controls on Government would be necessary." What is necessary is to transform and capacitate African public administration and management nexus to judiciously and implement the ideals of the UN Agenda and AU Agenda of giving quality welfare to the people on the continent. The paper shows in different ways of the continent's public administration and management system entering a new and critical stage in detecting, diagnosing, framing and implementing the solutions much needed by the continent in taking its rightful place within the global community. As such Africa needs as discussed in the paper to undertake constructive measures and implement far-reaching actions that ensures the realisation of Agendas 2030 and 2063.

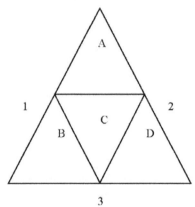

Fig. 3: African Public Administration Framing its Change and Transformation

Note a) frame the transformation   b) enable transformation
c) be the transformation   d) build capacity for transformation
1) catalyst for change committed to a mission
2) transform and strategise
3) develop: lead by example and accept responsibility   (Source: Forje: 2015)

The constructive measures for Africa's transformation of its public administration and management system should pivot within the contextual (i) frame of transformation; (ii) be the transformation; (iii) enable the transformation and (iv) build capacity for transformation as depicted in Fig. 3 – African Public Administration Framing its Change and Transformation. Fig. 3: attempts to identify a number of problems that negatively impact the practice of transforming public administration and management in many African countries.

Some of the factors include: (a) lack of capacity to meeting the growing public needs; (b) overstretched and underdeveloped public administration; (c) the increasing politicised nature of the bureaucracies and management systems; (d) public administrative systems that are quite vulnerable to political influences; and (e) public administrative systems that lack diversity/representativeness, appointments and staff from various and different ethnic groups. For example, the proportion of women in the top echelon of the administrative ladder is relatively low in many African countries. The need to create a more representative bureaucracy and functions as well as in which social ideals are as close as possible to the grassroots of the nation is very crucial in transforming public administration and contributing to equitable quality services delivery.

Framing the change and transformation requires redefining the structure of society within the changing national and global context; creating proactive efforts in meeting growing demands for welfare as well as building new knowledge; critical reassessment and reshaping the domestic order, ensuring meaningful changes within its corps, narrowing the disparity between the top and bottom segments of administrative personnel and creating a siren atmosphere; (ii) enabling transformation and change requires identifying strategic opportunities for policy engagement, leadership and working with other stakeholders; (iii) building for transformation and change, necessitates changing priority actions in meeting the diverse and complex challenges of national and global changes and social transformation; building human and institutional capacities and infrastructures; ensuring good pay-packets and working conditions as well as shunning inertia and corrupt practices, but gunning for effective, efficient quality services delivery; (iv) be the transformation and change.

Fig. 4: Administration / Leadership Nexus Impacting on Transformation and Development

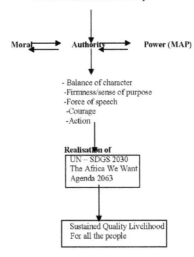

Source: Forje, 2015

This requires drastic measures – the public administration must itself be the centre or focus of transformation. Charity begins at home. The African Public Service Charter on the Principles and Values provides the code of ethics and behaviour which should be used as the bible for transformation and change in accelerating the realisation of envision goals. Importantly, it is pointless to ask the civil service to change if the government at the top is not setting an example. You cannot ask people to transform or to do something that you are not doing yourself. Leadership is at its best when the vision is strategic, the voice persuasive and the results tangible. The leader should show strength of character and have the moral authority to move others. Charisma without character leads to catastrophe.

Clearly, the leadership role is a vital part of any successful transformation or change activities and none more so than within the context of the continents crave for development. Therefore, the public administration like the 'leader' must command both moral, authority and power (MAP). **Moral** gives directions for ethical behaviour, sense of accountability and balance of character, as well as firmness of purpose; **Authority** is the leader's ability to use power rightly; authority is the ability to get others to do what you want because they recognise (through your life and words) that what you ask is legitimate and right; and **Power** is the ability to make others do your will rightly even if they would choose not to. The combination of moral, authority and power should create a new atmosphere for transformation as illustrated in Fig. 4: Administration/Leadership Nexus Impacting on Transformation and Development.

The public administration sector must change itself in the first place and be willing to accept changes that consolidate the holistic transformation and development nexus of the continent for the overall welfare and good of the people. Therefore Africa need to craft a public administration where the people continually expand their capacity and capability to create the results they truly desire, where new and expansive patterns of thinking are nurtured, where collective aspirations for the common good is set free and where people are continually learning how to learn and live together. I have been critical in my discourse on the theme, but within the contextual frame of us agreeing on a shared value system and acknowledging interdependency as the way for our future well-being as tied up together.

Conclusion and recommendations

In view of the ideas discussed here, the following are set out as measures needed to advance the course of transforming public administration and management in order to better realise the objectives and goals of UN Vision 2030 and AU Agenda 2063;

- Genuine demarcation between political party activities and public administration is necessary to create and effective and efficient public administration and management system that deliver's quality services to the nation
- Monolithic party blindness and public administration and management consciousness has to be addressed to restore sanity, hope and confidence in the system of governance;
- The continent through the African Public Service Charter on Principles and Values created the platform of dialogue, interexchange of ideas and best practices, as well as seek innovative, creative and entrepreneurial ways to constructively start *walking the talk* to ensure the genuine realisation of Agendas 2030 and 2063 respectively and in unionism;
- Strengthen the interface between the various stakeholders with a view to further improve measures underpinning the transformation initiatives
- Visionary servant political leadership is an imperative in transforming public administration and management style;
- Focus on training, merit and professionalism in the recruitment and promotion within public administration;
- Ensure a functional governance system that break down walls and build bridges across the politico-administrative divide.

References

Africa Association for Public Administration and Management (AAPAM (2015) Aide Memoire –"Transforming Public Administration and Management (PAM) in order to contribute towards Agenda 2063 within the context of the Sustainable Development Goals' The 37th AAPAM Annual Roundtable Conference, February 29th to 4th March 2016 (AAPAM Kenya-14 December 2015.

African Union (2014) African Union Agenda 2063: "The Africa We Want. Africa Is Consulting on Agenda 2063 Addis Ababa, Ethiopia, (Twitter: @_African Union #Agenda 2063: www.au.int.).

Africa Union (2011). The African Charter on Values and Principles of Public Service and Administration, Addis Ababa Ethiopia.

African Union Constitutive Act, (2002) 9th July 2002, Durban, South Africa.

Connolly William (1988).Political Theory and Modernity, University of Wisconsin Press, Madison.

Dia, Mamadou (1996) Africa's Management in the 1990s and Beyond – Reconciling Indigenous and Transplanted Institutions. World Bank, Washington DC.

Dodman, D. Ayers, J and Hug S. (2009) Building Resilience, In State of the World: into a Warming World. The World Watch Institute. (See: www.worldwatch.org/node/5984).

Economic Commission for Africa (ECA) (2005) "Striving for Good Governance in Africa. Synopsis of the 2005 African Governance Report, prepared for the African Development Forum IV. Addis Ababa.

Forje W. John (2009) The Challenges of Administrative Political and Developmental Renewal (Emerging Issues), Nova Science Publisher, Inc. New York, USA.

Forje W. John (ed.) (2013) Emerging Perspectives on Capacity Building. And Quality Public Services Delivery in Africa. Lambert Academic Publishing, Germany.

Cruikshank Barbara (1999). The Will to Empower: Democratic Citizens and Other Subjects. Cornell University Press, Ithaca and London.

Kaufman, Herbert (2001). "Major Players: Bureaucracies in American Government," Public Administration Review, 16 January/February: 18-42.

Kettl Donald (2002), "The Transformation of Governance: Public Administration for Twenty-First Century America", John Hopkins University Press, 03 September 2002.

Kingsley J. Donald (1944) Representative Bureaucracy: An Interpretation of the British Civil Service, Antioch Press, Yellow Springs, Ohio, USA.

Kondlo Merriman Kwandiwe (2014) Perspectives on Thought Leadership for Africa's Renewal (2014) Africa Institute of South Africa, Pretoria, South Africa.

Neustadt Richard (1966) "White House and Whitehall," The Public Interest 11, reprinted in Richard Rose (ed.) (1969) Policy-Making in Britain, The Free Press, New York.

Nwanze Kanayo (2015) "Money Doesn't Always Talk", New African, No.553, August/September 2015, London 21pp.

Pahad Aziz, Garth le Pere & Miranda Strydom (2015) Promoting Progressive African Thought Leadership, African Institute in South Africa, Pretoria, South Africa.

Sisson, C. H. (1959) The Spirit of British Administration. Faber and Faber, London.

United Nations (1996).United Nations General Assembly Resolution 50/225/96, New York, United States of America.

World Social Science Form (WSSF) (2015) Transforming Global Relations for a Just World. (Theme of the 3rd WSSF 2015, Durban International Convention Centre, South Africa, 13-16 September 2015.

Chapter Six

Facing the challenges behind in the business race in Africa: Escaping the cross-roads of disaster and despair

Abstract

Behind ever successful enterprise lays a great little idea. These ideas are not limited to the male gender alone. Yet females with bright ideas for business-start-up often get bogged down due to numerous constraints compared to their male counterpart. The paper looks at some inherent factors constraining the start-up of small business in a transitional polity in developing world, Africa in particular. These hindrances as it affects the female gender contribute seriously to the non-transformation of the continent from a backward into a service delivery society. It goes further to advance the idea that the starting blocks for small business start-up should be the same for both male and female. Most of the funding bodies or providing start-up financial inputs often does not take women seriously at the initial stages. Such perceptions have deep seated roots in the structure of society where preferences are directed to the male gender. Women tend to be more averse to risk than men but most privileges and financial assistance have often been given to male and not female children from birth. Such age-old traditions need structural changes. The society today operates on the calling of 'power to the people with equal opportunities for all.' This should be streamlined process also for business start-ups in Africa. The conclusion is that age-old taboos should change with the changing times of our society; and more women encouraged and supported to become entrepreneurs. Recommendations include setting up a one-stop shop information centre to provide the necessary and up-to-date information related to the business climate; erasing some of the exiting taboos that make women shy-away from becoming entrepreneurs among other drawbacks. Confidence building among women is imperative.

Keywords: Starts-up; female, cultural taboos, chauvinism, opportunities, challenges, information, finances; policies, confidence building

Introduction: The search for fair play and creating equal opportunities for all

Breaking down male chauvinism and aged-old traditional taboos is must if Africa is to transform itself from a backward into a quality service delivery society. The start-up of small businesses in Africa should be given a fair chance for all entrants to benefit and progress from the unstopping forces of globalisation offering lasting benefits to all. Opening up to female entrepreneurs is creating new partnership for prosperity, growth, job creation and sustainable quality livelihood. Most women entrepreneurs or would be entrepreneurs in Africa are placed behind in the business race. Former British Chancellor and later British Prime Minister in 2005 noted that if Britain could achieve the level of creating 150.000 more firms each year as the USA of female entrepreneurs, it would gain 750.00 more new businesses (www.every woman.co.uk; www.prowess.org.uk). There are no reasons why each African country cannot create more new businesses headed by women yearly when they already dominate the informal sector. Most of these activities do not need huge start-up capitals.

Given that in many African countries women make-up more 52% of a country's population, getting more women into the entrepreneurial bandwagon will create many jobs in a continent currently trailing behind in the development and human welfare nexus. For this to be effectuated would require a number policy measures and new political will to increase numerous incentives, social policy and training for women. There are still cultural and practical obstacles that prevent many women from taking the plunge. More women would establish businesses if it was not for fear of failure, according to Global Entrepreneurship Monitor.

In Africa where women constitute the brain behind the informal sector, the growth of small enterprises will surge when there is an enabling environment. Creating a level play ground or starting blocks is necessary to spur the female gender into private businesses. For now, the starting blocks for women and men in Africa are not the same, see Fig 1. There is need for crafting the same starting block for all citizens, to recognise and properly utilise the potentials of every citizen in the development process. The lack of finance is always a major drawback; and female house/family chores restraints women from becoming entrepreneurs. Certain outdated cultural taboos constitute serious impediments holding back the contribution of the female gender in transforming the process of development in African countries. It is also clear that men and women are often turned down by banks when applying for business funding.

Fig.1. Starting Blocks should be the same for men and women in business start-up

Starting blocks: Fewer women go into business for themselves because of a perceived lack of access to finance and fear of failure

Source: (Picture Getty) BETHEBOSS; METRO, Tuesday 9 May 2006, London, (www.metro.co.uk) p30

There is a perception held by many people especially women that they would not be treated as favourably. There is some truth in that. But the reality is that the banks and leading institutions are more focused on seeing a well-articulated business plan than sex structure before considering lending money. A good business plan is worth its weight in gold. Banks would like deal with people who have a clear idea of what they want and how they going to administer their business. Important also to know how much of their own money is being invested in their ideas. Building confidence and providing access to financial information so that women who have business idea will be encouraged to properly fund their company from the start is vital.

Undressing issues of inequalities restraining female gender participation as entrepreneurs Edstrom et al (2014:1; Hawkins et al

2013) asserts: "the shifting field of men and masculinities in development and how men's often conflicted engagements with the feminist project of redressing gender inequalities might be deepened and radicalised, through a deeper analysis of patriarchy and our relationship to it, by also linking it to other struggles for sexual and human rights, or social justice." There is a need to ensure gender justice, the realisation of women's right as human rights – and in improving the transformation of the continent are closely entwined, interdependent goals. Solving the issue of job creation through entrepreneurial elated activities involves challenging the current goal development which permits – and is driven by – inequality.

Women's vast contribution to development, and their key role as consumers and family careers, is still largely misunderstood and underestimated (Sweetman, 2012). Women need equal access to funding in start-up business. A lack of networking opportunities and skills is another obstacle to female success. Women who literate and can draw up 'business plans' for funding are often out of the workforce for periods of time to look after children or elderly relatives. They lose contact with colleagues and miss out on training opportunities. When they come to set up business, it means there is less support for them to call on. Spall (2014:12) notes that development programmes focusing on masculinities have often been criticised for focusing too much on seeking to change the attitudes and behaviour of men at the individual level, rather than seeking to change the broader structural basis of gender inequalities and power relations.

Some of these key symptoms are deeply rooted in the unsustainability of the Africa's development path based on primary exports of peasant agriculture (export of raw materials) failure to develop a broad-based and competitive manufacturing sector; lack of domestic and external investor confidence; poor governance among other inhibiting factors. The challenges are further compounded by new trends of global liberalisation and international centralisation. The political, economic and social elements of the current crisis are locked in a downward spiral of mutual cause and effect which in different ways impact negatively on the female gender. In spite of these drawback or shortcomings, women are fighting back gradually, but surely as can be seen in the rising proportion of women in economic related activities at top policy levels and at the grassroots as many are gradually emerging as entrepreneurs.

Calling for equal treatment (to state the least) and closing the gender gap between men and women in education, employment, entrepreneurship and other aspects of life would boost economic growth in many African countries. African governments can do a lot to advance gender equality and mainstreaming by introducing wide-ranging policy reforms and actions plans to relieve women from the scourges of household chores. The first strategic approach is that of drastic change in mindset. Society must move away from old established cultural taboos of the female place being restricted in the home and confined to child-bearing related activities. Second, change in mindset means critical thinking and positive critical thinking leads to empowerment. A critical factor in empowerment is building the human capacity so that those who have been denied the ability to making strategic life choices acquire such abilities.

Gone are those days when the girl-child was refused basic education; the belief was harboured that such training was only improving the welfare of the family into which she would be married. Many cases across the continent show that the girl-child cares more for the family than the boy-child. Therefore the girl-child should no longer be subjected to the whips and caprices of outdated beliefs and cultural taboos. The age-old custom of dowry should be regarded as *an appreciation* of the bride's parents for bringing her up, and not as payment for a bought commodity. Today, the payment of dowry has become commercialised and exploitative doing more harm than good. Is the girl sold as a slave? Every individual should be given the opportunity to exploit, expand and properly utilise his/her potentials for self-esteem and the progress of others. Some countries have made tremendous strides toward achieving gender parity, others have not. For Africa there is quite some distance to cover in gender parity like Sweden as depicted in Sweden's Balancing Act, see Fig.2.

Fig 2: Sweden's Balancing Act

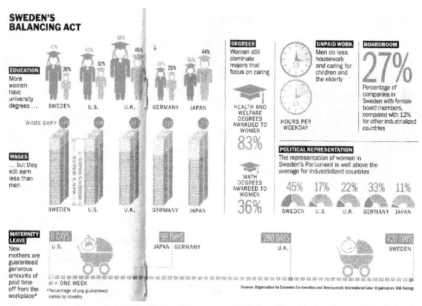

Source: Lisa Abend (2013) "Is It a Boy or a Girl? Sweden Embarks on Feminism's Next Frontier: Gender Neutrality", TIME, Vol. 182, No. 19, 2013, pp22-28

Some lessons can be drawn from the Scandinavian example, Sweden in particular.

Lisa Abenda (2013:24-28) posits that; "when in the early 1970s, the Swedish government began actively promoting women's rights, even feminists could hardly have imagined the successes to come; near parity in political representation, a near levelling of the playing field in the work place and fathers who share, if not equally then at least significantly, in the raising of their children. But if Sweden has gone further than almost any other country in the world to eradicate gender discrimination, it has not been content to rest on its laurels. In education, in the media, in sports and sex and shopping and even in its choice of pronouns, the Scandinavian nation is grappling in new ways with the boundaries that have traditionally defined the genders. Sweden has now reached a critical turning point, moving beyond mainstream feminist goals like equal pay and equal opportunity toward a society where gender doesn't matter."

No one is advocating a transfer of the Swedish model into Africa. All systems have their positive and negative sides. It is left for the continent to choose those aspects of Swedish drive for equality in the African context, blend or modify the positives for the development of Africa. For example, in terms of female representation in parliament, Rwanda tops the world. There are areas where we can empower the African women to contribute more positively to the transformation of the region. It is wrong as earlier noted to allow age-old and outdated cultural values preventing women from being equal partners in the development process. They have potentials like men. These potentials should be properly and adequately tapped into for the benefit of humanity.

The World Economic Forum Global Gender Gap Index, which measures discrepancies in 135 countries between men and women in pay, access to education and other factors, ranks Sweden fourth highest. In the 2010 national elections, women won 45% of the seats in Parliament (down from 47% in the previous elections), and currently 13 of the country's 24 ministers are women. Among women ages 15-64, 71.8% work outside the home, compared with 75% of men. On the whole, women earn 14% less than men, and when factors like education and profession are taken into account, make 94cents for every dollar that men do – which isn't perfect but compares favourably with 77cents average for American women.

Progress towards gender equality in Africa should be enshrined in law. For now the African woman has made tremendous progress ion fighting for gender equality. Thanks to the efforts of UN Women Conferences beginning with Mexico 1975, Copenhagen 1980; and especially Nairobi 1985 and Beijing 1990 backed by the gradual change in men's mindset in understanding and appreciating the role of women in nation-building. Across the continent traditional gender stereotypes are being upended in many ways. Many once male professions like medicine, law and journalism now have either equal numbers of box sexes or a slight female advantage. Many women are to be found in universities and secondary schools compared to before. For Africa to blurring the lines between the genders, it is perhaps the continent's approach to education that is most innovative (Mwamwenda & Lukhele-Olorunju (eds.) (201300: (Forje, 2016).

However, given the African traditional heritage, where male domination, taboos and other prejudices prevail very strongly, voices can be heard here and there against the notion of gender equality between the sexes. There are men who feel oppressed by the rapid push towards gender neutrality or equality in society; the tendency for this group is that society is turning against men, actively discriminating against them and undercutting what they see as their inherent right over women. For this group of thinkers, both men and women are trapped in their gender roles, and so must it remain. There is an apartheid attitude towards women. Nothing short of what blacks faced in apartheid South Africa.

Across the continent, women can be found in professions like the army, the police force, the warders, the fire-fighters, carpenters, engineers and name the rest. The one good thing in Cameroon is that women and men are paid equally in the public service but this does not mean that women are not discriminated against. The African woman still has a long distance to cover in terms of gender parity or equality. The position and place they hold today signify, of course, that significant grounds have been covered with much work to be done. It is clear that the majority of African men however, is on board with the ideal of closing the gender gap, and is prepared to see that current and future government policies in this domain are carried through.

Opportunities for women could alleviate inequalities and unleash the region's growth potential. For now numerous legal restrictions and customary taboos on women's economic activity remain (World Bank, 2015) which discourages women from saving in a formal institution and borrowing for business activities. These restrictions account for as much as 5 percentage points of the labour market participation gender gap in some countries of the region (Hallward-Drieneier and Hasan, 2013, Gonzales et al, 2015; Gonzales et al 2016).Despite some progress since the 1990s, eight countries in Sub-Saharan Africa still have 10 or more restrictions, including the need for her husband's consent before a woman can open a bank account or start a new job. Gender inequality and economic outcomes are intertwined, research shows☺ stronger growth advances gender

208

equality, and gender equality boosts growth (Duflo, 2012 and see Chart 1).

Chart 1: More Equality, Higher Growth

More equality, higher growth

High gender inequality appears to be hindering sub-Saharan Africa's growth, even after taking into account each country's level of development.

(United Nations Gender Inequality Index and GDP per capita growth not explained by level of development, 1990-2010)

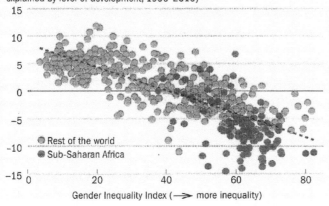

Gender Inequality Index (⟶ more inequality)

Sources: UNDP Human Development Report; World Bank, World Development Indicators; and IMF staff estimates.

Note: Countries showing growth above zero are growing faster than can be explained by their per capita income, and those that exhibit growth lower than zero are growing more slowly.

There are many reasons to believe that gender equality lifts growth, Closing world-wide gender gaps in education would give a tremendous boost to global human capital and reduce income inequality. Women tend to spend more of their household income on the education of their children and grandchildren than men do, so that closing the pay gap between men and women could translate to higher school enrolment for children, in turn leading to higher growth, And more women in the workforce means a larger pool of capable workers and entrepreneurs. According to the United Nations (UN) Gender Inequality Index, which measures inequality in the labour market, morality and fertility rates, education, and employment, many countries in Sub-Saharan Africa – notably Mali and Niger – stand out as having some of the world's highest gender inequality? Income inequality is also high in sub-Saharan Africa. In the past 15 years, rapid growth in the region has boosted per capital income, and poverty rates have fallen But wide income disparity across the population remains and has even increased in many countries, making incomes in the region the most unequal in the world after Latin America and the Caribbean (see Chart 2) – **High Income Inequality.**

Chart 2: High Income Inequality

Chart 2

High income inequality

Despite strong growth in sub-Saharan Africa, inequality has fallen little—and unevenly across countries.

(change in Gini coefficient, a measure of inequality)

Real GDP per capita growth, 1995-2011

Sources: World Bank, World Development Indicators database; and Solt (2014).
Note: Change is between 1995 (or next earliest available year) and 2011 (or latest available year). Data labels in the figure use International Organization for Standardization (ISO) country codes.

Greater income equality can encourage economic growth because it increases low-income household's ability to invest in education and physical capital. It can also reduce sociopolitical instability and poor governance, which discourage private investment (Barro, 2000). Opportunities for women have generally improved – but not enough. For example, male and female primary school enrolment has risen since the turn of the century, driven by the UN Millennium Development Goals (MDGs). But only 91 girls for every 100 boys are enrolled in primary or secondary schools, and only 73 women for every 100 men are at the postsecondary level. The reasons for these gaps range from lack of basic infrastructure, which means more time spent (mainly by females) on household related activities to high adolescent fertility rates and early marriage, which bind girls to household work at an early age. In Niger, for example, there are more than 200 births for each 1,000 girls ages 15 to 19, only 15 percent of girls are enrolled in secondary education.

In many African countries, women are behind in access to financial services, even though the percentage of the population with an account at a financial institution has increased immensely in recent years. Private financial banking services, like the Credit Unions and Express Union Banks are facilitating the opportunities for women to have access to credit loans and other financial services. The percentage has increased in recent years, but more so for men than for women. Indeed, gender inequality itself generates some income inequality. With more and more women entering the job markets (formal employment or in the informal sector) things are bound to change. The informal sector in Africa is on the rise across the African continent mostly dominated by women creating opportunities for economic growth.

Addressing the problems and exploiting opportunities

Getting the female gender on the plus side of the development continuum will open up opportunities for low-income households for women to alleviate inequalities and unleash the continent's growth potential. The inequality gap needs to be confronted holistically. The approach should not mean suppressing men and elevating women, but that of the sexes working in partnership for a common purpose – improving the quality of livelihood.

Better access to education for the female gender can in no small way address some of the problems of inequality. Women need to be empowered financially and education wise to be significant partners in the development process. Access to financial services will equally empower women to start-up small business. Legal instruments are imperative in this process as well. Policies and laws that are tilted to favour men's economic activities over women's activities need to be revisited. Some sub-Saharan African countries have taken measures to level the playing ground for women. In 1996, for instance, Namibia removed a number of legal barriers constraining women and female labour force participation rose by almost 8 percentage points in the decade that followed. Within the past three years, many sub-Saharan African countries have changed their laws to foster equality. For instance, Guinea's new labour code now includes a clause on nondiscrimination based on gender; Kenya the new law on matrimonial property gives both spouses equal rights to administer point property; and South Africa's law now mandates equal pay for work of equal value (Deieterich et al, 2016; World Bank 2015, Zeinullayev Tilek et al 2015). Building and improving on infrastructure like farm-to-market roads will aid women in the agriculture and informal sectors to transport their farm produces to urban centres. In line with this, making use of new technologies such as mobile banking can facilitate access to financial services in remote regions for women as well as help farmers to know current prices of products. The continent's inadequate infrastructure limits Africa's economic progress. Furthermore, reducing inefficiencies could substantially increase the economic dividends from public investment. Furthermore, improvements in infrastructure, better access to electricity and water, will affect growth both directly and by increasing the time girls and women have to participate in education and market activities. When girls spend half as much time fetching water their school attendance rises by 2.4 percent on average, with larger effects in rural areas (Nauges and Strand, 2013).

References

Abenda Lisa (2013). "Boys Won't Be Boys. Is Sweden's Push for Gender Neutrality a Noble Project or Political Correctness Gone Overboard?" The Time Magazine, Vol. 182. No. 19, 2013, pp24-28.

Barro J. Robert (2000). "Inequality and Growth in the Panel of Countries," Journal of Economic Growth, Vol. 5. No. 1, pp,5-32.

Dieterich Christine and Dalia Hakura (2015). "Inequality Gender Gaps and Economic Growth: Comparative Evidence for Sub-Sahara Africa," Chapter 3 of IMF's October 2015 Regional Economic Outlook: Sub-Saharan Africa, IMF Working paper, by Dalia Hakura, Mumtaz Hussain, Momique Newiak, Vimal Thakoor, and Fan Yang, Washington, USA.

Dieterich Christine Dalia Hakura, and Monique Newiak (2016). "In The Driver's Seat: Gender Equality Can Boost Growth in Sub-Saharan Africa", Finance and Development, June 2016, Vol. 53. No. 2, International Monetary Fund, Washington, USA, pp22-24.

Duflo, Esther (2012). "Women Empowerment and Economic Development," Journal of Economic Literature, Vol. 50, No. 4, pp1051-79.

Edstrom Jerker, Abhijit Das & Chris Dolan (2014) Introduction: Undressing Patriarchy and Masculinities to Re-politicise Gender". IDS Bulletin, Vol.45, No.1, January 2014, London, pp1-19.

Forje W. John (ed.) (2016). Gender Empowerment, Equality and Economic Development as African Solutions to African Problems. Lambert Academic Publishing, Germany.

Gonzales, Christian, Sonali Jain-Chandra, Kalpana Kochhar and Monique Newiak (2015). "Fair Play: More Equal Laws Boost Female Labour Force Participation," IMF Staff Discussion Note 15/02 Washington: International Monetary Fund, USA.

Hawkins, K: Kelbert , Pacheco, M. A; Edstrom, J; Nesbit-Ahmed, Z. (2013).Undressing Patriarchy: Redressing Inequalities, Report of An International Symposium, 9-12 September 2013, IDS, Brighton, UK.

Mwamwenda Tuntufye & Phindle Lukhele-Olorunju (eds.) The Triumph and Prosperity of Education in Africa. African Institute of South Africa, Pretoria, South Africa.

Nauges, Celine and Jon Strand (2013). "Water Hauling and Girls' School Attendance: Some New Evidence from Ghana," World Bank Policy Research Working Paper 6443 (Washington USA).

Spall John (2014). "(Money Has More Weight than The Man: Masculinities in the Marriages of Angola War Veterans", IDS Bulletin, Vol.45, No.1, January 2014, pp11-19.

Sweetman Caroline (2012). "Innovative Approaches to Gender And Food Security: Changing Attitudes, Changing Behaviours", Insights, Issue 82, January 2012, IDS, (Institute of Development Studies, University of Sussex, Brighton, Knowledge Service Publication Oxford, UK.

World Bank (2015). Women, Business and the Law 2016 – Getting to Equal. Washington, United States of America.

Zeinullayev Tilek et al (2015). |Catalyst for Change: Empowering Women and Tackling Income Inequality," IMF Staff Discussion Not 15/20, Washington International Monetary Fund.

Chapter Seven

Unleashing people's power: The promise of a new democratic revolution and evolution for Africa

Abstract

Historical events do not come with labels upon them, telling us precisely how important they are. Only the passage of time can do that, and it may take years. The sad but heroic act of the hawker in Tunis and the subsequent spell-over effect in early February 2011 unleashed the power of the people, creating a new political and governance dawn in the annals of Africa's democratisation and governance process. A new Africa in the making can no longer be stopped. The end of dictatorial, life serving presidency in Africa is over. The paper critically and objectively looks at the challenges and promise of a new democratisation process in Africa since the collapse of the global bipolar system: the intensification of the globalisation process which mobilises and enhances peoples' power to regain lost and rightful authority as the true custodians of power in society and the only force capable of dismantling entrenched centralised authoritarian regime structures under the canopy of President for Life Syndrome (PFLS). It argues that building strong institutions and political processes such as elections, strong and vibrant civil society, and not strong individuals remains critical in ensuring a sustainable democratisation and governance process for the continent. Strong institutions and not strong individuals provide the take-off for a continent that has stuck on the political/development runway for five decades. The African democratisation and governance architecture through the unleashing of "Peoples Power" should be seen as providing an opportunity to engage and develop appropriate capacity and responses to the continent's governance and development challenges. But the emergence of peoples' power should convert to constructing or perpetuating a state of anarchy. It should be for the liberation of the people from the bondage of centralised authoritarian regime structure characteristic of many African countries. The paper concludes that the principal governance challenge facing Africa is visionary servant leadership deficit and how to embrace a self-nourishing relationship between authority, accountability, participation, inclusion and responsibility. Sustaining the unleashed power of the people, acts as checks and balances, to the emerging geo-political-governance for a beleaguered continent stuck on the runway for too long. Unleashing people's power is the start of a new political

215

era. Change is coming to Africa. The people must embrace change and be conduit to the new transformation process.

Keywords: strong institutions, political process, inclusion, civil society, electoral process, change, justice.

Introduction: Understanding the political dynamics of change

The Arab Spring of 2011 unleashed an avalanche of chain events. A new continent was in the making. Significantly, the event brought to the forefront the consequences of the politics of neglect, exclusion, and articulate-self-interest. Above all, it accelerated the need for and process of institutional reforms in the governance structure of African countries. A new revolution and new continent was in the making through the dynamic forces and power of the people (Forje 2009). The take home message is clear – a new dynamic political evolution, "Flight 2011 Peoples Power" is on the runway ready for take-off to a new state construct on the continent.

When Presidents are brought into a Court of Law in a cage, or on stretchers, no condition can be deemed to be permanent. Importantly, no one is above the law. The state is the people. And the people as custodian of the state possess the final say in state construction. The "Arab Spring" or the fall of any regime should be seen within this context. Things fall apart; Achebe (1958) was categorical on the way things crumbling in the political construct of the continent.

When will constructive and encompassing change begin to take hold on the continent? The question is when will the African "summer or winter" begin? Regime change being is touted as not just about government, but also will systematic regime change take hold on the continent? For now good governance is touted as not just about government, but also about political parties, parliament, the judiciary, the media, and civil society. It is about how citizens, leaders and public institutions galvanised and relate to each other in order to make democratic change successful and sustainable (Ngwa in

216

Tanjong 2012 xiii) When will the "Arab Spring" or "calm before the storm" start its South of the Sahara descent?

The rise of peoples' power in search of a new holistic and inclusive governance system constitutes a new political development in Africa fifty years after independence. The continent descended into a 'bottomless pit' with centralised dictatorial regimes having a free playing ground. The 'Arab Spring' resurrected a new political jigsaw. Governance system and politics will never be the same again on the continent. Understanding the secret of democratic governance in Africa; unlocking the continent's future requires a proper understanding of the past, to better understand the present and gunning for a governance system of inclusion, shared-government, shared-obligations, responsibilities, and shared-prosperity in the construction of a sustainable future (Forje 2011:128).

A new renewal in the public sphere construed on the inalienable dictum and synergy of 'inclusion'; and 'popular participation through polycentric planning replacing the structurally-defective centralised governance arrangements since independence no longer could be stopped. The challenge now is to avert a resurgence of the strongman phenomenon. Above all, for Africans to understand and appreciate the long-term consequences and implications of NATO's assault on Africa North of the Sahara. Unleashing of peoples' power must have a vision and a focus geared towards (a) creating a capable and sustainable state: (b) sustainability in the living standards of the population: (c) protecting its independence and owning its development roadmap: (d) ensuring the rule of law, justice, equity in the distribution of the wealth of the nation: and (e) national unity, cohesion, constructive engagement of the various stakeholders among others.

The *"Arab Spring 2011"*, leading to NATO's destruction of Libya constitutes a challenge of global democracy. Above all, African solidarity and unity is put into serious questioning. While unleashing peoples' power for redressing the ills inflicted to society by centralised authoritarian regime structures is welcome: but unleashing peoples' only to permit foreign recolonalisation is absorbed and defeats the good intention that goes along with the ideal orientation of "power to the people and equal opportunities" for all in a new social construct. Unleashing peoples' power represents the final authoritative allocation of values for the common good, or else the purpose is defeated. Contrast the rapid mobilisation of forces by the UN and NATO towards Libya compared with the slow response by these bodies towards the plight of the suffering masses in Somalia or during the genocide in Rwanda. Few countries are coming to the aid of Kenya currently bearing the burden of refuges from Somalia. The international community has become a community of paradoxes. Articulate self-interest takes priority over collective interests. The West is not interested about the future of Libya but what it stands to gain from the conflict of destabilisation. No one supports a centralised authoritarian regime structure that defines the basic fundamental human rights and liberties of people. The double standards of the West are what are questionable. The hypocrisy of African unity is questionable at this stage. Is the agenda of African unity by 2017 still tenable (Forje 2011?).

Akinola (2011:1) is explicit on this point. His assessment is that centralised authoritarian governance system engendered orchestrated politics of exclusion, neglect and increasing deprivation in the continent. The public sphere dominated by the few elite with 'particularistic' concerns at the exclusion of the people, The trend of corruption among public officials clearly points in the failure of centralised governance arrangements underlines the inherent facts behind the "Arab Spring" and may be South of Sahara's "Hot Autumn" or whatever may occur.

African leaders for decades adopted a governance system of disconnect, contradictions, and dissonance between the political subcultures of the postcolonial (state) on the one hand and that of 'the people' on the other. A governance system of 'president for life (PFL) was established under the canopy of a monolithic party structure which rested on ethnic hegemonic forces. "Majority of citizens were pushed to live outside the post-colonial state, but also under the currents of the continuous struggle of groups within the state to redefine political spaces and identities in order to have a place and a voice in the public sphere, as well as, a share in the allocation of public resources" (Pul 2011:163-4). In short, inclusion and shared-prosperity were denied the vast majority of citizens. There is no trickle-down effect from top (or haves) to the bottom (have nots).

Apparently, democracy and state construction seems to have evolved on a wrong note in Africa. In addition, the question of visionary leadership remains a thorny sore in the transformation process of the continent. For now, Africa is littered with "served" and not "servant" leadership. In the face of existing mosaic of predatorialism there is need for responsible leadership and the implanting of a democratic and good governance culture in Africa, including the development of and appropriate utilisation of human capacity and natural resources.

Why the urge of maintaining the status-quo of holding on to power for too long in Africa? Why is it only Africa with stay-put presidents? Political sociology has an important contribution to make to the understanding of the inter-relations between political power and other institutions as the feature of the functioning of the political system. This is a very worrying aspect of the output functions of the governance structure in Africa. The political gurus and other analysts must begin the search for the right cure to the endemic cancer of 'sit-tight presidents' that has gripped the structure-functional dynamics of politics and governance on the continent.

Stay-Put Presidents in the World 2012

Country	Leader	Years in Office
Angola*	Eduardo des Santos	32
Burkina Faso*	Blasé Compaore	24
Cambodia	Hun Sen	26
Cameroon*	Paul Biya	30
Chad*	Idriss Derby	21
Ethiopia*	Meles Zenawi+	20
Equatorial Guinea*	Obiang Nguema	32
Gambia*	Yahya Jammeh	18
Kazakhstan	Nurusltan Nazarbayey	21
Iran	Ali Khamemi	30
Sudan*	Mar al-Bashir	22
Uganda*	Yoweri Museveni	26
Yemen	Ali Abdullah	33
Zimbabwe*	Robert Mugabe	32

Source; Forje [Forthcoming 2013] Complied from different sources including International database, US Census Bureau 2011; *Indicate African Countries; + Meles Zenawi died in August 2012 , *Yahya Jammah was defeated in a General elections in December 2016, and a new President Adama Barrow Sworn in February 2017

Africa is locked in the vicious cycle of poor governance which accelerates the state of underdevelopment. Since the 1990s, issues of 'Good Governance and Democratisation' have taken centre stage in the transformation process of the continent. Currently, the continent is submerged in witnessing the new onslaught of "people's power" to counter the action of 'hegemonic centralised authoritarian regime system'. Served leadership in Africa failed in responding appropriately to the needs and aspiration of the citizens. Popular participation (Adedeji 1997) was denied the people. The ruling regimes shied away for a people-centred developmental approach (Adedeji 2000).They went for a foreign dominated and control developmental approach that paid-off for the ruling elites and regime structure and foreign articulate self-interest. That is why Africa is stuck on the runway compared to the Asian Tigers.

The ongoing events in North Africa are indication of the uncompleted activities of the 1990s return to democratic governance and the imperative need for constructing a capable developmental state. The pending question is whether the 'Arab Spring' will generate new optimism, momentum and hope for change in Africa's fragile states within the contextual framework of "Good Governance" (Mkandawire 1995; Shivji 2006:338-220). The trajectory of post-colonial African democracy currently stuck within the realm of dictatorship and in light of the growing quest towards new forms of democratic governance has been subject to fundamental discourses calling for significant reconstruction and a new mindset. The analytical frameworks, three in number, are construed on exclusion, marginalisation and leadership. Poor leadership contributes to articulate self-interests paving the way for structured exclusion, exploitation, marginalisation and underdevelopment. The rule of law is shelved aside to ensure maximum exploitation of the people by a handful elite class.

Conceptual Premises

The conceptual framework and premises of departure, builds on 'problem-solving and problem-seeking,' in view of Pye's six crisis of development approach. As a result of inherent weakness in centralised-authoritarian structurally-defective governance system, people are provided with the vast opportunities to recapture their stolen inalienable rights or custodianship and as the focal-point of effecting constructive change as well as accelerating the process of development. As a result of the inability to resolve these crises of development, the continent is stuck on the runway unable to take-off to an industrial and eventually, a service delivery society.

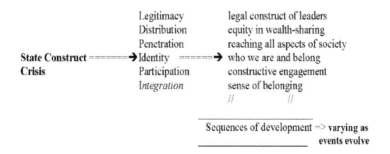

Holding citizens under a state of siege for a long-time, is bound to back-fire especially with the penetrating impact of the power of information and communication technologies (ICT's') in the era of a global village gaining more grounds and educating the people on their basic needs and fundamental rights. A form of disconnect exists between leadership and society which affects the orientation and realisation of a capable developmental state guaranteeing sustainable quality livelihood for its citizens. Sit-tight or Presidents for Life makes the government to lose its legitimacy. Fraudulent or dirty elections contributes to citizens' losing confidence and trust in the regime structure. Citizens' harbour and rightly so, the belief that their votes do not count: they are not participants in the transformation process.

Their sense of belonging and identity is seriously question and challenged. Apathy is ensued and frustration arise creating and injecting elements of destabilisation in the smooth functioning of the state machinery. When services delivery do not exist or pitched on ethnic lines, distribution and identity crisis begin showing its ugly face. The call for national unity goes unanswered. This equally reflects on the call for an African federation which goes on answered. No wonder many of Africa's secessionist movements are finding their way online to bring their plight to a wider audience. These secessionist groups arise due to government's inability in addressing the crisis of development in a most satisfactory way encompassing the best possible distribution, and inclusion indicators.

There are too many foreign interests with varied hidden agendas but with the common goal of destabilising the sustainable socioeconomic-political transformation of the continent. Two factors stand out clearly in the disconnect or destabilisation process.

- First, the ruling elite are disconnected from the realities of the society within the global context. The ruling class operates on the agenda of self-articulate interests which often is the interests of foreign bodies – part of the forces of neo-colonialism:
- Second these foreign bodies operate under a hidden agenda made to represent the interests of the ruling class. This problem of alienation tends to affect the mental picture, decisions-making ways of life and behaviour of these actors in their day-to-day operations. Politically, the public sphere is dominated by the few elites with 'particularistic' concerns at the exclusion of the silent majority of the people.

These alienating divisions between stakeholders in development (the elite and the people) are legacies of colonialism which were adopted by successive post-colonial African governments. As expected, most economic and political decisions in the continent do not reflect the aspirations of the people simply because government operations are excessively centralised and not people-focused. Without the citizens playing active roles in decision-making, governance process would continue to exclude and marginalised them" (Akinola 2011:3). It is equally important to guard against the 'blame theory' fifty years after independence. Rather the blame theory runs the risk of being a boomerang to the continent. Africa was ahead or at par with some Asian Tiger countries fifty years ago. Where is Africa compared to the Asian Tiger region today?

How objective is western media presenting the true image of Africa's struggle for sovereignty and independence? Has Africa felt encouraged from the Western media coverage? Developing a positive mindset is one of the most powerful life strategies there is to achieving anything. Therefore, if the aim of unleashing peoples power is to bring about constructive and inclusive restructuralisation or meaningful change, which is the mindset of the people, positive affirmation and coverage by Western media, would help develop a powerful and positive attitude to the quality of the living standards of the now oppressed majority. With such power and mindset we can turn failure around into success.

It is no secret that Africa has long been deprived of affirmation from the Western media: it would not be much to ask if we request that the continent be given proper and correct coverage for a change; expose those leaders bleeding their countries to death and are in the good books of the West for the inherent silent destruction of the continent. Africans are now tired of the protection and support given by the West to African dictatorial regimes that have no interest in their citizens but theirs and foreign articulate self-interests in mind. The 'blame theory' cannot be rejected in this case. Western developmental approach towards the African people is biased, but positive towards African leaders who are stooges of the West. Any African leader vocal and positive towards the development of the people is toppled within a twinkle of a second. On the other hand, Africans themselves must learn to distinguish between the leaders working for the collective good, not for the good of the West. The constant negative reports on the continent break the spirit and undermine people's ability to make positive change or attract goodness into their life. On the other hand, these negative reports should be a determinant factor for the people to unleash their power and take full control, own their development and show the world the real side of the African continent.

The state construct model advanced by (Edigheji 2010; Mkandawire 1995; Akinola 2011) in various ways streamline the missing links between African governments and African realities in the process of state construction. The missing dimensions in the development process of the continent being the people. Applying the

International Analysis and Development (IAD) framework, the paper situates and discusses the recent structural changes in Africa North of the Sahara and eventual fundamental changes likely to occur in other parts of the continent. Mainstreaming models of state building assumes establishing state legitimacy and avoiding state collapse through international intervention combined with military presence, huge amounts of aid, and democratic elections. The events in North Africa calls for a serious rethinking of the foundations of state construct in Africa.

Developments in North Africa are part of the uncompleted political structural changes of the 1990s and state inability to deliver quality services to citizens. The peoples' revolt for change constitutes a paradigm shift, from maladjusted states to democratic service delivery states. The paper is grounded on three structural changes; namely: (a) new growth theory or capability expansion; (b) institutional approaches; and(c) capability theory. The credibility of many African leaders can be faulted on these interrelated approaches to transformation. Sharing the views of Akinola (2011), regardless of the system of government practised, the type of relationship that a state has with the people and their community institutions, to a large extent, determines the outcome of democratic process. In short, a country gets the type of government it deserves. But a country can equally work itself out of the predicaments created. Unleashing people's power is an attempt to redress the existing impasse between the state, government, leadership, civil society and the private sector.

The inability of many African states to consolidate democratic governance or even simply create some form of stable political order invites a range of questions: Such as the reasons for the chronic crisis of legitimacy and participation afflicting Africa states. The failure to develop a sense of collective identity, vision and goal as the way forward for the people to reclaim their dignity and livelihood in building a sustainable and viable c The failure of formal political institutions; widespread exclusion of substantive groups harbouring critical opinions about the existing governance system and the need to put in place of functional system addressing the press8ing needs of the people. Such questions require in analysis that goes beyond formal institutional evolution and perhaps delves into the more sustentative socio-cultural dimensions of African governance conundrum" (Bujra and Lando, 2011: xii).

African states in their present constellations are uncheckable with unfettered power and thus become predatory as well as destructive to the sustainable transformation of the country. Foreign aid, economic and technological dependence is institutionalised through the *"donor-sustainability dichotomy"* with increased poverty in spite of the vast natural resources potential of the continent. Wrong priorities, the misuse of funds, and dependence on foreign assistance leads to disconnects between the state and civil society. The "donor sustainability dichotomy" (DSD) must be adequately addressed. Dependence on 'donors' for development restrains any form of sustainability, increases dependency and vulnerability, of the state as it exposes it to external exploitation and manipulation. Chaos, discontent, loss of trust and confidence in the government prevails, leading to a structurally-defective pattern of governance. The continent must get rid of the "donor dependency" attitude to cultivating a "sustainability – development" attitude. The present "donor-sustainability" dichotomy is destroying the continent. Dependency on donor is not healthy for the socio-economic transformation of the continent. Africa should move away from the 'donor' mentality to greater reliance on mobilising and proper utilisation of domestic resources. Dependency on indigenous effort is a sustainable development approach which must be encouraged.

North "Africa's Spring" unleashing of peoples' power and its eventual spill-over on the continent should be localised and contextualised within the following factor areas characterising the continent's governance style.

Wrong priorities, wrong development strategies, wrong approaches;

Political party patronage, clientelism, winner-takes-all attitude, ethnic affiliation, personality cult-worship and greed etc.

Poor Governance
═══════➔ Failure of civil society acting as custodians of the state, people's power, and rights:

Prevalence of centralised, authoritarian, ethnic regime structures,

Failure of governments in meeting the basic needs of the people;

Interferences from external bodies condoned by governing elites for articulate self-interests;

                //   //   //

Discontent, exclusion, alienation, fear, mistrust, and social injustice manifesting in various sectors of society and seriously impacting on the health of the state thereby jeopardising its legitimacy, sovereignty, independence, functionality and existence

        //   //   //

Failed States; Collapsed States; Under-developed Economies; Exploitation

The people of Africa deserve better than what their leaders have crafted for them. Unleashing their powers should be a constructive and sustainable developmental approach and not for destructive purposes. The "black man's burden" should be converted into the "black man's pride, governance and development." It means rethinking Kwame Nkrumah (1965) in its true perspective like rethinking Karl Marx to better understand Adam Smith's 'Wealth of the Nation', and the degree of rising frustration of the people. Karl Marx writes: Modern bourgeois society, with its relation of production, of exchange and of property, a society that has conjured up such gigantic means of production and of exchange, is like the sorcerer who has no longer able to control the powers of neither world that he has called up by his spells" While the ruling elites may rejoice in their current victory, they have cast a black spell they cannot recall – "The Arab Spring" may be just the beginning. The forces behind unleashing the power of the people should equally draw valuable lessons from Myrdal's (1957:99) assertion: *"Underdeveloped countries should not accept the inherited Western economic theory uncritically but remould it to fit their own problems and interests"* If Africa has a dearth of good leadership is it God's design? The truth remains, if we want to clean things up, we need to be clean ourselves. The absence of many local services, government must reflect its development priorities and provide meaningful strategic answers to the plight of the people. To be candid is it *government of, by and for the people* or **government against the people.**

Is there an emerging African lion?

These and other related inadequacies ties with serious development challenges facing the continent as well as the inadequacies of these response over the years – the leadership problem and positive citizenry responses to good leadership. What were the responses to the brilliant ideological ideals of "Nyerere's Ujamma? How did Africans react to Nkrumah's stand on a Union Government for Africa? This is the continent's greatest deficit. Is there something within the African environment that is so unique as to make the development challenge especially intimidating? Is the environment too 'hard' or 'harsh' to permit the occurrence of anything positive for the sustainable development and transformation of the continent? Is the "Arab Spring" the type of activities promoting a mindset that is antagonistic or favourably disposed to change – the type of change that uplifted the Asian Tigers from poverty to affluence, and from authoritarian rule to increasingly open government. It equally challenges the reader to ponder over the relationship between the prevailing chid-rearing practices, on the one hand, and the emergence of visionary leadership (as against follower-sycophant) personality type or personality cult worship, on the other (Balogun 2011.see also Bjura and Buthelezi 2002).

Constructive structural changes in mindset, behaviour, attitude and style of work are imperative for the emergence of an African Elephant, Lion or Leopard. For now, the very opposite of these virtues are at work It was hoped the collapse of the East-West conflict will drive a new sense of direction into the minds and behaviour of the people of the continent to constructively engage themselves towards a new beginning in a long walk to genuine independence and sovereignty. Two decades after it is still the old sing-song. Things not only continue "falling apart", but it remains a 'long walk to freedom'. The harsh reality is the very opposite of rising standards of living and new freedoms for the African poor. There are severe, potentially catastrophic economic inequities between the

North and South. The G-7 powers have very largely ignored these, but they have not conveniently gone away, rather they have become steadily worse. With such widening gap why should the oppressed not revolt – The Arab Spring for example. Following Erskine Childers, the statistics show,

- for example in 1960 the richest one-fifth of the world's population enjoyed 30 times the income of the poorest fifth;
- by 1989 the richest fifth was receiving 50 times the income of the poorest:
- the ratio of 20:80 or worse, dominates our world today:
- as the 1990s opened, the 20 per cent Northern minority of humankind had 82.7 percent of world gross national product: 81.2 per cent of world trade. Had 94:6 per cent of all commercial lending: 80.6 per cent of all domestic savings: 80.5 per cent of all domestic investment: and 94 per cent of all research and development:
- the 60 per cent majority of humanity in the South get the 20 per cent (or les) scraps from the tables of the affluent:
- in the South, some 1.2 billion people now live in absolute poverty, on the very margins of survival itself:
- more are driven into this condition every day, 40 per cent more in the last 20 years: they include over 560 million rural women whose numbers in such misery are running faster than men, with 75 million women the sole heads of rural households containing over 500 million children and older people.
- over 15 million of the rural poor die each year from starvation and disease aggravated by malnutrition;
- not less than 24000 children still die wholly unnecessarily every day:
- an African woman has a 1 in 14 chance of dying in childbirth, and in large parts of Asia a scarcely better chance:
- here in the North a woman has only 2:1 in 4000 chance:
- in many Northern countries only 2:1 in 7000 chance of dying while giving birth:
- new pandemic health threats like AIDS made 20000 children orphans in 1992 in Uganda alone, while mosquitoes breeding their own immunity against pesticides have made malaria present again in over 100 countries infecting over 260 million people, especially in

Africa (Childers Erskine 2011:19: UNDP Human Development Report 1992:) show the state of gross inequality between the two worlds.

On almost every indicator of social and ecological life – from health protection, literacy development, pipe born water supply, and future vocations for the youths to maintenance of biodiversity and the planet's security of air, water, soil and climate – the restructuring of societies for corporate globalisation has been increasingly life-destructive. Africa is most vulnerable in this setting. The road is indeed long and winding, requiring perseverance, patience and many other virtues to cope with the setbacks and disappointments without capitulating or resignation. Importantly, is bridging the deepening North-South divide. Both North and South must undergoing comprehensive structural reforms (CSR) to achieve equality among nations and peoples, small and big. Such a move will sealed the jigsaw puzzle causing conflicts, wars and instability within the global system. There is need to holistically tackle the system's weaknesses – poor governance, inequality and uneven development enhancing the divide between nations and peoples of the world.

Given such a structural setting, how can an African elephant, lion, leopard emerge? There is no disease without a cure. The plants, roots, are there and provide the hidden answer to the problems. We need just a determined will to search for the cure. We lack that determined will and mind for research and solution seeking. Our solution search is dependence on "handouts" which further subjects us to greater dependency and exploitation. The cult of dependency and exploitation is built on the endless repetition of "free-market mantras (liberalisation, privatisation and encouraged foreign trade and transnational corporation) combined with attacks on the cult's enemies – protectionism, government interference, capital controls, in short centralised authoritarian regime structures. Increase citizen participation by revamping, strengthening and deepening the governance system provides the way for constructive engagement leading to sustainable development.

The salience of the preceding sections raises the issue of a conflicting situation between unleashing people's power and centralised authoritarian regime structure in Africa. As earlier noted, failing to address the crisis of development subjects the people to the state of rising destructive frustration against the rise of collocation of personalities and circumstances whose behaviour cannot be logically explained or predicted with any degree of certainty. Apparently, the behaviour of such leadership is overcrowded with the vices of inherent powers of articulate self-interests. On the other hand, these actions depicts two things; (i) frustration with their leaders for failing to deliver the quality services needed; and (ii) their poor judgment in selecting their leaders. Based on these postulations, one can deduce the following hypothesis.

- Poor judgment on the part of citizens produces leadership selection that can be disastrous to society in the long-end;
- The relation between leadership and development arise from the realisation that the latter is most unlikely to happen unless the leadership selection, succession and development questions facing many African countries are fully resolved.
- External influences are a contributing factor to the continent's crisis of development.

The marriage between these three areas is simply, a country gets the type of government it deserves. External factors (the blame theory) at this stage some fifty years or more after independence does not hold in my opinion. It is a contributing factor depending on the angle of approach and space in time. Available evidence indicates that Africa's record in effecting smooth transfer of power has been largely dismal. Between 1960 and 2004, over half (51.5 percent) of the continent's heads of state lost their jobs in military coups, wars or invasions; with only 7.8 percent leaving office after electoral defeat, and another 12.2 percent opting for voluntary retirement. Military coups and one-party dictatorships have become an anachronism, but they continue to cast an ominous shadow on the leadership selection process in a number of African countries (Balogun, 2011:11).

Staying too long in office without proper service delivering and people's participation is a good recipe for chaos and violent system change. The top-bottom approach cannot satisfy the aspiration of the people: rather it alienates as it destroys a sense of national unity, cohesion and belonging. The two hypotheses merge into a blame theory based on the articulate self-interests of former colonial lords. Adopting this theory is an escapist approach to the problem. Because the citizens are unable to fashion a comprehensive and concerted inward looking approach for their well-being, room is created for external bodies to advance their articulate self-interests. Incidentally, local governing elites join the bandwagon of foreign articulate interests in bleeding their own society to death. In short, the ruling elites are stealing from the future, thereby impoverishing future generations. The governing elites have adopted what could be called 'appropriated carrying capacity" (ACC) which basically means the rich are living off the resources of the poor.

Analytically, the people demonstrate poor judgment in the selection of their leaders. The leaders when selected or elected respond inadequately to the demands of society. When basic needs are not provided people respond in a violent destructive frustrated manner. Incorporating the second hypothesis, Africa lacks visionary transformational leadership to inspire motivation, facing existing challenges from a holistic perspective and in the ultimate interest of the people. The relation between leadership and development arise from the realisation that the latter is most unlikely to happen unless the leadership selection, succession and development questions facing many African countries are fully resolved.

Leadership hinges on personalities, and, by implication, on accidents of history. It will take a long time for the continent to have visionary leadership style like that rendered by Nelson Mandela, Kwame Nkrumah, and Julius Nyerere (3Ns) as persons capable of transforming environments and influencing the course of history or at the very least, guaranteeing political order in rapidly changing societies and circumstances. These three African personalities exhibited what may be termed visionary political-will hypothesis which holds that the viability of the environment and of existing institutional arrangements depends on the protective cover provided by the incumbents.

Visionary servant leadership is a necessary but insufficient condition for the transformation of social systems. It must incorporate constructive engagement with the people as an inherent part and the beneficiary of change. Citizens must be ideologically and psychologically educated on their roles and missions for constructive change. The failure to harness and integrate leadership talents from different sources accounts for the lack of progress on various fronts in Africa. Corruption is one big challenge that remains impregnable due to the prevailing assumption that all it takes is 'leadership' or 'political commitment' (Forje 2003).

Leadership is not sufficient. The leader as a "general" needs strong support from the 'foot soldiers'. The marriage between a "visionary servant leadership" and "proactive positive responsive citizenry" constitutes the anvil for the emergence of a capable developmental state. Africa has to learn from the experiences of the East Asian Tigers – Singapore, Hong Kong, South Korea, Taiwan, Malaysia, Indonesia and Thailand within a generation transformed their economies significantly contributing to improving the quality of livelihood of the citizens. Some of these countries were apart or below the economic status of some African countries in the 1960s. In the eyes of the developed countries, East Asian states were dirt-poor and contemptible.

By the 1990s the dirt-poor countries had exhibited phenomenal growth rates that bypassed those of the developed economies. With this, they gained their respectability and sustained their sovereignty. These countries are the envy the world over. Africa remains an eye sore in spite of its vast natural resources potentials. But natural resources require added value through human capital development, which Africa has failed to develop. Adam Smith (1776) is explicit on the correlation between natural resources and human capital development.

The Asian Tigers transformed themselves from a "third" into a "first" world status within a couple of decades. The government and people of Libya failed to learn from the Japanese and South Korean development approach. With the vast revenues flowing from oil, human capital development was not given a priority. Dependency on external workers only helped in fuelling animosity against the government. The crisis of penetration was not properly handled and resolved. The two salient input factors driving these countries were "visionary leadership" and "responsible responsive citizenry" accelerating their sprint into economic supremacy, namely:-

Building the ethos of discipline, hard work, and alertness into leadership and management selection and development programmes

Pursuing a state-led, and export-oriented growth strategy, rather than wait until "market forces determined when and how fast import substitutes would be produced;

Remaining focused on internally charted courses and being constantly alert, to, nay, prickly towards, external interference or distractions;

Useful tips from the Asian Tigers to ==➜ African Countries	Developing a zero-tolerance for mediocrity, ineptitude, slackness, and slovenly behaviour;
	Bartering democratic participation for the benefits of economic growth, and imposing discipline in place of organisational laxity;
	Giving high priority importance to thrift and savings at the initial stage, to allow for 'conspicuous consumption' later
{Sources: collude from Balogun 2011}	

Of course, external input factors equally played an important role. But these external factors were aided by internal forces looking for a sell-out on thirty pieces of silver, internal discontent and other related developments. A vibrant country-centred civil society would have stood its ground against external invasion, placed articulate national or collective interests first.

Conclusion: Strategies and visions for the future – Hope or Despair?

Confronted with social and economic inequalities, the people have rediscovered their power, a possible solace to change existing state construct. In short, there is a move of existential realism than an ideological socialism. This move should be backed by clear doctrinaire orientation broadly conceptualised with a new economic, legal and political order where the country's resources are equitably distributed and aggregated for the all over development of the country/continent. Political as well as economic vision is sustained

233

by a corresponding education system currently lacking in Africa. The cloud of despair hangs over the continent. Despair can easily lead to rising destructive frustration.

The take home message for Africa is simple: Hard work and sustainability and not "donor inclined to sustainability". Short and simple, with the determination of the leaders and backed with the commitment of the citizens (leadership and popular participation or constructive engagement with civil society and the private sector) an anaemic economy can grow into a manufacturing powerhouse producing first class products for the world market like the Asian Tigers. Where is Africa today? She is still running around with a begging cap in hand. The "donor driven development" attitude cannot lead to sustainability and improved quality living standards for the population. There is an urgent need for strong institutions to help democracy to emerge and be consolidated on the continent.

A new mindset, behaviour and attitude are called for. The first step is to ask ourselves whether we want transformation, how, when and by whom? Facing the reality is to understand and appreciate the fact that only Africans can develop Africa. External assistance is only assistance not the real thing. The Asian Tigers did not sit with folded arms waiting for 'aid' to flow in from Europe. They took the bull by the horn. China did the same. Why can Africa? No other country can do that for another country. Articulate national self-interests play a key role. The new found power of the people should be directed in that direction. We should change 'the ideal or reality of false start' into a genuine reconstruction for the birth and growth of a new continent.

Is the "Arab Spring" the forerunner to the emergence of an 'indigenous sustainability development strategy' or what? A third African revolution becomes imperative. The first revolution triggered the independence of the continent. The second saw the failed attempt towards genuine return to democratisation as witnessed in Cameroon in the early 1990s, Rwanda 1994; Kenya 2007, Zimbabwe 2008, and Ivory Coast 2010 for example. "Democratisation instead of allowing African citizens to re-appropriate the apparatus of the State had if anything reinforced the most destructive tendencies of African polities. In particular, democratic reforms imposed from the West had precipitated a string of failed states. Despite the rapid spread of competitive 'multi-party' politics and various other state institutions designed to moderate power, the formal political structures of the state system are more than ever alienated from African citizens. Moreover the constraints on African government's formal powers of patronage imposed by economic liberalisation, have not starved clientelist networks embedded in the state" (Bujra op cit).

For now, the crisis of underdevelopment in Africa and globalisation in the world is a unique opportunity for addressing some core issues of democracy and human development. Like centralised authoritarian regime structure practised by many African countries, it has invigorated a worldwide peoples' movement whose loud demands for change are attracting more and more attention and support from grassroots movements. The "Arab Spring" for example, may lead to a true, "African reconstituted democratic governance system". A governance system structured to break the camel's back of endemic poverty, wanton corruption, inertia, exploitation, marginalization, poor governance nexus and underdevelopment.

The collective power of the people to shape the present and construct a better future is greater now than ever before, and the need to exercise it is more compelling. However, mobilising that power to make life in the 21st century and beyond more democratic, more secure and more sustainable is the foremost challenge of this generation. Fifty years ago as the wind of change blew across Africa; the continent was on the road to recover from the cataclysmic events of the 'Slave trade" and "colonial rule". African leaders were inspired by the vision that a united, independent free Africa back with its vast natural resources potentials will be empowered politically and economically to construct a new society with vast opportunities and promise for a better future to be handed down to the next generation. The challenges are far wide ranging today than yesterday if we take into consideration the serious an extraordinary population expansion. For example, Wambe (20128:74) notes: "In 1950, Africa represented only 9% of the world's population, with 230m out of 2.5bn people. In 2015, the figure had risen to 16%, with 1.2bn out of 7.3bn worldwide. In 2050, the estimates are that it will be 25% of the global population, with 2.4bn out of the world population of 9.5bn. In 2100, the figure will be 50% of the world population of 11bn. In terms of individual countries, Nigeria will have 700m people; Congo nearly 400m; Tanzania 300m; Ethiopia 250m; Uganda 200m; Egypt 200m and Kenya 160m according to the UN's worst-case scenario".

These "founding fathers" agreed in principles and set up an institution (Organisation of African Unity – OAU) to give effect to their vision. Over the past five decades, that good vision crumbled into centralised authoritarian regime structures denying basic needs to the vast majority of people. Today, the people have no choice but to regain their stolen freedom. Karl Marx notes: *"the redeeming feature of war is that it puts a nation to the test. As exposure to the atmosphere reduces all mummies to instant dissolution, so war passes extreme judgment on social system that have outlived their vitality."* Unleashing peoples' power puts the continent to test. Will the new power brokers make or mar the emerging political construct in a direction for the common good or will they go the same way like the disposed old guards? The continent is entrenched in a *"conflict situation"* with a most *dysfunctional governance* system which must be resolved amicably to the good of all. Some vital issues to be seriously addressed include:

➢ the uneven distribution of benefits:
➢ developing its human capital as added value to its natural resources:
➢ the current ambiguous role of the state:
➢ the North-South divide as well as internal rich-poor, male-female dichotomy:
➢ the place of Africa within the global construct:
➢ Africa articulating, aggregating and owning its developmental path;
➢ taking cognisance that the continent's interests are given top-most priorities:
➢ eradicating the destruction notion of ethnic diversity as a stumbling block to the development of the region; rather, ethnic diversity should be seen as added input value to the holistic transformation of Africa;
➢ arresting poverty and putting an end to endemic corruption;

The kleptocratic management of the African state suppresses the emergence of the African Lion, Leopard, Crocodile or Elephant; constraining any form of the emergence of an engine of growth or the take-off to a capable developmental state structure. Africa's development is held back by the *'dependency theory'*; the driven *'donor-development'* approach and the privatisation of the state approach adopted by the governing elites including even the means of coercion (Ake 1998). Choices for good governance and sustainability must be articulated by the people, each stakeholder taking its share of responsibility. Are the people well equipped to make the necessary choices and stand by it? Has the state created the requisite enabling environment for the people to operate and regained their stolen liberties and rights? It is expected of us all to create an optimum and comfortable environment to manage the most fragile and economically challenged landscapes created by the forces of the region's complicated historical past There are vast opportunities that come with a huge population, for example markets, labour force and its implication for cultural influence. Of course, the labour force has been endowed with the necessary skills that make them competitive in the world market space. We are currently exporting labour (skilled and unskilled) in the most dysfunctional way as our young cross the Sahara desert and other dangerous trends for greener pastures in Europe, other emerging economies and the Middle East.

Without which unleashing *"Peoples' Power"* will fail to achieve the envisioned goals. What a shame if the new uprising for a new state construct falls on the way side. Remember, policies represent the final authoritative allocation of values. Peoples' Power is a reality in today's national and global politics. At the national level, it sends a clear signal to "sit-tight presidents for life" to drastically readjust to the virtues of the basic tents of democracy. The new generation of leaders must gun for open and accountable government that ensures transparency, inclusion, and quality services delivery, rule of law, justice and constructive engagement of the various stake-holders. The six crisis of development must be holistically addressed. Democracy maps the pressing needs of good governance in a perilous age. Africa is entering this new age of "Here the People Rule" (Forje 2009) for the ultimate good of the country.

In the light of Africa's protean environment, one can but emphasise 'self-reliance' and a well-thought open development approach as the means of meeting the peoples demands while still meeting the challenge of the major contradiction, it is part of planet earth with vast natural resources but underdeveloped and the people poor in the midst of plenty. On the other hand: Europe belongs to Europeans. Europe exploited Africa for its development. Similarly Africa belongs to the African people and cannot change the excellent situation in which the African people win successive victories in the struggle for sovereignty, liberation, liberty and development. Unlike Europe, Africa is not exploiting any part of the world for its development take-off. We must understand the aspirations of the African people and the realities of Africans held captive for centuries by external forces. Any form of analysis must be firmly grounded in recognition of the depth of African nationalism, unity, integration and sensitivity to the historical forces of imperialism and racism. Africa is a large and complex continent that has its own dynamics, a feature most noticeable among the grassroots for liberty and freedom.

Unleashing people's power has to be seen as a process aimed at the fulfilment of an ideal, the creation of a democratic and egalitarian society. Unleashing peoples' power is an ongoing process like democracy as a means to end of authoritarian or bad governance. To this extent, it is a process that seeks to attain an ideal. Because of the massive power of the state that is predicated on inequalities and a strong will to protect privilege, actors engaged in unleashing peoples power is trapped in a very difficult situation. Popular aspirations demand of them great sacrifices whereas the state denies them opportunity to realise the ideal. We need to contextualise fundamental policies in respect of:

i. equality of opportunity and access to all training and reward system:

ii. equitable distribution of resources:

iii ownership of our development path

Democracy is beginning to emerge on the African continent. It is imperative for the people mobilise the fight spirit like in the days of the independence struggle and ensure the consolidation of the virtues of democratic governance throughout the continent. The Arab Spring beacons for constructive reckoning and comprehensive reform to re-rail the continent on the right track of governance. The need to unlock the leadership deficit in Africa is now but with an ideological agenda for constructing a capable developmental state. It is only through a progressive forward looking Afrocentric agenda adequately implemented that the huge problems on the path of economic transition from a backward to a service delivery society can be constructed. The exploding population dichotomy also provides other opportunities – a vast labour force and market – which of course, require that proper planning should begin now.

Recommendations

The paper strongly argues that *'unleashing people's power'* properly articulated and implanted rightly should promote a new era in the construct of African states to better promote:-

- the concept of oneness, belonging, unity and national cohesion:
- the building of democratic organs where the people shall participate not only in the administration, but also in the planning of their education human capital:
- the development of an alternative curriculum moulded to suit the socio-economic and political environment in which education takes place:
- the ethos and practice of the rule of law, social justice and equity in prosperity-sharing:
- democratic management of the factors in the life of human society and ensuring sustainability in the living standard of the people:
- people of the same planet, and should co-habit as such:
- democratically governed world community and proper management of international cooperation for the wellbeing of all.

References

Achebe Chinua (1958) Things Fall Apart. London.

Ake Claude (1998) "The Feasibility of Democracy in Africa", African Books Collection & CODESRIA, UK and Senegal.

Alexei Adebayo (1997) "Popular Participation, Democracy and Development: Is there a Dialectical Linkage?" in Adebayo Adedeji and Otter Oniga (1997) Nigeria Renewal and the Roots. Seed Books, London and New York in association with African Centre for Development and Strategic Studies (ACDESS), Ijebu-Ode, Nigeria, pp3-39.

Adedeji Adebayo (2008)"The Way Forward: Operationalising the Six Fundamental Principles of People-Centred Systems of Local Government", in Adedeji Adebayo and Samidele Ayo (eds.) (2000) People-Centred Democracy in Nigeria? The Search for Alternative Systems of Governance at the Grassroots. Heinemann Educational Books, Nigeria Plc, Ibadan, pp135-251.

Akinola, S. R. (2011) "Restructuring The Public Sphere for Democratic Governance and Development in Africa: The Polycentric Planning Approach", in Abdalla Bujra (ed) (2011) Political Culture Governance & the State in Africa. DMPF Nairobi – Kenya, pp1-61.

Balogun, M. J. (2011) A Framework for Leadership and Management Development in the African Public Service. CAMPS Secretariat/UNDP, Nairobi, Kenya.

Balogun, M.J. (2009) The Route to Power in Nigeria: A Dynamic Engagement Options for Current and Aspiring Leaders. Palgrave, New York.

Bujra Abdalla & Samuel Lando (2011) "Introduction", in Bujra Abdalla (ed.)2011 Political Culture Governance & The State in Africa. DMPF, Nairobi-Kenya.

Bujra Abdalla & Buthelezi Sipho (eds.) (2002) Leadership, Civil Society and Decentralisation in Africa. DMPF, Nairobi – Kenya.

Childers B. Erskine (2011) "In a Time Beyond Warnings – Strengthening the United Nations System" in Marjolijn Snippe, Vijay Melita and Henning Melber (eds.) (2011) Erskine Barton Childers – For a Democratic United Nations and the Rule of

Law. Development Dialogue No.56, June 2011, Dag Hammarskjöld Foundation, Uppsala – Sweden.

Edigheji Omano (ed.) (2010) Constructing a Democratic Developmental State in South Africa: Potentials and Challenges, Human Science Research Council Press, Cape Town, South Africa.

Forje W. John (Forthcoming: 2013) Architecture of Democracy, Governance and Development; Challenges, Prospects and Opportunities: A Strategy For Africa – Finding the Way Foreword.

Forje W. John (2011). Century of Change. Symposium on African Unity. Nova Science Publishers Inc., New York.

Forje W. John (2011) "Rethinking Political Culture, Governance and the state in Africa. Situating Cameroon Within the Context of Getting Systems Right – Governance and Capacity Building" in Abdalla Bujra (ed.) 2011. Political Culture Governance & the State in Africa, DMPF, Nairobi-Kenya, pp127-161.

Forje W. John (2003) Cameroon without Corruption. The Search for a New Vision, Niba Publishing House, Bamenda, Cameroon (New and enlarged edition forthcoming)

Marx Karl ( ) The Communist Manifesto.

Mkandawire, T. (1995) "Beyond Crisis's Towards Democratic Development States" 8th CODESRIA General Assembly, Dakar-Senegal, 26 June – 2July 1995.

Myrdal Gunnar (1957) Economic Theory and Underdeveloped Nations. Duckworth Publishers London.

Ngwa George (2012) "Foreword" in Tanjong Enoh (2012) Media Balance in Sub-Saharan Africa's Fragile Democracy. Analysis of Journalism Practice in Cameroon. Design House, Limbe – Cameroon.

Nkrumah Kwame (1965) Neo-Colonialism: The Last Stage of Imperialism. Heinemann, London.

Pul A. S. Hippolyt (2011) "Cropping and Aning to the Promised Land: Cultural Disconnects and the Challenges to Nationhood, Governance and Development in Africa", in Abdalla Bujra (ed.) (2011) Political Culture Governance & the State in Africa. DMPF, Nairobi-Kenya, pp163-202.

241

Shivji, G. Is (2006) "Pan-Africanism or Imperialism? Unity And Struggle towards a New Democratic Africa", African Sociological Review 10(1) pp208-220.

Smith Adam (1776) The Wealth of A Nation, London.

Wambe Onyekachi (2018). "Africa's Population Time-Bomb", New African, N0 581, March 2018, London. P74.

Chapter Eight

Moving towards an integrated public governance: Improving socioeconomic aspects of migration, integration, development and poverty alleviation. Experience from Africa in light of western xenophobic attitude

Abstract

During *the past decade the issue of migration, integration and xenophobic tendencies have taken centre stage in the mainstream thinking and practice of governments and international organisations to develop holistic public policies for the integration of immigrant population. Integration policies relates to all public policies implemented to cater for the welfare of immigrants once they find themselves in another country. Their presence in host countries put enormous pressure on quality services delivery (health, education, housing etc.) intercultural issues, diversity and participation in the local life of their new environment. Countries are obliged to articulate and implement comprehensive policies to ameliorate the plight of immigrants, integrate them in their new setting, and create harmony between immigrants and citizens of host countries. Since the coming into office, President Donald Trump has evoked a policy xenophobic attitude towards foreigners. Could this be a blessing or a curse for Africa? What would his presidency mean for the continent? Such a cacophony delights those harbouring xenophobic tendencies towards other groups they consider not belonging to their own race or country. Argument of the paper is that power-sharing, inclusion, participation and social equity provides best options for addressing problems under contestation. It examines critical issues needing serious considerations and policy strategies in ensuring a Holistic Integrated Service Delivery (HISD) without reducing the quality of livelihood of the people. What roles city councils, civil society organisations, local, regional and national authorities play in response to the challenges and opportunities brought by migration. It is maintained that collaboration at all levels with the various stakeholders would accelerate the process of a Holistic Integrated Public Governance (HIPG) and (HISD) as well as helping to reduce programme fragmentation, promote seamless services and help to resolve difficult social problems, some of which include (i) the exercise of power; (ii) the erosion of powerbase and destruction of the socio-cultural values of the host countries (Kernaghen 2008; Gross*

(2007; Forje, 2013) and the erosion of the cultural value heritage of immigrants in their new setting. Sometimes governments and other stakeholders often fail to make the changes in power-sharing and resources allocation required for successful (5Cs) (Keast et al 2007). The management of migration is an important issue that has recently been placed at the top of policy agenda of many countries. The arrival of migrants into other countries highlights the different aspects to manage migration and to rethink the governance of states towards citizens as well as public policies relating to this crucial issue. For the most part, the focus on migration is Europe – Africans migrating to Europe; yet the phenomena is also within the African nexus, triggered by a number of interrelated factors including some countries becoming pools of attraction for one or the other reason. What these migrants encounter is not different from what is experienced in Europe or in other parts of the globe. So there is a common silver lining enhancing the notion of human beings as one creation in spite of differences in their colour of skin or diversity in new cultural settings which calls for a coordinated and collaborative policy approach to addressing the situation, and creating a harmonious peaceful society.

Premises of departure

In different socioeconomic context, discriminatory, racist and xenophobic reactions against migrants should be prevented through effective communication policies and social movements. The United Nations Sustainable Development Goals (SDGs) 2030, inter alia, SDG6 (Economic Growth and Decent Work) encompasses targets regarding the status of migrant workers; and SDG 16 – Peace, Justice and Strong Institutions) harps on human trafficking. AU Agenda 2063 – Aspiration 1 – Prosperous Africa Based on Inclusive Growth and Sustainable Development: Aspiration 3 – An African Good Governance Democracy, Respect for Human Rights, Justice and the Rule of Law, among other international and national conventions create structural basis for a holistic policy framework contributing to ensuring the sustainable welfare of citizens and orientation of leaving no one behind (Stuart, et al 2016) strengthening confidence-building and a common sense of people belonging to a society.

Migration is forced through the periscope of the politics of exclusion, having the feeling of non-belonging to society, non-existence of the rule of law, often **rusticated/provoked** by the practice of a poor governance system. The role of the media is crucial in constructing an informed society. People need credible information from the media that skilfully moderate debate and provoke meaningful dialogue contributing to transforming the African continent. The importance of free and independent media to inform the citizens of the world is crucial to the implementation and achievements of national, regional and international conventions. Ongoing tragedies, for example across the Mediterranean Sea, and the Saharan Desert, racist and xenophobic tendencies and conflicts in some countries streamline the need for 5Cs and the importance of developing emergency and solidarity mechanisms to handle these situations as it equally beacons government to ensure and practice a governance system that improves the quality livelihood of citizens to limit undue migration and stress in society. President Trump's policy attitude towards 'Muslims and others' send wrong signals to the idea of creating a harmonious world system.

Once the people develop and consolidate the feeling of belonging (i.e. participating and equity in benefit-sharing) the tendency for migrating is greatly reduced. For these reasons, the practice of good governance, adherence to the rule of law; participation, inclusion and benefit-sharing plays important roles in mainstreaming and enhancing the various positive aspects of migration, integration, development and poverty alleviation towards the quality livelihood of people. Policies have to be **holistic** with responsibilities and ethical challenges in tackling national and global migration and integration as well as building capacity to ensure smooth promotion of sustainable development and effective alleviation of poverty.

The Way Forward

Building better policy strategies requires placing the interest of people first; policies that leave no one behind and policies that depart from the premises of 5Cs among the various stakeholders. The conclusion of the paper focuses on the art of midwifing migration, poverty alleviation, integration and development calling for joint 5Cs, efforts of governments, international organisations, and civil society organisations working hands-in-gloves to resuscitate, redesign and reorganise policies that place the welfare of humans in the forefront of activities. Government should articulate policies, with the media injecting information about those policies to enrich the ideas and improve their implementation for the good of society. The problem cannot be solved by a single nation, regional communities or continent. It requires a universal effort by all the stakeholders enshrining policies that ensure the treatment of people as human beings regardless of whatever diversities that exist for the mother-in-labour to go through a successful delivery process and growth of the child.

Keywords: Public policy, integration, civil society organisations, coordination, collaboration, cooperation, governance, inclusion, governance, diversity and inclusion, media, migrants and indigenes

Introduction: The challenges faced by developing polities

Poverty, corruption, poor leadership and underdevelopment stand glaring as the continent's deficit. These factors trigger underdevelopment disintegration and migration of a large proportion, draining the continent of its vital human capital and natural resources. Poor services delivery becomes the order of the day. Quality livelihood cannot be improved. When a continent exports its human capital and natural resources it is bound to remain underdeveloped, exploited, marginalised forcing citizens searching for escape routes to what they see as greener pastures. In either ways, the migrants are faced with both a blessing and curse. Simply stated, the 'migration carnage' urging the international community to sit up to respecting the Fundament Human Rights Principles.

Contextualising in the right perspectives, something is clearly wrong with the leadership and governance nexus of the African society. Seen within this backdrop, the paper is predicated on the idea that a comprehensive public policy articulation on migration and integration departing from the premises putting *people first* can be sustained, hence the conceptual notion of *consensus, corporation, collaboration coordination and conciliation* (5Cs) even in countries facing daunting structural and cultural obstacles; poverty, inequality and deep ethnic, national or religious diversities can fan movements of people. Migration and mobility continue to attract much interest, but also growing concern According to the 2013 World Population Policies report, 'among 185 countries with available data in 2013, 80 per cent of government policies to lower rural to urban migration, an increase from 38 per cent in 1996' (United Nations 2013). This proportion is highest in low-and middle-income nations in Africa and Asia – the regions that are currently undergoing urban transitions.

Therefore, practical policy questions regarding international migration strike a deep chord in contemporary European politics that reverberates beyond the policy realm because they raise difficult theoretical questions about political identity; belonging to a polity, and membership in a state: Who are we? How do we draw the line between 'us' and 'them'? Can 'they' become 'us'? If so, how long does it take; what does it take? At first glance, these questions may seem relevant only to domestic politics and appear to have little to do with international politics. Living in a globalised world construct, migration within and without affects us all requiring comprehensive national and international administrative policies in addressing the problem because the nation-state and the political institutions associated with it developed many years ago with today's developed world being the net importer of people. Africa is losing both its human power and natural resources due to poor governance. This contributes to deepening the underdevelopment of the continent.

Conversely, these two continents (Africa and Asia) produce the highest number of immigrants to Europe; Regions confronted with serious socio-economic problems and poor quality services delivery. On the other hand migration into Europe equally contributes to shortages in the provision of adequate housing, basic infrastructure and services; also overcrowding and congestion as well as increasing exposure to environmental hazards. There is no doubt that a rapidly growing urban population and migration present serious challenges to national governments, international organisations and the global community if not properly handled. In this regard, African countries, civil societies and other relevant partners should engage in fundamental research on peace and security in Africa from different perspectives.

In doing so we should clearly distinguish between problems caused by colonialism to tear apart African societies, problems of governance, instability, poverty, corruption and the environment have been caused by African governments and people themselves, albeit sometimes with the encouragement of outsiders. This is necessary because Africa cannot build unity or secure peace, development and stability without paying due attention to *'bread and butter'* issues and to the challenge of globalisation. We must bear in mind that African unity and sustainable transformation and controversial destructive ideologies of hate and xenophobia are incompatible. To send into the ghetto intolerant ideological xenophobic ideals is to begin by improving the welfare of the African people, ensuring their security in all aspects of live. The people in return must equally adhere to the role of good citizenship and judiciously protect what they have.

Neither must we forget the historical patterns of aggressive fundamentalism established by exogenous forces in their penetrative engagements with Africa nor will the axis of evil that guided the Berlin Conference of 1884 partitioning the continent to suit the egoistic, oppressive and dominating of the West. As evident, the continent had been subjected to a sustained process of organised spoliation since she was systematically but aggressively contacted by the Western world in the 15th century. These forces, as flag-bearing representatives or advocates of elitist and exclusively bigoted groups, have enlisted the support of African foot-soldiers, servicemen and fifth columnists to forcefully impose on African civilisations overarching regimes whose worldviews reduced everything to a single monolithic logic. Such fundamentalist preoccupations have spawned elaborate but organised adventures responsible for far reaching spoliatory excesses committed on African peoples and resources, past and present. Whether the predatory projects were, in their respective temporal phases, the slave trade, imperialism, colonialism, or as is the case now, fundamentalist neo-liberal economic reforms, the fact is that they set in motion zero-sum processes of exclusive disenfranchisement on a broad scale (Timamy, 2007). The President of The United States and the leaders of Western countries are only following the strategies laid down by the architects of intolerant ideologies, organised spoliation and rationalised by a meretriciously-packed western view of global domination particularly of the African continent.

Attention is directed to conflict management as migration, intolerant ideologies, integration, poverty alleviation and development issues pose elements of conflicts: the role of strong political institutions and visionary leadership become apparent in providing endurable solutions. Two caveats feature here: first, emphasis on strong political institutions designed to help facilitate conflict management and contributing to mutual understanding; and second, a uniform institutional design is not prescribed, but strongly believing power-sharing and placing *people first* promoting Lijphart's (1984: 1999) *'consensus democracy' and the wave of powering-sharing democracy* as important elements for a harmonious national and world societal environment fit for human habitation. Although Africa won its independence many decades ago, what victory has she gained, and what has been our impact in this harsh and cruel world? There has been a gross failure in the process of nation-building contributing to state failure and with the different consequences it ushers on the livelihood of the people.

A heavy burden lies on the shoulders of Africans, for they are responsible for nothing less than the destiny of Africa, and its welfare. This obliges us all to chart a course of coherent action ensuring integrated and sustainable development of the region without leaving any one behind. The question arises; what kind of development for Africa? While only Africans have the answer to this critical question, the prospects for growth, development and peaceful co-existence in the global context, calls for a global framework, a grand design bearing the imprint of all nations working in harmony for the common good. Let us follow when history calls us away, as the flowers of tomorrow are the seeds of today, implying, placing *'people first'* remains the cardinal point of development and economic growth that is forceful and at the same time socially and environmentally sustainable.

This paper is not against the programmes of globalisation, privatisation, liberalisation, development and other reform measures that enhance sustainable transformation of Africa, improving the quality of livelihood of the people, but an analysis of the wisdom of African leaders embracing, sometimes reluctantly, the particular reforms that have been imposed on them to destabilised their countries. In short, agitating for a Renaissance Africa is a holistically call to approach things differently – placing Africa's interest first, and striving judicious to attain the set goals. Africa is only against meretriciously packaged devices that are systematically disempowering and systematically disenfranchising the people as human beings. The paper has to be seen with the context of a call on African countries to advance an economic theory of government and practice of good governance with the interest of the people as its top priority. That is per emphatically stresses that the prospects for Africa's economic renaissance and sustainable transformation lie at the altar of good governance and of systematic technologisation of the region making the best opportunity of *advantage of the later-comer advantage*. The battle now, is one structured within the premises for *fighting for inclusion, recognition and sovereignty* as well as making the best use of its natural and human resources. This equally compels African leaders and policy endeavours, economic planning should not be undertaken in isolation; on the contrary, deliberate mechanism must be catapulted to integrate science planning and technology planning into development planning as a whole. The urgent need for comprehensive Marshall Strategic Plan for Africa is strongly called for. (Forje, 1989; Forje &Yazini 2015:83-104).

Therefore, the adoption of a new development paradigm, enhancing accountability by public servants, protecting, safeguarding the rights and dignity of Africans, and need for morality and integrity in national and continental life is crucial. With such ideological orientation in mind and practice, Africans would be respected the world over. Failure in this line of thinking is what breeds the existing intolerant xenophobic attitude towards blacks and her descendants across the world. We can only build a strong renaissance base when the dignity of the African is greatly assured. Clearly, the issue of Renaissance African project does not need a 'top-down inter-state approach'; rather it badly needs the total mobilisation of grass-roots civil society forces to put pressure on both the individual states as well as the community itself. We need proactive policy strategies to deepening African integration, building mutual under-standing and peaceful coexistence among ourselves.

Today, if we wish to enter the era of dialogue of the 5Cs and to awaken to its possibilities, the dialogue nexus must first be keyed in and establish essentially among ourselves; and who can prepare us for it better than all the stakeholders (state, civil society, private sector, international community, policy-makers etc.) working in synergy with one another towards common objectives – quality services delivery and sustainable livelihood for all citizens. However, the absence of the 5Cs both at the national, regional, continental and international levels combined to frustrate concerted efforts towards articulating and implementing comprehensive policy strategies addressing issues of migration, integration, poverty alleviation and sustainable development.

In different socioeconomic context, discriminatory, racist and xenophobic reactions against migrants should be prevented through effective communication policies and social movements. *The United Nations Sustainable Development Goals (SDGs) 2030, inter alia, SDG6 (Economic Growth and Decent Work) encompasses targets regarding the status of migrant workers; and SDG 16 – Peace, Justice and Strong Institutions) harps on human trafficking. AU Agenda 2063 – Aspiration 1 – Prosperous Africa Based on Inclusive Growth and Sustainable Development: Aspiration 3 – An African Good Governance Democracy, Respect for Human Rights, Justice and the Rule of Law, among other international (*Geneva Conventions) and national conventions create structural basis for a holistic policy framework contributing to beaconing and ensuring the sustainable welfare of citizens and orientation of leaving no one behind (Stuart, et al 2016) strengthening confidence-building and a common sense of people belonging to a society. Here lies the essence of African Renaissance and within the framework of *'Ubuntu, Harambee, and Batho Pele'* as the pathway and guide revitalising and pushing forward Africa's developmental nexus. We have our developmental concepts. These are tools that are part of our cultural heritage which we should use to accelerate the transformation of the continent. We hate all that is part of us but embrace things foreign to us. It is time we grow-up and appreciate what we have and properly use it to improving our livelihood.

Addressing the underlying problems call for close collaboration and co-production of a holistic public administration at the national, regional, continental and global levels. As policymakers and social providers, they are at the forefront of managing the dynamics for inclusive growth and local development as well as providing quality services that continuously improves the welfare of citizens (Kobia, 2013). In this regard, Fig 1: reposition cardinal issues within the public services derailing the provision of quality services delivery to citizens, absence of which induces the movement of people within and between countries.

Fig 1: The Impact of Poor Leadership and Governance on Migration and Quality Services Delivery is the result of a number of interrelated factors impacting differently on citizens' welfare;

• Absence of transparency and accountability;	Absence of the rule of law;
• Absence of independent judiciary;	Absence of strong independent institutions;
• Weak constitutional reforms;	Policy inconsistency
• Poverty, growing insecurity;	Unemployment;
• Poor economic performance;	Corruption; Inertia
• Poor services delivery;	Poor infrastructure;
• Exclusion, non participation of citizens;	Conflicts

Poor Quality Livelihood

//

Migration, Disintegration; Destructive Frustration, and Underdevelopment

The movement of migrants from Africa to Europe will continue as long as the economic crisis and poor quality services delivery in the continent prevails. Curbing migration requires consolidated democratic governance, economic growth, job creation and employment among others. Socio-economic inequality fuels migration and curbing the fleeing citizens from South to the North requires joint policy articulation and implementation. The continent's population is getting younger and fleeing. On the other hand, today's reality is that migration has become a hot-button issue around the world, not least because of the recent surge in refugees, in the case of Africa, *'economic migrants'* risk their lives through dangerous terrains. Rising expectations has now converged into rising destructive frustration, and disappointment leading to serious and gross mistrust in government, loss of hope and confidence in individual psychics.

How can national and the international community ensure that the global economy continues to develop in a way that is socially inclusive, curbs unnecessary migration and promotes sustainable world development, and peaceful coexistence?

The rising expectation of independence or hyper-optimism dashed away because of the myriad of issues – such as the lack of good governance, services delivery and endemic corruption among others contributing to civil unrests and holding back efforts at sustainable development. The truth is the litany of Africa's woes is awful, painful and agonising. While the rest of the world is modernising, Africa remains a museum piece. The outcome of this coercive and alternative situation has seriously worsened prospects of development, heightened the real for migration, and promotes intolerant ideologies of xenophobia and hatred leading to yet more alienation, coercion, destruction and oppression (Forje, 2002:41-60).

African countries are stuck in a poverty and governance trap even though some remarkable economic and political progress have been made over the past decade, but not sufficient enough to ensure inclusive quality services delivery: such as core functions of government in the provision of social services, health care and education, the provision of infrastructure: such as roads, ports, power, the protection of individuals from crime and violence and creation of new jobs and employment opportunities. Both national and global economies have created fabulous wealth and extreme poverty – with the poorest of the poor facing the daily life-and-death challenges of insufficient nutrition, lack of health care, unsafe shelter, unemployment, lack of drinking water and sanitation (Sach 2015) to list but a few of essential basic needs. The large majority of Africans are disconnected from whatever is seen as economic growth in these countries. Several of Africa's resource-rich countries remain at the bottom of the international league-table for human development. Africa registers some of the world's largest inequalities in wealth and in wellbeing, as captured by indicators such as life expectancy, health care and education.

Migration: taking Rickety Boats to Europe Africa Renewal p.28, Special edition 2017

Migrants from Africa and elsewhere rescued from a smuggler's boat by an Italian naval ship in the Mediterranean. UNHCR/A. D'Amato

Source: Africa Renewal 2017: Migration: Taking Rickety To Europe, Special Edition, on Youth 2017, p28-29

So far, the benefits of economic growth have been skewed and disproportionately shared. A small group of less than 4% captures a large chunk of the income and wealth in the continent's rapidly changing tide of capitalist progress. In this landscape, *a nouveau ruche* has arisen, a transnational capitalist elite class who are the primary beneficiaries of Africa's economic growth. Many wonder if Africa is growing, why are some Africans desperate to escape to Europe by sea, at great risks to their lives. To add insult to injury, some see the Western media reports of these desperate migrants as containing an element of sarcasm. If Africa is growing, one would have thought that the incentive would have been for its people to stay at home and contribute to its transformation (Adejumobi, 2014: 46). This is not the case implying that growth is not sufficient, and services delivery is poor inducing people to move where they hope to get the basic life sustaining means. Many people, especially the disadvantaged are left behind. Other parameters improving the quality of livelihood of citizens should be taken into consideration.

Policy articulation should originate not only from the national; but global level as economic development depends heavily on international trade, cooperation or linkages among nations to ensure sustainable development. Such cohesive policies approach will promote a proper understanding of the world as a complex interaction of economic, social, environmental, and political systems that leads to a well-functioning society, one that delivers wellbeing for its citizens today and for future generations. The immigrants moving northwards remain a symbol of many failures requiring common policy solutions. The need for the pursuit of a strong, common but aggressive administrative policy supported by deeper regional integration underpinned by an African leadership providing clear visionary as well as total mobilisation of all sectors of society behind a common development approach remains imperative for constructing an inclusive African society.

The Green Card phenomenon

Therefore, addressing the fundamental issues of migration and inequality can be a 'win-win' situation both for the powerful and powerless in society. The present situation of Africans falling victims to slavery is the result of poor services delivery at home. The American Green Card is another form of slavery though this could and is a difference in offering Africans a means of improving their welfare denied them at home. The large number of Africans risking their lives across the Sahara Desert and Mediterranean seas to reach Europe in search of greener pastures is issues linked to bad governance back home. The coming into being of the New American Government under President Donald Trump brings into the fore the need for greater African unity, integrated development and proper utilisation of our resources – human and natural (Forje 2017). Whether they could be positive trend in the new administration towards Africa is an issue of wait and see.

Poor utilisation of human capital resources leads to serious drainage of potential human potential that can contribute to performance management and serviced delivery. Fig1: Emigration from Sub-Saharan Africa depicts a tip of the iceberg.

255

Fig 1 Emigration from Sub-Saharan Africa

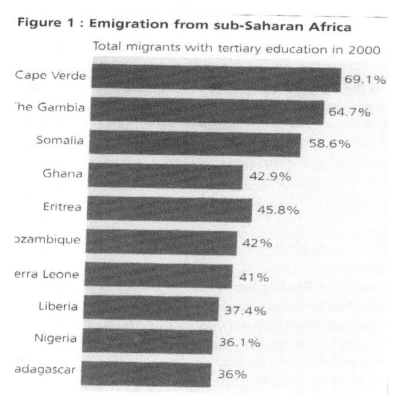

Figure 1 : Emigration from sub-Saharan Africa

Total migrants with tertiary education in 2000

Country	Percentage
Cape Verde	69.1%
The Gambia	64.7%
Somalia	58.6%
Ghana	42.9%
Eritrea	45.8%
Mozambique	42%
Sierra Leone	41%
Liberia	37.4%
Nigeria	36.1%
Madagascar	36%

ce: *Measuring the International Mobility of Skilled Workers (1990-
)), Policy Research Paper 3381, World Bank: Washington, Frédéric
juier and Abdeslam Marfouk, 2004*

The situation is even worse, calling for serious policy actions in the proper utilisation of human capital in the development process. Proper training and utilisation breeds proper public sector effectiveness. A critical challenge for performance management and higher education in Africa is reversing the brain drain even though the 'brain drain' can be 'brain gain' for the continent in the long-run. In many cases attracting these skilled human capital have failed, the trend is now moving towards using intellectual's migrants in host countries to strengthen teaching and research back home through graduate advising, joint research schemes, and creating networking skills and opportunities. For example, the South Africa Network of Skills Abroad aims to link highly-skilled South Africans living abroad and working in academic, cultural and commercial sectors.

Since the 1990s, increasing migration through political and economic in different countries place transit counties of the Maghreb by irregular migrants have intensified border patrolling of the Straits of Gibraltar and host European countries under serious strain as well as contributing to xenophobic attitude. Migrants cross from more easterly places along the Mediterranean ports in Senegal and Mauritania (see Map 1 – Migration Routes from Sub-Saharan Africa to Europe).

Map 1: Migration routes from Sub-Saharan Africa to Europe

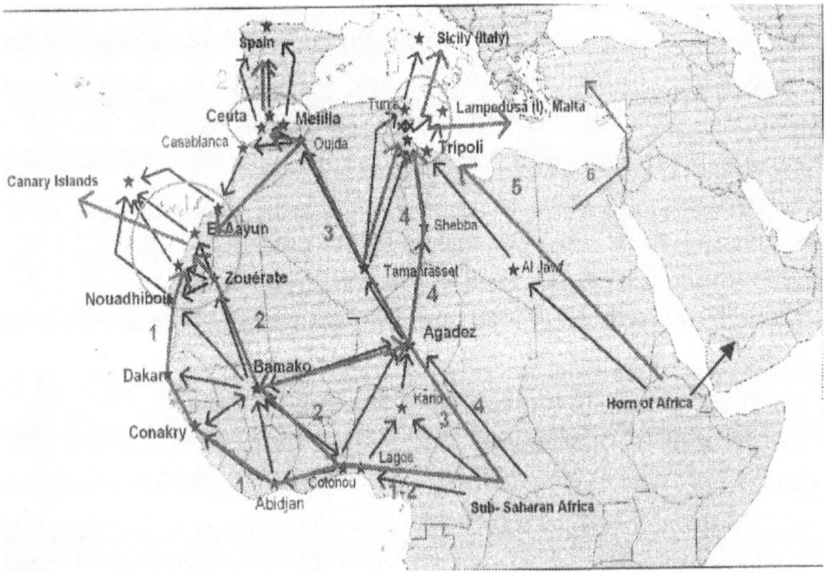

Source: Van D. Moppes (2006) The African Migration Movement: Routes to Europe. Working Papers, Migration and Development Series, Report No.5 Nijmegen: Radboud University.

Between January and September 2004, almost 4,000 irregular migrants were apprehended in Spanish territorial waters while seeking to enter the European Union (EU) territory (European Commission, 2005). This is a serious great loss of human resources – particularly of youths in the prime of their productive capacity, who waste their lives away in foreign land, struggling endlessly but unsuccessfully to enter European countries clandestinely. Some engage in illicit activities and fall prey to traffickers' rackets in their desperate search for survival. Many now languish in jails. The numbers simply keep increasing, attesting to the energy, perseverance and desperation of these migrants as well as intensify social conflicts, and xenophobic attitudes in the various European countries towards African foreigners. But perhaps the highest cost of irregular migration is the loss of life itself. Irregular immigrants face double jeopardy: they run the risks of dehydration during the long trek across the Sahara desert and of shipwreck during the sea crossing and many lose their lives (Adepoju2008:22-23; Boubakri 2004).

These trends of development raise the issue of African Renaissance and Unity within and beyond the African continent. President Trump like all other American governments fail to understand that the *'green card'* phenomenon helps in building the human capital of the United States, keeping it ahead of other nations in terms of development and world domination. Most of the Noble Prize Laureates topped by America are foreigners who have acquired United States citizenship. Africa like other parts of the world exports its human capital for the sustainable development of the United States though there is *win-win* for the entire world through the knowledge contributed to the transformation of the universe. In spite of the hatred against the 'Black' population, lies the tendency of encouraging African immigrants to the United States. By 2015, there were 2.1 million African immigrants living in the United States. (See Fig 2: New African Immigrants to the USA since 1970).

Following Dovi (2017:29-29) There are different reasons why people migrate, but sometimes it's like jumping without a parachute. You have no other choice. Poverty and lack of opportunities force African youths to risk all in search of jobs abroad. Countries topping the migration traffic list include Nigeria, Gambia, Ivory Coast, Guinea, Mali, Senegal and, to a lesser extent, Ghana, in that order. Still, some of these African migrants manage to reach Europe by the Mediterranean on life rafts or overloaded boats, paying USA$3.000 to USA$5,000 per person per trip. Many others die trying. In 2015 alone some 171,000 migrants arrived in Italy from North Africa, the highest number ever recorded, beating the 2014 record of 170,100 according to Italian authorities, The year 2016 broke another record – as the deadliest for those trying to reach Europe by sea. IOM's Missing Migrants Project recorded 5,085 migrants and refugee deaths in the Mediterranean, compared to 3,777 the previous year and 3,279 in 2014.

Fig. 2: New African Immigrants to the USA since 1970;

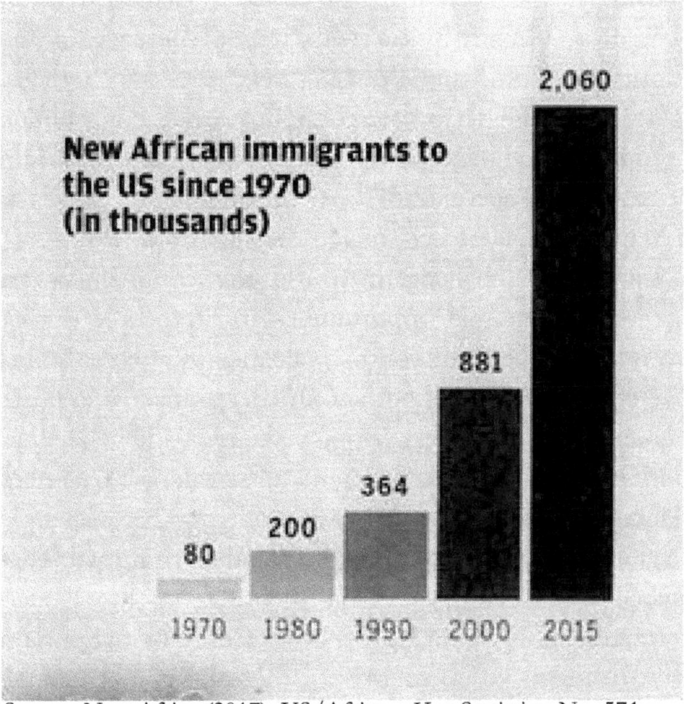

New African immigrants to
the US since 1970
(in thousands)

	1970	1980	1990	2000	2015
	80	200	364	881	2,060

Source: New Africa (2017). US/Africa – Key Statistics, No. 571, April 2017, London, p25

According to Galbraith 91979:109-110), migration, we have seen, is the oldest action against poverty. It selects those who most want help. It is good for the country to which they go; it helps to break the equilibrium of poverty in the country from which they come. What is the perversity in the human soul that causes people so to resist so obvious a good? The resistance has two sources – perhaps three. Social disturbance and conflict have usually followed mass movement from poor countries to the rich. The second arises from a classical error in economic calculation – on that economists have rightly sought to combat, with slight success, for nearly a century; and finally, there is resistance of a sort from the countries from which the people go. There is pride in the ambition to take care of one's own."

At the same time, the African Growth and Opportunity Act (AGOA) created 350.00 jobs for Africans on the continent. While in return, Africa has exported goods worth USA$697bn since 2000. The Number of USA embassies in Africa stands at 46 with the following countries having no USA embassies, Algeria, Central African Republic, Comoros, Guinea-Bissau with virtual presence in the following Libya, Sao Tome and Principe, Seychelles and Somalia. More than 600 US firms have invested in South Africa, contributing to an estimated 10% of GDP, and employ more than 1000,000 South Africans for example. The value of US Foreign Aid top Africa is depicted on Map 1 – Value of US Foreign Aid to Africa.

African leaders are challenged to use the continent's vast resources to create economic opportunities to lift people out of endemic poverty and to keep the youth, a valuable resource, at home. Migrants have come to believe that the only way to make it in life is to leave the country which is a very wrong perception and behaviour. Why the continent should be exporting its most valuable resources at this era. Here has been a sharp increase in the number of people on the move globally in pursuit of better lives and work abroad. That number reached 244 million by 2015, according to the United Nations; International Migration Report 2015. Contrary to common perceptions, Africans make up to 14% of the total number, or 34 million migrants in 2015. Africa is the major host for intra-regional migration. Kenya and South Africa, with their better-performing economies, b are major recipients of mixed migration-refugees and irregular and economic migrants – from other African countries, according to the Regional Mixed Migration Secretariat (RMMS), that supports agencies in the Horn of Africa and Yemen in managing and protecting migrants.

The only way to out-trump – *Trump's axis of evil xenophobic'* developmental strategic attitude towards Africa is to ensure that the continent develops the way it wants by bringing to the forefront a comprehensive integrated national development strategy linking it up with UN Sustainable Development Agenda (SDGs) and African Union Agenda 2063. Two things are essential in driving the transformation agenda constructively and holistically forward for the continent to gain its place in the new global-based knowledge economy: (i) building the human capital of the continent, as well as improving the health of the people: and (ii) developing the infrastructure of the region through a proper utilisation of its human and natural resources potentials. The reality is that if all the so-called illegals in the United States were suddenly to return home, the effect on the American economy would also be little less than disastrous. A large amount of useful, if often tedious work in New York and other northern cities would go unperformed. Fruits and vegetables in Florida, Texas, and California would go unharvested. Food prices would rise spectacularly and so on and forth. It is not only Americas that will suffer this fate. The European countries would have to face the brunt of dispatching away the immigrants. In short without these immigrants, the economy of Western Europe and the United States of America would suffer. The German economy would be in serious trouble without the Turks, Yugoslavs, and Italians.

Map 2: Value of US Foreign Aid to Africa

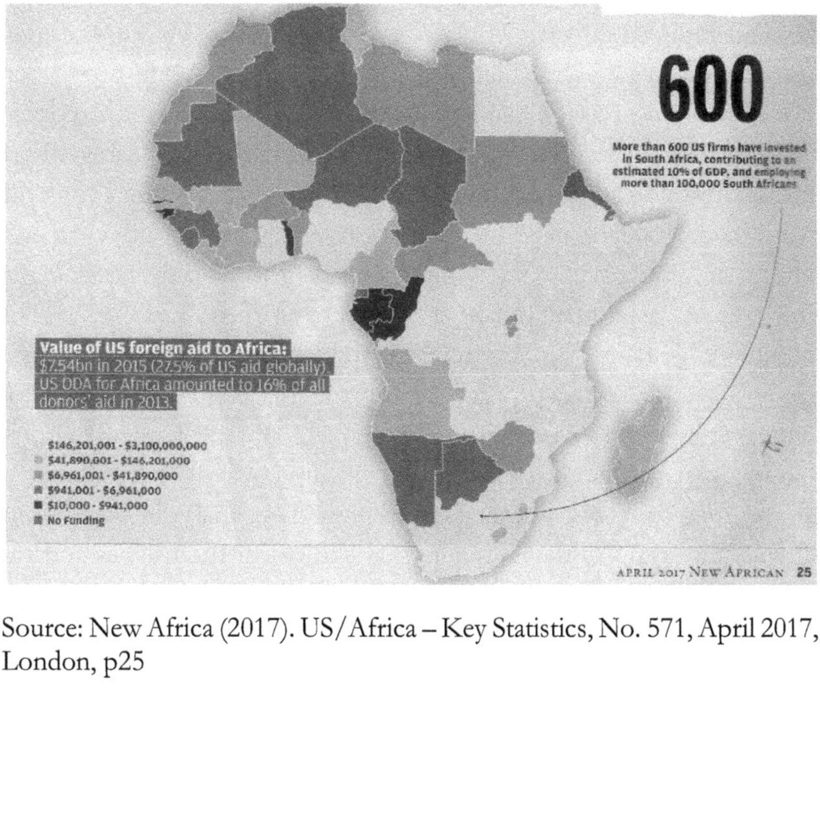

Source: New Africa (2017). US/Africa – Key Statistics, No. 571, April 2017, London, p25

Engaging in building the infrastructural base of the region through projects like energy (to drive the industrial engine); transportation (roads, railways, harbours, seaports, air transports etc., to facilitate the free movements of people and goods); telecommunication (connecting the continent with itself and the outside world) and other sources like the internet in building and enhancing human capital and knowledge, and strengthening trade links. These activities will create jobs, employment opportunities as well as contributing to improving the living standards of the people. Though immigration cannot be totally eliminated for this does augur well for world integration. It can be drastically reduced and made more humane to encourage world cohesion and mutual relationship. And for Africa to avoiding losing its human capital most essential for its transformation as well as benefiting from the globalisation nexus of our time. Any society at the threshold of development that exports its human capital and natural resources is doomed to perpetual underdevelopment, occupation and exploitation.

In many African states this point remains unacknowledged and appreciated and governments seek to accomplish vastly more than they have the capacity to implement successfully. More often than not they recruit foreign experts at very high costs instead of training and utilizing their own human capital. Particularly in states where administrative and technical capacity is low, the leadership should be wary of selecting a path of development that is too 'government-intensive'. Policymakers must make choices for the public sector and they must establish priorities for government activities. The continent is faced with a fundamental choice of that between a capitalist and socialist organization of the economy and tailor whatever choice so made to meet the needs of the people. A choice has to be made in choosing between shrimp cocktail or tomato soup as the first course at dinner people have died, many in vain, while attempting to make that fundamental choice for themselves and for others, including of course others not yet born.

Envisaged actions – Shaping Africa's future – Reversing the push factor

The energies contained in Africa's strengths must be potently released in targeted actions against isolation and deprivation, and poor quality livelihood. Africa's actions must be seen in the living standards of its population. No external advantages can supply the place of self-reliance. The force of one's own being, if it has any force, must come from within. That is why good leadership, governance and people involvement in mapping, constructing and owning their welfare is important. It provides the way for people to have faith, confidence and trust in their governments as well as consolidating their desire to remain home which belongs to them. The push factors (few economic opportunities in their own countries and hope for a better future' as the major drivers) attracting Africans abroad has to be reversed.

Remember that not only Africans are migrating. Looking back in history, a good case is Sweden. In the last century Sweden (then in union with Norway was one of the poorest countries in Europe. Some 90 percent of the people lived in the countryside – the characteristic equilibrium of poverty. After 1860, paralleling in the development of public education but aided also in the sixties by serious food shortages and hunger, accommodation was increasingly rejected. In the half century between 1861 and 1910, more than a million Swedes moved to the United States. This and the companion escape to local industry broke the equilibrium of poverty in the Swedish country. Rural Sweden, once so poor, became prosperous. In the ninety years after 1846, some 52 million people are estimated to have left Europe for other lands. In roughly the same period (1821-1832), 32 million can to the United States (Galbraith, 1979:101-102).

South Africa once the pride of Africa is fading. Former ECA Executive Secretary Prof. Carlos Lopes (2017:22-23) in situating the decline prowess of South Africa notes: "The G7/8 acknowledged the power of this influential player and so did other world groupings, including G20. South Africa was ever present in the international for a, where its contributions were taken seriously and it was easily recognized as the voice of Africa. South Africa's international clout did not come only because it was an economic powerhouse, but perhaps more because it was prepared to send peacekeepers, defend and advanced governance system and shape international debates without pulling its punches. But that was then – when South Africa stood tall not only in Africa but among the more advanced emerging nations. Sad to say, things have gradually gone downhill since the golden period."

Challenging developed countries xenophobia towards Africa calls for a new mindset among Africans and a new leadership style for the continent. Leadership that is not devoid of the people but one focused on putting first the interest and welfare of citizens' top on the development priority pyramid. First of all, Africa is changing in a rapid changing, hostile and complexed world. This requires a new kind of political and business leadership style to engrave the continent within the changing global environment. Second for Africa to make progress especially within the context of sustainable interferences between national development plans (NDPs), the UN (SDGs) Agenda 2030, and AU Agenda 2063. Third, development process should be *'bottom-up'* not *'top-bottom'* as ids the case to ensure that no one is left behind; and for the people to participant and owning their development trajectories. With good government, Africa can move mountains and build a new continent. Four, cracking the code by unlocking Africa's secret to wealth and development (natural resources). Here is where AU Agenda 2063, UN Agenda 2030 and NDPs have to be exploited to the best interest of the people.

Only by cracking the code of underdevelopment and unlocking the developmental potentials, and exploiting global opportunities can the region begin too seeing the light in the tunnel of underdevelopment and exploitation nexus. Five, poor action destroys the present and future of Africa giving ample room for the spread of xenophobic attitude. Speaking truth to the centres of power in Africa and the rest of the developed world is crucial for the re-emergence of the continent as a veritable player in the world. That is why Renaissance Africa and Unity of the continent needs to be reinforced by the Batho Pele concept of 'consultation, service, standards, access,

264

courtesy, information, openness and transparency, redress and value for money'; so that we can create a society were *we belong, we care and we serve*. These concepts should the powerful arsenals for fighting destructive ideologies. They should equally get Africa out of what has been known as *failures of development and the failures in the management'* of our human environment. Unfortunate, Africa has fallen victim of its neglect of its rich cultural values. Our callous neglect is our doing and underdevelopment, with intolerant xenophobic attitude vent on us as the result creating a threatened future for the continent.

Migration can be a bumper harvest when properly coordinated that brings greater dividends and happiness to all parties. Unfortunately, human greed pushed forward by sycophantic, individualistic and xenophobic attitudes prevents us from seeing the positive sides of immigration. There is push and pull factors propelling the desire to go from one place to another, internally and externally, within and between countries. No one can really state that one part is more important than the other. But likewise, all must be the developmental agenda of the developing polities and the conscience of the developed nations. As the two converge, it should be in the ultimate interest of propelling the welfare humankind; and the people to live a peaceful coexistence world construct without destroying the generations future of generations yet to come.

Shaping the future of Africa requires a new strategic approach to addressing the continents developmental challenges which should be prioritised and structured on placing the *'people first'*, leaving no one behind. No doubt some progress has been made since the wind of change took a tsunami crusade across the continent in the late 1950s and 1960s. But the progress so far achieved could have been most pronounced if only we had applied some of cultural values heritage such as the concepts of *'Batheo Pele, Harambee and Ubuntu'* in our development strategies. We did not and continue to rely heavy on alien concepts, though useful, not understood by the vast majority of citizens has not propelled the continent to the state of maturity. Apparently, the fact that on understood western concepts has kept the region at bay all this while requiring serious structural changes. Adopting best practices from other places is not bad. There is a bit.

Such best practices should be codified and integrated into the cultural values of its new environment. This has and continues triggering the fleeing of young Africans from the continent. The journey so far though with some substantive progress needs to be to rekindle and consolidated paying greater attention towards the envisaged areas listed here;

- building the human and institutional capacity most need for by the human capital and institutional capacity of the continent;
- strengthen, deepening and sustaining progressive political leadership and consolidating the achievements made so far;
- improving on the health status of the people(i.e. addressing the heavy burden of diseases; building a healthy society, for economic growth, eradicating endemic poverty as its sustainability requires a healthy citizenry) to be productive and competitive;
- strengthening the private sector and placing the youths and women on the plus side of the development continuum;
- learning from best practices from different parts of the continent and world at large;
- bringing women to the plus side of the development continuum as well as creating a greater participatory for the youths as future custodians of the progress of the continent;

Conclusion; What does the future hold?

The issue of immigration and xenophobic tendencies cannot be solved by a single nation. It requires national and international policy frame works in getting to the bottom of the issues that divide people and nations. Join efforts by the developed and developing countries are required to achieve meaningful and underlying structural changes in economic, cultural and social transformation. Without joint efforts the consolidation of one world different states would lead to chaotic ending. Trump or no Trump, the cancer of exclusion based on race, colour or creed needs to be adequately addressed. The underlying pressure of migration internal or external, and how it is played out in practice, remains the Achilles heel determining how viable in the long run is the world organised into nation states diverging ever further in income levels and standards of livelihood.

This is the hour to awaken the "Renaissance Spirit" and to activate our cultural values systems by deploy the concepts of (ubuntu, harambee, and batho pele) among others as the key to fighting xenophobic and other intolerant ideologies in driving forward a New African Order for Development (NAOD) as the first step towards wooing and winning the developed world into understanding, appreciating and utilising our value added concepts as tools for balanced development; and in creating a more humane world society. Is the West prepared to forego what they see as an inherent hegemonic attitude of superiority and domination? Or are we working in unionism furthering the common understanding and common spirit of responsibility so clearly needed in a divided world.

So far, much off the real energy of the continent, and its future, lies outside present government structures. What the people need is to cut themselves from donors and from corrupt government and nonfunctioning states. Two questions that can be asked: How do Africans stand their fragile, failed and corrupt governments, and how do they survive in these economies? Turn to the first question the answer is that they ignore their governments. And the reason they ignore government is the answer to the second question: they have their own economy. Variously called the *'informal sector'* or the *'parallel economy'*, it is the real engine of life. The people survive because the 'informal sector'. There are plenty of things to be undertaken by the state and people to build a strong and united country as the agony of the continent rolls-on.

Importantly as noted by Zeleza (1997:423), "If Africa's new democracies are to be sustainable they must be moulded from Africa's progressive historical and contemporary traditions (*and concepts like ubuntu, batho pele, harambee etc.*) those that rooted in the proliferation and richness of associated life" giving dignity and sovereignty to the people. African countries will be judged by the ability to deliver economic wellbeing to their citizens. We have to move away from those strongly advocating and practising Afro-pessimism to embracing an ideological oriented Afro-optimism of brighter days ahead. The continent's development should not be

267

construed within the salvation premises of benevolent recolonisation based on periodic charities of handouts and 'Band Aids' that ridicules the sovereignty and dignity of the people.

Fighting intolerant ideologies that promote unhealthy migration (what is happening at the Mediterranean Sea, Sahara Desert) and xenophobic ideologies presents the greatest challenges facing the transformation of the continent. It is important to note that the domestic environment is not necessarily independent of the international. Intervention from all quarters is necessary in dealing with the issue. Let us hope that as income disparities widen, globalisation forces proceeds, and the immigration, intolerant ideologies of hate and xenophobic tendencies mounts, and the fall-out forcing constructive and reasonably change in thinking the world over for a geographical scope of governmental responsibilities for balanced economic development and social welfare for all. Trump or no Trump, Africa must concentrate on consolidating the forces for African Renaissance and building the future she wants her own way. Hope and not despair should guide the continent as it moves forward in realising AU Agenda 2063, UN SDGs 2030 and in conjunction with proactive forward looking national development Agendas.

We cannot deny the reality that immigration has both the positive and negative sides. How can the countries the world over build on the positive sides to make the movement of people positive to all. What is important now is to sensitise the public at home and abroad on the role, and contributions of migrations to host and home countries. There are positive and negative sides of the coin. The negative sides of the movement have to be looked into in a holistic pattern so that the movements of people bring greater and positive dividends to society. Migration and development policies need to be properly synchronies to have a better chance of succeeding if the dynamics and underlying factors of migration, in both countries of origin and of destination were fully taken into account (Van Dalen & Esveldt 2003). Sub-Saharan Africa is facing daunting challenges in respect of increasing irregular migration, migrants' rights, human trafficking and the migration of skilled professionals. On the other hand, the challenges of migration are seriously aggravated by the ageing of population in the North and the spiralling growth of populations and hence of the labour force in Sub-Saharan Africa. The two need each other. To succeed they must articulate a holistic strategic policy approach to the benefit of both sides. Integrating populations and communities is essential as a prerequisite for building a healthy world environment.

The process of integrating immigrants into new communities, to take one timely example, often falters not because any technical capacity is lacking in the community, but because new arrivals are seen to be 'other' by those who are more established, and are treated as such. Successful integration, like many other areas, requires the ability to establish shared priorities and summon the collective will of a diverse and evolving community. Education is essential to the construction of a thriving nation. We need to educate the society to create a healthy community and to contribute to the common good. Unfortunately, what is ongoing in many African countries, a confuse rush for creating higher educational establishments for money making. Otherwise, how can we explain the establishments of these institutions with dilapidating infrastructures or non-existence of infrastructures? The rise of mushroom institutions of higher learning with poor and inadequate quality of teaching staff only makes a mockery of improving the standard of human development in the country. Development is limited if the human capital development nexus evolves on the wrong footing. That is why improved education and training remain critical. Education remains the key to accelerating the development process, ensuring equality in society and creating the solid anvil for quality livelihood for all.

A time for constructive and holistic action is now. The continent is blessed with vast opportunities to pursue the reforms much needed to ensure prosperity for decade's reigns over the continent. Government should make all necessary efforts to stimulate job creation, trade and investments. To be blunt, African governments should articulate and execute agendas for inclusive growth, equity in prosperity-sharing; short, medium and long-term action plans that offer practical solutions to pressing priorities that restore confidence of investors and hopes for citizens for a brighter today and tomorrow. The following levers are critical and must be keyed into all actions geared towards transformation: sound fiscal policy, financial inclusion, reform of the labour market and the education system, improved governance, strong business environment and the empowerment of women and other marginalized groups in society.

With such vision in mind, it will equally enable governments and other stakeholders to rethink their growth and development strategies as well as implement more equitable social contracts that enhance social cohesion and inclusion in society. The point is that inaction, or the politics of exclusion remains disastrous breeding economic stagnation, fuelling protracted conflicts and social tensions and divide, rising unemployment, intensifying migration and other social ills. This is the hour and moment to transverse from goals to action. Attaining SDGs, AU Agenda 2063 or NDP's will therefore not be sustainable without accelerating the pace of reforms, with democratic governance and economic inclusion as primary goals. Africa now finds itself in a unique opportunity to accelerate its development nexus from the right perspective. A sustained political will is most needed for economic transition to ensure an entrenched stable and prosperous African society. The people should be educated and informed that its cultural, ethnic and religious diversities should be regard as strength rather than a weakness. This remains the most added values to the continent's development.

References

Adejumobi Said (2014). "The Pain of Inequality in Africa", New African, No. 541, July 2014, IC Publication, London, pp46-47.

Adepoju Aderanti (2008) Migration in Sub-Saharan Africa. Current African Issues. The Nordic Africa Institute, Uppsala, Sweden.

African Union (2015) AU Agenda 2063: The Africa We Want, Special Third Edition, Addis Ababa, Ethiopia.

Boubakri, H. (2004): Transit Migration between Tunisia, Libya and Sub-Saharan Africa: Study Based on Greater Tunis." | Paper for Regional Conference on Migrants in Transit Countries: Sharing Responsibility for Management and Protection. Istanbul 30 September – 1 October.

Dovi Awo Efam (2017). "Youth And Migration – Migration: Taking Rickety Boats to Europe", Africa Renewal, Special Edition 2017 – Invest in Youth, United Nations, New York, pp28-29.

European Commission (2005). Visit to Ceuta and Melilla – Mission Report Technical Mission to Morocco on Illegal Immigration (7-11 October 2005), MEMO/05/380. Brussels.

Forje W. John (ed.) (2017) Withering or Constructing African Unity; Lambert Academic Publishers, Germany.

Forje W. John (2013) Emerging Perspectives on Capacity Building and Quality Public Services Delivery in Africa, Lambert Academic Publishing, Germany.

Forje W. John (1989) Science and Technology in Africa. Vol. 10. Longman Guide to World Science and Technology, Longman Group UK Limited, Harlow, Essex.

Forje W. John (2002). |"The Disappointment of Independence|", in Future Research Quarterly, Fall 2002, Vol. 18, No. 13, World Future Society, Maryland, USA, pp41-60.

Forje John &Yazini April (2015). "Rethinking Africa's Development through Science and Technology: A Partnership Opportunity for South Africa and China", in Funeka Yazini April & Garth Shelton (eds.) (2013) Perspectives on South Africa-China Relations. Africa Institute of South Africa / Human Science Research Council, South Africa. Chapter Six, pp83-104.

Galbraith Kenneth John (1979). The Nature of Mass Poverty. Penguin Books Ltd, Harmondsworth, Middlesex, England, United Kingdom.

Gross, Sue (2007) "How Far Have We Travelled Towards a Collaborative State?" in Niamh Gallagher and Simon Parker (eds.) (2007). The Collaborative State. How Working Together can Transform Public Service, pp38-47, Demos.

Keast R, Brown K, and Mandell, M.P. (2007) Getting the Right Mix: Unpacking Integration Meanings and Strategies", International Public Management Journal, 10(1) 9-33.

Kobia Margaret (2013). "Towards Creating An Entrepreneurial Public Service As A Strategy for Realising National Vision" in Forje (ed.) (2013) Emerging Perspectives on Capacity Building

And Quality Public Services Delivery in Africa. Lambert Academic Publishing, Germany, pp107-120).

Kernaghan, Kenneth (2008). Integrated Service Delivery, Barriers and Benchmarks, Toronto: Institute for Citizen-Centred Service.

Lijphart Arend (1984). Democracies: Patterns of Majoritarian and Consensus Government in Twenty-one countries. Yale University Press, New Haven, USA.

----- (1999) Patterns of Democracies: Government Forms and Performances in 36 Countries, Yale University Press, New Haven.

Lopes Carlos (2017). "Where Is the Pot of Gold at the Rainbow's End?" New Africa, No. 572, May 2017, AN IC Publication, London.

Sach D, Jeffrey (2015) The Age of Sustainable Development, Columbia University Press, Columbia, United States of America.

Stuart Elizabeth et al (2016) Leaving No One Behind. A Critical Path for the First 1000 Days of the Sustainable Development Goals (SDGs), Overseas Development Institute, London, July 2016.

Timamy M. H. Khalil (2007). The Political Economy of Technological Underdevelopment in Africa. Renaissance Prospect, Global Tyranny, and Organised Spoliation. Concept publications (Press Division) Lagos, Nigeria.

United Nations (2013). World Population Policies 2013m Department of Economic and Social Affairs, New York.

United Nations (2015) Sustainable Development Goals Agenda 2030, New York.

Van Dalen, H. P. and Esveldt, I. (2003). "Migratie Out of Africa", Maandschrift Economie, 67(3):254-65.

Zeleza Tiyambe Paul (1997). Manufacturing African Studies and Crises, CODESRIA Book Series, Dakar, Senegal.

Acknowledgement

I would like to acknowledge with deep appreciation the authors, journals and books used in aiding the write-up of this paper. The inadequacies herein remain my responsibility.

Chapter Nine

Unlocking Africa's economic heart

Abstract

In spite of its resources potential, Africa remains the least developed continent on Planet Earth. The paper props into issues promoting or inhibiting the sustainable transformation of the region. It does so by critically unleashing fundamental issues delaying its transformation nexus. The geo-construct of these landlocked states calls for specially designed economic approach. To respond to a set of socio-political and economic developments on the continent for over 500 years of European colonialism influencing the pattern of governance of African countries and they continue to do so. .Colonialism established ruling hierarchies and entrenched forms of poor citizenship which were both blatant (as under apartheid) but also subtle (as in forms of Orientalism). Colonialism also produced ways of knowing and meaning-making which imposed particular forms of reasoning and, at the same time, marginalized or silenced alternative ways of understanding the world. Western colonialist domination imposed an artificial backwardness on African countries and her people. It caused both an abnormal stagnation of cultural development and even cultural retrogressions. The effects of these western-centred influences on developing nations have been a 'set of facts'. These 'facts' are widely employed as evidence that purportedly proves certain delusions – Africa is poor because it is poor to begin with. Therefore, the paper has two objectives, (i) to discredit and discard widely held delusions concerning the poverty of the continent, delusions widely spread among both European and African circles; and (ii) in place of those delusions, supply an applicable set of policies, a set of policies made comprehensively for practical realization of the sustainable transformation of Africa. It adopts a progressive Afrocentric approach rather than the Eurocentric development strategy that has dominated the economic transformation of the continent. Poor governance backed by poor leadership remains the underlying factors of the continents underdevelopment. A sea of confusion clouds the socioeconomic transformation of the continent. The focus of the paper is on African states in general and in particular landlocked states, leadership and resources use in the transformation of the continent so that the people benefit from their natural resources. It is clear that countries on the coast line are of advantage, the existence of poor leadership can equally be a curse to these countries. The cases of Nigeria and Cameroon illustrate a good example (Omotola 2006;

273

Forje 2011; Asonganyi 2015). Putting western influence in Africa to one side, how do we aid Africans in achieving the most rapid realization of the people's mental potentialities, for mastering the advanced technologies African industry and agriculture urgently require to improve on the welfare of the people?

Keywords: Landlocked states, development, leadership, failed states, human capital development, resources, skills

Introduction: Unleashing Potentials for Transformation

"A people without a positive history are like a vehicle without an engine. They always live in the shadows of a more successful society"

(Steve Biko)

Africa's 54 states are bedevilled with many potentials as well as obstacles related to the state of socio-economic transformation. Some are landlocked, with or without resources; delays and bureaucratic red tapes; some have built-in trading disadvantage such as high transport costs, poor governance and other obstacles inhibiting economic growth of these countries. Yet the underlying factor that sentences the continent to perpetual underdevelopment is bad governance and poor leadership. To this can also be added external factors that can be overcome through the practice of good governance, unity and the determined resilience of the people to improve on their wellbeing. The integration and unity of the people provides the requisite anvil of increasing economic prosperity and political stability in Africa. Yet, looking at the present situation of the continent, the question arises, "is this a realistic option? Is Africa not a continent in crisis, whose future will be characterized by economic instability, famine, political confusion, unrest and continuous ethnic or even regional wars?

Contextualising the African continent in genuine socio-economic transformation terms, we can do so from essentially two different analytical standpoints, namely; (Eurocentric which builds on the concept of *'Free Trade'* or *'Free Market Economy'* with the ground work

274

long laid by Adam Smith school of thought; and the other, Afro-centric, strongly grounded by Nkrumah and a host of others as the practical basis for the political and economic independence and sovereignty of the continent. Depending on which of these two different conceptual approaches one takes, one arrives at different conclusions as the present state and future prospects of the continent. The significance of this is best captured by an ambiguous illustration presented here (Fig 1: Looking into the African Crystal Ball).

What first attracts you looking at the picture is a vase; yet at the same glance the heads of two persons looking at each other. The primary cause for your alternating perception lies in your mental effort synthesising the various features of the picture into a definite gestalt. Once you have comprehended that your perception is a function of your mental activity, it is possible for you to shift, by a small mental effort, your point of view to the one or the other perception (Bandmann 1980:10). Having the right mindset, common and collective mentality efforts lead to conceptualising the right solutions to the socio-economic and political economic problems of the continent. For now, the continent seems to be condemned to the ghetto of poor quality livelihood. There is need for developing a 'grand design' for the integration and industrialization of Africa. What future awaits a continent when it exports both its raw natural resources and human capital? Poverty and underdevelopment will never disappear in Africa if this the kind of entrenched policy approach adopted by the leaders A comprehensive new structural adjustment has to put in place to reawaken the desire of building an Africa that response to the desires and needs of the citizen to better improve on their quality livelihood. We must into the crystal ball with a different pair of lenses and new mindset. Involvement of the people through a participatory approach is imperative. Therefore, it is time to put an end to the current top-bottom development approach by embracing and consolidating the bottom-up developmental approach.

Fig. 1 Looking into the African Crystal Ball

Source: Credit Bandmann Hans (1980). "Opening Address to the FEF Conference on the Industrialisation of Africa". In Fusion Energy Foundation (1980). The Industrialisation of Africa. Campaigner Publications, Wiesbaden, Germany.

Africa and the rest of the world are looking at each other in conceptualising the economic and political problems of the continent in such a way that we come to a conceptual starting point for considering the development of Africa. It is also within this context that *'landlocked African countries'* and *'coastal states'* are looking at each other to create the enabling environment and perspective of increasing free movements of persons and goods; to usher prosperity and political stability for the sustainable development of Africa. The vase is the crystal ball Africans must look into, sought out their differences/predicaments and articulate a common policy strategy and implementation action plan to advance a progressive Afro-centric developmental approach. Such a new plan of action should ensure a new approach to the education of citizens and building their capacity and workforce, a cultural renaissance or the technical aspects of articulating and implementing a forward-looking strategy for developing Africa.

Therefore the poor and rich, the urban and rural areas should be looking at each other with the goal of ensuring balanced development, equity in benefit-sharing as the right approach to the new economic perspective for Africa. What does the two different approaches – Eurocentric and Afro-centric concretely mean for the economic and political perspectives for Africa? The publication, Africa in the 1980s: A Continent in Crisis (Legum and Zartman, 1979) directly or indirectly show-case the Eurocentric and Afro-centric undercurrents reflecting some of issues addressed here. The economic crisis of the 1980s (Structural Adjustment Programmed– SAP) was a deliberate ploy that Africa is not worth the development and industrialization. This was a tacit comprise by the West that Africa should be left as ghetto to fight is battles. In short, constructed/comprehensive development should not see daylight in the region.

It was a French politician who remarked in the 1930s; *"there are no crises in Africa, they only serve as an excuse for those who do not want to leave the old track"* (Legum and Zartman, 1979). To take up the challenge of its underdevelopment, Africa must open up the interior and link with the coastal regions to facilitate its industrialisation nexus. Only by linking the coastal region with the interior that a new Africa can be discovered to face current challenges. Such a linkage and industrialisation will give it a new kind of riches and fertility as well as improved welfare. Africa will no longer be thrown into the ghetto. A successfully implemented grand Afro-centric design linkage and industrialisation under united coordinated policy concepts will change the face of the continent for the better. The need for an African New Order (ANO) can no longer be emphasised.

The paper stresses the fact that poor governance and served leadership in fragile states underscores the main problems limiting the sustainable transformation of the continent. Conversely, good governance and leadership offers a more realistic approach in transforming the continent and improving the welfare of citizens. It should also be noted that good governance (GG) and economic development (ED) are impended by weak public institutions because public institutions are weak (Rothstein & Teorell, 2008) in these countries dominated by an all-powerful served leaders. The continent is in urgent need of servant leaders out to serve the people and not to be served. Thus a servant leader is one who knows the way, goes the way, and shows the way Therefore, as captain (s)he looks for results not salutes. The paper shows that the necessary dimensions of an industrialization of Africa and the problems which result from that must be Afro-centric.

Only through an Afro-centric development agenda can Africa concretize what an economic policy approach based on the *'industrial system'* means for Africa, as opposed to the current Eurocentric approach dominating the discussions on 'development' strategies for Africa. The basic consideration is this: the basis of all economic consideration is the population in its development-dynamic. Development has to be people-oriented and focused on constantly improving on the welfare of citizens. Some seventy or more years ago, China was one of the poorest countries in the world, populated mostly by rural peasants, and still suffering from more than a century of internal turmoil and international humiliation, Today China is a rapidly modernising economic dynamo with growing global influence. Africa can with good governance and visionary leadership accomplish the same form of development (Nye 2010; Joseph (ed.) (2010). China for example has lifted people out of poverty than anywhere else in the world: its per capita income increased five-fold between 1990 and 2000, from USA$200 to USA$1,000. Between 2000 and 2010, per capita income also rose by the same rate, from USA$1,000 to USA$5,000, moving China into the ranks of middle-income countries. Between 1990 and 2005, China's progress accounted for more than three-quarters of global poverty reduction and is the reason why the world reached the UN Millennium Development Goals (MDGs) of halving extreme poverty. This incredible success was delivered by a combination of a rapidly growing labour market, driven by a protracted period of economic growth, and a series of government transfers such as the above urban subsidy, and the introduction of a rural pension (Stuart, 2015).

Looking at the crystal ball (Fig 1), the African situation depicts a sorrowful picture. For example the Goldman Sachs in a more up-to-date honest report on South Africa (one of Africa's economic giant) stated that 'South Africa is one of the most unequal societies in the world. By 2008, 85% of Africans were still in the impoverished or lower income categories, receiving less than R1,400 per month (USA$120) compared to 87% of whites who occupied the middle and upper income categories. Unemployment too has barely moved from the 23% inherited in 1994 to a post-Apartheid average of 24.5%. With 70% of the unemployed under 34, the young are disproportionately affected. Job and export-creating mining and manufacturing almost halved their share of GDP to 23% since 1986, while banking and real estate doubled to 24% (Commey 2015:48). Rapid population increase without corresponding economic growth and sustainable employment nexus impedes the transformation of the continent. The Chinese example should spur Africa to have an integrative and inclusive society, a productive and dynamic economy and sustainable welfare structure catering for all citizens. In short, only Africans can build up Africa.

The same picture can be painted of other African countries. How can a continent possessing most of the world's resources be the poorest and least-developed at the same time? This is because Africans have refused to own their resources. Above all, they seem to bath in the enchanted waters of their ignorance being their weakness. Thus there is a common virus spreading across the length and breadth of the continent that must be arrested. The *'ignorance virus'* must be eradicated without which progress cannot be made. So far, Africa remains the continent to explode, needing a little ignites to spark it and everything will go into flames. Ironically, the people spend long periods defining who Africans are which is time wasting for the people but of great benefit to the rich while the real issues – the dispossession of our poverty hangs over our heads remaining unresolved and undermining the sovereignty of the continent.

Therefore, African governments must reduce inequality, empower women, increase employment, especially amongst the youth and defend the gains made so far. The way forward is to improve and increase public sector productivity output, efficiency and effectiveness. The challenges the continent faces, are that of race, ethnicity, class, poor human capital development, skills disparities, entrepreneurship deficits, immigration problems, poverty, unemployment, wrong use of resources and the lack of access to capital play major roles in making the continent poor in the wakes of plenty. This remains a deadly cocktail and why the continent must search for a new crystal ball to unlock its development deficiency. Interesting enough, the continent has the resources – human and natural - and even capital to do what needs to be done, yet it is not acting in that vein. Why? It is clear that a high degree of dissatisfaction with the pace of economic growth and inequality in the benefit or prosperity-sharing persist encouraging a tense political temperature, contestation and finger-pointing that gives rise to competing centres of power and loggerheads in society. Finger pointing as noted by (Mashamaite 2014) only divide rather than unite society. Unity, confidence and trust among African states will rapidly address the plight of landlocked countries as well as accelerate its transformation from an underdeveloped to a developed society. Afro-centric agenda is the 'blue-print' necessary for changing the economic and political conditions for an industrialization of Africa. Unless the face of Africa is comprehensively changed, the people will have no quality livelihood.

The greatest pride a continent has is its independence, social cohesion and strong economic growth under the canopy of good governance and rule of law. In unlocking is development predicament it equally needs an entrepreneurial and skilled human capital base (Juma 2015; Muchie 2015). Unfortunately, Africans worship everything foreign. To paraphrase Djanie (2015), Africans love everything foreign. Their love and worship for anything foreign helps in destroying their ability to progress as it entrenches and deepens their dependency. As a result, they hang on the 'blame' theory for their failure. The result is that they waste time defining things that should no longer be defined in the interest and benefit of the West rather than forging ahead for the benefit of Africa. The real issue facing Africa is dispossession of Africans and the glorification of the West – thus the cause of the continent's poverty – which remains unresolved.

In a chaotic and confused development environment, (like what exist in the African polity-space, change can only come from within and through a new mindset and the determination to brave all odds. Africa is yet to arrive; the entire society to produce sustainable development and this entails moving away from exporting raw materials to establishing industries. In short embracing the Afro-centric rather than the Eurocentric agenda is what the continent needs. It is envisaged that a progressive Afro-centric agenda properly executed denotes what UN Secretary-General coins, *'2015 to be a year if transformation in leaving no one behind and ensuring lives of dignity for all."* The Afro-centric agenda should be to end poverty and hunger, put an end to isolation and to achieve sustainable development goals (SDGs) in all totality through promoting inclusive economic growth protecting the environment and promoting social inclusion.

Interesting enough, Africa's landlocked states possess the bulk of Africa's natural wealth. Thus unleashing their potentials (landlocked countries like empowering women and exploiting the prowess of youths) could transform Africa's socio-economic development. The continent has the resources but not the capacity to become and industrial entity. For now, the economy of African countries is diversified to a merely very slight degree. The extractive economic sectors still dominate, largely as a heritage from the colonial period, i.e. agriculture, forestry, fishing (to a slight degree), and mining. Agriculture often soaks up more than 70% of the total labour power of a country. Productivity in must economic sectors is extremely low; and therefore their contribution to the total economic net surplus is also low. This is primary due to insufficient human capital development, but especially due to lack of an efficient scientific and technological base (Fusion Energy Foundation 1980:84-5).

Not many African countries succeeded in attaining the Millennium Development Goals (MDGs) apart from Mauritius, Cape Verde, Rwanda, Botswana and Seychelles. The leaders are challenged to ensure the realisation of the call *'Africa's transformation'* and the main African Union (AU) Development Strategy, Agenda 2063. If they has ever been a time to fight for the continent's economic independence is now, which means stopping exporting hides and skins, coffee, tea, cocoa and even crude oil and other materials in their raw form. For now, the biggest challenge remains how to process these raw materials and how to transport their exports and imports most effectively and efficiently with minimum cost and how to connect with other African countries. We must infuse the process of development and connectedness and grow to replace all the left-over refuse we carry into the initial phases of the present great undertaking. This is the key to fostering the most rapid advancement of the continent and deploying the powers of scientific and technological to accelerate Africa's economic development and quality livelihood for all.

The current economic model (Eurocentric agenda) which excludes value addition, is exploitation of the highest order and we cannot continue that way" (Kabukuru 2015). For Africa's transformation to be truly realized and millions lifted out of poverty a new push is needed to reach seven percent economic growth which requires developing and maintaining new infrastructures. That is why it is extremely important to unlock the continent's economic heart for sustainable development goals. Getting into the depth of the interior, creating access for free movements of people and goods and processing its natural resources remain vital for Africa's development.

Methodological and conceptual approach

The paper builds on secondary data, participant observation and discussions with a wide cross section of the population. To this is added the political, economical, social, technological, environmental and legal (PESTEL) and the SWOT analysis (strength, weaknesses, opportunities and threats) are used to determine the positive and negative potentials relevant for the continent in its transformation process indicating as well as some factors influenced by internal and external conditions.

Fig 2: PESTEL and SWOT Analysis

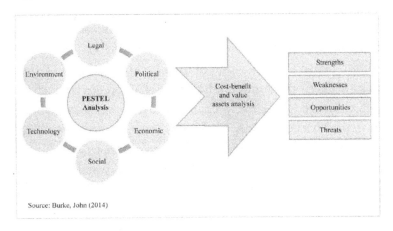

Source: Burke, John (2014)

This is illustrated on Fig 2: PESTEL and Fig. 4: SWOT Analysis Map respectively (see Sofaniadi 2015:18). The interrelationship or combination between PESTEL and SWOT, cost-benefit and socio-economic analyses illustrates the sustainable livelihoods framework which shapes the socio-economic analysis of African countries. The sustainable livelihoods framework demonstrates that vulnerability to poor resources use, poor infrastructural and institutional networks, bad governance and articulate served leadership among others will of course impact on the status of a society.

Institutional structures, processes and rule of law are necessary to improve on the value of livelihood – human, natural, financial, physical and social. These assets are vital livelihood drivers for improving quality of welfare for all. Good governance, servant leadership style are catalyst to sustainable development. The path to Africa's economic development and technological progress provides the indispensable environment in which to foster consciousness of scientific and technological transformation of the continent. Building the human capital of the people is developing the creative potentials of the individual mind. It is the sum total of this collective individual mind development under the state of good governance and rule of law that has the transforming mechanism for the region. Presently, it is a wishful delusion or thinking to speak of the development of Africa without committing ourselves to the replacement and eradication of factors of economic doctrines impeding the sustainable transformation of the continent. The question of landlocked African countries and industrialisation of the region provides an occasion for replacing the Eurocentric model with a new approach.

A comprehensive combination of the PESTEL and SWOT show how the prowess of the continent lies through good governance and leadership which constructively change the face of Africa and its population within a generation. The dynamics of the economies have changed as landlocked countries face more obstacles and hurdles than their maritime neighbours. Growing political instability within coastal states makes the importation and exportation of goods extremely difficult. It is noted that transport costs for landlocked countries are as high as 77% of the value of exports. Unit costs of road transport in Africa are in the region of 40% -100% more than rates in Southeast Asia. The challenge is how to use PESTEL to improve on its status (strength and opportunities) and to wade off existing threats and weaknesses impeding the sustainable development of the region.

The relationship between Governance, Leadership and Development

Many argue that good governance, leadership and development nexus of the 1990s, has evolved to be unrealistic, overloaded and too ambitious (Grindle, 2002). Others point to the rather technical approach often being imposed from outside (Chhotray & Hulme, 2009) about the socioeconomic transformation of the continent. It is not a question of theory but improving the welfare of the people. Here Sachs (2015) notes that 'sustainable development is both a way of looking at the world with a focus on the interlinkages of economic social and environmental change, a way of describing our shared aspirations for a decent life, combing economic development, social inclusion and environmental sustainability.

What is required is a reconstituted best mindset rather than focusing on establishing and operating on the 'blame' theory. The post 2015 agenda or the Sustainable Development Goals (SDGs) should spur Africa towards a new engine of growth strategy – hence the emphasis on a progressive Afro-centric approach. Adopting the reality theory which establishes the constructive and progressive way forward for the linkages between good governance, leadership and development in unlocking Africa's economic heart is the better alternative. Of course, we cannot escape the realities of the peculiarities and essential difficulties of some African states – for example, landlocked or resources deficient countries. The Kenya-Uganda railway remains in tract with plans to extend the line to Kigali in Rwanda. In the colonial era, roads and railway lines led from the interior to the coast. In the vast Congo territory, Belgium used the might Zaire River to transport initially rubber, later copper and other minerals to sea outlets and thus transform itself from an impoverished state to a wealthy, powerful nation. Cecil Rhodes dream of *'opening up Africa'* to the world by building roads and railway lines that connected the coast of Africa with the interior – the Cape-to-Cairo railway link that would have feeder branch-lines going east and west, north and south in each country should be kept alive with a difference.

The salient factor is that good governance and leadership play important roles in transforming the socioeconomic status of a country. This can be supported from experiences in countries that are resources deficient but able to pull themselves out of the poverty nexus. Poor governance and leadership breeds a vicious circle of underdevelopment characteristic of contemporary Africa. Responding to the plight of the people, the continent needs to protect, adapt, relocate and progressively responding to the changing times under the great influence of advances in science and technology. Thus PESTEL plus SWOT plus the late-comer advantage forms the constructive structural-base for Africa's transformation and ensuring a strong place within the globalization nexus of our time. Given that 'globalisation' is the highest stage of scientific imperialism and with the continent's deficiencies in human capital development and industrial base, it cannot be a veritable player in harvesting the benefits of this new knowledge-based economy.

Taking the case of Africa's landlocked countries, (Botswana, Burkina Faso, Burundi, Chad, Central African Republic, Ethiopia,

Lesotho, Malawi, Mali, Niger, Rwanda, Swaziland, Uganda, Zambia and Zimbabwe) these countries can be seen as least developed yet endowed with abundant resources potential. There are many reasons why landlocked countries are poor. To begin with, they are relatively isolated from the world even though advances in technology ushers greater communication connectivity among nations. The spread of telecommunications via the humble mobile phone and increasingly the Internet has greatly reduced the 'isolation factor' in landlocked countries. In the second place, distance from the sea entails extra costs, more complicated logistics, more bureaucracy, higher insurance premiums and more dependence on the goodwill and stability, of neighbours with sea outlets. For example, the civil war in Cote d'Ivoire impacted seriously on cotton exports from Mali and Burkina Faso.

Assuming Cameroon being an unstable polity, this would impact seriously on the economies of Chad and the Central African Republic. Botswana emerges as the star of the world's landlocked countries. It is the world's largest producer of gem-quality diamonds which, after refining, are negligible in volume but hold enormous value. These are transported to the world's buying centres by air. Like Zambia, Zimbabwe and South Africa, it also produces excellent beef, but getting this to markets abroad is a more expensive exercise. Zimbabwe holds the largest platinum reserves in Africa and is an important producer of gold and other minerals. Zambia is one of the world's major producers of copper. Mali, once the centre of the trans-Saharan trade, is slowly regaining its lustre as one of the continent's important gold producers – although this time, the direction of travel for its export is towards the Atlantic rather than the Red Sea. Niger has the second largest reserves of uranium in the world. Chad has emerged as an oil producing country through a pipeline to the Atlantic coast via Cameroon. All these show the importance of rails, ports, roads and air transportation to the economy of the continent.

To disenclave these land locked territories, the construction of both a Trans-African Railway line and Road Communication network is essential. The development of the following, Fig.3: Projected African International Railway links are important; just as the importance of a comprehensive Trans-African Road (Cairo to Cape, Banjul to the Horn) network. In line with this are the urgent improvements in harbour infrastructures within the coastal states and improvements of river ways to ease the plight of landlocked territories.

Fig 3. Suggested/Projected African International Railway Lines.

Trans Sahara Link	Fes-Bechar – Niamey	2700	km
Atlantic Line	Makurdi-Douala-Kinshasa-L aunda-Windhuk	4000	km
Trans West Africa	St. Louis-Kankan-Parako-Ngaoundere-Bangui	4400	km
The Cairo –Cape	Cairo-Cape line	8000	km
Trans Sahelien	Bamako-Niamey-N'Djamena-Nyala	3600	km
West African Coastline	Dakar-Freetown-Abidjan-Lagos-Douala	3800	km
Trans Centralafrica	Yaoundé-Bangui-Pakwach	2400	km
Trans Eastafrican	Addis Ababa-Nairobi-Quelimane	3600	km
Pacific Line	Mombasa-Da-Beira-Maputo	3000	km

Source: Forje (2015) compiled from Fusion Energy Foundation (1980) The Industrialisation of Africa.

The construction of an interconnected continental rail network will help regions far from the coasts and locked countries will obtain effective connections to the ports, and thus to the world markets; international lines will connect individual national networks to each other, and will thus form the backbone of the economic and political unity of Africa. To facilitate the export of goods from the continent will equally require expansion of existing main ports and constructions of new ones. West, Central and Southern African countries have great potentials in ports construction. The most comprehensive construction harbour projects will be in Abidjan, Dakar, Lagos, Accra, Niger Delta, Limbe (Cameroon), Luanda, and Banana through which for example, the largest part of trade of inland states of Mali, Upper Volta, Niger, Chad, Central African Republic will be rooted. The navigation of rivers like Niger, Benue, Cross River, and Volta etc. will be great help to landlocked economies as well as the interior parts of countries. Improvements of Eastern and Southern African ports, Mozambique, Mombasa, Mtwara, Beira, Durban, Cape Town, Port Elizabeth, Massawa, etc. will supply a large inland region, the South of Sudan, East and South of Zaire, Zambia,

Malawi, Zimbabwe. Egypt has already expanded the Suez Canal. The integration of the African population still living outside the nuplexes, together with a steady growth of exports and imports will increase the transportation of goods.

It means that their exports cost more to get on board ships and imports become more expensive. Within this context, it is even cheaper to transport goods from the United States and Europe, Nigeria, Cameroon, Ghana and Senegal than to move the same items from these countries to a neighbouring landlocked country. In short, the actual cost of transportation along Africa's trade corridors is no anywhere else higher than it is anywhere else in the world but the transport that the price of transport is the highest. Long delays, poor infrastructure, and above all, gross inefficiencies and bureaucratic red tape at the border crossings all conspire to make the movement of goods and people in Africa among the most expensive in the world. The lack of seaboard, ports and harbours, railway way lines and road infrastructures are a major constraint on the economic development of landlocked countries in particular and the continent in general.

Airlines are significantly increasing their role of connecting countries and peoples, making long-distance travels easier and better. For landlocked African countries, airlines have been the saving grace. Countries like Ethiopia, Zambia and Malawi can airfreight their horticultural produce and flowers to virtually any destination in the world and still sell at high competitive prices. Apparently, Africa's regional integration is gradually picking up and transport corridors are reaching out to countries deep in Africa's hinterland. Many airlines are pushing up plans to link the entire continent by opening new routes. Once the whole of Africa is connected up, the sky is the limit for this incredibly rich continent. Africa's aviation industry is growing at 4.7%, faster than any other region and passage numbers are expected to double to 300 million in the next two decades according to Brock, 2015. This increase is not an increase in domestic flight, opening the interior and linking it with the capital cities, except in countries like South Africa, Kenya, and Ethiopia.

The irony is that the greater share of the continent's natural resource wealth and its commodities lies in the landlocked heart (Dowden 2010). Why unlocking and unleashing Africa's potential is essential for the development and improving the welfare of citizens. In addition, inequality remains a big issue and must be tackled. Significant gender and regional inequalities, implying that governments need to do more to target women and people living in rural areas (as well as other groups such as disabled) to ensure that no one or state is left behind. The governance and democracy structure needs to be revived (Knight et al 2002; Ake 1996; Forje, 2011). To stretch the issue further, equitable growth will of course need to be a sustainable kind that cuts across rather than increases the existing divide in society. Connecting the continent through proper infrastructural construct will ease the plight not only of the landlocked countries but equally accelerating development related activities within and between nations.

Old trade routes from ancient civilization of Great Zimbabwe to the shoes of Mozambique, from North Africa to the Atlantic coast of the Gulf of Genuine and other transport infrastructure across the continent should be developed. Without the construction of a modern transport and communication system the developed economies could not have attained the characteristics which today place them beyond all other nations. This close insoluble connection between industrial development and the building up of effective transport systems hold true for Africa: they can be no real development unless massive infrastructural projects are made an integral part of the overall development process. No industrialization of Africa without infrastructure – it would be pointless repeating this obvious truth, if there did not exists certain circles and entrenched viewpoints which deny exactly such a connection.

The strategic approach of Eurocentric agenda is to retain Africa as suppliers of raw materials and established permanent markets for exports. The World Bank has not departed from that strategic orientation; Africa must be kept at the level of an underdeveloped raw materials supplier. With no industry to demand large transport volumes, railway transport systems are superfluous as the hidden agenda keeping Africa underdeveloped. There must be no *dark ages* for the African continent. No people of any nation must be pushed into zero-growth practices and ideologies. No longer must there be a system of unbalanced development, and ethnic divide, a combination of which threatens peace and development as well as undermines the quality livelihood of citizens. The World Bank position can be likening to European colonialist domination imposed an artificial backwardness on many nations and their people. This caused both an abnormal stagnation of socio-cultural-economic underdevelopment or retrogressions. Africa is forced to leave with the after-effects of the Berlin1884 human destruction conference. This is the hour for Africa to speak truth to centres of power in the West and to accept no such power imposition from the East either. We have the yam and the knife. Proper use of such advantageous gift should be made use to improve on the quality living standards of the population

Currently, the continent's greatest deficits are leadership, human capital building and commitments of transcending from underdevelopment to development. New thinking, new think-tanks and a progressive human capital development should form the foundation of walking the change. This requires carving a new niche in the continent's policy environment, of which the New Partnership for Africa's Development (NEPAD) through its African Peer Review Mechanism (APRM); Africa's Charter on the Values and Principles of Public Service Administration in Africa; African Charter on Democracy, Elections And Governance among others that craft a new road-map of development of achieving sustained quality living standards for the masses. The ideological spring board for Africa must be construed within the parameters of Africa's interest first, and strongly based on the continent's own emotionalism and sentimentalism with the framework of Pan-Africanism, anti-colonialism and anti-imperialism. The wellbeing of the African people, unity of purpose should supersede all other divide imposed on the people and for Africans to claim their political power and sovereign rights to build the continent they want.

Landlocked, resources deficient poor and other countries suffer from the same patterns of trade since time immemorial and under the canopy of 'cultural imperialism' and other refuse of western colonial office. The Europeans were mercantile – setting up bases along the coast, making forays into the interior to obtain whatever was of worth which they later exported to Europe. Africa provided an invaluable source of raw materials for their industries - gold, diamonds, ivory, slaves, tea, sugar, coffee, hardwood etc. The continent became the land of great opportunity – where fortunes could be made by any one sufficiently determined to do so. Africa has been and is central to and will continue to be essential to the vitality and growth of the global economy. Unless Africans control their resources they cannot make progress. Africa can never transition from poverty to wealth unless they move from export of primary products to the creation of industries. That is why Africa beginning from Ghana was talked out of the industrialisation agenda. In short, western agenda was based on a strategy of taking African eyes out rendering it impossible for the continent to find and map out the right compass for its transition. The strategic approach was maintaining the continent as a raw material exporting entity and market for western products. Should not the continent use UN Agenda 2030 (SDGs), African Union Agenda 2063 and national development goals to reconstruct a new continent within the global knowledge-based economy of our time? What is the continent waiting for? Is it another Brussels conference to further butcher the continent before we react or what?

Discussions and analysis

To begin with, Africans must fight for economic independence with the same zeal they fought for political independence. They draw examples from Asian countries. A new mindset is imperative. There is need to assimilate western technologies with African cultures, and move away from the idea of finished goods syndrome. Second, there is the lack of a political will to create a new body of knowledge works in the African society. Third, there is a gross lack of genuine public-private partnership in the continent's development agenda. African governments give little essence to supporting the private sector. There is the strong adherence to state-owned enterprise, which unfortunately is the avenue for corruption and of waste of state funds.

Of course, there is the fear that the private sector seems to owe allegiance to the government. Therefore, the continent needs a strong indigenous private sector which should equally be void of party politics influences. The World Bank Structural Adjustment Programme (SAP) did a lot to destroy the economic growth of the continent. This is enough reason for changing existing course. The only magic wane is digging deeper into the secrets why the West with no natural resources is developed and Africa with abundant resource is not developed. The second is learning from best practices as provided by China and the Asian Tiger Nations. It is time for the emergence of a *developmental state model* whereby the government controls, manages and regulates the economy on the continent. The Chinese economic model of success resonates with the Ethiopian current economic situation, given that China has gone through similar growth in recent history. Thirdly, to sum up courage, build a new political will to change and grow.

Apparently the challenge Africa has – weakness and threats – looked at these critically and objectively are actually strengths and opportunities. For example, infrastructure is a limiting factor but it is also an opportunity for local and external investors. Therefore weaknesses and threats can and should be converted into strengths and opportunities. It shows that Africa is on the winning side needing good governance, proper management nexus and determination to convert weakness into strength and threats into opportunities. Across Africa are lots of potentials for growth and behind the slums of every capital are ticked millionaires who can and should invest properly to change the face of the continent. Clearly, there is a lot that needs doing – and no doubt plenty of money to be made doing it which equally trickles down into improving the livelihood of the people.

Fig 4: Sustainable livelihood framework

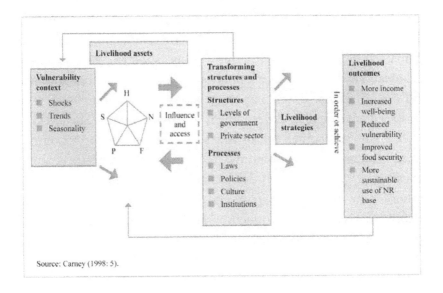

Source: Carney (1998: 5).

Africa remains vulnerable due to a number of interrelated inherent factors some of which have been discussed. Based on the reality that the continent holds most of the world resources, both the PESTE and SWOT create basis for reconsidering its current Eurocentric developmental approach and to embrace a progressive Afro-centric developmental agenda. The strength and opportunities of the region is clear. This gives it the structural basis for adequately addressing prevailing weaknesses and threats. From the paper, the weaknesses and threats are identified as poor governance, poor leadership, poor human capital development, exclusion and inappropriate utilisation of resources. Poor institutional construct and underdeveloped infrastructures impedes the sustainable transformation of the region into an economic powerhouse region. The need to invest in elevating the infrastructures of the continent cannot be exaggerated. Africa should take advantage of Gerschenkron (1962) 'late-comer advantage'; exploit its existing strength and opportunities to adequately address prevailing weaknesses and threats. African countries need a new technological approach, as this is what underlines the fundamental difference between 'developing' and 'developed' societies is technology. Therefore African countries ought to seek to achieve technology autonomy in its quest for positive transformations and prosperity for its people. The ways in which technology is developed, institutionalized, animated and celebrated, from the core of 'development' (human, economic, environmental, etc.) and ultimately civilization itself. But 'techno-spheres' are not only technical. They are also social, political, and ideological. For societies and countries that have long been kept from realizing their own prosperity and dignity, development is also liberation (Sheikheldin, 2018). The late-comer advantage should spur African countries towards technological autonomy. Technological autonomy is about attaining a high-level of self-determination in planning and mapping technological Affairs. Attaining endogenous capacity to guide and execute decisions on production and innovation; creating and transferring key technological products and services; steering relevant foreign and local investment as well as trade; setting own priorities of development free from external manipulation; are goals that must be central to such planning efforts, notes,(Sheikheldin op cit).

This calls for comprehensive and concerted action plans, for example, AU 2063 Agenda, national development plans which can best be unsurpassed technological knowledge and wisdom of its people. When the resources of the people are depleted, the people must make the transition to a technology-based economy as the only way forward in improving the livelihood construct of the people. Fig 4: Provides the way forward in changing the face of and lives of the people. Within these approaches (SPETEL, SWOT and Late-comer Advantage) lie the issues of financing these infrastructural developments. That is another area for research and discourse. What is important now is linking the coastal states and landlocked countries, industrialise, create more jobs and improve on the welfare of all citizens. Take the case of Ethiopia, for example. As a landlocked, Ethiopia relies heavily on Djibouti and Kenya for access to the sea. Today, it takes several days for freight trucks to haul containers from the port of Djibouti to Addis Ababa. But when the refurbished electric railroad connecting the two cities opens in 2016, it will reduce transport costs and cut delivery time from four days to just ten hours (Tafirenyika, 2015:4).

Creative and integrated development signifies changing the way one thinks and acts as well as through a constructive combination of the PESTEL and SWOT approaches. The significance of these approaches is that it correlates with the fundamental aspects of sustainable human progress, creating room for certain mechanisms to spot their strengths, weaknesses, opportunities and threats promoting or retarding their development related activities. With this, African countries are exposed to mastering the issues underscoring their transformation by abstract that aspect of his/her creative behaviour that correlates with successive advances in mastery of the transformation process. The various institutions or mechanisms provide the needed platform of gagging which way to follow that brings ultimate benefits to society.

This also creates the structural basis for transforming the minds of the people, building economic development and technological progress and foster consciousness for sustainable development related activities that promotes sustainable livelihood for all. Sustainable development goals and progress cannot be attained in an environment permeated with cultural and political barbarism. The continent cannot sustain development via technological barbarism. Development can only progressed through a well-coordinated input mechanisms and structures that improve income, wellbeing, reduced vulnerability and insecurity, improved food, health, shelter security; among others; where there is respect for the rule of law, good governance, strong institutions not individuals and where there exist harmonious relationship between the state, civil society and the private sector.

Currently, African countries are vulnerable to western manipulations. Therefore levels of state and private sector interface are important for promoting livelihood strategies and constraining some of the vestiges of western imposed transformation nexus that inhibit the sustainable development of the continent. Some of these issues are depicted in Fig. 3: Sustainable Livelihood Framework which also forms the holistic basis for a comprehensive analysis. A new mindset is imperative that should usher constructive reconstruction in 'attitude, behaviour and conduct' (ABC) at all levels of society, government and the private sector and as the touch-light to livelihood strategies leading to quality livelihood. Opening up the interior would lead to the industrialization of the region, which in turn would help transform and strengthen their economies. The lack of competitiveness of African manufacturing and the extent to which the scope for domestic value addition is left untapped are epitomized by the cotton's trade in raw materials. For example, follow the Economic Report on Africa by the UN Economic Commission for Africa (2012), while Africa accounted for about 16% of global cotton exports in 2012, only 1% of these exports, or about USA$400 million, was cotton that had been processes into fabrics. During the same period, the continent imported USA$0.4 billion worth of cotton and USA$4 billion of cotton fabrics.

The World Bank approach to education was and is destructive, laying strong emphasis to the arts and seeing technical, vocational as having no use to the continent. The International Monetary Fund (IMF) focused on education but ignoring vocational and technical training as the prime driver for change. General education focuses on reading and writing, but this does not take the continent anywhere in terms of development. The continent has failed to utilise knowledge and technology for its sustainable transformation. Knowledge and technology should propel creativity, innovation and entrepreneurial development as the underlying factors for transforming the continent. Looking back at history, with Africa as the cradle of civilization, the centre of university knowledge, and building on the indigenous knowledge of the people, the developing African should watershed itself in these words; *'because of the progress I bequeathed to my posterity to build upon, I ensure that my ancestors have not lived for nothing.'* Let us distinguish the essence of that matter in our contemporary development trajectories.

However, Africa can leapfrog into a new brave world by taking a long-look at the rise and fall of Timbuktu. Timbuktu as the first centre for university education in the world fell; Africa has fallen but can rise again. Men and women of wisdom are shinning torches in our darkness; they are torches that will guide us out of our ignorance. Stated differently, the greatest intellectual giants Africa has produced have emphasized on this. For example, Nnamdi Azikiwe (Nigeria) declared some years back; *'show the light and the people will find their way'*.

Kwame Nkrumah (Ghana) noted that *'socialism without science is void;'* and Philip Emeagwali (the Nigeria computer wizard), adding his voice notes that *"democracy without technology is void;' and paraphrasing Nyerere, while the West is heading to the moon, I am struggling to get to the village.'* Failed states exist because leaders make wrong decisions. Looking forward to another 50 years, of democracy and leadership in Africa plays a vital role in turning what could be seen as a *curse into blessing* for the transformation of the continent. The wealth and progress of the future of the continent will be derived from developing its intellectual capital (New African No.500, November 2010:97).

That intellectual capital will give added value to the natural resources potentials of the continent in such a way that neither land-locked nations nor nations with access to the coastal region should suffer. No part of the continent should be left behind. The Eurocentric agenda is the *'route of death'* for Africa. The progressive Afro-centric strategy provides the road map for Africa's sustainable development goals and development for the welfare of the people. It gives them the will, resilience and strength from rising from the aches of underdevelopment, exclusion, exploitation and poor livelihood. Africa must produce an elite and think-tank corps, not in the sense of a privileged stratum squatting on the shoulders of the less favoured; but an elite of servants, and elite of the dedicated modern agents providing the leadership and sense of direction and new vision for the continent. Only through such a vision can the continent can successfully unlock the continent's economic heart. To quote Patrice Lumumba (1961), *'Africa will write its own history, and in North and South that history will be seen to be one of glory and righteousness,'* significantly contributing the sustainable welfare of all citizens. The decision taken by the United Nations in 1989 in declaring 20 November as Africa Industrialisation Day with the goals to mobilize the commitment of the international community to the industrialisation of Africa should be taken seriously in order to transform and strengthen their economies. According to the ECA (2014) the continent must establish stronger institutions and adopt effective measures to enhance structural transformation. In short, deliberate and smart trade policies and practices would lead to the much-delayed industrialization of Africa.

The paper has briefly spanned the continent's status of underdevelopment, identifying its struggles, successes and failures. So far the continent faces serious challenges. Attending comprehensively to these issues means, Africa can still raise to greater heights. Africa remains the land of great opportunity, even though, for now, the continent's geography has not been kind to landlocked states. The paper set out to elaborate and prescribed some solutions to the plight of landlocked states and the industrialisation of Africa in general; it also had the mission to sharpen the judgement and perception of those forces concerning the right and the wrong concepts of development. Therefore, the paper calls on African governments and its people to exercise political will and courage as well as take the right steps to seek solutions to the problems of its underdevelopment through restructuring its governance system and leadership style.

A progressive Afro-centric approach is strongly recommended. Any other approach based on short-term considerations would in the long-run operate to the long-run political and economic detriment of Africa. This not what Africa of the 21st century and beyond wants? Africa wants leadership with bold ambition and a clear vision for sustainable quality livelihood for its citizens. African governments must pay serious attention to improved political space, access to media, viability of opposition parties, policies and politics of inclusion, rule of law and civic education. Order is necessary to enhance the state of cohesion, unity and sense of belong. Only through this can the people address the imperial presence and rape of the African continent. We should draw valuable lessons from Howard Thurman who asserts: *"A man must be at home somewhere before he can feel at home everywhere."* Africans can and must feel at home (Africa) before they can image belong elsewhere. The other is by St Francis of Assisi, who states: *"Where there is discord, may we bring harmony; where there is error, may we bring truth; where there is doubt, may we bring faith; where there is despair, and may we bring hope."* In short, Africa should being by rethinking its development nexus through the premises of extending the olive branch to all actors in the political spectrum. There has to be a holistic and inclusive approach to the development of the continent. Effective management of national resources is what defines successful leadership which transcends to sustainable development, quality services delivery culmination to sustained better livelihood.

The process in which this paper has engaged us is not mere economic-development, not merely a remedy for the hazards otherwise threatening the continent in this time. We are engaged, if we see that matter rightly, in a battle to finally solve the problem of the 'hinterlands'. The paper has guided us through the dilemma of a landlocked society and the overall issues of underdevelopment. And to place the present and future order of the continent under the rule of the 'Grand Design' of a strong, united and developed Africa by citizens especially consciousness of the development of the creative potentials of the individual mind for the common good. For this condition we must assign to our mind the function of developing a *'watcher'* who watches the 'watcher' and to optimally optimise scientific and technological advances for the transformation of the continent. Development is not just a common transformation. It also entails liberating the energies of the people; a country can grow without adequately providing basic freedoms and needs. The entire system and the entire survival over time could be questioned because the state has created a democratic society that aspires for a brighter future and wellbeing of the people. Political instability and state fragility have emerged as a tendency in African countries with poor resources management records. In many cases, the sheer volume of revenues generated from the mineral resources has also taken the attention of decision makers away from institutional and human development, export diversification and value addition at the expense of local production, thereby deepening inequality and exacerbating poverty. Throughout the continent, natural resources booms have only to a limited extent set off a dynamic growth process but exacerbated corruption. The continent cannot continue with such mentality and attitude towards development.

Conclusion and recommendations

African solutions to its predicament now demands urgent and radical measures. The continuation of a Eurocentric agenda for the continent implies the continued danger of irreversible damage to the continent. On the other hand, a progressive Afro-centric approach requires the political will which must be mustered in Africa by Africans and the Diaspora to engender a rapid accumulation of industrial capital to advance the continent. In this connection, this paper calls for political courage from all Africans and from the developed political, financial, and economic leaders to promote a New World Economic Order for global development, peace and stability. An African solution now demands urgent and radical global measures. The paper presents a blueprint for the sustainable development goals of Africa, by looking particularly at the plight of landlocked countries and Africa in general. The failure of government to address fundamental problems makes natural resource to be curse rather than a blessing to the people.

First, the paper attempts to re-interrogate the deepening crisis of the continent's development saga. The continued underdevelopment of the continent is attributed to poor leadership, governance and the misuse of natural resources. That landlocked territories suffer most as this adds to their cost bills, the general tendency is that of poor leadership and inadequate infrastructures across the continent. It is imperative correcting the flaws of the past to be well equipped to address the present and face the challenges of the future. Therefore African governments through a progressive Afro-centric approach and from holistic perspectives should champion a new sustainable development agenda to improve on the welfare of the people. The big challenge the continent faces is that poverty is still immense and unemployment is still high. Growth has to bring with it benefits to community. Africa must get its act together and rightly too.

Secondly, African governments are obliged in developing appropriate policies and institutional changes and adaptation technology to the character of each region. The squandering of opportunities, coupled with subsequent development as well as excruciating poverty and general conditions of living, accounts for the new form and character of frustration and the wave of migrations from the continent. This has become more devastating and worrisome under the nascent democracy. The trend, form and character of destructive frustration in the continent only attest to the failure of state (Asonganyi, 2015) and responses to the problem. There is, therefore, an urgent need for fundamental overhaul of the state of governance and resources use. This also requires change in leadership style as well as a strong call for a new mindset among the population. It was Friedrich Last (1841) who noted that *'the nation creates its productive forces out of the mental and physical powers of its individuals'*. This statement is a wake-up call for Africa to reinvent, reconstitute and reshape its development trajectories. Africa should draw valuable lessons from this statement and forge ahead with its transformation nexus. In other words, '2063 should not be a dream. Africans have the means to achieve AU objectives. All the continent needs is building self-confidence. Africa will not be saved or developed by an international committee. It must stop begging and dependent on grants. In addition, the illicit flight of capital must stop' (Nkosi, 2015:20).Only Africans can build up Africa. It involves the participation of all. Each individual should contribute his/her quota for a brighter future awaits the continent. The potential power of every African must be harnessed.

Thirdly, the state, civil society and the private sector need to articulate forward looking policy strategies to ensure that the best results arising out of the exploitation of the natural resources base are used in improving the sustainable welfare of the citizens. This means sustainable investments in human capital development, institutions building and infrastructure development. The Afro-centric agenda should be geared towards ending poverty and hunger and to achieve sustainable development through promoting inclusive economic growth, protecting the environment and promoting social inclusion. Africa is now a late-comer to development but with many advantages provided by advances in science and technology providing fundamental breakthroughs that cuts down Rostow's stages of development. Bold ambition and political assertiveness is what the continent needs to become a capable developmental state. It is time the continent flexes its economic muscle by giving comprehensive added value to its vast natural resources potential. They need also to come up with innovative financial products and establish effective and efficient national and regional financial institutions and services to sustain its related development activities for the overall wellbeing of the people.

Recommendations

- Addressing the root causes of the continents underdeveloped status requires a constructive rethinking in the governance and leadership construct of the region;
- Civil society and the private sector must develop a new mindset for the sustainable transformation of the continent.
- Only a comprehensive focus on good governance at all levels, that is efficient and people-oriented can make positive changes in the lives of the people;
- Reduce inequality within and among countries; as well as promote inclusive and sustainable economic growth, full and productive employment and decent work for all;
- Empowerment of the female gender as well as ensuring the youths are put into useful employment spree as the life-wire for Africa's development;
- Ensure economic integration within and between states; regional integration should be a win-win project for all its stakeholders beyond the tokenism of solidarity and charity.
- Africa should intensify its ongoing efforts to diversify the economy, build infrastructures, and connect with the interior or landlocked areas to rebuild the economy and welfare of the people.
- There is an urgent need to promote peace and inclusive societies for sustainable development, provide access to justice for all and build effective, accountable and inclusive institutions

The struggle continues with hope of victory in the end!

References

African Union (2011) African Charter on Democracy, Elections and Governance, Addis Ababa, Ethiopia.

African Union (2011). African Charter on the Values and Principles of Public Service and Administration, Addis Ababa, Ethiopia.

Ake Claude (1996) Democracy and Development in Africa. Brookings Institution, Washington DC. USA.

Agbu, Osita (2005) "Oil and Environmental Conflicts", in Saliu, Hassan A. (ed.) Nigeria Under Democratic Rule, 1999-2003, Vol.2, Ibadan University Press, Ibadan, Nigeria.

Asonganyi Tazoacha (2015). Cameroon: Difficult Choices in a Failed Democracy (Memoir) NGT Publishing, Madison, USA.

Brandmann Hans (1980)."Opening Address to the FEF Conference on the Industrialisation of Africa", Fusion Energy Foundation (1980). The Industrialisation of Africa Campaigner Publications, Wiesbaden, Germany.

Brock Joe (2015) "Shaking up African Aviation", The New Age, 17 September 2015, South Africa, p16.

Burke, John (2014) Introduces PESTEL and SWOT Analysis, Northumbria University, Newcastle, England

Carney, D. (ed.) (1998) Sustainable Rural Livelihoods: What Contribution Can We Make? UK Department for International Development (DfID).

Chhotray, V, & Hulme, D. (2009) "Contrasting Visions for Aid and Governance in the 21st Century: The White House Millennium Challenge Account and DFID's Drivers of Change', World Development 37(1):36-49.

Commey Pusch (2015) "South Africa: Looking into the Crystal Ball: New African, No. 553, August/September 2015, London, pp48-50.

Djanie Akua (2015)/ Why I Am Not Feeling Proudly Ghanaian, New African No. 553, August-September 2015, London, pp46-47.

Dowden Richard (2010), Africa: Altered States, Ordinary Miracles, Public Affairs, New York, N.Y. USA.

Economic Commission for Africa (ECA) (2014) Dynamic Industrial Policy for Africa. Addis Ababa, Ethiopia.

Forje W. John (2011) State Building and Democracy in Africa. A Comparative and Developmental Approach A CARAD Publication/Nova Science Publishes Inc., New York, USA.

Fusion Energy Foundation (1980) .The Industrialisation of Africa, Campaigner Publications, Wiesbaden, Germany.

Gerschenkron, A. (1962). Economic Backwardness in Historical Perspectives. The Belknap Press of Harvard University Press, Cambridge, USA.

Grindle, M. (2002) "Good Enough Governance: Poverty Reduction and Reform in Developing Countries', paper prepared for the Poverty Reduction Group of the World Bank, Kennedy School of Government, Harvard University, Boston, MA.

Joseph A. Williams (ed.) (2010) Politics in China. Oxford University Press, Oxford, UK.

Juma Calestous (2015) "Enterprises as Innovations Schools", New African No.553, August-September 2015, London, pp68-69.

Kabukuru Wanjohi (2015). "Post-2015: In Whose Hands is Africa's Future:" New African No.553, August-September 2015, London, pp10-16.

Knight Barry, Hope Chigudu & Rajesh Tandon (2002) Reviving Democracy: Citizens at the Heart of Governance. The Commonwealth Foundation, Earthscan Publishers, London

Legum, C. & Zartman, I.W. (1979). Africa in the 1980s (1980s Project – Council on Foreign Relation) McGraw-Hill Books. USA,

Mashamaite Moss (2014) The Moving Finder Writes Vol. 2, Chatworld Publishers, South Africa.

Muchie Mammo (2015) "Why Pan-African Education Should be Promoted", New African, No.553, August-September 2015, London, pp24-25.

New African (2010) "Africa Can leapfrog Into the Information Age", New African, No.500, November 2010, London, pp97.

Nkosi Ntombi (2015). "Shaping Africa's Future" The New Age, 17 September 2015, South Africa, p20.

Nye S. Joseph (2010). The Power to Lead. Oxford University Press. Oxford, UK.

Omotola Shola (2006) .The Next Gulf? Oil Politics, Environmental Apocalypse and Rising Tension in the Niger Delta. Occasional

Paper Series, Vol.1. No.13, 2006 ACCORD, Durban South Africa.

Rothstein, Bo and Teorell, Jan (2008) "What is quality of Government? A Theory of Impartial Government Institutions", Governance: An International Journal of Policy, Administration and Institutions 21(2):165-90.

Sachs D. Jeffrey (2015). The Age of Sustainable Development. Columbia University Press, USA.

Sheikheldin Gussai (2018) Liberation and Technology. Development Possibilities in Pursuing Technological Autonomy. Mkuki na Nyota Publishers, Tanzania.

Sofaniadi Safrinal, Rusmandi & Aniessa Delima Sari (2015) Protect, Adapt or Relocate? Responding to Climate Change in Coastal Indonesia, Working Paper Series 14:2015, IIED London.

Stuart Elizabeth (2015) "China Has Almost Wiped Out Urban Poverty. Now It Must Tackle Inequality'. Overseas Development Institute, (ODI) United Kingdom.

Tafirenyika Masimba (2015). "The Changing Face of Ethiopia", Africa Renewal, Vol. 29. No. 2, August 2015, United Nations, NY, pp4-5.

Conclusion

Getting away from scorn: Building a new mindset and decolonising foreign policy and influence in Africa

Introduction

"By the very nature of their role, incarnate leaders must plan to make an exit.|"

(David Mckenna)

"As weather shapes mountains, so problems make leaders."

(Warren Benniss)

"To lead is to struggle. In a world such as ours in history as we know it, to choose the path of leadership is to be on a collision course with conflict."

(Leighton Ford), 1991)

"Africa's weaknesses and incompetence's are the Western World's greatest assets used to keeping the continent at the underdevelopment barometer. Building new strategies to wither the storm is imperative. We have so far failed and there is time to search for true, genuine heroes to pilot the ship to the destination we want"

(John W. Forje, 24 June 2017 – Bali Nyonga)

Where have all the powers gone in overcoming the storm?

The state of the continent's exploitation and underdevelopment remain overwhelming disastrous and leads us to this cry of alarm beaconing African leaders to reconsider the transformation strategies used so far since the attainment of independence. Where has all the power gone? Why are we not using these powers to improve on the wellbeing of the citizens? Why is democracy and development evading the continent? Why do we fail in making the electorate sovereign? We are not to start another round of discourse but to continue stressing the candid reality the people remain supreme in any society. The people must be the focus of development. Until this sinks deep into our minds and actions progress cannot come the way of the people.

Within us there is a built-in resistance to change which seems to threaten our stability and challenge our power. Even if our current situation is unhappy, we still dig in our feet. As young woman with severe problems ironically responded, when challenged to undergo a spiritual conversion, 'I think I prefer the security of my misery!" The degree of resistance depends on how critical the change is. 'Crisis' is a word which comes from the Greek *krisis,* and implies a separating ort dividing. Every crisis brings about a polarization and reveals what is truly inside people," (Ford, 1991:252-3). Africa's state of underdevelopment is more than an enough crisis. What is inside the minds of Africans must emerge and above all be thoroughly addressed to the common good of all? We are challenged to know how to cope with the divisions within our continent, how to tone down the rhetoric, how to search for acceptable compromises, how to arrive at consensus, how to assist opposing parties to understand how the other perceives the problems and how to open the way for creative solutions. And in the words of Gardner (1986:12) 'go to the root of the communication breakdown whether it is anger, fear, mistrust or differing assumptions and definitions and the willingness to engage in a battle when necessary is a *sine qua non* of leadership." The willingness of Africans to constructively engage in transforming their poor living conditions into a better one is a sign of the growing reasoning and maturity of the people.

What the publication is all about is a call for genuine reform, fighting against the evils of underdevelopment, oppression, poverty, unemployment and corruption. The challenge is to transform the current crisis into victory, development; to stand fast and fight for sustainable development and democratic governance, inclusion and equity in the sharing of the national cake; defending the sovereignty of the country, your freedom and liberty. Be alert, stand firm and not to neither lose sight of the goals nor forgot what you set to achieve in the first place. The words of Arnold Toynbee (1946:547) summaries everything discussed throughout the book; "And now, as we stand and gaze with our eyes fixed upon the farther shore, a single figure rises from the flood and straightway fills the whole horizon, There is the Saviour; and the pleasure of the Lord shall prosper in his hands; he shall see of the travail of his soul and shall be satisfied."

It is worth pointing out, even ad nauseum, that development does occur in a vacuum. It can rightly be argued 'policies cannot be created and delivered in a political or historical vacuum' (Cummings, 1988:4). We have to bear in mind that development is a complex process which is closely linked with reinforcing inter-relationship with the objective and quantitative factors of production, on the one hand, and the economic factors – the political, social, cultural, psychological and institutional on the other. The continent seems to have failed in marrying these two crucial factors together. Indeed, any development strategy, whatever the economic advantages, must be politically viable. The point is that Africans are behaving like the Europeans did some three-hundred or more years ago. There have been obvious failures. Europe could colonise other parts of the world to have added advantage to their transformation. Today Africa can make the best opportunities of the 'late-comer advantage' to advance its developmental process. Is the continent actually taking that advantage? There is the gnawing problem about the extent of African countries financing their development related without depending on foreign finances. African leaders have yet to embark on the idea of self-financing their development activities by mobilizing domestic sources of resources.

We need to change and deepen our minds to better address our problems. Social progress and development, on the one hand, is not only influenced strongly but it is determined by two factors; the growth of human knowledge, and the necessary sufficient conditions that favour this growth of human knowledge. The publication lays heavy weight on building the human knowledge of the continent. In doing so we equally trigger other aspects of change, progress and development that transforms the human being. The so-called underdevelopment of Africa cannot be viewed merely as a form of

309

stagnation (in the context of linear and spiral developmental processes) but rather as constituting a challenge to the theory of social evolution. For many centuries, Africa has and continues suffering from the devastating effects of the great rhythms of history –conquest, invasions, and migrations such that the very conditions that promote the growth of human knowledge, and therefore, of progress and development, have been bedevilled by that formidable crisis of identity (a natural sequence) which engulfs the culture, the society and the individual (Lartey 1977).

Change is rapidly taking place all the time in human societies. The Africa of today is not what it was fifty or more years ago and would not be the same fifty or more years to come. Pockets of progress can be recorded here and there. Africa could have taken advantage of its 'latecomer to the development nexus' to achieve greater things since the attainment of independence. It failed to do so. To get away from the scorn the people must rethink their role and activities in the past fifty years and forge ahead with a new structured agenda. It is going to be a safer world when Africa is not left behind. It is therefore of the utmost of the developed world to rally resources and construct a new mindset towards the people of Africa and not to continue treating them as non-human beings. Leaving Africa or any part of the world behind is creating an unsafe world system. The world construct today is either all nations drown or swim together.

Our survival or destruction depends upon how we pull together or go our separate ways. We have to create a better world for present and future generations. Seen within this perspective, I draw from the views of Professor James A. Dator a futurist of The University of Hawaii states: "For centuries we were taught to worship our ancestors and to be true to our traditions, and it was good that we did so. But now, given the novelty and quantity of the challenges rushing at us from the future, we need to do something we have never had to do before, and which I fear we may not be able to do now: we must worship our descendants; we must love our grandchildren more than we love ourselves."

Africa is facing serious crisis. The entire human race is facing crisis too, but that of Africa is more devastating. The continent is on a cross-road, one way leading towards a certain catastrophic future and the other offering the hope of a sustainable future. Our focus here is to gun on a hopeful future for all even though fierce battles are fought throughout the continent. How to wade off foreign domination is the tall question we must holistically confront before it is too late. For now, the ball is firmly in the court of African countries. Only a united front from and speaking with one voice can the continent can help bring constructive change. To get change requires internal structural changes as well. But with *'sit-tight'* presidents, (who is the country and the country the president) it is difficult to see how such changes can be effected.

However, granted that these sit-tight-presidents are firmly in control, it equally remains true that the doors are not necessarily all shut. It is the place of the population to exploit any existing windows of opportunity to effect constructive change. Perhaps a glimmer of hope will emerge. However, given the current international policy climate, unless there is an African United Front (AUF) to provide a sense of vision and direction, no single African country can brave the stormy seas alone. A common and united front is imperative. At the same time inaction places the continent at a serious risk of being swallowed by a United Developed World (UDW).

Nations must turn away from the destructive logic of an 'arms culture' and focus instead on their common future. The level of armaments and the destruction they could bring about bear no relation to the political conflict that triggered the arms competition in the first place. Nations must not become prisoners of their own arms race. They must face the common danger inherent in the weapons of the nuclear age. They must face the common challenge of providing for sustainable development and act in concert to remove the growing environmental sources of conflict (The Brundtland Report 1987:304).

Africa can only maintain its relevance in the new century and world order if it rises to the new challenges of the time as well as preparing for the future by meeting the expectations of the people. These challenges, of course, include the establishment of an enabling environment for the furtherance of democratization, economic recovery and growth, and the creation of viable institutions to consolidate democracy, popular participation and good management and the promotion of fundamental human rights as well as the provision of basic needs to all; as well as the management of intricate internal conflicts, the maintenance of national cohesion, peace, security and stability throughout the continent. For now, the continent is caught between the trappings of *'sting rich'* and *'sting poor'* phenomenon. It is important to escape the route of *'sting poor'* and begin walking on the path of quality livelihood for all.

Fig.1 Pyramid of Capitalist System or the Existing True Face of Capitalism

The point is that capitalism triggers a welcome focus on the global problem of growing inequality. It was capitalism that triggered the evil axils of colonialism, splitting the continent into bits and pieces to suit Western maximization of the resources of Africa countries for their profits and well-being. For now the penetrating dimensions of the capitalist system and the general dependence of Africa on the *'big brother – North'* needs a new focus. African countries have been brainwashed to such a degree that they have become totally impotent to the acute problems facing them. Capitalism though an aged-old system has planted lasting factors within African countries difficult to eradicate overnight - see **Fig.1 Pyramid of Capitalist System or The True Face of Capitalism.** The current system is oriented within the following framework:

With Capitalism ➔We rule you ➔ We fool you ➔ We shoot at you ➔ We eat for you ➔ We feed all (and if I may add) =➔ *We destroy you*

This portrays the true face of capitalism. But capitalism can be given a human face by allowing a trickledown effect to uplift the quality livelihood of the down-trodden swimming in abject poverty. For example, should Cameroon, Democratic Republic of Congo or Nigeria wish to benefit from their extensive material wealth, it must increase its capacity to promote human security and national cohesion. If the structural problems confronting these countries – such as underfunding, poor human development building capacity, low morale and other ills are not addressed, the development and security of the country is likely to continue to deteriorate. So long as the civil society in these countries continue to distrust the authorities and perceive them as personally-interested actors rather than guarantors of social wellbeing, ethnic strife, regional conflicts and the competition for inclusion in the sharing of the national resources will continue to be the dominant narrative in the politics of these countries. The new capitalism with a human face should take a new and well refine structural construction depicted below. The *Human Face of Capitalism* should take the following or a much better form of construction. The new capitalism with a *human-face* should take a new-structural construct as depicted below.

With the new Capitalism➜we cooperate with you ➜we work with you ➜we help you ➜ we share with you to grow ➜ we make our profits with you➜we build a more secured world with you.

It is hoped such orientation will lead to justice and equity, for without justice and equity they can neither peace nor peaceful coexistence among people and nations. The absence of justice and equity is what has contributed and sustains the conflict between the Jews and Palestine, was the source to the Rwanda genocide, the Biafra war in Nigeria. The ongoing divide between Southern Cameroons and La Republique du Cameroun is the major source of conflict between the two parts of the country to mention but a few cases. It is what sustains the division between the rich and poor or developed and developing countries of the world. Poverty can be erased on the African continent by putting aside articulate self-interests and place 'people first' as the goal and vision for development. Are we prepared side-lining articulate self-interest and gunning for the collective articulate interest of the people and the progress of society?

Keeton Gavin (2015) of Rhodes University notes that; *'inequality inevitably increase because capital assets gain value faster than economic growth. The owners of capital, the rich, therefore become wealthier and their wealth always rises faster than the wages of the poor. To help the poor catch up a global tax on wealth is needed.'* So we need a new capitalism order – *Capitalism with a Human Face* – that tries to narrow the gap between the 'haves and have-nots. For Africa, improving on their human capital and being people focused will go a long way in narrowing the gap between the *'sting rich'* and the *'sting poor'*.

Fig.2: Peri-urban agricultural activities lead to food system

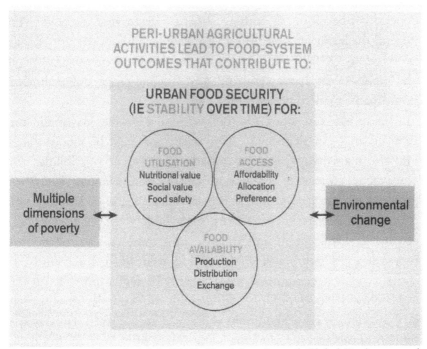

Source: Ingram, J. et al. (eds.) (2010). Food Security and Global Environmental Change. Earthscan, London

While we cannot do away totally with capitalism and must live with, a new form of capitalism with a *'human face'* needs to be effectuated since the current form and practice of capitalism is the sources of growing inequality. As a latecomer to the development syndrome, socialism has not yet succeeded in eroding the imprints of exploitative profit-making dimensions embodied with capitalism (Forje, 1990:46). Could we have a capitalist system geared towards the following orientation even though not perfect in its present formulation? Where capitalism allows for a sustainable degree of trickle-down effects to improve the quality livelihood of the people? Here is a challenge for the African State capacity to empower the people as indicator of resilience to external pressures. The gap in human capital is the largest contributor to income equality. Inequalities in education perpetuate huge disparities in human capital. The gap is widening requiring new actions which should include political awareness and consciousness of the people to articulate, execute and own their development nexus. Dependency is killing Africa. We have to grow up; stand on our feet and feed ourselves. To depend on handouts is nothing short of destroying ourselves. To depend on fertilisers as a means of meeting our food security needs is disastrous. What are the side effects of fertilisers on our body, soil and plants? Why have we abandoned organic crops but embraced non-organic planted crops?

There is a dire need for transformative policies to bridge the rural-urban, poor-rich divide. The rural poor must be incorporated into the mainstream of development. One set of possibilities for constructive forms of integration across these agendas, based on greater attention to rural-urban transformations and dynamics in the divide should be to support more sustainable food production and ecosystem management, and for agriculture to be a major contributor to poverty alleviation and ensuring food security for the country. It is now widely accepted that food security depends not only on the availability of food but on entitlements of particular groups that enable them to have economic and social access to it. Thus as the definition of food security entails the ability of individuals to obtain adequate nutritional value from food which helps to address the link between poverty undernutrition and malnutrition can better explored by intensifying agricultural production and proper distribution ensuring it reaches all parts of the country at affordable prices.(Marshall and Randhawa, 20117:21-22). Creating that link between the farmers and consumers underpins the alleviation of multiple dimensions of poverty acting as a safety net to keep producers out of poverty. From these perspectives, the role of agriculture as contributing factor to food security is depicted in Fig 2: Per-Urban Agricultural activities.

The challenges dogging the continent lay not so much in the weakness of the policies or indeed inability to rule but in the general attitude of African leaders who have developed the habit of replacing the colonial masters. The founding fathers did make some mistakes but where committed to the total liberalization of the continent. Today's leaders are not committed to genuinely working for the welfare of the people; rather they have adopted the *'sit-tight'* attitude to buttress their welfare. There has to be a concerted as well as comprehensive *'mindset shift'* across the board which looking at the politics of the day looks virtually impossible or the machinery towards that direction is grinding very slowly or not grinding at all. The attitude of *'sit-tight'* presidents or leadership constitutes a serious mayhem for the continent. The continent cannot continue which such mayhem; and the best prospects for putting an end to the current impasse faced is a combination of the intervention of peoples' forces and genuine national dialogue with all the stakeholders resolved with the strong commitments and conviction for building the Africa we want and that next generations to come would be proud off. Lessons should be drawn from the example set by Africa's first Woman (Johnson of Liberia) elected president for handing over power to new democratically elected president.

The politics of poverty is different from the politics of affluence. It has been hard for politicians of the affluent countries and of the ruling elites in Africa to perceive. People of affluence and associated capacity for expression have recourse against the state – they can be heard in condemnation of political behaviour of which they disapprove, and they have the sanction of sacking the offender. Their politicians and officials respond to their behaviour, act with a caution, decorum, attention to individual rights that come to be assumed. The poor in the poor country have no similar capacity for assertion. Poverty makes the task of daily survival far more compelling (Galbraith. 1979).

Here is where we call for capitalism with a human face, and ruling African elites to behave with a human face and feelings towards the 'have nots'. The forces and bells of liberation are ringing and the process of decolonization and many instances where the imperialist and neocolonialist powers have used and continue using force or he threat of it have proved beyond all doubt that the has passed when 'peace and security' could be thrust on nations. The great wisdom of our founding fathers who struggled for decolonization and the immense pride of those who believe in the equality of humankind and unity of the African continent consist in the fact that peace, security and development can only be achieved by joint efforts and for everyone alike.

More than fifty years have passed since the *'wind of change'* started blowing across the African continent. Even though, it could be said to be a comparatively short period for history, and the Organisation of African Unity (OAU) and the African Union (AU) could be seen as completely new phenomenon in the history of the continent. Nonetheless, the OAU/AU embodies the ideals which many sceptics regard as premature, given the existence of such diverse socio-economic and political systems and state formations characterising the body. Sages of many countries and nations teach that humankind cannot exist if (s) he has nothing pleasant to look forward to. Lev Tolstoy the Great Russian writer noted that life must and could be a ceaseless joy. If life does not grant you great joy it is merely because the path you are following leads in the wrong direction. After all, it is our attitude to what surrounds us that brings us joy or otherwise.

It is my strong believe that the AU will and must play its role in the salvation of the African continent. And that human intellect will be victorious and will not permit the death of African civilisation and its place in contributing to world development, peace, justice and prosperity for all. A transformed leadership backed a responsive proactive citizenry will enhance capabilities through advancing the agility level by improving the decision making and implementation processes to be more efficient and highly effective in service delivery. A transformed leadership is required to unlock, harness, enhance and sustainably deploy the continent's vast resources for the development of Africa leading to the improvement of the people's living standards.

Even though a country may achieve economic growth without development, it is not possible for real development to occur without economic development. We can hardly run away from the point that development is a collective responsibility in which all have to share in its labour as well as its fruits. This publication challenges us to make people, their freedom and human dignity the focus of analysis and transformation. The publication equally scorns the premise that the progress of African countries lies in 'the mindless imitation of western models'. Rather, it beacons and points in the direction that the salvation of African countries rest in an intelligent use of local and human resources The words of Adedeji Adebayo (1982:29) should be seriously taken as he observed:

"we need to set in motion a development process that puts the individual at the very centre of the development effort; a development process that is both human and humane without necessarily softening the discipline that goes with development but which enhances man's personality; a development process that does not alienate man from his society and culture but rather develops his self-confidence in himself and identifies his interest with those of his society and thereby develops his ability and willingness for self-reliance."

We need a holistic approach to development seen within the context of development being a whole; an integral, value-loaded, cultural process encompassing the natural, environmental and social relations – education, production, consumption and well-being.

The continent's future is not predetermined. It has to be constructed, with the benefits of analysis, planning and programming that go to the roots of political, economic, cultural and social reality. African leaders must demonstrate greater unity, cohesion, confidence as well as instil hope in the people for a better and brighter tomorrow and for the people to exploit the strategic economic and geopolitical strengths and opportunities which the continent commands in the rapidly fast changing and hostile global world construct of our time. Africa should draw from its historical past, articulate prioritised articulate strategic and policy framework for constructing that betters tomorrow for all not a select few. There is a general recognition that many African countries have relatively weak institutions, low human development status, poor public financial management, and inadequate oversight, and poor governance that leads to endemic corruption and low productivity. The anecdote of from a crooked timber of humanity no proper thing can be ever be constructed, tells us to embark on the path of 'right game changer' to pilot the country on a new and comprehensive path.

The profound ineptitude of Africa's response to Western interference in the development trajectories of the continent will continue as long as Africa fails in its unity and integration efforts. Africa must not undermine the democratic process. Equally important is to pull civil society in the right direction as he greatest assets to fighting our common enemies, if we are to construct a new Africa our own way and the way we want and own. Such a mindset guarantees that our foes will always have the upper hand. The developed world succeeds because Africa fails to construct a united front. Africa fails to take advantage of its new strength and make new improvements in its available opportunities. Africa continues to capitalize on its weakness and threats directed against her. What Africa is doing is subsidizing the military industrial and economic powerful West. Take the case of African countries receiving USA$162bn in 2015 mainly in loans, and personal remittances. But at the same time, USA$203bn being taken away from the continent either directly or through multinationals repatriating profits or illegally moving money into tax havens or by cost imposed by the rest of the world through climate change adaptation and mitigation. Following Kavier McVeigh of the Guardian, African countries received USA$29bn a year stolen illegally, logging fishing and trade in wild life and plants. According to a report, 'Honest Account' and by the same token, 47 African countries suffered an annual financial deficient of USA$41.3bn whose population remains trapped in endemic poverty and stinking corruption dichotomy. While it is clearly evident the African continent is subsidizing the rich nations to the tune of USA$41bn per year, rightly the citizens can pose the simple but challenging question, can Africa afford to waste money, subsidizing the rich in the West when it should be spending this amount on the needy people of the continent.

Why are African leaders taking Africa away from Africa and the people? As we continue to degenerate the role of citizens in the development process as well as stripping of our cultural values from the development process, we are actually destroying our cultural heritage to be eventually evicted from the continent In short, which such attitude and behaviour Africa can never ever made it into the club of the developed It will remain a continent without a history with no future. Yet, it remains the continent for the future of the world. This should force African leaders and people to start looking for the politics and economics of reasoning that advances policies for improving the welfare of the people – politics and economics for the common good. The book by Jean Tirole (2017) – Economics for the Common Good – should provide a pointer for African governments. Reaching Poor People and silencing for good, the politics and acts of corruption and poor governance is a tall order for African governments. But these vices must be overcome for the region to make progress. Bias and barriers must be must be eradicated if the continent will provide sustainable development and proper livelihood to its rapidly increasing population. For now Africa is lagging behind but has a promising market for the future.

None of these issues of development is an invitation to complacency. It calls for hard work; increasing widespread of the use of new financial technologies, broadening human knowledge, skills, and participation, provides huge opportunities, intense competition, increase productivity, creativity and innovative attitudes to improve on the welfare of the people. It is a tall order of mixed activities with no room for complacency. The outreach is the people and nothing but the wellbeing of all in society. This is the only way the agony of Africa can be holistically addressed. We have grown up with the orientation of too much talk, with not enough progress to forge ahead a new order. All African's are called upon to act decisively against the ongoing genocide that has been inflicted on Africa. The creation of an African Free Trade Area is a beginning, an eye of the political and economic storm but enough to ensure the unity, and integration of the continent. Africa continues weeping as the scramble continues. Africa is changing but still intertwined into old and new configurations.

The sad thing for Africa is that it has leaders for whom the greatest general good of the people seem to be little more than an afterthought to their own grandiose interest and political ambitions. There is need for a new caravan of hope and trust to forge a new social contract that should turn around the plight of the vas continues to suffer. A new social contract between the state and people to get rid of historical hindrances that keep the African people from constructing its national unity and cohesion, which has impeded the sustainable development of the continent. We need to pull together – harambee' and build a strong sense of shared-struggle, and communalist spirit and ideals to sustain our political and cultural heritage as the anvil for the common good of today's generations forth coming ones. It means making the turn of the century one of

Africa's more promising one. AU Agenda 2063 should be seen as the torch light to that goal.

I hope you have had a wonderful time browsing through these views of mine as I hope hearing from you on how we can improve on the ideas advanced. Let us start the debate for a better Africa we all want leaving no one behind and being each other's keeper. We need to be proactive not reactive in our policy strategies and actions. We must not squander the heritage of present and future generations but hand a better constructed and well-refined Africa to future generations. We have no choice but to make our *great great grandchildren* the order of the day. Having our great, great grandchildren in today's development agenda, means facing the underdevelopment crisis from a more focused perspective that requires the following points of departure; which are not exhaustive? Africa is fast over-reaching the 1billion population status. How to provide for the wellbeing of that rapidly increasing population calls for serious thinking and comprehensive policy actions and implementation process. Many ideas abound. Let us share these wonderful ideas; and grow like the developed West with a special difference, the Africanness in us.

➤ the need for people's participation at all levels of social, economic, political and cultural transformation;

➤ it is imperative to allow the people much greater access to a larger resource share, as an indispensable condition for a people's centred development, for genuine democratic transformation and for irreversible control of economic and political power by the people. The more control the people exercise over their natural resources, the more empowered they are. Empower the people and they will green the land and overcome their misery;

➤ we need to pay special attention to the rate of population growth; proper birth planning system is needed. In order to appreciate the seriousness of the population, the issue of rapid population growth should be tackle as a major developmental problem, but not exclusively so. This is not to deny that the mere demographic aspects also deserve attention and are relevant to the problem of underdevelopment;

➢ we should pay attention to environmental concern as Africa is gradually, but relentlessly annihilating its positive cultural and educational values, namely collective and individual solidarity, self-help (ubuntu, harambee, batho pele, etc.) equity, organic relation to nature, etc. which is being overwhelmed by the onslaught of the global 'consume more' culture which has already cast its spell and subdued Eastern Europe and has fast invading the humble minds and attitudes of the world's poor especially in Africa.

➢ we should pay adequate attention to the supremacy of the human being as the priority objective of development in all our activities;

➢ also important is to focus on the implications of the arbitrary division of political borders, the resulting heterogeneous ethnic composition of the population, which in conjunction with economic and environmental degradation are causing bloody conflicts across the continent reinforcing the poverty and poor quality livelihood of the people;

➢ the ongoing attempt of forcing industrial and non-industrial economies into globalised knowledge-based world economy is not profitable for the currently in Africa where the people subject under great stress.

➢ the continent should seriously rethink its development strategy, priority and action plans; some of the actions need include; stronger links among African countries; integration and cooperation, good governance and management.

➢ Sustainable development in Africa requires setting and agreeing on the essential priorities for immediate action, and committing ourselves from here and now to begin implementing them immediately within and among our own countries.

The new caravan and signs of hope

There is need for a constructive change of political, economic, social and cultural culture construct to take the continent to higher heights, without which we shall the region is doomed for ever.

"Under a dictatorship, a country ceases to exist. All that remains is a fiefdom, a planet of slaves regimented by aliens from outer space."

(Wole Soyinka, Nigeria and Winner of the Nobel Prize for Literature)

"We must walk rapidly but not run. We must not be opportunists, nor allow our enthusiasm to make us lose the vision of concrete reality."

(Amilcar Cabral, Former President, Guinea-Bissau and Cape Verde. One of Africa's Greatest Political Revolutionaries)

"It took the madmen of yesterday for us to be able to act with extreme clarity today. I want to be one of those madmen. We must dare to invent the Future".

(Former President Thomas Sankara, Legendary Leader of Burkina Faso)

"Gone are the day when the only way to view your continent was one of despair and indignity"

(President Uhuru Kenyatta of Kenya)

"I'm trying to tell you that there is a new wave on the continent. A new wave of openness and democratization in which, since 2000, more than two-thirds of African countries have had multi-party democratic elections. Not all of them have been perfect, or will be, but the trend is very clear."

(Dr Ngozi Okonjo-Iweala, Former Finance Minister, Nigeria)

"It's important to debunk the myths of Africa being this benighted continent civilized only when white people arrived. In fact, Africans had been creators of culture for thousands of years before. These were very intelligent, subtle and sophisticated people, with organized societies and great art."

(Henry Louis Gates – Harvard Academic)

To control a people you must first control what they think about themselves and how they regard history and culture. And when your conqueror makes you ashamed of your culture and your history, he needs no prison walls and no chains to hold you"

(John Henrik Clarke: Afro-American Historian and Pan-Africanist)

"Civil society organizations are very important. They can protest. They can speak out. They can demonstrate. They can pressurize the government"

(Hailemariam Desalegn, Former Prime Minister, Ethiopia)

"Old carts can be repainted but they still keep moving in the same old ruts"

(Mongo Beti (of Blessed Memory – Cameroonian Writer and Political Essayist)

"If we not taking action to make our lives better, if we are not walking, if our feet are not moving, then there is no footprint for people to follow"

(Oliver Mtukudzi, Zimbabwean Musician and Human Rights Activist)

"The impoverishment inflicted on the Southern world, in neither large part by an economic disequilibrium imposed by neither reason nor foresight by northern consumer society, must go. It is both a chief cause and chief effect of a massive and growing environmental destruction that ultimately threatens all of us. Furthermore, it has a human cost that contains the seeds of future instability and conflict, and is morally repugnant."

(Gro Harlem Brundtland, Oslo, March 1990)

"Not enough is being done to adapt recent innovations in materials technology, energy conservation, information technology, and biotechnology to the need of development countries. These gaps must be covered by enhancing research, design, development, and extension capabilities in the Third World."

We have just presented the tip of the iceberg. We have to look back into the future and to make the future better for generations yet to come.

(John W. Forje, Bali-Nyonga, Cameroon)

References

Adedeji Adebayo (1982). "Development and Economic Growth in Africa to the Year 2000: Alternative Projections and Policies", in Shaw M. Timothey (ed.) 1982, Alternative Future for Africa, Westview Press, Boulder, Colorado.

Brundtland Gro Harlem (1987) The Brundtland Report - Our Common Future, World Commission on Environment and Development. Oxford University Press.

Cummings, K. Stephen (1988). "Facing Africa's Development Challenges", in Africa's Development Challengers and the World Bank: Hard Questions, Costly Choices, in Cunnings K Stephen (ed.), (1988), Boulder, Colorado, Lynne Rienner, p.4.

Ford Leighton (1991). Jesus: The Transforming Leader, Hodder and Stoughton Publishers, London.

Forje W. John (1990).Development Policy and Politics in Africa", Philosophy and Social Action 16(1)1990:39-56, India.

Forje W. John (2002). "The Disappointment of Independence." Future Research Quarterly, Fall 2002, Vol. 18. No.3.Bethesda – Maryland, USA, pp41-60.

Galbraith Kenneth John (1979). The Nature of Mass Poverty. Penguin/Pelican Books Ltd, Harmondsworth, Middlesex, England.

Gardner W. John (1986). The Task of Leadership, Leadership Papers 2 (Washington, DC: Leadership Studies Program, Independent Sector.

Ingram, J. et al. (eds.) (2010). Food Security and Global Environmental Change. Earthscan, London.

Keeton Gavin (2015). "Poor Education is the Cause of Inequality", Business Day, Thursday 17 September 2015, South Africa, p13.

Lartey Wilhelm George (1977). The Fourth Dimension: The Argument against the Theory of Evolutionary Stages of Social Development. The Department of Political Science, University of Lund, Sweden.

Marshall Fiona and Pritpal Randhawa (2017). India's Peri-Urban Frontier: Rural-Urban Transformations and Food Security. IIED/IFAD Working Paper, London.

Tirole Jean (2017). Economics for the Common Good. Princeton University Press, Princeton University Press, Princeton, NJ. USA.

Toynbee J. Arnold (1946). A Study of History. Oxford University Press, (London / New York).

CARAD Publications

Withering or Constructing African Unity: (2017) Lambert Academic Publishing, Germany ISBN: 978-3-330-31786-4.

Gender Empowerment, Equality and Economic Development (2016). Lambert Academic Publishing, Germany, ISBN: 978-659-71046-9.

Perspectives on Democracy and Good Governance in Africa (2015). Lambert Academic Publishing, Germany, ISBN: 978-3-659-56679-0.

Emerging Perspectives on Capacity Building and Quality Public Services Delivery in Africa (2013) Lambert Academic Publishing, Germany, ISBN: 978-3-659-38368-7.

State Building and Democracy in Africa: A Comparative and Developmental Approach (2011). Nova Science Publishers, Inc. New York, USA. ISBN: 978-1-61209-025-2.

Cameroon without Poverty: Civil Society Empowerment: Growth and Poverty Eradication. Mapping New Strategies for the Future. (2010). Lambert Academic Publishers, Germany. ISBN (78-3-8433-6951-0).

Here The People Rule: Political Transition and Challenges for Democratic Consolidation in Africa (2009). Nova Science Publishers, Inc. New York, USA. ISBN: 13: 978-1-60692-706-9.

The Challenges of Administrative Political and Developmental Renewal in Africa: Essays on Rethinking Government and Reorganisation (2009). Nova Science Publishers, Inc. New York, USA. ISBN: 13:978-1-60741-266-3.

The Challenges of Administrative Political and Developmental Renewal in Africa: Emerging Issues (2009). Nova Science Publishers, Inc. New York, USA., ISBN-13:978-1-60741-265-6.

Small Business Development in Cameroon, Problems and Prospects in a Historical Context: A Case Study. (2006) School of Business Management. The University of Reading, United Kingdom.

Multinationals and Cultural Clashes in a Developing Country: A Case Study of Cameroon. (1995) (City University Business School, Department of Business Studies, London, UK).

Science and Technology in Africa. (1989). Vol. 10. Longman Guide to World Science and Technology, Longman Group UK Limited, (ISBN) 0-582-00086-6.

Science, Technology and Development Policy in Cameroon. (1987). Presstationen, Skandiahuset, Lund – Sweden, ISBN 91-7810-970-1 ISSN: 0280-2902.

The One and Indivisible Cameroon. Political Integration and Socio-Economic Development in A Fragmented Society, (1981) Department of Political Science, Lund Political Studies No. 35, University of Lund, Printing Pres, Lund-Sweden (ISBN) 91-7222-450-9.

Third World Development and The Myth of International Co-operation.

The Challenge of African Economic and Technological Development and the Influence of International Forums, Lund – Sweden (1979).

The Rape of Africa at Vienna: African Participation in the 1979 United Nations Conference on Science and Technology for Development, (1979) AV-Centralen, Lund – Sweden.

Planning For Development: Cameroon's Five –Year Development Plans (1977). Department of Economic History, University of Lund – Sweden Bokforlaget Doxa, Lund, Sweden.

Forthcoming

➢ Unchaining African Development:
➢ Shaping Africa's Future. Transform Africa and Global Relations for a Just and Stable World.
➢ The Future of Africa: Decline or Reform and Development.
➢ Aborted Development. The Betrayal of Africa.

Lightning Source UK Ltd.
Milton Keynes UK
UKHW022017170320
360497UK00008B/258